BUSINESS ROMANIAN DICTIONARY

Romanian-English
English-Romanian

A Publication Supported and Funded by the British Government's Know How Fund

BUSINESS
ROMANIAN
DICTIONARY

Romanian-English
English-Romanian

by Alex Macedonski

PETER COLLIN PUBLISHING

First published in Great Britain 1996
by Peter Collin Publishing Ltd
1 Cambridge Road, Teddington, Middlesex, TW11 8DT

British Library Cataloguing-in-Publication Data

A catalogue record for this book is available from the British Library

ISBN 0-948549-45-9

Text computer typeset by PCP, Teddington

Printed by Looseleaf Company, Wiltshire

PREFACE

The aim of this work is to give the user a basic business vocabulary in Romanian and English with translations into the other language.

The vocabulary covers the main areas of day-to-day business usage including banking, telecommunications, sales and purchases, as well as some legal terms used in these areas.

The dictionary gives many examples of usage both to show how the words are used in context and how they can be translated.

PREFAȚĂ

Lucrarea de față se adreseasă celor interesați în dobândirea unui vocabular de bază al limbajului folosit în afaceri, în domeniile economic și comercial în română și engleză, cu traducerile respective.

Vocabularul cuprinde termeni folosiți zilnic în comerț, operațiuni bancare, telecomunicații, tranzacții de vânzare-cumpărare, ca de altfel și un număr de termeni juridicifolosiți în aceste domenii, oferind utilizatorului posibilitatea de a efectua traduceri dintr-o limbă în cealaltă.

Dicționarul oferă numeroase exemple pentru a arăta cum cuvintele sunt folosite în context și felul în care pot fi traduse.

ACKNOWLEDGEMENTS

I should like to record my thanks to Mr Peter Collin for his professional help; without his expertise the publication of this dictionary would have not been possible. I also wish to thank Val Petcu and Florin Nicolaescu for their precious suggestions and support and Grant & Cutler Ltd for allowing me to use their computers.

MULȚUMIRI

Aș dori să mulțumesc domnului Peter Collin pentru ajutorul profesional acordat, fără a cărui expertiză publicarea acestui dicționar ar fi fost imposibilă. Aș dori de asemenea să mulțumesc domnilor Val Petcu și Florin Nicolaescu pentru prețioase sugestii și sprijin, ca de altfel și companiei Grant & Cutler pentru permisiunea de a folosi calculatoarele lor din dotare.

Român-Englez
Romanian-English

Aa

abandona *vb* to abandon sau to leave; **a abandona serviciul (de bună voie)** = to leave *sau* to quit (one's job); **şi-a abandonat slujba ca să-şi continue studiile** = she quit her job to continue her studies; **şi-a abandonat slujba din Bucureşti când i s-a oferit un post avantajos la o firmă din Braşov** = he left his job in Bucharest when he was offered a good position with a firm in Braşov

abandonare *sf (renunţarea la proprietate în favoarea altei părţi)* abandonment; **abandonarea mărfurilor în vamă** = abandonment of goods in customs

abatere *sf (deviere)* deviation

abona *vb* **a (se) abona (la o publicaţie)** = to subscribe (to a magazine); **s-a abonat la revista ei preferată** = she subscribed to her favourite magazine

abonament *sn* **(a)** subscription (to newspaper, magazine) **(b)** *(de călătorie)* season ticket

abonat *sm* subscriber

absent *adj (de la locul de muncă sau o întrunire)* absent; **nu am putut începe şedinţa pentru că preşedintele era absent** = we could not start the meeting as the chairman was absent; **absentează din motive de sănătate** = he is off sick; **persoană care absentează nemotivat** = absentee

absenteism *sn (termen denumind totalitatea absenţelor nemotivate)* absenteeism

absolut *adj* absolute; *(situaţia teoretică în care un singur producător controlează în totalitate piaţa de desfacere)* **monopol absolut** = absolute monopoly; **conducător absolut** = autocrat

absolvent *sm* graduate

absorbţie *sf* absorption

abţine *vb* **a se abţine** = to hold back

abundenţă *sf* glut

abuz *sn* misuse

academie *sf* college; **academie de comerţ** = commercial college

acapara *vb* **(a)** to buy up **(b)** to capture; **a acapara 20% din piaţă** = to capture 20% of the market

accelera *vb* to accelerate

accepta *vb* to accept; **a accepta (şi respecta) condiţiile unui contract** = . to accept the conditions of a contract

acceptare *sf* acceptance; **acceptare bancară** = bank acceptance; **acceptare parţială** = partial acceptance

acces *sn* **(a)** entrance; **cale de acces** = access **(b)** reach

accesibil *adj* accessible; within reach; **preţuri accesibile** = reasonable prices

accesibilitate *(acces) sf* reach

accesoriu *sn* **(a)** *(garnituri)* fittings **(b)** *(echipament)* equipment; **accesorii de birou** = office equipment

accident *sn* *(natural sau provocat)* catastrophe; *(stricăciune)* breakdown

aceleaşi *adj & pron* same; **la acelaşi nivel** = par; **cu aceeaşi valoare** = on a par with; **în aceleaşi condiţii** = pari passu

acerb *adj* stiff; **competiţie acerbă** = stiff competition

achita *vb* **(a)** to pay; **a achita o notă de plată** = to pay a bill *sau* to foot the bill **(b)** to pay off; to liquidate; **a achita plata ipotecii** = to pay off a mortgage; **a achita o datorie** = to liquidate a debt; **a-şi achita datoriile** = to square up; **a (se) achita de o datorie** = to pay off a debt; **datorie care nu va fi achitată** = bad debt **(c)** *(a rambursa)* to pay back; **a achita un împrumut** = to amortize sau to pay back a loan; **împrumutul trebuie achitat în 2 ani** = the loan must be paid back within 24 months

achitare *sf* liquidation; **achitarea unei datorii** = settlement

achitat *adj* paid; **achitat anticipat** = prepaid

achiziţie *sf* purchase *sau* buy; acquisition; **achiziţie cu numerar** = cash purchase; **achiziţie cu plata în rate** = hire purchase; **achiziţii en gros** *sau* **cu ridicata** = bulk purchase; **comandă de achiziţie** = purchase order; **contract de achiziţie** = purchase agreement

achiziţiona *vb* *(a cumpăra)* to purchase; to acquire; **a achiziţiona o companie** = to take over a company; **proprietatea a fost achiziţionată de un cumpărător anonim** = the property was acquired by an unknown buyer

achiziţionare *sf* acquisition; **achiziţionare masivă de acţiuni la deschiderea bursei** = dawn raid

achizitor *sm* purchaser; purchase officer

acompania *vb* to accompany

acont *sn* deposit; **condiţiile de vânzare sunt: 10 % acont şi 12 rate lunare de 20.000 lei** = the terms of sale are: 10% deposit and 12 monthly payments of 20,000 lei

acoperi *vb* to clear; **afacerea lui a fost un eşec total de vreme ce el nu şi-a acoperit nici măcar cheltuielile** = his venture was a disaster as he did not even clear his expenses

acoperire *sf* cover

acord *sn* **(a)** **a fi de acord** = to accept *sau* to agree; **cele două companii au căzut de acord în ceea ce priveşte capitolul siguranţă** = the two companies agreed on the safety issue **(b)** contract; deal; *(aranjament)* agreement; *(angajament)* engagement; *(învoială)* bargain; *(tratat internaţional)* treaty; **cele două părţi au semnat acordul** = the two parts signed the deal; **a încălca un acord** = to break an engagement; **acord comercial** = marketing agreement; **acord comercial internaţional** = commercial treaty; **acord de clearing** = clearing agreement; **acord de transfer** = transfer agreement; **acord particular** = private treaty

acorda *vb* **(a)** to grant; to award; **a acorda unui debitor răgaz de a plăti** = to allow a debtor more time to pay; **a acorda un împrumut** = to grant a loan **(b)** to award; **a acorda despăgubiri** = to award damages

Acordul General de Tarife şi Comerţ *sn* General Agreement on Tariffs and Trade (GATT)

acreditiv *sn* letter of credit (L/C)

act *sn* *(document)* document; *(document legal)* act; *(contract sau testament, etc.)* întocmirea unui act oficial = act in law; *(acord în scris, semnat şi parafat de ambele părţi)* deed; **act de transferare a acţiunilor** = deed of transfer; **act de vânzare** = bill of sale; **act notarial** = notarial deed

activ 1 *sn* **activ curent** = current assets; **active nete** = net assets 2 *adj* **(a)** operative **(b)** *(ocupat)* active; energetic **(c)** *(angajat)* employed **(d)** *(productiv sau eficient)* productive; **bani activi** = active money; **capital activ** = productive capital; *(de comerţ sau de plăţi, etc.)* **balanţă activă** = active balance

actual *adj* **(a)** *(curent)* current; **preţ actual** = current price **(b)** *(în vigoare)* actual **(c)** *(la zi)* up to date

actualiza *vb* *(a moderniza)* to update; **actualizăm banca de date la două luni** = we update our data base every other month

actualizare *sf* update

acţiona *vb* to act

acţionar *sm* shareholder; **adunare a acţionarilor** = shareholders' meeting; **capital al acţionarilor** = shareholders' equity

acţiune *sf* **(a)** *(faptă)* action **(b)** *(titlu)* share; **acţiuni** = shares *sau* stock; **deţine acţiuni în valoare de 2,000,000 lei într-o companie de distribuire a gazului metan** = he holds 2,000,000 lei worth of shares in a gas company; **acţiuni ale administratorilor** = qualifying shares; **acţiune gratuită** = bonus share; **acţiune nominală** = registered share; **acţiuni obişnuite (la bursă)** = equities; **acţiuni ordinare** = ordinary shares *sau* common stock; **acţiuni preferenţiale** = preferred stock; **acţiune privilegiată cumulativă** = cumulative preference share; **acţiuni cu valoare mai mică de 10 pence**

sau $1 = penny shares *sau* *(US)* penny stock; **acţiune de vânzare contra numerar** = cash share; **acţiuni pe termen (care urmează să fie valorificate la o dată ulterioară)** = futures; **alocare de acţiuni** = share allotment; **capital în acţiuni** = share capital; **certificat de acţiuni la purtător** = stock certificate to bearer; **a cumpăra acţiuni în scopul revânzării** = to stag; **deţinere de acţiuni** = shareholding; **deţinător de acţiuni** = shareholder *sau* stockholder; **emiterea de acţiuni** = share issue; **societate pe acţiuni** = stock company **(c)** *(proces)* **acţiune legală** = action *sau* case; **acţiuni în justiţie** = legal proceedings; **acţiune civilă** = suit *sau* lawsuit; **(într-un litigiu) a ajunge la un acord înainte de a porni acţiunea judecătorească** = to settle out of court

acumula *vb* **a (se) acumula** = to accumulate; **a acumula stoc** = to stock up

acumulare *sf* **acumulare de stoc de rezervă** = stockpiling

acut *adj* *(intens)* keen

acuzare *sf* **act de acuzare** = indictment

acuzat *sm* *(pârât)* defendant

acuzaţie *sf* charge; *(act de acuzare)* indictment; **ei riscă acuzaţia de furt din magazin** = they face a charge for shoplifting

adaos *sn* addition

adapta *vb* **a (se) adapta** = to adapt

adaptabil *adj* flexible

adăuga *vb* to add; **valuare adăugată** = added value

adăugare *sf* addition

adjunct *sm* deputy; **director adjunct** = deputy manager

administra *vb* to administer; **a administra necorespunzător** = to mismanage *sau* to maladminister; **a administra o afacere** = to manage; **a administra un magazin (pentru realizarea de profituri)** = to keep a shop

administrare *sf* administration; **administrarea proprietăţilor** *sau* **mijloacelor fixe** = property administration

administrativ *adj* administrative; *(de conducere)* managerial; *(funcţionăresc)* clerical; **personal administrativ** = office staff

administrator *sm* administrator

administraţie *sf* administration; *(guvern)* government; *(fisc)* **administraţie financiară** = revenue office; *(Fiscul)* **Administraţia Financiară** = *(în Marea Britanie)* Inland Revenue *(în SUA)* Internal Revenue Service; **administraţia locală** = local government

admite *vb* to admit; *(a recunoaşte)* to acknowledge

admitere *sf (recunoaştere)* admission

adopta *vb* to adopt; **consiliul directorilor a adoptat noua propunere** = the board of directors adopted the new proposal; **a adopta o lege** = to pass a law

adresa *vb (unui grup, etc.)* **a (se) adresa** = to address

adresă *sf (locaţie)* address; **adresă prescurtată** = telegraphic address

aduce *vb* **a aduce dobânzi** = to earn; **acest cont îi aduce o dobândă rezonabilă** = this account earns him a decent interest

aduna *vb* **(a)** to add; *(o coloană de cifre, etc.)* to add up (a column of figures) **(b)** *(în armată)* to assemble **(c)** *(a strânge)* **a aduna bani** = to rake in (money)

adunare *sf* **(a)** *(sumă)* addition **(b)** assembly; **adunare generală anuală** = annual general meeting (AGM)

advers *adj* adverse

aer *sn* air; **echipat cu aer condiţionat** = air-conditioned; **transport de mărfuri pe calea aerului** = air freight; **a expedia pe calea aerului** = to airfreight

aerian *adj* air; **companie de transport aerian** = airline; **linie aeriană** = airline

aeronavă *sf* aircraft; **aeronavă de transport de mărfuri** = commercial aircraft

aeroport *sn* airport; **vom ateriza la aeroportul Bucureşti-Otopeni la ora 1.55** = we will land at Bucharest-Otopeni Airport at 1.55 pm

afacere *sf* **(a)** *(tranzacţie)* deal; **afacere favorabilă** = bargain; **a încheia o afacere avantajoasă** = to strike a bargain **(b)** *(tranzacţie comercială)* venture; affair; **el a propus o nouă afacere** = he came up with a new business proposition **(c)** **femeie de afaceri** = businesswoman; **om de afaceri** = businessman; financier; *(comerciant)* trader; **a face afaceri** = to trade; to do business

afacerist *sm* racketeer

afecta *vb* to affect; **majorarea impozitelor nu va afecta compania noastră** = the tax increase will not affect our company

afgan(ă) *s & adj* Afghan

Afganistan *sm* Afghanistan; Notă: capitală: **Kabul**

afilia *vb (a (se) ataşa)* **a (se) afilia** = to affiliate

afiliat *adj (înrudit)* related; **companie afiliată** = affiliated *sau* associate *sau* subsidiary company

afirma *vb* to affirm *sau* to state

afirmaţie *sf* affirmation

afiş *sn* poster; **afiş publicitar** = handbill

afreta *vb* to charter

Africa de Sud *sf* South Africa; Notă: capitală: **Pretoria;** monedă: **rand sudafrican** = South African rand

agendă *sf* diary; **agendă de birou** = desk diary

agent *sm* **(a)** *(mijlocitor)* go-between **(b)** *(împuternicit)* attorney **(c)** agent; **agent de asigurări** = insurance agent; **agent imobiliar** = estate agent **(d)** broker; **agent comercial** = broker; **agent de plasare** = employment agent; **agent de schimb** *sau* **agent de bursă** = stockbroker

agenţie *sf* **(a)** agency; **agenţie de plasare** = employment agency; **agenţie de schimb valutar** = bureau de change; **agenţie publicitară** *sau* **agenţie de publicitate** = advertising agency *sau* publicity bureau; **agenţie de turism** = tour operator; **agenţie de voiaj** *sau* **agenţie turistică** = travel agency **(b)** *(filială sau sucursală)* branch office

agrafă *sf* **agrafă de birou** = paper-clip

agrar *adj* **reformă agrară** = land reform

agricultură *sf* agriculture

ajunge *vb* to reach; **a ajunge la o înţelegere** = to reach an agreement

ajusta *vb* to regulate

ajustat *adj* *(corelat)* index-linked

ajuta *vb* to aid *sau* to assist *sau* to help; **împrumutul de la bancă l-a ajutat să înfiinţeze propria sa întreprindere** = the bank loan helped him to start his own business

ajutor *sn* **(a)** help; **a sări în ajutor** = to step into the breach; **ajutor financiar** = financial help *sau* aid *sau* backing **(b)** *(de stat)* benefit; **ajutor de şomaj** = unemployment benefit; **ajutor financiar plătit de asistenţa socială în caz de boală** = sickness benefit **(c)** assistant

alb *adj* **în alb** = blank; **andosare în alb** = blank endorsement; **cec în alb** = blank cheque

albanez(ă) *s & adj* Albanian

Albania *sf* Albania; Notă: capitală: **Tirana;** monedă: **lek albanez** = Albanian lek

alcătui *vb* **a alcătui un plan** = to plan

aleatoriu *adj* random; **eroare aleatorie** = random error

alegător *sm* voter

alege *vb* **(a)** to choose; to pick; **alegeţi, vă rog** = take your pick please; **clienţii au putut alege dintr-o gamă largă de sortimente** = customers could choose from a good range of products; **şeful serviciului personal a ales pe cel mai potrivit candidat pentru postul vacant** = the personnel manager picked the most suitable candidate for the vacancy **(b)** *(prin vot)* to elect; **a alege un preşedinte al unei societăţi** = to elect the chairman of a society

alegere *sf* **(a)** *(selecţionare)* pick *sau* picking *sau* choice **(b)** election *sau* poll; **alegeri generale** = general election **(c)** *(opţiune)* option; **a exercita dreptul de alegere** = to take up an option

alfabetic *adj* **ordine alfabetică** = alphabetical order

Algeria *sf* Algeria; Notă: capitală: **Alger** = Algiers; monedă: **dinar algerian** = Algerian dinar

algerian(ă) *s & adj* Algerian

aliment *sn* *(şi plural)* food

aloca *vb* to grant; to allocate; *(fonduri)* to earmark; **a aloca fonduri pentru cercetare** = to allocate funds for research

alocare *sf* allotment; **alocare de acţiuni** = share allotment

alocaţie *sf* (a) allocation (b) allowance; **alocaţie de stat** = child benefit; *(în Marea Britanie)* **alocaţie acordată mamei la naşterea fiecărui copil** = maternity benefit

alocuţiune *sf (cuvânt)* address

alterna *vb* to alternate

alternativ *adj* alternative

alternativă *sf* alternative

amaneta *vb* to pawn; **a amaneta ceva** = to put something in pawn; **pentru a face rost de bani a trebuit să-şi amaneteze ceasul** = he had to pawn his watch in order to get some cash; **obiect de amanetat** = pawn; **a recupera un obiect amanetat** = to take something out of pawn

amănunt *sn* (a) detail; **veţi afla toate amănuntele în ultimul nostru catalog** = you will find all the details in our latest catalogue; **a descrie în amănunt** = to detail; **i s-a cerut să descrie în amănunt planul său** = he was asked to detail his plan (b) **comerţ cu amănuntul** = retail *sau* retail trade; **a desface** *sau* **a vinde cu amănuntul** = to retail; **preţ cu amănuntul** = (i) all-in rate; delivered price; (ii) retail price; **indice de preţuri cu amănuntul** = retail price index; **vânzător** *sau* **negustor cu amănuntul** = retailer

amănunţi *vb (a detalia)* to itemize

amâna *vb* to postpone; **a amâna plata** = to postpone payment; **a amâna o şedinţă** = to put back a meeting; **şedinţa a fost amânată pe săptămâna viitoare** = the meeting was postponed to next week

amânare *sf* postponement

ambala *vb* to pack

ambalaj *sn* package; packaging *sau* packing; **ladă de ambalaj** = packing-case

ambalare *sf* packaging; **preţul pentru francare şi ambalare** = postage and packing (p & p) (cost)

ambasadă *sf* embassy

ambasador *sm* ambassador

ambiţie *sf* ambition; *(energie)* drive

ambiţios *adj* ambitious; **persoană ambiţioasă** = high flier

ameliora *vb* **a se ameliora** = to pick up *sau* to improve

amenda *vb* (a) to fine (b) *(o lege)* to amend

amendă *sf* fine; *(penalizare)* penalty; **compania de asigurări a fost somată să plătească o amendă de 5.000.000 lei** = the insurance company was asked to pay a 5,000,000 lei fine

amortiza *vb* to amortize; to depreciate; *(costuri sau cheltuieli)* to clear; **costul investiţiei ar trebui amortizat în 10 ani** = the cost of the investment *sau* the investment cost is to be depreciated over 10 years *sau*

amortizare *sf* redemption; **amortizare anticipată** = redemption before due date; **amortizare a fondurilor fixe** = depreciation; **amortizarea unei ipoteci** = redemption of a mortgage; **amortizare uniformă** = straight-line depreciation; **coeficient de amortizare** = depreciation rate; **fond de amortizare** = sinking fund

amortizat *adj (rambursabil)* **care poate fi amortizat** = redeemable

an *sm* year; **câştigă 200.000 de lei pe an** = he gets 200.000 lei per annum (p.a.); **an calendaristic** = calendar year; **an fiscal** *sau* **financiar** = financial year

analist *sm* analyst; *(programator)* programmer

analiza *vb (a examina)* to analyse; **a analiza un cont** = to analyse an account

analiză *sf* analysis; **analiză comparativă** = comparative analysis; **analiză dinamică** = dynamic analysis; **analiză statică** = static analysis; **rezultatul unei analize** = analysis

ancheta *vb* to inquire into

anchetă *sf* inquiry; **o anchetă oficială prvitoare la modul în care fondurile au fost folosite** = an official inquiry into how the funds were used

ancoraj *sn* anchorage

ancorare *sf* anchorage

Andora *sf* Andorra; Notă: capitală: **Andorra la Vella** currencies: **franc francez** = French franc; **peseta spaniolă** = Spanish peseta

andoran(ă) *s & adj* Andorran

andosa *vb* to endorse

andosare *sf* endorsement; **andosare în alb** = blank endorsement; **andosare prin procură** = procuration endorsement

anexa *vb* to attach; *(a pune în plic)* to enclose; **a anexat fotocópii ale documentelor** = he attached photocopies of the documents

angaja *vb* **(a)** to staff **(b)** to employ *sau* to engage *sau* to hire *sau* to recruit; **ei au angajat un inginer de sistem pentru a pune la punct reţeaua de calculatoare** = they engaged a computer expert to set up a computer network; **firma angajează personal sezonier în perioadele de vârf** = the firm hires extra staff for the busy season; **odată cu creşterea cifrei de afaceri compania a angajat personal nou** = as the business grew the company employed more staff; **vom angaja 20 de persoane pentru noul depozit** = we will recruit 20 staff for the new warehouse; **compania a angajat 200 de muncitori** = the company took on 200 hands

angajament *sn* **(a)** *(acord)* engagement **(b)** commitment

angajare *sf* employment; **angajare cu normă întreagă** = full-time employment; **contract de angajare** = employment contract; **a face cerere de angajare** = to apply for a job

angajat 1 *adj* employed; salaried 2 *sm* employee; *(muncitor)* hand; *(salariat)* wage-earner; **angajat al unei întreprinderi** = member of staff

Anglia *sf* England; Notă: capitală: **Londra** = London; monedă: **lira sterlină (£)** = pound sterling (£)

Angola *sf* Angola; Notă: capitală: **Luanda;** monedă: **kwanza**

angolan(ă) *s & adj* Angolan

angrosist *sm* **(a)** stockist **(b)** *(în SUA)* jobber **(c)** wholesaler

anotimp *sn* season

antedata *vb* to backdate

anterior *adj* prior; **acord anterior** = prior agreement

antet *sn* letterhead; **hârtie (de scris) cu antetul companiei** = headed paper

anticipa *vb* to anticipate

anticipat 1 *adv* *(în avans)* beforehand 2 *adj* advance; **plată anticipată** = advance payment; **profit anticipat** = anticipated profit

antiinflaţionar *adj* anti-inflationary *sau* counterinflationary

antrepozit *sn* warehouse; *(magazie)* store

antreprenor *sm* **(a)** entrepreneur *sau* contractor **(b) antreprenor de pompe funebre** = undertaker

antrepriză de construcţii *sf* building contractor

anual 1 *adj* annual *sau* yearly; **adunare generală anuală** = annual general meeting; **cost anual** = annual cost; **raport anual** = annual report; **revizie contabilă anuală** = annual accounts 2 *adv* annually *sau* yearly

anuar *sn* yearbook

anula *vb* to annul *sau* to cancel *sau* to rescind; *(un contract, decret, etc.)* to void; *(plata unei datorii)* to write off; *(a opri)* to call off; **contractul a fost anulat de ambele părţi** = the contract was annulled by both parties; **el a telefonat să anuleze comanda** = he phoned to cancel his order; **tranzacţia a fost anulată** = the deal is off

anulare *sf* cancellation; **anularea unei rezervări** = cancellation of a booking

anunţ *sn (public)* advertisement; **anunţuri la mica publicitate** = classified advertisements

anunţa *vb* **(a)** *(a informa)* to advertise **(b)** *(a notifica)* to notify; **a anunţa (preţuri) oficial** = to schedule **(c)** to publish; **noile valori ale dobânzilor nu au fost anunţate încă** = the latest interest rate changes have not yet been published

anvergură *sf* span; **de mare anvergură** = on a large scale

aparat *sn (dispozitiv)* device

apartament *sn (la hotel)* suite; **a rezervat un apartament la hotel pentru el şi familia sa** = he booked a hotel suite for himself and his family

aparţine *vb* to belong

apel *sn* **(a)** *(chemare)* call **(b)** appeal; **a face apel** = to make an appeal

aplica *vb* **(a)** to apply; to enforce; **a aplica condiţiile unei înţelegeri** = to enforce the terms of an agreement; **a aplica o lege** = to enforce a law; **a aplica o regulă** = to apply a rule **(b) a se aplica** = to operate

aplicare *sf* enforcement

aplicat *adj* applied; **economie aplicată** = applied economics

aprecia *vb* **(a)** to appreciate; **clienţii apreciază rabatul comercial întotdeauna** = customers always appreciate getting a good discount **(b)** to estimate *sau* to rate *sau* to appraise *sau* to gauge

apreciere *(estimare) sf* estimation

aproba *vb* **(a)** to approve *sau* to sanction; **a aproba oficial** = to ratify **(b)** to pass; **a aproba un document** = to pass a document

aprobare *sf* **(a)** endorsement; approval; **aprobare tacită** = tacit approval; **cheltuieli fără aprobare** = unauthorized expenditure **(b)** *(permisiune)* sanction; **are nevoie de aprobarea primăriei pentru a deschide o creşă** = she needs the sanction of the council to open a nursery **(c)** *(ratificare)* ratification; **contractul va fi prezentat spre aprobare** = the agreement will be presented for ratification

aproviziona *vb* to supply; to furnish

aprovizionare *sf* supply

apt *adj* fit

aptitudine *sf* *(calificare)* qualification; **aptitudini profesionale** = professional qualifications

Arabia Saudită *sf* Saudi Arabia; Notă: capitală: **Riyadh;** monedă: **riyal arab saudit** = Saudi Arabian riyal

aranja *vb* to fix; **a aranja obţinerea unui împrumut** = to raise a loan

aranjament *sn* agreement; **a ajunge la un aranjament** = to reach a compromise

aranjat *adj (deseori, în culise)* fixed

arăta *vb* to show *sau* to point

arbitra *vb* to adjudicate

arbitru *sm* umpire

arenda *vb* to let

arendaş *sm* **(a)** tenant farmer **(b)** *(în Marea Britanie)* bailiff

Argentina *sf* Argentina; Notă: capitală: **Buenos Aires;** monedă: **peso argentinian** = Argentinian peso

argentinian(ă) *s & adj* Argentinian

argint *sn* silver; **argint cu puritate de 92,5%** = sterling silver; *(sau din aliaj de cupro-nichel, de culoarea argintului)* **monedă de argint** = silver

arhivar *sm* **(a)** filing clerk **(b)** registrar

arhivă *sf* file; records; **a clasa dosare în arhivă** = to file; **toate cópiile facturilor sunt păstrate în arhiva companiei** = all the copy invoices are kept in the company's records

arie *sf* **(a) arie productivă într-o clădire** = floor space **(b)** *(unde guvernul intervine pentru atragerea de noi activităţi industriale)* **arii de dezvoltare** = development areas

armator *sm* *(proprietar de vase)* shipowner

artă *sf* art; **arta de a vinde** *sau* **arta de a convinge cumpărătorii** = salesmanship

articol *sn* **(a)** article; item; *(plural)* goods; **articole (de comerţ)** = commodity; **articole de lux** = luxury goods; **articole de uz casnic** = household goods **(b)** *(in newspaper)* **articol de fond** = editorial

artizanat *sn* cottage industry

arunca *vb* to throw; **a arunca încărcătura în mare** = to jettison; **a arunca la gunoi** = to scrap

arvună *sf (avans)* key money

asambla *vb* to assemble

asamblare *sf* assembly

ascensor *sn* lift; *US* elevator

ascunde *vb* to keep back

ascuns *adj (secret)* hidden; **avarie ascunsă a unei nave** = hidden damage; **viciu ascuns** = inherent vice

asesor *sm* consultant

asigura *vb* **a (se) asigura** = to assure *sau* to insure; **a asigura din nou** = to reinsure; **persoană asigurată** = the policy holder *sau* the insured

asigurare *sf* **(a)** insurance *sau* assurance; **asigurare totală** = full cover; **agent de asigurări** = insurance agent; **companie de asigurări** = assurance company; insurer; **poliţă de asigurare** = insurance policy; **poliţă de asigurări auto** = car insurance *sau* motor insurance; **a încheia o poliţă de asigurări** = to insure; **a încheia o nouă asigurare** = to reinsure; **a-şi scoate o poliţă de asigurare** = to underwrite **(b)** *sfpl (ajutor de stat pentru bătrâni, şomeri, bolnavi, etc.)* **asigurări sociale** = social security

asistent *sm* assistant

asocia *vb* to associate; to combine

asociat **1** *sm* associate *sau* partner; **asociat principal** = senior partner; **a deveni asociat** = to associate **2** *adj* corporate

asociaţie *sf* **(a)** association; federation; **asociaţie de sindicate** = federation of trade unions **(b)** combine

asociere *sf* partnership

aspect *sn* element; **au studiat cu atenţie toate aspectele înţelegerii** = they studied carefully all the elements of the agreement

aştepta *vb* **a se aştepta** = to anticipate; **a se aştepta la** = to bargain for; **ne aşteptam la o întârziere de două săptămâni pentru livrarea comenzii** = we anticipated a delay of two weeks in delivering the order

aşteptat *adj* due; **următoarea livrare este aşteptată în două zile** = the next shipment is due in two days

atac *sn (brusc)* raid

ataşa *vb (a anexa)* to attach; **a (se) ataşa** = to affiliate

ataşat *sm* attaché; **ataşat comercial** = commercial attaché

atelier *sn* workshop; shop; **atelier mecanic** = machine shop; **atelier de reparaţii** = repair shop

atenţie *sf* care; **atenţie cuvenită** = due care

atenua *vb* to diminish

ateriza *vb* to land

aterizare *sf* landing

atesta *vb* to certify

atestat *sn (recomandare)* testimonial

atinge *vb* to reach; **a atinge un preţ ridicat** = to reach a high price

atrage *vb* to draw; **a atrage atenţia cuiva** = to draw someone's attention

aur *sn* gold; **aur de 24 de carate** *sau* **pur** = 24 carat gold; **lingouri de aur** = gold ingots *sau* gold bars; **mină de aur** = gold-mine; **monede de aur** = gold coins; **rezerve în aur** = gold reserves; **a face comerţ cu aur** = to deal in gold

aurifer *adj* **bazin aurifer** = gold-field

austeritate *sf* austerity; **buget de austeritate** = austerity budget

Australia *sf* Australia; Notă: capitală: **Canberra;** monedă: **dolar australian** = Australian dollar

australian(ă) *s & adj* Australian

Austria *sf* Austria; Notă: capitală: **Viena** = Vienna; monedă: **şiling austriac** = Austrian schilling

austriac(ă) *s & adj* Austrian

autentic *adj* authentic *sau* real

autentifica *vb* to authenticate; *(a certifica)* to attest

autobuz *sn* bus

autofinanţare *sf* autofinancing *sau* self-financing

autofinanţat *adj* self-financed

autohton *adj* indigenous; homegrown; **industrie autohtonă** = homegrown industry; **produs autohton** = indigenous product

automatic *adj* automatic

automatiza *vb* to automate

automatizare *sf* automation

automobil *sn* car

autonom *adj (pe cont propriu)* self-employed

autor *sm* author; **drept de autor** = copyright; **drepturi de autor** = royalties; **a-şi asuma drepturi de autor** = to copyright; **protejat de dreptul de autor** = copyrighted *sau* copyright

autoritate *sf* authority

autoriza *vb* **(a)** to authorize **(b)** to commission; to empower **(c)** to license

autorizaţie *sf* **(a)** *(permis)* permit; *(licenţă)* licence; **autorizaţie de construcţie** = planning permission; **autorizaţie de comercializare a băuturilor alcoolice** = liquor licence; **autorizaţie de import** = import permit **(b)** *(document oficial)* warrant **(c)** commission **(d)** go-ahead

autoservire *sf* **magazin cu autoservire** = self-service store

autostradă *sf (în Marea Britanie)* motorway

autoturism *sn (personal)* private car; **autoturismul companiei** = fleet car; company car

avans *sn* advance; *(arvună)* key money; **în avans** = beforehand *sau* in advance; up front; **plată în avans** = advance payment; money up front; **a plăti în avans** = to advance *sau* to pay in advance

avansa *vb* to advance

avansare *sf (promovare)* advancement *sau* promotion

avantaj *sn* favour; *(circumstanţă favorabilă)* advantage; *(bonificaţie)* **avantaje oferite unor salariaţi** = perks

avarie *sf* damage

avere *sf* **(a)** asset **(b)** wealth; **impozit pe avere** = wealth tax

avertisment *sn* notice; **a da un avertisment (oficial) cuiva** = to serve notice on someone

avion *sn* plane; **avion de transport comercial** = freighter; **colegul meu va sosi la Bucureşti cu avionul de ora 3 de la Heathrow** = my colleague is arriving in Bucharest on the 3 o'clock plane from Heathrow; **par avion** = airmail; **a expedia par avion** = to airmail; **coletul trimis par avion a ajuns la destinaţie în numai patru zile** = the package sent by airmail reached its destination in only four days

aviz *sn sau* **avizare** *sf* note *sau* notice; **aviz de debit** = debit advice; **aviz de expediere** *sau* **aviz de expediţie** = advice note; **aviz de primire** = advice of delivery

aviza *vb* to notify; **directorul general a avizat sindicatul că măsuri de reducere a personalului aveau să fie puse în practică în curând** = the managing director notified the union that further job cuts were to follow shortly

avizier *sn* notice-board

avocat *sm* **(a)** lawyer; barrister; attorney **(b)** counsel **(c)** solicitor

avocatură *sf* the legal profession

Bb

bac *sn* ferry; **a traversa cu bacul** = to ferry; **am luat bacul de la Brăila** = we took the ferry from Brăila

bacşiş *sn* gratuity *sau* tip; **a da bacşiş** = to tip; **a fost admonestat pentru primirea de bacşiş** = he was told off for accepting gratuities; **i-a dat şoferului de taxi un bacşiş generos** = he gave the taxi driver a generous tip

bagaj *sn* baggage; **bagaj de mână** = hand luggage

Bahamas (Insulele) *sfpl* The Bahamas; Notă: capitală: **Nassau;** monedă: **dolar bahamez** = Bahamian dollar

bahamez(ă) *s & adj* Bahamian

baissier *sm* bear

balanţă *sf* (a) balance; **balanţă activă (de comerţ** *sau* **de plăţi, etc.)** = active balance; **a avea balanţă negativă în bancă** = to be overdrawn; **balanţă de plăţi** = balance of payments; **balanţă (de plăţi) negativă** = adverse balance (of payments) (b) *(cântar)* scales

bancă *sf* (a) bank; **are un cont la banca Ţiriac** = he banks with Ţiriac (Bank); **a depune** *sau* **a depozita bunuri sau bani la bancă** = to bank (money) *sau* to deposit money in a bank; **a ţine banii în bancă** *sau* **a avea cont în bancă** = to bank *sau* to have a bank account; **bancă comercială** = High Street bank; **bancă comercială (pe acţiuni)** = joint-stock bank;

acceptat de bancă = bankable; **director de bancă** = bank manager (b) **bancă de date** = data bank

Banca Angliei *sf* Bank of England

Banca Centrală Suedeză *sf* Riksbank

Banca Federală Germană *sf* Bundesbank

Banca Franceză *sf* Banque de France

Banca Naţională Italiană *sf* Banca d'Italia

Banca Naţională a României (BNR) *sf* Romanian Central Bank

Banca Română de Comerţ Exterior *sf* Romanian Foreign Trade Bank

bancar *adj* bank *sau* banking; **cont bancar** = bank account; **costuri bancare** = bank charges; **rate de bază ale dobânzilor bancare** = bank base rate; **operaţii bancare** = banking

bancher *sm* banker

bancnotă *sf* banknote; **bancnotele s-au dovedit a fi false** = the banknotes proved to be forged

Bangladeş *sf* Bangladesh; Notă: capitală: **Dacca** = Dhaka; monedă: **taka**

bangladeş(ă) *s & adj* Bangladeshi

bani *smpl* money; *(fonduri)* finances; **bani avuţi la îndemână** = ready cash; **bani de buzunar** = pocket-money; **bani falşi** = counterfeit money; **bani gheaţă** = (i) cash *sau* hard cash; (ii) active capital; **bani în mână, disponibili pe loc** = cash in hand; **bani peşin disponibili** = ready money; **avans în bani gheaţă** = cash advance; **a câştiga bani (muncind)** = to earn money; **a depune bani la bancă** = to put money into the bank; **ofertă în bani peşin** = cash offer; **a plăti cu bani peşin** = to pay in cash; **a plăti un avans în bani peşin** = to put money down; **sumă de bani aflată în casă la deschiderea magazinului** *sau* **sumă de bani păstrată într-un cont de economii (pentru dobânzi)** = float

bar *sn* bar; **după şedinţă s-au dus la barul hotelului** = after the meeting they went to the hotel bar

bara *vb* *(a interzice)* to bar; **cec barat** = crossed cheque

bară *sf* *(a claviaturii unei maşini de scris sau calculator)* **bara de spaţiu** = space bar

barieră *sn* barrier; **bariere vamale** = tariff barriers

baril *sm* barrel; **patronii restaurantului au importat 10 barili de vin din România** = the owners of the restaurant imported 10 barrels of red wine from Romania

BASIC *(limbaj simplu de programare a calculatoarelor)* BASIC (Beginner's All-purpose Symbolic Instructions Code)

baza *vb* **a (se) baza** = to base; **a se baza pe** = to calculate on *sau* to base one's calculations on; **ideile sale de marketing se bazau pe speculaţii** = his marketing ideas were based on speculation

bază *sf* base; **de bază** = basic; **salariu de bază** = basic pay

bănesc *adj* pecuniary; **recompensă bănească** = pecuniary reward

Belgia *sf* Belgium; Notă: capitală: **Bruxelles** = Brussels; monedă: **franc belgian** = Belgian franc

belgian(ă) *s & adj* Belgian

belşug *sn* *(bogăţie)* wealth *sau* affluence

beneficia *vb* to benefit *sau* to profit; **toată lumea cu un venit mic va beneficia de pe urma noilor măsuri** = everyone on low incomes will benefit from the new measures

beneficiar *sm* recipient; **beneficiar al plăţii** = payee

beneficiu *sn* (a) advantage (b) *(profit)* benefit *sau* profit; proceeds; **beneficiu contabil** = book profit; **beneficiu de exploatare** = operating profit; **marjă de beneficiu** = profit margin; **participarea la beneficii** = profit-sharing

benzină *sf* petrol; **o maşină cu consum scăzut de benzină** = car with low petrol consumption

bifa *vb* *(verifica)* to check

bilanţ *sn* account; balance sheet; **analiza bilanţului** = balance sheet analysis

bilateral *adj* reciprocal; **contract bilateral** = reciprocal contract

bilet *sn* (a) fare; **bilet de dus** = single ticket *sau* single fare; **tarif** *sau* **costul biletului de călătorie** = fare; **costul biletului de călătorie dus şi întors** = return fare; **costul biletului de călătorie pentru dus** = single fare; **casă de bilete** = booking office; **preţ al biletului de intrare** = entrance fee; **preţul biletului la stadion** = gate money (b) *(titlu cambial ce conţine o promisiune de plată)* **bilet la ordin** = promissory note

bilunar *adv & adj* fortnightly; în **România salariaţii sunt plătiţi**

bilunar = in Romania, employees are paid fortnightly

birocraţie *sf* bureaucracy *sau* red tape

birou *sn* (a) bureau *sau* office; **accesorii de birou** = office equipment; **birou de plasare** = job centre; **birou de informaţii** = information office (b) desk; **am nevoie de un birou nou cu mai multe sertare** = I need a new desk with more drawers; **s-a aşezat la birou şi a început să lucreze** = he sat down at his desk and began working; **PC** *sau* **imprimantă care poate fi aşezat pe birou** = desktop computer *sau* printer

bizui *vb* **a se bizui pe** = to reckon on *sau* to bargain on

bloc *sn* bloc; **bloc de locuinţe** = block of flats

bloca *vb* to block *sau* to freeze; **a bloca accesul la credite** = to freeze credits; *(în caz de pierdere sau furt)* **a bloca o filă de cec** = to stop a cheque; **cec blocat** = order not to pay; **cont blocat** = account on stop

blocadă maritimă *sf* blockade; **spărgător de blocadă** = blockade runner

bogat *adj* affluent

bogăţie *sf* wealth *sau* affluence

boicot *sn* boycott

boicota *vb* to boycott; **a boicota un produs** = to boycott a product

Bolivia *sf* Bolivia; Notă: capitală: **La Paz;** monedă: **peso bolivian** = Bolivian peso

bolivian(ă) *s & adj* Bolivian

bon *sn* (a) *(chitanţă)* voucher; **bon de casă** = cash voucher; **bon de rambursare** = refund voucher (b) bond; **bon de tezaur** = treasury bond *sau* government bond

bonificaţie *sf (avantaje oferite unor salariaţi)* perk; **bonificaţie de producţie** = incentive payment

boom *sn* boom

bord *sn* board; **la bordul unei nave** = on board (a) ship; **peste bord** = overboard; **a arunca încărcătura peste bord** = to throw the cargo overboard

borderou *sn (foaie de pontaj)* tally sheet

bovine *sfpl* cattle

Brazilia *sf* Brazil; Notă: capitală: **Brasilia;** monedă: **real**

brazilian(ă) *s & adj* Brazilian

breaslă *sf* guild; **breasla meşteşugarilor** = craft guild

breşă *sf* breach

brevet *sn (licenţă)* patent

breveta *vb* **a breveta o invenţie** = to patent an invention

brevetat *adj* proprietary; **produs farmaceutic brevetat** = proprietary drug

Britanie (Marea) *sf* Great Britain; Notă: capitală: **Londra** = London; monedă: **liră sterlină (£)** = pound sterling (£)

britanic(ă) *s & adj* British

broker *sm (agent de schimb)* (stock) broker

broşură *sf* booklet; **am ales această excursie din broşura publicată de agenţia de voiaj** = we picked this trip from the booklet issued by the travel agent

brut *adj* gross; pre-tax; **beneficiu brut** = gross margin; **a obţine beneficii brute** = to gross; **profit brut** = gross profit *sau* pre-tax profit; **salariu brut** = gross salary; **banca a declarat un profit brut de peste 500 de miliarde de lei** = the bank reported a pre-tax profit of over 500 billion lei

bucată *sf* piece; **la bucată** = by the piece; **cost per bucată** = unit cost

buget *sn* budget; **buget alocat pentru publicitate** = advertising budget; **buget echilibrat** = balanced budget; **buget general** = ordinary budget; **buget militar** = military budget; **proiect de buget** = draft budget; **a repartiza din buget** = to budget

bugetar *adj* budgetary; **estimaţie bugetară** = budget estimate

buletin informativ *sn* journal; **buletin informativ intern** = newsletter

bulgar(ă) *s & adj* Bulgarian

Bulgaria *sf* Bulgaria; Notă: capitală: **Sofia;** monedă: **leva** = lev

bun *adj* good; **bună credinţă** = good faith

bunăstare *sf* welfare; **bunăstare socială** = social welfare

bunuri *snpl* goods; *(produse)* commodity; **bunuri de consum** = consumer goods; *(marfă)* merchandise;

bunuri fără un proprietar evident = bona vacantia; **bunuri de folosinţă îndelungată** = consumer durables *sau* durable goods; **bunuri imobiliare** = estate; **bunuri necesare** = staple commodities; **bunuri personale** = goods and chattels; **bunuri personale (mobile)** = effects; **bunuri transportate pe calea aerului** = air cargo; **bunuri în tranzit** = goods in transit

bursă *sf* (a) **Bursa** = Stock Exchange; **bursă de valori** = stock market; **bursă de mărfuri** = commodity exchange; **bursa neagră** = black market *sau* black economy; **agent de bursă** = jobber; **joc la bursă** *sau* **operaţiuni de bursă** = speculation; **a juca la bursă** *sau* **a face speculaţii la bursă** = to speculate; **operaţiuni de bursă după ora oficială de închidere** = after-hours trading; **societate comercială cu acţiuni la bursă** = quoted company **(b)** grant; **bursă de studii** = student's grant

butoi *sn* barrel

buzunar *sn* pocket; **a băga în buzunar** = to pocket; **calculator de buzunar** = pocket calculator; **ediţie de buzunar** = pocket edition

Cc

cabină *sf* booth; **cabină telefonică** = callbox *sau* telephone booth *sau* telephone kiosk

cabinet *sn* **cabinet medical particular** = medical practice *sau* doctor's surgery; **cabinet stomatologic particular** = dental practice; **Doctorul X şi-a deschis un cabinet medical particular pe Strada Mihai Eminescu** = Dr X opened a practice on Mihai Eminescu Street

cablu *sn* cable; **telegramă prin cablu (transoceanic)** = cable; **televiziune prin cablu** = cable television

cadastru *sn* land register

cadou *sn* (a) gift *sau* present; **colegii i-au făcut cadou un ceas când a ieşit la pensie** = his colleagues gave him a watch as a present when he retired (b) handout

cadran *sn* dial

cadre *snpl* personnel

calcul *sn* (a) estimate; **a efectua calcule** = to process figures; **calcul aproximativ** = rough estimate; **greşeală de calcul** = miscalculation (b) **expert în sisteme de calcul** = computer specialist; **oficiu (centru) de calcul** = computer bureau

calcula *vb* (a) *(a socoti)* to calculate *sau* to work out the figures; *(a estima)* to figure out *sau* to reckon; **a calcula**

greşit = to miscalculate (b) to compute

calculare *sf* calculation; **risc calculat** = calculated risk

calculator *sn* (a) *(ordinator)* computer; **operator (de) calculator** = computer operator (b) **calculator electronic (de buzunar)** = (pocket) calculator

cale *sf* way; **cale de acces** = access; **cale ferată** = rail *sau* railway; **pe calea aerului** = by air; **pe cale maritimă** = by sea

calendar *sn* calendar

calendaristic *adj* **an calendaristic** = calendar year; **lună calendaristică** = calendar month

califica *vb* to qualify

calificare *sf* *(aptitudine)* qualification; **cu înaltă calificare** = highly qualified

calificat *adj* qualified; **muncă calificată** *sau* **mână de lucru calificată** = skilled labour

calitate *sf* quality; **calitate inferioară** = bad quality; **calitate superioară** = good quality; **control tehnic de calitate** = quality control; **de calitate** = good; **de calitate inferioară** = cheap *sau* second-class *sau* second-rate; **aceşti pantofi sunt de calitate inferioară şi urâţi** = these shoes are cheap and ugly; *(despre comerţ, desfacere, servicii, etc.)* **de calitate**

modestă = downmarket; **de prima calitate** = first-class

calomnia *vb* to libel

calomnie *sf* libel; **acțiune civilă pentru calomniere** = action for libel

camătă *sf (dobândă)* usury

cambie *sf (tratā)* bill of exchange

Cambodgia *sf* Cambodia; Notă: capitală: **Phnom Penh;** monedă: **riel**

cambodgian(ă) *s & adj* Cambodian

Camera de Comerț *sf* Chamber of Commerce

Camera Comunelor *sf (în Marea Britanie - cameră inferioară a Parlamentului Britanic)* House of Commons

Camera Lorzilor *sf (în Marea Britanie - cameră superioară a Parlamentului Britanic)* House of Lords

Camerun *sm* Cameroon; Notă: capitală: **Yaoundé;** monedă: **franc CFA** = CFA franc

camerunez(ă) *s & adj* Cameroonian

camion *sn* lorry *sau* truck

camionetă *sf* pickup truck

campanie *sf* campaign; **campanie de creștere a vânzărilor** = sales campaign; **campanie de economisire** = economy campaign; **campanie de reducere a costurilor** = economy drive; **campanie publicitară** = publicity campaign

Canada *sf* Canada; Notă: capitală: **Ottawa;** monedă: **dolar canadian** = Canadian dollar

canadian(ă) *s & adj* Canadian

canal *sn* channel

Canalul Mânecii *sn* the Channel *sau* the English Channel; **tunel** feroviar sub Canalul Mânecii (care leagă Marea Britanie de Franța) = the Channel Tunnel

candidat *sm* candidate; **candidații la postul de director au susținut un examen riguros** = the candidates for the post of director had to take a stiff examination

candidatură *sf* application (for a job *sau* a post); **a (-și) depune candidatura** = to nominate

cantitate *sf* quantity; number; **cantitate considerabilă** = (i) a great deal *sau* a good deal; (ii) bulk; **a obținut un bun scont cumpărând o cantitate mare de articole de papetărie** = he got a good discount by buying a large quantity of stationery

capabil *adj* (a) *(apt)* fit (b) efficient; **lucrător capabil** = efficient worker

capacitate *sf* capacity; **capacitate de producție** = throughput; **capacitate instalată** = installed capacity; **capacitatea totală de încărcare a navei** = deadweight; **capacitatea deadweight (de încărcare) a unei nave** = deadweight capacity of a ship

capăt *sn (limită)* border; **capăt de linie** = terminal

capital *sn* capital *(participare)* stake; **capital de rezervă** = reserve capital; **capital fix** = capital equipment; **capital lichid** = active capital; **capital neproductiv** *sau* **neinvestit** = dead capital; **capital operativ** = working capital; **cheltuieli de capital** = capital expenditures; **a procura capital (prin emiterea de acțiuni) pentru înființarea unei companii** = to set up a company

capitală *sf* capital; **București este capitala României** = Bucharest is the capital of Romania

capitalism *sn* capitalism

capitalist *sm* capitalist

captiv *adj* **piaţă captivă** = captive market

captura *vb* *(a acapara)* to capture

captură *sf* capture

caracter *sn* **(a)** *(literă)* character; **caracter tipografic** = letter; **caractere chinezeşti** = Chinese characters **(b)** *(personalitate)* character

caracterizare *sf* *(certificat de conduită sau calificări)* testimonial

carat *sn* carat; **aur de 24 de carate** = 24 carat gold; **inel cu diamant de 5 carate** = 5 carat diamond ring

carenţă *sf* lack; want

cargobot *sn* cargo boat; bulk carrier

carieră *sf* career; **el a avut o carieră remarcabilă ca profesor** = he had a remarkable career in teaching

carnet *sn* **carnet de cecuri** = cheque book; **carnet de depuneri** = bank book *sau* paying-in book; **carnet de economii** = pass-book

cartă *sf* *(document)* charter

carte *sf* **(a)** book; **carte tehnică** = operating manual; **carte tehnică (de exploatare)** = user's manual **(b)** **carte de acoperire a cecului** = cheque card; **carte de credit** = credit card; **titular** *sau* **deţinător al unei cărţi de credit** = cardholder **(c)** **carte poştală** = postcard **(d)** *(certificat de asigurare auto pe timpul călătoriilor în străinătate)* **cartea verde** = green card

cartel *sn* cartel; combine; ring; **cartel internaţional** = international cartel

cartelă *sf* card

cartier *sn* **(a)** neighbourhood; **cartier rezidenţial** = housing estate **(b)** *(zonă)* estate

casa *vb* **(a)** *(o sentinţă)* to avoid **(b)** **a casa mijloace fixe** = to write off

casă *sf* **(a)** *(într-un magazin)* desk *sau* cash desk *sau* pay desk; *(în supermagazin)* checkout; **a plătit pentru cumpărături la casă** = he paid for the goods at the desk; **casă de bilete** = booking office *sau* box office; **maşina de casă** = cash register; **sold de casă** = cash balance **(b)** *(imobil)* house **(c)** **casă de ajutor reciproc** = credit cooperative **(d)** **casă de bani** = vault *sau* strongbox; **casă de economii** = savings bank

casetă video *sau* **video-casetă** *sf* videotape *sau* videocassette

casetofon *sn* **(a)** dictating machine **(b)** tape recorder

casier *sm* cashier; teller

casnic *adj* domestic; **aparate de uz casnic** = domestic appliances

catalog *sn* catalogue *sau* list; *(listă de preţuri)* price list; **preţ de catalog** = list price

catastrofă *sf* catastrophe; **acea companie de asigurări recunoaşte următoarele tipuri de catastrofă; cutremure, inundaţii şi furtuni violente** = that insurance company recognizes the following types of catastrophe: earthquakes, flood and storms

categorie *sf* **(a)** category; **hotel categoria lux** = first-class hotel **(b)** denomination **(c)** rank

cauţiune *sf* bail; **a elibera pe cauţiune** = to bail

caz *sn* case

cazare *sf* accommodation

cazier *sn* **cazier judiciar** = criminal record

cădea *vb* to collapse *sau* to fall

cădere *sf* collapse *sau* fall; **căderea regimurilor totalitariste în Europa de Est oferă oamenilor de afaceri străini noi posibilităţi de investiţii**

= the collapse of the totalitarian regimes in Eastern Europe offers the foreign investors new business prospects

călător *sm* traveller

călători *vb* to travel

călătorie *sf* travel *sau* journey; **cec de călătorie la purtător** = traveller's cheque

călăuză *sf* guide

cămătar *sm* **(a)** pawnbroker **(b)** usurer

cămătărie *sf* usury

căpitan *sm* *(de vas comercial sau de pasageri)* captain; *(de vas comercial)* seacaptain; **căpitan al unui vas comercial** = ship's officer

cărăuş *sm* bearer

căsuţă poştală *sf* post office box *sau* P.O. Box

căuta *vb* to look; **a căuta de lucru** = to look for a job

cântar *sn* **(a)** balance **(b)** *(balanţă)* scales

cântări *vb* **(a)** to consider **(b)** to consult **(c)** to weigh; **acest colet cântăreşte 3,5 kilograme** = this parcel weighs 3.5 kilos

câştig *sn* **(a)** bread **(b)** earnings; **capacitate de câştig** = earning capacity *sau* earning power; **potenţial de câştig** = earning potential **(c)** profit *sau* gain; *(slang)* **câştig neaşteptat** = killing; **a specula şi câştiga (la bursă)** = to make a killing

câştiga *vb* *(muncind)* to get; to earn *sau* to make; to gain; *(a obţine net)* to net; **a câştiga bine** = to earn a good wage; **ei câştigă 90.000 de lei pe lună** = they earn 90,000 lei per month; **un contabil poate câştiga 2 milioane de lei pe an** = an accountant may get 2 milion lei a year; **a câştigat 10 milioane de lei din**

vânzarea acţiunilor sale = she made 10 million lei by selling her shares; **magazinul câştigă bani frumoşi din vânzarea de suveniruri turiştilor** = the shop makes a lot of money from the sale of souvenirs to tourists; **a câştiga mulţi bani** = to rake it in

ceartă *sf* dispute

cec *sn* cheque *sau* US check; **acest magazin acceptă numai bani şi cecuri** = this store accepts cash and cheques only; **cec barat** = crossed cheque; **cec clarificat** = cleared cheque; **cec de călătorie la purtător** = traveller's cheque; **cec poştal** = girocheque; **carnet de cecuri** = cheque book; **a completa un cec** = to write a cheque *sau* to draw a cheque

ceda *vb* **(a)** to cede **(b)** to make a concession

cedare *sf* cedarea proprietăţii creditorilor = cession

ceh(ă) *s & adj* Czech

Cehă, Republica *sf* Czech Republic; Notă: capitală: **Praga** = Prague; monedă: **coroană cehă** = Czech koruna

Celsius *s* *(scală de măsurare a temperaturii)* **temperatura va atinge 10° Celsius azi** = today the temperature will reach 10° Celsius

cent *sm* cent *(în SUA)* **monedă de 10 cenţi** = dime; **monedă de 5 cenţi** = nickel; **monedă de 25 de cenţi** = quarter

centimetru (cm) *sm* centimetre (cm)

centraliza *vb* to centralize; **economie centralizată** = centralized economy

centralizare *sf* centralization

central *adj* central; **bancă centrală (de stat)** = central bank

centrală (a) *sf* centrală telefonică = (i) switchboard; (ii) telephone exchange; **centrală electrică** = power station; *(pentru încălzirea locuinţelor)* **centrală termică** = central-heating plant (b) headquarters

centru *sn* (a) centre; **centru comercial** = (i) shopping centre; (ii) commercial district; **centrul oraşului** = town centre *(în SUA)* downtown (b) point; **centru de vânzare** *sau* **desfacere** = point of sales

cerceta *vb* (a) to research (b) to examine

cercetare *sf* (a) examination (b) research *sau* inquiry; **cercetare aplicată** = applied research; **compania a decis alocarea unei sume de 1 miliard de lei pentru cercetare** = the company decided to allocate 1 billion lei to research; **institut de cercetări** = research institute

cercetător *sm* researcher *sau* research worker

cere *vb* (a) *(a ruga)* to ask; **curs cerut** = asking price (b) *(a solicita)* to request (c) to demand; to exact; **a cere datorilor să plătească** = to exact payment from debtors

cerere *sf* (a) request; *(solicitare)* **cerere în scris** = application; **formular de cerere** = application form; **la cerere** = on request; **cerere de plată pe loc** = payment on demand; **a face cerere** = to apply; **a face o cerere pentru** = to put in a request for; **a făcut cerere de împrumut dar a fost refuzată** = he applied for a loan but was refused; **cererea ei de împrumut a fost aprobată** = her request for a loan was granted; **ca să obţineţi un împrumut, trebuie să faceţi cerere la bancă** = you have to make an application to the bank in order to get a loan (b) demand; *(teorie economică)*

consumer demand; **cerere diversificată** = composite demand; **cerere excesivă a unui produs pe piaţă** = excess demand; **cerere flexibilă** = elastic demand; **curba (structura) cererii** = demand curve; **inflaţie generată de cerere excesivă** = demand-led inflation (c) *(rugăminte)* appeal

cerinţă *sf* requirement

certifica *vb* *(a autentifica)* to attest *sau* to certify

certificat *sn* certificate; **certificat de acţionar (la purtător)** = share warrant; **certificat de căsătorie** = marriage certificate; **certificat de naţionalitate a unei nave** = certificate of registry; **certificat de naştere** = birth certificate; **certificat de sănătate** = medical certificate

cesionar *sm* assignee

cesiune *sf* assignment

charter party *sf* charter party; **cursă charter** = charter flight

chei *sn* (a) quay (b) *(de mărfuri)* wharf

cheie *sf* key; **factor cheie** = key factor

cheltui *vb* to spend; **şi-a cheltuit aproape toţi banii pe cumpărarea unei case noi** = he spent most of his money buying a new house; **a cheltui excesiv** = to overspend; **a cheltui mai mult decât este prevăzut în buget** = to overspend one's budget; **a cheltui mai puţin decât prevede bugetul** = to underspend

cheltuială *sf* (a) expense; outlay; **au stat la hotel pe cheltuiala companiei** = they stayed at the hotel at the company's expense (b) spending; **bani de cheltuială** = spending money (c) cost *sau* expenditure *sau* outgoings; **revizorul a cerut un raport detaliat al cheltuielilor** = the auditor asked for a breakdown of the expenses; **cheltuieli administrative** = administrative costs; **cheltuieli comune** = joint costs; **cheltuieli de capital** = capital expenditure; **cheltuieli de constituire** *sau* **preliminarii** = preliminary expenses; **cheltuieli de călătorie** = travelling expenses; **cheltuieli de expediţie** = handling charges; **cheltuieli de exploatare** = running costs; **cheltuieli de fabricaţie** = manufacturing overheads; **cheltuieli de întreţinere** = overhead expenses; **cheltuieli fixe** = fixed costs *sau* oncosts; **cheltuieli generale** = overheads; *(chirie sau impozite, etc.)* **cheltuieli globale** = overall cost; **cheltuieli marginale** = marginal costs; **cheltuieli ocazionale** = incidental expenses; **cheltuieli publicitare** = advertising outlay; **cheltuieli uzufructuare** = user costs; **cont curent de cheltuieli** = expense account

chema *vb* to call

chemare *sf* call

chestiona *vb* to query

chestionar *sn* questionnaire; **clientul a fost rugat politicos să completeze chestionarul** = the customer was kindly asked to fill in the questionnaire

chestiune *sf (problemă)* question; issue

chibzui *vb* to consider; **a chibzui asupra unei oferte** = to consider an offer

chibzuială *sf* **(a)** *(judecată)* consideration **(b)** *(economie)* economy

chibzuit *adj (econom)* careful with money *sau* penny-wise

chilă *sf* keel

Chile *sf* Chile; Notă: capitală: **Santiago (de Chile)**; monedă: **peso chilian** = Chilean peso

chilian(ă) *s & adj* Chilean

chilipir *sn (achiziţie la un preţ avantajos)* bargain buy; *(afacere favorabilă)* bargain

China *sf* China; Notă: capitală: **Beijing**; monedă: **yuan**

chinez(ă) *s* Chinese

chinezesc *sau* **chinezească** *adj* Chinese

chioşc *sn* kiosk; **chioşc de ziare** = newspaper kiosk

chiriaş *sm* tenant; **chiriaş liber să rezilieze contractul de închiriere la cerere** = tenant at will

chirie *sf* rent; **a da cu chirie** = to hire out *sau* to rent out; **chirie contractuală** = contractual rent; **reglementarea chiriei** = rent control; **chirie exorbitantă** = rack rent

chitanţă *sf* **(a)** receipt; **chitanţă de vânzare** = sales receipt; **chitanţă vamală** = customs receipt **(b)** *(recipisă)* slip *sau* voucher; **chitanţă de depunere** *sau* **depozitare** = certificate of deposit; **chitanţă de salariu** = pay slip; **a arătat chitanţa de vânzare şi a cerut rambursarea banilor** = he produced the sales slip and asked for a refund

chitanţier *sn* receipt book

ciclu *sn* **(a)** cycle; **ciclu economic** = business cycle **(b)** chain

cifra *vb* to code

cifră *sf* figure; **cifra de vânzări** = sales figures; **cifră de afaceri** = turnover; **cifră de plan** = target figure; **număr din două cifre (de la 10 la 99)** = double figures; **sumă din şase cifre (peste 100.000)** = six-figure sum

cifru *sn* code; combination; **închizătoare cu cifru** = combination lock

cinste *sf* faith; *(lealitate)* honesty

ciocan *sn* hammer

ciocănel *sn* *(la licitații)* hammer

cipriot(ă) *s & adj* Cypriot

Cipru *sm* Cyprus; Notă: capitală: **Nicosia;** monedă: **liră cipriotă** = Cyprus pound

circula *vb* to circulate

circulație *sf* **(a)** circulation; **a pune bani în circulație** = to put money into circulation **(b)** flow; **circulația banilor** = cash flow **(c)** traffic; **agent de circulație** = traffic warden

circulant *adj* circulating; **capitaluri circulante** = circulating capital

circular *adj* circular

circulară *sf* *(notă)* circular *sau* circular letter; **compania a trimis o circulară oferind livrare gratuită tuturor clienților fideli** = the company sent out a circular offering free delivery to all established customers

cita *vb* to subpoena

citație *sf* *(la tribunal)* summons; *(ordonanță)* writ; subpoena; **citație preliminară** = originating summons; **i-a telefonat avocatului ei după ce a primit citația** = she rang her lawyer after receiving the summons

civil *adj* civil; **acțiune civilă** = civil action; **a se constitui parte civilă (în procese)** = to bring a civil action; **construcții civile** = civil engineering; **drept civil** = civil law

clar *adj* *(evident)* clear

clarifica *vb* *(a lămuri)* to clear; **discursul omului de afaceri a clarificat orice dubiu** = the businessman's speech cleared the doubts

clasă *sf* class; **clasa întâia** = first class; **clasa a doua** = second-class; *(în călătoriile cu avionul sau vaporul)* **clasă**

turistică *sau* **clasa a doua** = economy class *sau* tourist class; **bilet clasa întâia** = first class ticket; **a călători cu clasa a doua** = to travel second-class; **ei vând calculatoare numai din clasa procesorului 586** = they only sell computers in the 586 category

clasifica *vb* to classify *(în ordinea importanței)* to rank; to grade

clauză *sf* *(prevedere)* clause; **clauză adițională** = rider; **clauză de eschivare** = escape clause; **clauza tarifului progresiv** = escalator clause; **una din clauzele contractului interzice grevele** = one of the contract's clauses forbids strikes

clădire *sf* building; *(imobile)* property

clearing *sn* **acord de clearing** = clearing agreement

client *sm* *(cumpărător)* client *sau* customer; **client vechi** *sau* **al casei** = regular customer; **mulțumirea clientului** = customer satisfaction

clientelă *sf* clientele

club *sn* *(organizație; societate mondenă)* society; **club select** *sau* **exclusivist** = exclusive club

coadă *sf* queue; **a sta la coadă** *sau* **a forma o coadă** = to queue; **a se așeza la coadă** = to join the queue

COBOL *(limbaj de programare a calculatoarelor)* COBOL (Common Business Oriented Language)

cod *sn* code *(în Marea Britanie)* **cod al impozitului pe venit** = tax code; **cod poștal** = postcode; *US* zip code

codice *sn* code

coeficient *sn* rate; **coeficient de amortizare** = depreciation rate

colabora *vb* to collaborate; **fabrica de calculatoare a colaborat cu compania de software în realizarea unui nou calculator** = the computer manufacturer collaborated with the software company on a new machine

colaps *sn (prăbuşire)* collapse

colecta *vb* **(a)** collect **(b)** to raise ; *(pentru abonamente)* **a colecta cotizaţii** = to raise subscriptions

colectiv 1 *sn (grup)* collective 2 *adj* collective; **noul produs a fost rezultatul muncii colective** = the new product was the result of collective work

colectivism *sn* collectivism

colector *sn (cont bancar inactiv)* dead account

colecţionar *sm* collector

coleg *sm* colleague

colegiu *sn* college

colet *sn (pachet)* package *sau* packet *sau* parcel; **colet poştal** = postal packet; **coletul a fost livrat la domiciliul ei** = the package was delivered to her door

coletărie *sf (mesagerie)* parcel post

coloană *sf (de grafic)* bar; *(de cifre)* column; **a aduna o coloană de cifre** = to add up a column of figures

colonialism *sn* colonialism

Columbia *sf* Colombia; Notă: capitală: **Bogotá**; monedă: **peso columbian** = Colombian peso

columbian(ă) *n & adj* Colombian

comanda *vb* **(a)** *(a ordona sau a da ordine)* to command *sau* to order **(b)** to order; **au comandat un cântar electronic nou pentru registratură** = they ordered new electronic scales for the mail room

comandă *sf* order; **am făcut comandă de mobilier de birou** = we placed an order for office furniture; **a onora o comandă** = to fulfil an order; **a reînnoi o comandă** = to reorder; **comandă de import** = indent;

comandă neonorată (încă) = outstanding order; **comandă prin telefon** = telephone order; **comandă suplimentară** = reorder; **de comandă** = made to order *sau* bespoke; **formular de comandă** = order form; **registru de comenzi** = order-book

comanditar *adj* asociat comanditar = sleeping partner

combina *vb* to combine

combinaţie *sf* combination

comercial *adj* commercial *sau* mercantile; **acord comercial** = trade agreement; **centru comercial** = shopping centre; **complex comercial** = shopping mall; **deficit comercial** = trade gap; **flotă comercială** = merchant fleet; **funcţionar comercial** = accounts clerk; **lege comercială** = mercantile law; **marină comercială** = merchant navy *sau* mercantile marine; **partener comercial** = trading partner; **port comercial** = commercial port; **societate comercială** = trading company; **valoare comercială** = market value

comercializa *vb* to commercialize; to merchandize; *(a vinde)* to market; **a comercializa un produs** = to merchandize a product

comercializare *sf* commercialization; **planuri de comercializare** = marketing plans

comerciant *sm* dealer *sau* merchant; *(proprietar de magazin)* shopkeeper; *(om de afaceri)* trader *sau* businessman; **comerciant individual** = sole trader

comerţ *sn* commerce; trade *sau* trading; business; *(vânzări)* market; *(subiect de studiu în academiile comerciale)* commerce; **balanţă de comerţ pozitivă** = favourable balance of trade; **bancă de comerţ** = merchant bank; **comerţ exterior** = foreign trade; **comerţ ilicit** = *(bursa neagră)* black

economy;   *(contrabandă)* racket;
(escrocherie) racketeering; **comerţ**
interior = domestic trade *sau* home
trade; **comerţ liberalizat** = free
market; **comerţ multilateral** =
multilateral trade; **comerţ de schimb**
= barter; **a face comerţ** = to trade

comis voiajor *sm* commercial
traveller

comisie *sf sau* **comitet** *sn* board;
commission *sau* committee; **comisie**
consultativă = advisory board;
guvernul a înfiinţat o comisie de
investigare a acuzaţiilor de
corupţie = the government set up a
commission to investigate the
corruption allegations

comision *sn* commission; rake-off;
comision bancar = banker's
commission; **comision de asigurări** =
insurance commission; **comision**
ilegal = kickback; **agenţia a câştigat**
un comision de 5 milioane de lei
pentru serviciile prestate = the
agency got a 5 million lei rake-off for
its services

comitet *sn* committee; **membru al**
unui comitet = member of a
commitee

companie *sf* company; **lucrează în**
această companie de 30 de ani = he
has been working in this company for
30 years; **majoritatea companiilor**
caută să reducă costurile de
producţie = most companies are keen
to cut production costs; **companie de**
contrucţii = building contractor;
companie de transport aerian =
airline; **companie fantomă** = bogus
company; **companie subsidiară** =
subsidiary company; **secretarul**
companiei = company secretary

compensa *vb* to compensate; to
make up (for) *sau* to offset; to equalize;
a compensa dividende = to equalize
dividends; **a compensa o pierdere** =
to make up a loss; **pierderile de anul**
trecut au fost compensate parţial

de creşterea comenzilor de anul
acesta = last year's loss was partly
compensated for by the increase in
orders this year

compensaţie *sf* **(a)** compensation
sau indemnity; **a primit o**
compensaţie de £1000 pentru
pierderile de comision = he received
£1000 in compensation for the loss of
commission; **compensaţie pentru**
concediere = severance pay **(b)**
restitution

competent *adj* competent

competenţă *sf* competence;
consultantul financiar şi-a dovedit
competenţa oferind numeroase căi
de economisire = the financial
adviser proved his competence by
offering various ways of saving money

competitiv *adj* competitive; **piaţă**
competitivă *sau* **de concurenţă** =
competitive market; **preţ competitiv**
= competitive price *sau* keen price

competiţie *noun (concurenţă)*
competition; **competiţie ardentă** *sau*
intensă = keen competition;
competiţie loială = fair competition

complet **1** *adj (întreg)* complete;
(general) omnibus; **ediţie completă** =
omnibus edition **2** *adv (total)*
completely

completa *vb* to complete

completare *sf* completion; **vă**
rugăm să expediaţi cererea după
completare = please send your
application upon completion

complex **1** *sn* complex; **complex**
comercial = shopping mall; **complex**
industrial = industrial complex **2** *adj*
(complicat) complex

component *sn (piesă)* component;
element; **procesorul este cel mai**
important component al unui
calculator = the processor is the most
important component of a computer;

(software sau program) **componente logice** = software

compromis *sn* compromise; *(cu creditorii)* accommodation; **a ajunge la un compromis** = to reach a compromise; **a ajunge la un compromis cu creditorii** = to reach an accommodation with creditors; **a face un compromis** = to compromise *sau* to effect a compromise

compromite *vb (a primejdui)* to compromise

computeriza *vb* to computerize

comun *adj* common; **cont comun** = joint account; **proprietate comună** = joint ownership; **în comun** = jointly

comunica *vb* to communicate; *(la telefon)* to get through; **el comunica cu succes cu clienţii săi** = he communicated very successfully with his customers

comunicare *sf (înştiinţare)* communication

comunicat *sn* news release; **comunicat (de presă)** = press release

comunism *sn* communism

comunist *sm & adj* communist

Comunitatea Economică Europeană (CEE) *sf* European Economic Community (EEC)

concedia *vb* to axe; to sack *sau* to dismiss; **a concedia personal** = to make staff redundant; **a concedia temporar** = to lay off; **a fost concediată din cauză că nu era punctuală** = she was sacked for bad time-keeping; **datorită scăderii bruşte a vânzărilor magazinul a trebuit să concedieze temporar doi vânzători** = because of a sharp drop in sales the shop had to lay off two assistants; **ea a fost concediată pentru lipsă de politeţe faţă de clienţi** = she was dismissed for being impolite to customers

concediat *adj* redundant; **a fi concediat** = to get the sack

concediere *sf* redundancy; **compensaţie pentru concediere** = severance pay

concediu *sn* leave; *(vacanţă)* holiday; *US* vacation; **numărul de zile de concediu la care un lucrător are dreptul** = holiday entitlement; **are dreptul la un concediu anual de 25 de zile** = he is entitled to an annual leave of 25 days; **banii de concediu** = holiday pay; **concediu plătit** = holidays with pay; **concediu medical** = sick leave; **indemnizaţie de concediu medical** = sick pay

concentra *vb* to centralize

concentrare *sf* centralization

concesie *sf* concession *sau* compromise

concesiona *vb* to lease

concesionare *sf (franşiză)* franchise

concesiune *sf* **(a)** lease **(b)** concession; **concesiune de exploatare a minereurilor** = mineral concession

conciliere *sf (mediere)* conciliation

concluzie *sf* decision

concorda *vb* to tally

concordanţă *sf* **a fi în concordanţă cu** = to check with

concret *adj* effective; **cerere concretă** = effective demand

concura *vb* to compete; **vom înfrânge concurenţa cu aceste preţuri reduse** = we will beat our competitors with these low prices; **acum putem şi noi face concurenţă celorlalte companii pe piaţa sistemelor audio** = we can now compete with other companies on the audio systems market

concurenţă *sf* (a) competition; **a face concurenţă** = to compete; **concurenţă neloială** = unfair competition; **concurenţă sănătoasă** *sau* **constructivă** = healthy competition; **piaţă de concurenţă** = competitive market (b) *(rival în afaceri)* competitor

condiţie *sf* condition; **condiţii favorabile** = facilities; **condiţie implicită** *sau* **subînţeleasă** = implied condition; **condiţii ale contractului de muncă** = conditions of employment; **condiţii de plată** = payment terms *sau* terms of payment; **condiţii de schimb** = terms of trade; **condiţii de vânzare** = terms of sale

condiţional *adj* conditional

condiţionat *adj* conditional *(a bunurilor, etc.)* **acceptare condiţionată** = conditional acceptance *sau* qualified acceptance; **ofertă condiţionată** = conditional offer

conduce *vb* *(a îndruma sau a dirija)* to conduct *sau* to direct; *(a guverna)* to head *sau* to govern; *(a organiza)* to run *sau* to manage; *(a dirija sau a forţa)* to drive; **a conduce necorespunzător** = to mismanage; **conduce delegaţia** = he heads the delegation; **directorul conduce şedinţa** = the manager chairs the meeting *sau* the manager conducts the meeting; **el conduce filiala noastră din Londra** = he directs our operations in London *sau* he manages our branch in London

conducere *sf* management; **de conducere** = managerial; **a fi numit într-o funcţie de conducere** = to be appointed to a managerial position; **echipă de conducere** = management team; **preluarea majorităţii acţiunilor într-o companie de către echipa de conducere** = management buyout (MBO)

conducător *sm* *(şef)* leader; boss

conduită profesională *sf* code of practice

conecta *vb* to interface

conexiune *sf* (a) connection; **conexiune periferică a unui calculator** = port (b) *(interfaţă)* interface

conferinţă *sf* conference; **conferinţă de presă** = press conference; **sală de şedinţe** *sau* **conferinţe** = conference room

confident *sm* confident

confidenţial *adj* confidential; **vă rog să ţineţi minte că tot ce am discutat este strict confidenţial** = please remember that what we discussed is strictly confidential

confirma *vb* (a) *(primirea bunurilor, plăţii, etc.)* to acknowledge (b) to confirm; **a confirma o rezervare** = to confirm a booking; **i s-a cerut să confirme în scris comanda telefonică** = he was asked to confirm his telephone order in writing (c) to endorse; **a confirma prin semnătură un cec** = to endorse a cheque (d) *(a valida)* to validate

confirmare *sf* confirmation; acknowledgement; **confirmare în scris** = letter of acknowledgement; **scrisoare de confirmare (de primire, etc.)** = (i) letter of acknowledgement; (ii) letter of confirmation

confirmat *adj* confirmed; **credit confirmat irevocabil** = confirmed irrevocable credit

confisca *vb* to impound; *(bunuri)* to distrain; *(a sechestra)* to sequester; **vameşii au confiscat marfa contrabandistului** = the customs officials impounded the smuggler's goods

confiscare *sf* impounding ; *(sechestrare)* sequestration

conflict *sn* **(a)** dispute; **conflict de muncă** = industrial dispute **(b)** *(litigiu)* litigation

conforma *vb* **a se conforma** = to comply

conformitate *sf* compliance; **în conformitate cu rugămintea dumneavoastră** = in compliance with your request

confruntare *sf* challenge

Congo *sm* Congo; Notă: capitală: **Brazzaville;** monedă: **franc CFA** = CFA franc

congolez(ă) *s & adj* Congolese

conosament *sn* consignment note

consecinţă *sf (efect)* aftermath

conservator 1 *sm* conservative 2 *adj* conservative

considera *vb* to consider; to judge; **consider sugestiile Dvs. foarte folositoare** = I consider your suggestions very useful

considerabil *adj (important)* considerable

consilier *sm* adviser *sau* consultant

consiliu *sn* **(a)** board; **consiliu de administraţie** = board of directors *sau* management; **şedinţă de consiliu** = board meeting **(b)** council; **consiliu municipal** = town council

consimţământ *sn (permisiune)* consent

consimţi *vb* to accept *sau* to consent

consolida *vb* to consolidate

consolidare *sf* consolidation

consorţiu *sn* consortium

constant *adj (stabil)* constant; *(regulat)* regular

constantă *sf* constant

constructiv *adj (practic)* constructive

construcţie *sf* building *sau* construction; **clădirea se afla în construcţie când au cumpărat unul din apartamente** = the building was under construction when they bought one of the flats; **construcţii civile** = civil engineering; **expert în construcţii civile** = specialist in civil engineering; **antrepriză de construcţii** = construction company

construi *vb* to build *sau* to construct; **noua linie de metrou a fost construită de un consorţiu de companii britanice şi franceze** = the new underground line was constructed by a consortium of British and French companies

consul *sm* consul

consular *adj* consular

consulat *sn* consulate

consulta *vb* to consult; **el nu va lua o hotărâre până când nu se va consulta cu asociatul său cel mai apropiat** = he will not make any decision until he has consulted his closest associate

consultant *sm* adviser

consum *sn sau* **consumaţie** *sf* consumption; **bunuri de consum** = consumer goods

consuma *vb* to consume *sau* to eat

consumator *sm* consumer; **grup de consumatori** = consumer group; **profitul consumatorului** = consumer's surplus; **studiul comportamentului consumatorilor** = consumer research

consumaţie *sf sau* **consum** *sn* consumption

cont *sn* **(a)** account; **cont bancar** = bank account; **cont curent** = current account *sau* drawing account; **cont curent personal** = cheque account; **cont de capital** = stock account; **cont de depozit** = deposit account; **cont**

de economii = savings account; **extras de cont bancar** = bank statement **(b) cont de exploatare** *sau* **de exerciţiu** = trading account; **contul de profit şi pierderi** = profit and loss account; **cont de protocol** = entertainment account; **cont curent de cheltuieli** = expense account; **cont deschis** = charge account; **extras de cont** = statement of account

contabil *sm* **(a)** accountant; **contabil-şef** = accounts manager; *(în Marea Britanie)* **contabil atestat** *sau* **calificat** = certified accountant; **serviciu contabil (financiar)** = accounts department; **revizor contabil** = auditor; **sistem contabil (manual sau computerizat)** = accounting system **(b)** bookkeeper

contabilitate *sf* **(a)** accountancy **(b)** bookkeeping **(c)** accounts department

contact *sn* contact

contacta *vb* *(a ţine legătura)* to contact; **a contacta pe cineva la telefon** = to contact someone by phone

container *sn* container; **transportul de mărfuri în containere** = container traffic *sau* unitized handling

contesta *vb* **a contesta o decizie** = to appeal against a decision

contingentare *sf* **sistem de contingentare** = quota system

continua *vb* to proceed *sau* to keep on; **au continuat să lucreze în ciuda faptului că erau epuizaţi** = they kept on working in spite of the fact that they were worn out

contra *adv* *(împotriva)* against; **contra ramburs** = carriage forward; **plata contra ramburs** = cash on delivery (COD)

contrabalansa *vb* to offset

contrabandă *sf* racket; *(trafic ilegal de mărfuri)* contraband; smuggling; **a face contrabandă** = to smuggle

contrabandist *sm* smuggler

contract *sm* *(în scris sau verbal)* contract; deed *sau* agreement; **a semna un contract** = to make a deal; **contract bilateral** = bilateral contract; **contract de împrumut** = loan agreement; **contract de închiriere** = tenancy agreement; **contract ilegal** = illegal contract; **contract oficial** = formal contract; **contract unilateral** = unilateral contract; **contract verbal** = verbal agreement *sau* consensual contract

contracta *vb* to contract

contrafăcut *adj* counterfeit; **cec contrafăcut** = defaced cheque

contramanda *vb* countermand

contramandare *sf* cancellation

contraofertă *sf* counterbid

contrar *adj* adverse

contribuabil *sm* taxpayer

contribui *vb* to contribute; **ei au găsit un sponsor care să contribuie la acoperirea costurilor de cerecetare** = they found a sponsor to contribute to the cost of research

control *sn* check *sau* control; *(inspecţie)* inspection; **control inopinat** = spot check *sau* snap check; **control (tehnic) de calitate** = quality control; **controlul alocării devizelor sau controlul schimbului valutar** = rationing of foreign exchange

controla *vb* *(a verifica)* to control; *(a regula)* to regulate; **preţuri controlate de guvern** = government-regulated prices

controlor *sm* inspector

conţine *vb* to contain; **această cutie conţine aparatul video, cabluri şi instrucţiuni de folosire** =

this box contains the video recorder together with leads and instructions

conţinut *sn* **(a)** contents; **conţinut al unui dosar** = contents of a file **(b)** *(într-un plic, scrisoare, etc.)* enclosure

conveni *vb* to agree; **preţ convenit** = agreed price

convertibil *adj* **monedă** *sau* **valută convertibilă** = convertible currency; *(despre mijloace fixe)* **convertibil în bani lichizi** = realizable

convertibilitate *sf* convertibility

convinge *vb (prin cuvinte)* to assure

convorbire *sf* **convorbire telefonică** *loco sau* **urbană** = local call

cooperativă *sf* cooperative; **cooperativă agricolă de producţie** = collective farm *sau* agricultural cooperative; **cooperativă de consum** = consumer's cooperative

copia *vb* to copy *sau* to photocopy (a document)

copiator *sm* copier *sau* photocopier *sau* copying machine

copie *sf* copy; **copie la indigou** = carbon copy; **copie ilegală** *sau* `pirat' **a unei casete video** = a pirate copy of a video

copropietar *sm* part-owner *sau* joint owner

corect *adj* **(a)** *(precis sau exact)* correct *sau* exact **(b)** **practici comerciale corecte** = fair dealings; **preţ corect** = fair price

corecta *vb (a îndrepta)* to correct *sau* to amend

Coreea (Republica) *sf* South Korea; Notă: capitală: **Seul** = Seoul; monedă: **won corean** = Korean won

corean(ă) *s & adj* Korean

corela *vb (a indexa)* to link

corelat *adj (ajustat)* index-linked; **pensii corelate cu majorarea preţurilor** = index-linked pensions

coresponda *vb (a scrie scrisori)* to correspond

corespondenţă *sf* **(a)** correspondence **(b)** *(scrisori, pachete, etc.)* correspondence *sau* mail *sau* post; **prima lui îndatorire este deschiderea corespondenţei în fiecare dimineaţă** = his first task is to open the correspondence every morning; **corespondenţă care conţine broşuri publicitare** = junk mail

corespondent *sm* counterpart

corespunde *vb (a se potrivi)* to correspond *sau* to fit *(a fi în concordanţă cu)* to check with; to tally; **cifrele nu corespund** = the figures do not tally

corporativ *adj* corporate

corporaţie *sf* guild; corporation

corupe *vb* to corrupt

corupţie *sf* corruption; bribe

cost *sn* cost; *(tarif)* charge; **cost anual** = annual cost; **cost de desfacere** = selling cost; **cost de producţie** = cost of production *sau* production cost; **cost mediu unitar** = average unit cost; **costul biletului (de intrare)** = admission charge; **costuri bancare** = bank charges; **preţ de cost** = cost price; **raport cost-beneficiu** = price-earnings ratio

costa *vb* to cost

Costa Rica *sf* Costa Rica; Notă: capitală: **San José;** monedă: **colón**

costarican(ă) *s & adj* Costa Rican

costisitor *adj (scump)* expensive *sau* dear; **o nouă reţea de calculatoare s-a dovedit a fi mai costisitoare decât se prevăzuse** = the new computer network proved to be more expensive than they had expected

coş *sn* basket; **coş de cumpărături** = shopping basket

cotă *sf* (a) quota; **cota la export** = export quota; **cota la import** = import quota; **restricţii la cotele la import sau export** = quota restrictions (b) *(participare)* share; **cotă din piaţă** = market share; **cotă din profit** = share of profit (c) quotation

cotidian 1 *sn* *(ziar)* daily (newspaper) 2 *adj (zilnic)* daily

cotiza *vb* to contribute

cotizaţie *sf* contribution; **cotizaţie plătită de un membru de partid** = political levy

cotor *sn* stub *sau* counterfoil; **cotorul carnetului de cecuri** = cheque stub

crea *vb* to create; to build; *(a forma)* to form; **proiectul a creat 100 noi locuri de muncă** = the project created 100 new jobs

crede *vb* *(a gândi)* to believe; **el crede că a fost grăbit în semnarea contractului**= he believes he was rushed into signing the contract

credinţă *sf* **bună credinţă** = bona fides; **cu bună credinţă** = in good faith

credit *sn* *(împrumut)* credit; **a acorda credit** = to credit; **credit deschis** *sau* **nelimitat** = open credit; **credit fix** = fixed credit; **carte de credit** = credit card; **limită a creditului** = credit limit

credita *vb* to credit

creditor *sm* creditor

crescător de animale *sm* stock breeder

creşte *vb* to grow; *(a (se) majora)* to increase; *(a escalada)* to escalate; *(a spori)* to rise *sau* to accumulate; *(a se ameliora)* to pick up; *(despre preţul acţiunilor)* to boom; **a creşte forţat** = to boost; **deverul companiei a**

crescut considerabil decând un nou director general a fost angajat = the company's sales have grown a great deal since the arrival of the new managing director; **profiturile noastre au crescut substanţial anul trecut** = last year our profits increased substantially; **vânzările au crescut din nou după o perioadă de stagnare** = sales have picked up after a bad patch

creştere *sf* growth; *(majorare)* increase *sau* rise; *(în valoare)* gain; *(plusvaloare)* increment; *(mărire a profitului)* accrual; **creştere a capitalului** = capital increase; **piaţă în criză, când oferta este mai mare decât cererea** = depressed market

criză *sf (depresiune)* **criză economică** = depression *sau* slump; recession; *(lipsă)* scarcity *sau* shortage; **criză de materii prime** = scarcity of raw materials; **criză energetică** = shortage of energy

Croaţia *noun* Croatia; Notă: capitală: **Zagreb;** monedă: **dinar**

croat(ă) *s & adj* Croatian

cronometra *vb* **a cronometra timpul de lucru** = to clock in

crud *adj* raw

Cuba *sf* Cuba; Notă: capitală: **Havana;** monedă: **peso cubanez** = Cuban peso

cubanez(ă) *s & adj* Cuban

cultiva *vb* (a) to farm (b) to grow; **ei cultivă legume în grădina din spatele casei** = they grow their own vegetables in the back garden

cumpăra *vb* to buy *sau* to purchase *sau* to acquire; **a cumpăra o casă în valoare de 15 milioane de lei** = to buy a property for 15 million lei; **a cumpăra mai mult decât necesar** = to overbuy; **a cumpăra o afacere în întregime** = to buy out; **a cumpăra pe loc (la un preţ avantajos)** = to snap up; **a cumpăra tot; a cumpara masiv** = to buy up

cumpărare *sf* purchase; **putere de cumpărare** = buying power *sau* purchasing power; spending power

cumpărător *sm* **(a)** shopper; client; **magazinul încearcă să-şi menţină cumpărătorii mulţumiţi** = the shop tries to keep its clients happy **(b)** *(al unei proprietăţi)* purchaser *sau* vendee **(c)** *(persoană care acceptă o ofertă)* taker

cumpărături *sfpl* shopping; **a face cumpărturi** = to shop; **coş de cumpărături** = shopping basket

cunoaşte *vb* to know; **îşi cunoaşte meseria** = he knows his trade; **abilitatea de a cunoaşte ceva în mod deosebit** = know-how

cunoaştere *sf* knowledge

cunoştinţă *sf* contact *sau* connection; **a reuşit să obţină audienţa printr-o cunoştinţă** = he managed to obtain the appointment through a connection; **are multe cunoştinţe în lumea editurilor de carte** = he has many contacts in the publishing business

cunoştinţe *sfpl* knowledge; *(ştiinţifice, tehnice)* know-how; **cunoştinţe elementare** = basic knowledge

cuprins *sn* *(tablă de materii într-o carte)* contents

curat *adj* clear; **conştiinţă curată** = clear conscience

curator *sm* *(adminstrator fiduciar)* trustee

curând *adv* early

curent 1 *sn* flow 2 *adj* **(a)** *(actual)* current; **preţ curent** = going rate **(b) cont curent** = current account

curier *sm* courier

curs *sn* **(a)** course; **curs în care teoria alternează cu practica (în producţie)** = sandwich course; **curs de reciclare** = refresher course **(b)** price; **curs cerut** = asking price; **curs cerut la licitaţie** = bid price; *(la bursă)* **cursul la închidere** = closing price; **primul curs** = opening price **(c)** rate; **curs fix de schimb valutar** = fixed exchange rate; **cursul de schimb valutar** = exchange rate

cursă *sf* **(a)** race; **cursă de cai** = horse race; **sumă de bani pariată la curse** = stake **(b) cursă charter** = charter flight

curte *sf* *(incintă)* yard

custodie *sf* *(păstrare)* safe-keeping

cuşetă *sf* sleeping-car

cutie *sf* box; **cutie poştală** = letter box

cuvânt *sn* *(alocuţiune)* address

Dd

dactilografă *sf* typist

dactilografia *vb* to type; *(în cadrul unei întreprinderi)* **birou de dactilografie** = typing pool

dactilografiere *sf* typing; **greşeală de dactilografiere** = typing error

Danemarca *sf* Denmark; Notă: capitală: **Copenhaga** = Copenhagen ; monedă: **coroană daneză** = Danish krone

danez(ă) 1 *s* Dane 2 *adj* Danish

dar *sn* gift *sau* present

data *vb* to date

dată *sf* date; **toate documentele primite prin poştă sunt ştampilate cu data respectivă** = all the documents received through the post are stamped with the day's date; **a pune data (pe un document, etc)** = to date (un document, etc.); **a uitat să pună data pe cec** = he forgot to date the cheque; **fără dată** = undated

date *sfpl (informaţie)* data; **bancă de date** = data bank

dator *adj* indebted

datora *vb (bani)* to be in debt; to owe; **îmi datorează 10.000 de lei** = he owes me 10,000 lei

datorat *adj* due; *(demult)* overdue; **bani datoraţi unei firme, de primit** = accounts receivable; **sumă datorată** = indebtedness

datorie *sf* **(a)** debt; indebtedness; **achitarea datoriei** = debt amortization; **agenţie de colectare a datoriilor** = debt-collecting agency; **datorie care nu va fi achitată** = bad debt; **datorie externă** = external debt; **datorie flotantă (pe termen lung)** = floating debt; **datorie naţionlă** = national debt; **datorie permanentă** = permanent debt; **datorie publică** = public debt; **datorie temporară** = temporary debt *sau* short-term debt; **a se îngloda în datorii** = to run into debt; **a plăti o datorie** = to settle an account *sau* to pay an account; **a-şi plăti datoriile** = to meet one's obligations; **plătirea de dobânzi pentru o datorie** = debt servicing; **fără datorii** = out of debt **(b)** *(obligaţie)* burden; **datoria faţă de contract** = the burden of the contract **(c)** duty *sau* obligation; **datorie de onoare** = debt of honour; **datorie morală** = moral obligation **(d)** *(sarcină)* assignment **(e)** liabilities

daune *sfpl* damage; *(pentru încasarea primei de asigurare)* **daune cauzate intenţionat** = malicious damage

dărui *vb* to present

debarca *vb* to land

debarcare *sf* landing; **talon de debarcare** = landing card

debit *sn* debit; **aviz de debit** = debit advice

debita *vb* to debit; **a debita un cont** = to debit an account

debitare *sf* **notă de debitare** = debit note

debitor 1 *adj (datornic)* debtor; **cont debitor** = debit account; **naţiune debitoare** = debtor nation; **sector economic debitor** = debtor economic sector 2 *sm (datornic)* debtor

debuşeu *sn* outlet

decalaj *sn* time lag

decădere *sf* decline

decepţie *sf (înşelăciune)* deceit

decepţiona *vb* to cheat

decide *vb* (a) *(a hotărî)* to decide (b) **a (se) decide** = to elect *sau* to appoint

decis *adj (hotărât)* determined; **erau decişi să termine treaba înainte de sfârşitul anului** = they were determined to finish the work before the end of the year

decizie *sf (hotărâre)* decision

declara *vb* to state; to declare; to affirm; **la vamă au spus că nu aveau nimic să declare** = at the customs they said they had nothing to declare; **a declara nul** = to cancel; **a se declara vinovat sau nevinovat** = to plead; **declararea falimentului** = declaration of bankruptcy; **valoare declarată (la vamă)** = declared value

declaraţie *sf* (a) declaration; affirmation; statement; **avocatul omului de afaceri a emis o declaraţie privitoare la incident** = the businessman's lawyer issued a statement regarding the incident (b) **declaraţie a pârâtului ca răspuns la acuzaţia adusă** = plea (in court) (c) **declaraţie oficială** = official return

declin *sn* decline

declina *vb (a refuza)* to decline

deconta *vb* to discount

decret *sn (lege)* decree

decreta *vb* to decree; **a guverna prin decrete** = to rule by decree

deduce *vb (costuri)* to deduct *sau* to set against; **a deduce o sumă pentru cheltuieli** = to deduct a sum for expenses; **a deduce pierderi din impozite** = to offset losses against tax

defalca *vb* to break down

defalcare *sf* breakdown

defect *sn* fault; **defect mecanic** = mechanical fault; *(despre un produs, etc.)* **cu defecte** = imperfect

defectuos *adj* faulty; **tehnicianul a fost chemat să schimbe cablul de alimentare defectuos** = the technician was called to replace the faulty power cable

deficit *sn* deficit *sau* loss; **compania are un deficit de 10 milioane lei** = the company has a 10 million lei deficit; **defict al balanţei de plăţi** = balance of payments deficit; **deficit bugetar** = deficit spending

definitiva *vb* to finalize; **a definitiva un contract** = to finalize a contract

deforma *vb (realitatea, fapte, etc.)* to misrepresent

deformare *sf* misrepresentation

degrada *vb* **a (se) degrada** = to downgrade

degradare *sf* **degradare fizică** = physical *sau* internal deterioration; **datorită degradării avansate, clădirea a trebuit să fie demolată şi înlocuită cu una nouă** = due to advanced structural deterioration, the building had to be demolished and replaced by a new one

deîmpărţit *sn* dividend

delapida *vb* to embezzle

delapidare *sf* embezzlement

delega *vb (a împuternici)* to delegate

delegat *sm* **(a)** *(trimis)* delegate **(b)** proxy

delegaţie *sf (procură)* proxy

demisie *sf* resignation; **a-şi da demisia** = to resign *sau* to quit; **şi-a dat demisia** = he tendered his resignation

demisiona *vb* to resign *sau* to tender one's resignation

demnitar *sm* official; **oameni de afaceri britanici s-au întreţinut cu înalţi demnitari de stat pe timpul vizitei lor** = British businessmen met high officials during their visit

democraţie *sf* democracy

demodat *adj* out of date; old-fashioned; *(depăşit din punct de vedere tehnic)* obsolescent; **maşinile de scris demodate au fost înlocuite cu calculatoare şi imprimante** = old-fashioned typewriters have been replaced by computers and printers

demografie *sf* demography

demonetiza *vb (a scoate o monedă din uz)* to demonetize

demonstra *vb* to demonstrate

demonstrare *sf (prezentare)* demonstration

demonstraţie *sf* demonstration

denaţionaliza *vb (a privatiza)* to denationalize; **guvernul va denaţionaliza sectorul transportului în comun** = the government will denationalize the public transport sector

denaţionalizare *sf (privatizare)* denationalization

deosebi *vb (a diferi)* **a se deosebi** = to differ

deosebire *sf* difference; **care e deosebirea dintre cele două oferte?** = what is the difference between the two offers?

departament *sn* **(a)** *(secţie)* department *sau* division; **departamentul de marketing** = marketing division **(b)** *(minister)* government department; *(în Marea Britanie)* office **(c)** bureau

depăşi *vb* to exceed; to surpass; **a-şi depăşi suma din cont** = to overdraw; **capacitate depăşită** = excess capacity

depăşit *adj* **(a)** excess **(b)** out of date; obsolete; **depăşit din punct de vedere tehnic** = obsolescent; **la ora actuală calculatoarele 286 sunt considerate depăşite** = these days 286 computers are considered obsolete

dependent *adj* dependent

depinde *vb* to depend; **depindem de capacitatea furnizorului de a livra materia primă la timp** = we depend on the supplier to deliver the raw materials in time

deponent *sm (martor în procese)* deponent

depou *sn* depot; **depou feroviar** = train depot

depozit *sn* **(a)** *(depunere)* deposit; **cont de depozit** = deposit account **(b)** depot; yard; **depozit de mărfuri** = goods depot **(c)** *(magazie)* warehouse; stockroom; **depozit vamal** = bonded warehouse; **şef de depozit** = warehouse manager

depozita *vb* to store; to warehouse

depozitare *sf* storage; warehousing

depoziţie *sf (mărturie)* deposition

deprecia *vb (a pierde din valoare)* **a (se) deprecia** = to depreciate; **monedă depreciată** = undervalued currency

depreciere *sf (a mijloacelor fixe)* writedown

depresiune *sf (criză economică)* depression *sau* slump

deprimat *adj* depressed

depunător *sm* depositor

depune *vb (bani la bancă)* to deposit

depunere *sf* deposit; **depunere pe termen** = fixed deposit; **foaie de depunere** = deposit slip; **carnet de depuneri** = bank book *sau* paying-in book

deputat *sm* deputy

deranjat *adj* out of order

desăvârşi *vb* to accomplish

descărca *vb* to land *sau* to offload; **a descărca bunuri în port** = to land goods at a port

descentralizare *sf* decentralization

deschidere *sf* opening

descreşte *vb (a (se) reduce)* to fall away; *(a se micşora)* to diminish

descurca *vb (a reuşi)* **a se descurca** = to manage to; to get on

desemna *vb* to designate; **a desemna (într-o funcţie** *sau* **post)** = to appoint (someone to a position)

desen *sn* design

desena *vb* to design

desenator *sm* designer

desface *vb* to dissolve

desfacere *sf (debuşeu)* **piaţă de desfacere** = outlet; **cheltuieli de desfacere (vânzare)** = selling cost

despăgubire *sf* **(a)** compensation **(b)** *sfpl* **despăgubiri** = damages; **a acorda despăgubiri** = to award damages; **a cere despăgubiri** = to claim (damages); **a conveni asupra plăţii unei despăgubiri** = to settle a claim; **a pretinde bani drept despăgubiri** = to claim money in damages; **cerere de despăgubiri a** persoanei asigurate = insurance claim; **cerere de despăgubiri pentru pierderi parţiale** = damage claim; **l-a dat în judecată pe fostul patron pentru despăgubiri** = he sued his former employer for compensation; *(reclamant)* **persoană asigurată care cere despăgubiri companiei de asigurări** = claimant

destinatar *sm* addressee

destinaţie *sf* **(a)** *(punct terminus)* destination; **a ajunge la destinaţie** = to arrive **(b)** arrival; **staţie de destinaţie** = arrival station

desuet *adj (demodat)* old-fashioned; obsolescent

detalia *vb* to itemize; *(a descrie în amănunt)* to detail; **factură detaliată** = itemized invoice

detaliere *sf* breakdown

detaliu *sn* particulars; *(amănunt)* detail

deteriora *vb* to deface

deteriorare *sf* **deteriorarea calităţii produselor (alimentare)** = deterioration

deteriorat *adj* **monede** *sau* **bancnote deteriorate** = defaced coins *sau* notes

determina *vb* to determine

deturnare *sf* **deturnare de fonduri** = defalcation

deţinătoare de teren *sf (proprietăreasă)* landlady

deţinător *sm (proprietar)* owner; *(posesor)* holder; *(uzufructar)* **deţinător de drept (al unei proprietăţi)** = beneficial owner; **deţinător de obligaţiuni** = debenture-holder; **societate anonimă deţinătoare de acţiuni** = holding company

deţine *vb* to hold; **preşedintele deţine 50% din acţiunile**

companiei sale = the chairman holds 50% of the shares in his company

devaloriza *vb* a (se) devaloriza = to devalue

devalorizare *sf* devaluation

deviere *sf* (abatere) deviation

deviz *sn* (estimare) estimate *sau* quotation; a întocmi un deviz = to quote *sau* to estimate

devize *sfpl* (valută) foreign currencies

dezacord *sn* difference

dezamăgi *vb* to fail; partenerul său l-a dezamăgit = his partner failed him

dezavantaj *sn* (inconvenient) drawback

dezbate *vb* to dispute

dezbatere *sf* dispute; dezbateri = proceedings

dezechilibrat *adj* unbalanced

dezechilibru *sn* imbalance

dezinforma *vb* to misinform

dezinformare *sf* misrepresentation; dezinformare frauduloasă = fraudulent misrepresentation

dezintegrare *sf* disintegration

dezmembra *vb* to break up

dezonora *vb* to dishonour

dezvălui *vb* to disclose

dezvolta *vb* a (se) dezvolta = to develop *sau* to expand *sau* to grow; economia se dezvoltă într-un ritm constant = the economy is expanding at a constant rate

dezvoltare *sf* development *sau* expansion *sau* growth; (avânt economic) boom; ajutor de dezvoltare = development aid; dezvoltarea comerțului exterior = expansion of foreign trade; dezvoltare economică = economic development *sau* economic growth; dezvoltare industrială = industrial development; industrie cu potențial rapid de dezvoltare = growth industry; rata dezvoltării = growth rate; țări în curs de dezvoltare = developing countries *sau* emerging countries

diagramă *sf* diagram; chart; flow chart

dicta *vb* to dictate; a dicta o scrisoare unei secretare = to dictate a letter to a secretary

dictafon *sn* (casetofon) dictating machine

diferență *sf* difference; diferență de prețuri = price difference

diferențial *adj* differential; discriminare *sau* tratare diferențială = discrimination; salarizare diferențială = differential pay

diferi *vb* (a) to differ (b) (a varia) to range

diferit *adj* different

dificil *adj* (greu de îndeplinit) difficult; sarcină dificilă = difficult task

dificultate *sf* (a) difficulty (b) (pericol iminent) distress

diminua *vb* (a) to diminish (b) (a reduce) to reduce (c) (activitatea economică) to depress

diminuare *sf* (a) abatement; diminuarea cererii = reduction in demand (b) reduction; (scădere) decrease

dinamic *adj* go-ahead

direct 1 *adj* direct; acțiune directă = direct action; cheltuieli directe = direct cost; plata prin debitarea directă a contului curent personal = direct debit payment; vânzare directă = direct sale 2 *adv* direct; a vinde direct = to sell direct

directivă *sf (sarcină)* directive; *(indicaţie)* guideline; **a aplica directivele guvernamentale** = to follow the government guidelines

directoare *sf* manageress

director *sm* director *sau* manager; executive; **director general** = managing director; **director al direcţiei contabilitate** = accounts manager

dirija *vb* **(a)** to direct; **monedă dirijată** = managed money **(b)** *(a forţa)* to drive; **a dirija nivelul preţurilor** = to drive prices up or down

disc *sn* disk *(dischetă)* **disc floppy** = floppy disk; *(disc intern într-un calculator)* **hard disc** = hard disk

discernământ *sn* discretion

dischetă *sf (disc floppy)* floppy disk

discreţie *sf* discretion; **această afacere reclamă discreţie şi tact** = this job requires discretion and tact

discriminare *sf (tratare diferenţială)* discrimination

disponibil *adj* available; **venit disponibil** = disposable income; **facturile nu sunt disponibile pentru verificare** = the invoices are not available for checking

dispozitiv *sn* device

dispoziţie *sf* **(a)** *(reglementare)* regulation **(b)** **dispoziţie de plată** = bank mandate *sau* banker's order

distanţă *sf* **(a)** mileage **(b)** distance; **distanţa de la Londra la Bucureşti e prea mare pentru o călătorie cu maşina** = it's a long haul from London to Bucharest by car

distribui *vb* to distribute; **cataloagele noi au fost distribuite tuturor clienţilor noştri importanţi** = new catalogues were distributed to all our important customers; **a**

distribui în părţi egale = to share *sau* to parcel out

distribuitor *sm* distributor; *(angrosist)* stockist

distribuţie *sf* distribution; **cheltuieli de distribuţie** = distribution costs; **reţea de distribuţie** = distribution channels; **teoria distribuţiei** = Theory of Distribution

district *sn* district

divers *adj* diverse; **articole diverse** = sundries *sau* sundry items

diversificare *sf* diversificare a produselor = differentiation

diversitate *sf* variety; **diversitate de articole şi preţuri** = variety of items and prices

dividend *sn* **(a)** dividend; **dividend acumulat** = accumulated dividend; **dividend intermediar** = interim dividend **(b)** yield

diviziune *sf* division; **diviziunea muncii** = specialization

divulga *vb* to disclose; **băncile nu ar trebui să divulge detalii privind conturile clienţilor lor** = banks should not disclose any details about a customer's accounts

dizolva *vb* to dissolve

dizolvare *sf* dissolution

dobândă *sf* **(a)** interest; **acest cont oferă dobândă de 4,5%** = this account pays 4.5% interest; **dobândă de întârziere** = penalty interest; **dobândă negativă** = interest charge; **dobândă netă** = net interest; **dobândă preferenţială** = prime rate; **dobândă retroactivă** = back interest; **împrumut fără dobânzi percepute** = interest-free loan; **dobânzi compuse** = compound interest; **dobânzi creditoare** = interest earned; **rata dobânzii** = interest rate **(b)** usury

dobândi *vb* to gain; **a dobândi experiență** = to gain experience

doc *sn* dock; **doc de încărcare** = loading dock

docher *sm* docker

document *sn* (a) record (b) *(act)* document; *(autorizație)* warrant; **document legal** = act *sau* deed; **document oficial** = legal document (c) *(cartă)* charter

documentar *adj* documentary

documentare *sf* documentation

documentație *sf* documents *sau* documentation; literature; **după ce a studiat documentația a întocmit raportul** = after studying the documentation he wrote his report

dolar *sm* dollar; **dolarul american** = American dollar *sau* greenback

donator *sm* donor

donație *sf* donation; handout

dosar *sn* (a) file; **a clasa documente la dosar** *sau* **a pune dosare în arhivă** = to file documents; **i s-a cerut să aducă dosarul cu vânzările pe anul trecut** = he was asked to fetch last year's sales file (b) folder; **a pus actele într-un dosar** = he put the documents in a folder (c) brief

dota *vb* to equip; **biroul era dotat cu calculatoare puternice** = the office was equipped with powerful computers

dovadă *sf* evidence

dovedi *vb* *(a atesta)* to certify; to authenticate

Dow Jones *(la bursa din New York)* **indice Dow Jones** = Dow Jones Index

drapel *sn* flag

drept 1 *sn* (a) law; **drept civil** = civil law; **drept penal** = criminal law (b) right; **dreptul de negociere a contractului colectiv** = right to bargain; **dreptul la grevă** = right to strike (c) claim; **drept legitim** = legal claim; **nu are drept legal asupra acestui teren** = he has no claim to this land 2 *adj* just

dubios *adj* dubious *sau* questionable; **metode dubioase** = dubious practices

dubla *vb* **a (se) dubla** = to double; **numărul clienților aproape s-a dublat în cursul anului trecut** = the number of customers has almost doubled over the past year

dublu *adj* double; **impunere dublă** = double taxation

duplicat *adj* duplicate; *(în două exemplare)* **(în) duplicat** = two-part

dur *adj* stiff

duty-free *adj* **magazin duty-free** = duty-free shop

duzină *sf* dozen; **măsură de 12 duzini** = gross

Ee

echilibra *vb* to balance

echilibru *sn* equilibrium; **echilibru parţial** = partial equilibrium; **preţ de echilibru** = equilibrium price; **sumă de echilibru** = equilibrium amount

echipa *vb* to fit out; **au echipat atelierul** = they fitted out the workshop

echipaj *sn* crew

echipament *sn* (a) equipment; **închiriere de echipament** = equipment leasing (b) *(bunuri personale mobile)* effects

echipat *adj (despre o casă, birou, etc.)* **complet echipat** = self-contained

echitabil *adj (just)* fair; **tranzacţie echitabilă** = square deal *sau* fair deal

echivalent 1 *sn* equivalent 2 *adj* equivalent; **a fi echivalent cu** = to be equivalent to; **o pintă este echivalentul a 0,548 litri** = one pint is the equivalent of 0.548 litres

echivalenţă *sf (paritate)* equivalence

econom *adj* economical; *(chibzuit)* careful with money *sau* penny-wise

economic *adj* economic; **conflict economic** = economic warfare; **creştere** *sau* **dezvoltare economică** = economic growth *sau* economic development; **eficienţă economică** = economic efficiency; **geografie economică** = economic geography; **indicator economic** = economic

indicator; **planificare economică** = economic planning; **politică economică** = economic policy; **sancţiune economică** = economic sanction; **sistem economic** = economic system; **tendinţe economice** = economic trends; **teorie economică** = economic theory

economic(os) *adj* (a) economical *sau* inexpensive; **consum economic de carburanţi** = economical fuel consumption; **ştiinţe economice** = economics (b) energy-saving

economie *sf (chibzuială)* economy; **după prăbuşirea regimului comunist ţara încearcă să îşi reconstruiască economia** = the country is trying to rebuild its economy after the collapse of the communist regime; **economie capitalistă** = capitalist economy; **economie de comandă** = command economy; **economie dezvoltată pe de plin** = mature economy; **economie politică** = economics

economii *sfpl* savings; **casă de economii** = savings bank; **cont de economii** = savings account

economisi *vb* to save *sau* to economize; **a economisi bani** = to save money *sau* to set money aside; **a economisi materii prime** = to economize on raw materials; **el economiseşte ca să-şi cumpere o maşină nouă** = he is saving to buy a new car; **pentru a economisi timpul, au cumpărat o imprimantă**

cu viteză de lucru mai mare = in order to save time they bought a faster printer

economisire *sf* saving

economist *sm* economist

Ecuador *sm* Ecuador; Notă: capitală: **Quito**; monedă: **sucre**

ecuadorian(ă) *s & adj* Ecuadorian

edita *vb* to edit

editor *sm* publisher

editorial 1 *sn* *(articol de fond)* editorial; **sarcina sa principală este redactarea unui editorial pentru ediția duminicală a ziarului** = his main job is writing editorials for the Sunday edition of the newspaper 2 *adj* editorial

ediție *sf* edition; *(număr)* issue; **ediție de buzunar** = pocket edition

educa *vb* to train

efect *sn* effect *sau* impact; aftermath; **efectul majorării ratei dobânzilor nu putea fi prevăzut imediat** = the effect of the rise in interest rates could not be foreseen immediately; *(repercusiune)* **efect secundar** = knock-on effect

efectiv *adj* effective

efectua *vb* *(a face)* to effect; **a efectua o plată** = to effect a payment *sau* to make a payment

eficace *sau* **eficient** *adj* (a) efficient; **sistem eficient** = efficient system (b) productive; **consum eficient** = productive consumption

eficiență *sf* efficiency; **eficiență economică** = economic efficiency

egal *adj* equal; **șanse egale (pentru toți)** = equal opportunities; **a fi egal cu** = to equal *sau* to be equivalent to; *(în aceleași condiții)* **în ritm egal** *sau* **în etape egale** = pari passu; **în părți egale** = fifty-fifty

egala *vb* to equal

egalitate *sf* equality; *(la același nivel)* par

egaliza *vb* to equalize

Egipt *sm* Egypt; Notă: capitală: **Cairo**; monedă: **liră egipteană** = Egyptian pound

egiptean(ă) *s & adj* Egyptian

elastic *adj* elastic *sau* flexible

elasticitate *sf* *(flexibilitate)* elasticity; **cerere lipsită de elasticitate** = inelastic demand

electrocar *sn* *(stivuitor)* forklift truck

electronic *adj* electronic; **transfer electronic de fonduri** = electronic funds transfer

electronică *sf* electronics

element *sn* (a) element (b) factor (c) unit

elevator *sn* lift; *US* elevator

eligibil *adj* eligible

Elveția *sf* Switzerland; Notă: capitală: **Berna** = Bern; monedă: **franc elvețian** = Swiss franc

elvețian(ă) *s & adj* Swiss

embargou *sn* embargo; **a pune embargou asupra** = to embargo something *sau* to put an embargo on something

emigra *vb* to emigrate

emigrant *sm* emigrant

emigrare *sf* emigration

emisie *sf* issue

emite *vb* (a) *(a pune în circulație obligațiuni, etc.)* to issue; **a emite o factură** = to raise an invoice (b) *(a transmite)* to network

emitere *sf* issue; **preț de emitere** = issue price

energetic *adj* *(plin de vitalitate)* energetic; *(dinamic)* go-ahead

energie *sf* (a) energy *sau* force (b) energy *sau* power; **energie electrică** = electric power; **a aproviziona cu energie (electrică)** = to power; **a folosi raţional energia (electrică)** = to save energy; **compania încearcă să economisească energia (electrică)** = the company is trying to save energy; **factor de economisire a energiei** = energy saving; **măsuri de economisire a energiei** = energy-saving measures (c) *(ambiţie)* drive

englez(ă) 1 *s* Englishman, Englishwoman 2 *adj* English

enumera *vb* to list

epavă *sf* wreck; **bunuri recuperate de pe o epavă** = wreckage

epuiza *vb* **a epuiza stocul** = to sell out

epuizat *adj* out of stock; *(despre publicaţii)* out of print; **stocul de cărţi pe care doriţi să le comandaţi s-a epuizat** = the books you wish to order are out of stock

ermetic *adj* airtight

eroare *sf* (a) *(greşeală)* error *sau* mistake; *(scăpare)* slip-up; **a comite o eroare** = to make a mistake; to slip up (b) *(eşec)* miscarriage; **eroare judiciară** = miscarriage of justice

eroda *vb* *(a (se) uza)* **a (se) eroda** = to erode

eroziune *sf* erosion; **eroziunea solului** = soil erosion

escalada *vb* to escalate

escaladare *sf* escalation; **escaladare a preţurilor** = escalation of prices

escală *sf* **a face o escală** = to call; **vaporul va face escală la Constanţa** = the ship calls at Constanţa; **scurtă**

escală = stopover; **a face o scurtă escală** = to stop over

escorta *vb* to accompany

escroc *sm* (a) racketeer (b) *(trişor)* cheat

escrocherie *sf* *(comerţ ilicit)* racketeering

esenţial *adj* essential *sau* basic

estima *vb* (a) to reckon; to figure out; **a estima cheltuielile** = to reckon the costs; **vânzări estimate** = projected sales (b) to forecast

estimare *sf* (a) *(apreciere)* estimation (b) *(deviz)* quotation (c) forecast; **estimare a cheltuielilor** = forecast of expenses

Estonia *sf* Estonia; Notă: capitală: **Tallinn**; monedă: **krona**

estonian(ă) *s & adj* Estonian

eşalona *vb* to stagger; **concedii eşalonate** = staggered holidays

eşec *sn* (a) *(nereuşită)* failure *sau* defeat; **în cele din urmă el a trebuit să-şi recunoască eşecul** = eventually he had to admit defeat (b) miscarriage (c) default

eşua *vb* to fail *sau* to collapse; **întreprinderea sa a eşuat datorând milioane de lei** = his business collapsed owing millions of lei; **eforturile sale de a întemeia o afacere au eşuat** = his effort to set up his own business failed

etaj *sn* floor; **contabilitatea se află la etajul trei** = the accounts department is on the 3rd floor

etalon *sn* gauge

eticheta *vb* (a) to label (b) to brand

etichetă *sf* (a) label *sau* sticker (b) brand

Etiopia *sf* Ethiopia; Notă: capitală: **Addis Abeba** = Addis Ababa;

monedă: **birr etiopian** = Ethiopian birr

etiopian(ă) *s & adj* Ethiopian

eurocec *sn* Eurocheque

euroobligaţiune *sf* Eurobond

Europa *sf* Europe

european *s & adj* European; **Uniunea Europeană (UE)** = European Union (EU)

europiaţă *sf* Euromarket

evalua *vb* to appraise *sau* to estimate *sau* value; *(a stabili preţul)* to price; *(a judeca)* to assess; *(a aprecia)* to rate; **a evalua valoarea unei proprietăţi** = to assess the value of a property; **proprietatea a fost evaluată la 15 milioane lei** = the property was valued at 15 million lei

evaluare *sf* valuation; estimate; **evaluare a cheltuielii** = estimate of costs; **a cerut evaluarea colecţiei sale de bijuterii** = she asked for a valuation of her jewellery collection; **specialist în evaluări** = valuer

evaluator *sm* valuer

evaziune *sf* evasion; **evaziune fiscală** = tax evasion; **a fost găsit vinovat de evaziune fiscală** = he was found guilty of tax evasion

evident *adj* evident *sau* clear; **era evident că preţul locuinţelor va creşte din nou** = it was clear that house prices would rise again

evita *vb* to avoid *sau* to get round; **nu a putut să evite traficul intens de pe autostradă** = he could not get round the traffic jam on the motorway; **el încearcă să evite cumpărarea de echipament costisitor** = he tries to avoid buying expensive equipment

exact *adj* exact *sau* accurate

examen *sn* examination *sau* test; **examen medical** = medical

examina *vb* (a) to examine; **clientul a examinat minuţios maşina înainte de a o cumpăra** = the customer examined the car thoroughly before buying it (b) to analyse

examinare *sf* *(expertiză)* examination; **vameşul a continuat examinarea camionului suspect** = the customs official continued their examination of the suspect lorry

excedent *sn* surplus

excepta *vb* to except

exces *sn* excess; **exces de personal** = overmanning; **plată în exces** = overpayment; **stocuri în exces** = excess stock *(în SUA)* overstocks; **a plăti în exces** = to overpay

excesiv *adj & adv* redundant; **a acumula stocuri excesiv** = to overstock; **a cheltui excesiv** = to overspend; **preţ** *sau* **tarif excesiv** = overcharge

exclude *vb* to exclude; **preţurile citate exclud TVA** = the prices quoted exclude VAT

exclusiv *adj* exclusive *sau* sole; **contract de vânzare exclusiv** = exclusive sales agreement; **drepturi exclusive** = sole rights; **reprezentanţă exclusivă** = sole agency

excursie *sf* package tour; excursion *sau* trip

executa *vb* to carry out *sau* to execute; **a executa un ordin** = to execute an order

executiv *adj* executive; **consiliu executiv** = executive; **persoană cu putere executivă** = decision-maker

executor *sm* (a) *(al unui testament)* executor (b) *(persoană de încredere)* fiduciary (c) **executor judecătoresc** = official receiver

exemplar *sf* **(a) formular în două exemplare** = two-part form **(b)** sample; **exemplar gratuit** = free sample

exerciţiu *sm* **exerciţiu financiar** = accounting period *sau* financial period

exod *sn* **exodul intelectualilor peste graniţă** = brain drain

exorbitant *adj* exorbitant; **preţuri exorbitante** = fancy prices

expansiune *sf* expansion

expedia *vb* to send *sau* to dispatch *sau* to consign; **bunurile au fost ambalate şi expediate** = the goods have been packed and dispatched; **bunurile au fost expediate acum două zile** = the goods were consigned two days ago; **a expedia mărfuri** = to ship; **a expedia o scrisoare** = to post a letter; **a expedia par avion** = to send by airmail *sau* to airmail; **a expediat coletul par avion** = he sent the parcel by airmail; **a expedia pe calea aerului** = to airfreight

expediere *sf (expediţie)* shipment *sau* shipping; *(trimitere)* dispatch *sau* dispatching; consignment; mailing; **expedierea de material publicitar clienţilor potenţiali** = direct mailing

expeditor *sm* sender; shipper

expediţie *sf* shipping; mailing; *(secţie, oficiu)* dispatch department; **aviz de expediţie** = advice note; **notă de expediţie** = dispatch note; **funcţionar răspunzător de expediţie** = shipping clerk

experienţă *sf* experience; background; **avem o experienţă bogată în domeniul vânzării de carte** = we have a lot of experience in selling books; **datorită experienţei sale în microelectronică el a dobândit un post bine plătit** = his background in the microelectronics industry allowed him to get a well paid job

expert 1 *sm* expert *sau* specialist; **a cerut sfatul unui expert financiar** = he asked the advice of a financial expert; **expert în legislatură fiscală** = specialist in tax law 2 *s & adj* proficient

expertiză *sf* **(a)** expertise; proficiency; **expertiză financiară** = financial expertise **(b)** examination

expira *vb* to expire; **poliţa lui de asigurări va expira în trei luni** = his insurance policy will expire in three months; **poliţă de asigurări expirată care nu a fost reînnoită** = lapsed insurance policy

expirare *sf* expiration; **expirarea unei poliţe de asigurări** = expiration of an insurance policy

exploatare *sf (funcţionare)* running; **beneficiu de exploatare** = running costs; *(a intra în vigoare)* **a intra în exploatare** = to become operative

exponat *sn* exhibit; **exponatele lor au fost foarte apreciate** = their exhibits were highly praised

export *sn* export; **bunuri de export** = goods for export; **cotă de export** = export quota; **licenţă de export** = export licence; **subvenţii la export** = export bounty

exporta *vb* to export; **exportăm utilaje şi importăm materii prime pentru industria alimentară** = we export machinery and import foodstuffs

exportator *sm* exporter

expoziţie *sf* exhibition *sau* show; *(târg)* fair; **expoziţie comercială** = trade fair; **expoziţie de echipament de calcul** = computer show; **reprezentantul nostru merge la Expoziţia de Carte din Frankfurt în fiecare an** = our representative goes to the Frankfurt Book Fair every year; **sală de expoziţii** = showroom

expune *vb* **(a)** to lay out **(b)** a **(se) expune** = to exhibit

extensie *sf* extension

exterior *adj* foreign; **comerţ exterior** = foreign trade; overseas trade

extern *adj* foreign

extinde *vb* **(a)** to spread *sau* to extend **(b)** a **(se) extinde** = to expand **(c)** to branch out

extraordinar *adj* extraordinary; **cheltuieli extraordinare** = non-recurring expenses

extras *sn* **extras de cont bancar** = bank statement

Ff

fabrica *vb* to manufacture *sau* to make; to develop; **a fabrica un produs nou** = to develop a new product; **fabricat în Anglia** = made in England

fabricant *sm* manufacturer *sau* maker; producer; **fabricant de automobile** = car maker *sau* car producer; **preţ minim de vânzare recomandat de fabricant** = manufacturer's recommended price

fabricaţie *sf* manufacture *sau* manufacturing *sau* making; **cheltuieli generale de fabricaţie** = manufacturing overheads

fabrică *sf* **(a)** *(uzină)* factory *sau* factory uni;t *(de textile)* mill; **în această fabrică se produce mobilă destinată exclusiv exportului** = in this factory they only make furniture for export; **fabrică de încălţăminte** = shoe factory; **fabrică de hârtie** = paper mill; **preţ de fabrică** = factory price **(b)** *(întreprindere)* works

facilitate *sf* *(posibilitate)* facility; **facilitate de descoperit** = overdraft facility

facsimil *sn* *(fax)* facsimile *sau* fax

factor **1** *sm* agent **2** *sn* factor; **factor ciclic** = cyclic factor; **factor de cost** = cost factor; **factor decisiv** = deciding factor; **factori de producţie** = factors of production

factoring *sn* *(finanţare similară creditului)* factoring

factura *vb* to invoice *sau* to bill

facturare *sf* invoicing; **birou de facturare** = invoicing department

factură *sf* invoice

facultate *sf* college; **facultate de comerţ** = commercial college

facultativ *adj* *(opţional)* optional; **asigurarea în caz de şomaj este facultativă** = the redundancy cover is optional

Fahrenheit *(scală de măsurare a temperaturii, apa îngheaţă la 32° şi fierbe la 212°)* Fahrenheit

faliment *sn* failure; bankruptcy; *(a înceta activitatea)* **a da faliment** = to fail *sau* to go under; to close down; **întreprinderea lui a dat faliment după doi ani de eforturi zadarnice** = his venture failed after struggling for two years; *(falit)* **care a dat faliment** = bankrupt; **ordin (judecătoresc) de declarare a falimentului** = adjudication order

falit *sm* (i) insolvent; (ii) bankrupt; **el a fost declarat falit** = he was declared bankrupt

fals **1** *adj* **(a)** false; bogus **(b)** *(forged)* counterfeit; **alarmă falsă** = false alarm **2** *sn* forgery; counterfeit

falsifica *vb* **(a)** to manipulate; **a falsifica intrări contabile** = to manipulate accounts **(b)** to forge; **a falsifica bani** = to counterfeit; **a**

falsifica o semnătura = to forge a signature

falsificare *sf* **(a)** falsification; **falsificarea de conturi** = falsification of accounts **(b)** forgery

fantezist *adj* fancy; *(care atrag clienţi prin insolit)* **bunuri** *sau* **articole fanteziste** = fancy goods

faptă *sf* act *sau* action

far *sn* lighthouse

favoare *sf* **(a)** favour; **a cere o favoare** = to ask for a favour; **toţi membrii consiliului de administraţie sunt în favoarea angajării de personal sezonier pentru perioada de Crăciun** = all members of the board are in favour of taking on more staff for the Christmas season **(b)** benefit; **rata dobânzilor era în favoarea lui** = the interest rates were to his benefit

fax *sn* *(facsimil)* fax; **a transmite prin fax** = to fax

federal *adj* federa;l *(sistem bancar american, format din 12 bănci)* **Sistemul Federal al Resurselor** = Federal Reserve System

federaţie *sf* *(asociaţie)* federation

feedback *sn* feedback

fel *sn* *(modalitate)* form

feribot *sn* ferry

ferm *adj* firm; **ofertă fermă** = firm offer

fermă *sf* farm; **mică fermă agricolă** = smallholding

fermier *sm* farmer

fezabilitate *sf* feasibility

fictiv *adj* fictitious; **fonduri fictive** = fictitious assets

fiduciar *adj* **adminstrator fiduciar** = trustee; **companie fiduciară** = trust company

fiecare *adj* **în fiecare zi** = every day; **citesc un ziar în fiecare zi** = I read a newspaper every day

fier *sn* iron; **fier vechi** = scrap metal

fierărie *sf* hardware (shop)

filială *sf* *(sucursală; agenţie)* branch *sau* branch office; **această bancă are 200 de filiale în ţară** = this bank has 200 branches throughout the country

Filipine *sfpl* Philippines; Notă: capitală: **Manila;** monedă: **peso filipinez** = Philippine peso

filipinez(ă) *s & adj* Filipino

final *adj* **(a)** *(ultim)* final; **produs final** = end product **(b)** terminal

financiar **1** *adj* **(a)** financial; **ajutor financiar** = financial assistance; **an financiar** = financial year; **centrul financiar** = financial centre; **centrul financiar al Londrei** = the City; **consilier financiar** = financial adviser; **criză financiară** = financial crisis; **exerciţiu financiar** = accounting period *sau* financial period; **resurse financiare** = financial resources; **situaţie financiară** = financial position; **societate financiară** = finance house **(b)** **Administraţia Financiară** = revenue office *sau* tax office; *(în Marea Britanie)* Inland Revenue; *(în SUA)* Internal Revenue Service; **inspector financiar** = revenue officer **2** *adv* financially

finanţa *vb* to finance; **sectorul particular va finanţa construirea noii linii de metrou** = the private sector will finance the construction of the new underground line

finanţe *sfpl* **(a)** finance **(b)** banking

Finlanda *sf* Finland; Notă: capitală: **Helsinki;** monedă: **marcă** = markka

finlandez(ă) *adj* Finnish

finlandez(ă) *s* Finn

firesc *adj* natural

firmă *sf* **(a)** *(întreprindere comercială)* firm; *(instituţie)* establishment **(b) firmă de magazin** = shop sign

fisc *sn (administraţie financiară)* revenue office

fiscal *adj* fiscal; **an fiscal** = tax year *sau* fiscal year; **evaziune fiscală** = tax evasion; **inspector fiscal** = inspector of taxes *sau* tax inspector; *(în SUA)* tax assessor; **politică fiscală** = fiscal policy

Fiscul *sn* revenue office *sau* tax office; *(în Marea Britanie)* Inland Revenue; *(în SUA)* Internal Revenue Service

fişă *sf* filing card; **fişă de magazie** = stock control card

fişier *sm* computer file

fix *adj* fixed *sau* set; **cheltuieli fixe** = fixed costs; **mijloace fixe** = fixed assets; **preţuri fixe** = set prices; **procentaj fix** = flat rate; **schimb valutar fix** = fixed exchange rate; **tarife fixe** = fixed charges

fixa *vb* **(a)** *(a menţine)* to fix *sau* to set; **a fixa data unei şedinţe** = to fix a meeting **(b)** *(preţuri)* to set; to peg

flexibil *adj* flexible; **acord flexibil** = open-ended agreement; **buget flexibil** = flexible budget; **program de lucru flexibil** = flexitime; **sistem tarifar flexibil** = flexible tariffs

flexibilitate *sf* elasticity *sau* flexibility; **flexibilitatea cererii** = elasticity of demand; **flexibilitatea ofertei** = elasticity of supply

flotă *sf (militară)* navy; **flotă (comercială)** = merchant fleet

fluctuaţie *sf (oscilaţie)* swing; **fluctuaţii periodice** = periodic swings

foaie *sf* **foaie de pontaj** = time sheet; **foaie volantă** = flier

folos *sn sau* **folosinţă** *sf* use

folosi *vb* **a (se) folosi** = to employ *sau* to use

folosire *sf* usage; **folosire deficientă** = misuse

folositor *adj* useful

fond *sn (sumă de bani)* fund; **compania nu are fondurile suficiente pentru deschiderea unei alte filiale** = the firm lacks the necessary funds to open another branch; **fond de acoperire** *sau* **protector** = protective cover; **fond pentru cheltuieli minore** *sau* **fond de piaţă** = petty cash; **fond de rezervă** = contingency fund; **Fondul Monetar Internaţional (F.M.I)** = the International Monetary Fund (I.M.F.)

fonda *vb (a înfiinţa)* to set up

forma *vb* to form; **a forma şi înregistra o companie** = to incorporate a company

formal *adj* formal

formalitate *sf* formality; **formalităţi vamale** = customs formalities

formă *sf* form

formular *sn* form; **a completa un formular** = to fill in a form; **formular de cerere** = application form; **formular de contract (tipărit)** = standard agreement

forţa *vb* **(b)** *(a conduce sau a dirija)* to drive; **a forţa un contract dezavantajos** = to drive a hard bargain **(b)** *(a sili)* to force; **compania a fost forţată să plătească o amendă substanţială** = the company was forced to pay a substantial fine

forţă *sf (putere)* force; *(resurse)* energy; **forţă de muncă** = manpower *sau* work force

fost *adj* former; **fostul director general a ieşit la pensie acum 5 luni** = the former managing director retired 5 months ago

fracţie *sf* fraction

fracţiune *sf* fraction

fragment *sn* fragment *sau* scrap; *(parte)* part

fraht *sn* *(scrisoare de trăsură)* waybill

franca *vb* to stamp *sau* to frank; **maşină de francat** = franking machine *sau* postal meter

francez(ă) *adj* French

francez *sm* Frenchman

franşiză *sf* franchise

Franţa *sf* France; Notă: capitală: **Paris;** monedă: **franc francez** = French franc

franţuzoaică *sf* Frenchwoman

fraudă *sf* fraud; **a obţine profituri prin fraudă** = to gain profits by fraud

fraudulent *adj* fraudulent; **dezinformare fraudulentă** = fraudulent misrepresentation

frecvent *adj* common; **greşeală frecventă** = common mistake

frontieră *sf* border

funciar *adj* **impozit funciar** = property tax; **rentă funciară** = ground rent

funcţie *sf* *(poziţie)* function

funcţiona *vb* **(a)** to function *sau* to run; *(deranjat)* **care nu funcţionează corespunzător** = out of order; **a observat că ordinatorul nu funcţiona corespunzător** = she noticed that the computer was not running properly; **această imprimantă nu funcţionează**

corespunzător = this printer does not function properly **(b)** *(ca interpret, etc.)* to act (as)

funcţionar *sm* clerical worker; white-collar worker; **funcţionar comercial** = accounts clerk; **funcţionar de bancă** = bank clerk; **funcţionar oficial** = civil servant; **funcţionar de stat** = civil servant *sau* public servant; **luna trecută toţi funcţionarii de stat au primit o mărire de salariu de 3%** = all the civil servants got a rise of 3% last month

funcţionare *sf* *(exploatare)* operating *sau* running

funcţionăresc *adj* *(administrativ)* clerical

fund *sn* bottom; **fund dublu (al unei valize)** = false bottom; **a atinge fundul (despre un vas)** = to bottom

fundamental *adj* fundamental *sau* basic; *(principal)* prime

furgonetă *sf* *(camionetă)* pickup (truck)

furnizor *sm* supplier; **furnizorul a livrat comanda la timp** = the supplier delivered the order in time

furt *sn* theft; **furt de către custode** = defalcation

fuziona *vb* to merge; **cele două companii rivale au fuzionat anul trecut** = the two rival companies merged last year

fuzionare *sf* union

fuziune *sf* merger

Gg

Gabon *sm* Gabon; Notă: capitală: **Libreville;** monedă: **franc CFA =** CFA franc

gabonez(ă) *s & adj* Gabonese

galon *sn (unitate de măsurare a lichidelor egală cu 4,54 litri în Marea Britanie și 3,78 litri în SUA)* gallon

gamă *sf* **(a)** *(sortiment)* range; **vindem o gamă largă de unelte electrice =** we stock a wide range of power tools; **gamă de produse =** product range *sau* product line **(b)** *(scară)* scale; **gamă de prețuri =** scale of prices

garaj *sn (de autobuze)* bus depot

garant *sm* guarantor; underwriter

garanta *vb* **(a)** to guarantee; to warrant; **prețuri agricole minime garantate =** guaranteed prices **(b)** to secure; **a garanta plata unei datorii =** to guarantee a debt **(c) garanta o plată =** to underwrite **(d)** to vouch for

garanție *sf* **(a)** guarantee; **certificat de garanție =** guarantee certificate *sau* warranty; **condiții de garanție =** express warranty; **garanție implicită =** implied warranty; **garanție de 12 luni =** twelve-month guarantee *sau* warranty; **pentru acest televizor aveți garanție de un an de zile =** with this TV set you get a twelve-month guarantee; **persoană care primește o garanție =** warrantee; **service în garanție =** after-sales service **(b)** security; **fără garanție =** unsecured; **împrumut fără garanție =** unsecured loan **(c)** *(acont)* deposit; cover

gară *sf* railway station

garderobă *sf* cloakroom

gazdă *sf* hostess

general *adj (total)* general; **acord general =** general agreement *sau* omnibus agreement; **alegeri generale =** general election; **director general =** general manager; **grevă generală =** general strike; **medie generală =** general average

german(ă) *s & adj* German

Germania *sf* Germany; Notă: capitală: **Bonn;** monedă: **marcă germană (DM) =** Deutschmark (DM)

gestiune *sf* management

Ghana *sf* Ghana; Notă: capitală: **Accra;** monedă: **cedi ghanez =** Ghanaian cedi

ghanez(ă) *s & adj* Ghanaian

ghid *sm* **(a)** guide **(b)** *(îndrumar)* directory

ghișeu *sn* desk; **ghișeu de informații =** information desk *sau* office

gir *sn* endorsement

gira *vb* to endorse; *(emiterea de acțiuni)* to underwrite

girant *sm sau* **garant** *sm* (i) guarantor; surety; (ii) underwriter

giro *sn* remittance

grad *sn* rank; grade

gradat *adj* gradual

grafic *sn* chart; diagram *sau* graph; **grafic circular** = pie chart; **grafic de vânzări** = sales chart

gram *sn* *(1000 g = 1Kg)* gram *sau* gramme

graniţă *sf* border

gratificaţie *sf* (a) gratuity (b) *(primă de export)* bounty (c) *(primă sau recompensă financiară)* bonus

gratis *sau* **gratuit** 1 *adj* free; *(servicii speciale cu prefix 0800 în Marea Britanie, cu prefix 800 în SUA)* **serviciu telefonic gratuit** = freephone; **a utliza un serviciu telefonic gratuit** = to call freephone; **acţiune gratuită** *sau* **titlu gratuit** = bonus share; **catalogul este gratuit** = the catalogue is free; **exemplar gratuit** = free sample; **livrare gratuită** = free delivery 2 *adv* **a telefona gratuit** = to call freephone; *(în SUA)* to call toll free

grăbi *vb* **a se grăbi** = to jump; **a se grăbi să accepte o ofertă** = to jump at an offer

grec *sau* **greacă** *s* Greek

grec(esc), grecească *adj* Greek

Grecia *sf* Greece; Notă: capitală: **Atena** = Athens; monedă: **drahmă** = drachma

grefier *sf* court clerk

greşeală *sf* mistake *sau* error; **a face o greşeală** = to make a mistake; **din greşeală** = by error; **greşeală de tipar** = printing error

greşi *vb* to make a mistake *sau* to make an error; to slip up

greşit *adj* false; **calcul greşit** = false calculation

greu *adj* heavy; **industria grea** = heavy industry; **pierderi grele** = heavy losses

greutate *sf* weight; **greutate maximă admisă** = weight limit; **greutate brută** = gross weight; **greutate netă** = net weight

grevă *sf* strike *sau* stoppage (of work); *(despre un sector economic, serviciu, etc.)* **ajutor de grevă** = strike pay; **convocare la grevă** = strike call; **a face grevă** = to strike *sau* to go on strike; **grevă cu ocuparea întreprinderii** = sit-down strike; **grevă generală** = general strike *sau* all-out strike; **grevă simbolică** *sau* **grevă de avertisment** = token strike; **grevă la scară naţională** = nationwide strike; **paralizat de grevă** = strikebound; **spărgător de grevă** = blackleg *sau* scab *sau* strikebreaker

grevist *sm* striker

grijă *sf* care; **a avea grijă de** = to care; *(adresă pe plic)* **în grija** = care of (C/O); **Domnului Jones în grija Domnului Scott** = Mr Jones, care of (C/O) Mr Scott

gros *adj* (a) **en gros** = wholesale; **achiziţii en gros** = bulk purchase; **comerţ en gros** = wholesale trade; **scont pentru achiziţii en gros** = quantity discount; **preţ de mic gros** = trade price (b) *(brut)* gross; pre-tax

grup *sn* (a) group *sau* association; party; **grup de persoane cu interese comune** = interest group; **grup de lucru** = working party; **grup de specialişti** = panel of experts; **grup operativ** = task force (b) *(concern industrial)* group (c) board; **grup conducător** = governing body (d) cartel (e) collective

grupa *vb* **a (se) grupa** = to group

Guatemala *sf* Guatemala; Notă: capitală: **Guatemala City** = Ciudad de Guatemala; monedă: **quetzal guatemalez** = Guatemalan quetzal

guatemalez(ă) *s & adj* Guatemalan

guvern *sn* government; cabinet; **şedinţă de guvern** = cabinet meeting

guverna *vb* to govern

guvernamental *adj* governmental

Guyana *sf* Guyana; Notă: capitală: **Cayenne;** monedă: **dolar guyanez =** Guyana dollar

guyanez(ă) *s & adj* Guyanese

Hh

Haiti *sn* Haiti; Notă: capitală: **Port-au-Prince; monedă: gourd haitian** = Haitian gourde

haitian(ă) *s & adj* Haitian

hardware *sn* computer hardware

harnic *adj (muncitor)* industrious

hartă *sf* chart

hârtie *sf* paper; **hârtie de împachetat** = wrapping paper; **hârtie liniată** = lined paper; **hârtie milimetrică** = graph paper; **pungă de hârtie** = paper bag

heliport *sn* heliport

hidraulic *adj* hydraulic; **energie hidraulică** = water power

hotărî *vb* to decide; **s-a hotărât să încerce o nouă stratagemă de atragere a clienților** = he decided to try a new strategy for attracting customers

hotărâre *sf* decision; **a ajunge la o hotărâre** = to reach a decision

hotărât *adj* determined

hotel *sn* hotel; **director de hotel** = hotel manager; **nota de plată a camerei la hotel** = hotel bill; **a plăti și părăsi hotelul** = to check out (of a hotel)

hrană *sf* food

Ii

ideal *adj* ideal *(optim)* optimum

ieftin *adj* cheap *sau* inexpensive; **acest calculator este mai ieftin comandat prin poştă** = this computer is cheaper by mail order; **mână de lucru ieftină** = cheap labour; **a cumpăra ieftin** = to strike a bargain

ierta *vb* **a ierta (o datorie)** = to write off a debt

ilegal *adj* illegal *sau* unlawful; *(pe sub tejghea)* under the counter

ilegalitate *sf* illegality

ilicit *adj* illicit *sau* unlawful; **comerţ ilicit** = illicit trading; **câştig ilicit** = illicit gain

imagine *sf* image; **imagine publică a unei întreprinderi** = corporate image

imigrant *sm* immigrant

imitaţie *sf* counterfeit

imobil 1 *sn (clădiri)* house; property; **vrem să cumpărăm un imobil pentru noua noastră filială** = we are looking to buy a property for our new branch 2 *adj* immovable

imobiliar *adj* **(a) agent imobiliar** = estate agent *(în SUA)* real estate agent *sau* realtor; **agenţie imobiliară** = estate agency; **proprietate imobiliară** = real estate; house property *(în SUA)* realty; **societate imobiliară** = property company **(b)** **bunuri imobiliare** = estate; **proprietate imobiliară** = real estate

imobiliza *vb (a transforma capital lichid în mijloace fixe)* to immobilize (capital)

impact *sn* impact

impar *adj* odd; *(3, 5, 7, etc)* **numere impare** = odd numbers

impas *sn* deadlock; **negocierile sunt în impas** = the negotiations have come to a standstill *sau* the negotiations have reached a deadlock

imperfect *adj (cu defecte)* imperfect; **librăria a returnat editurii exemplarele (de carte) imperfecte** = the bookshop returned the imperfect copies to the publisher

imperialism *sn* imperialism

impermeabil *adj* waterproof

implementa *vb* to implement; **planul va fi implementat anul viitor** = the new plan will be implemented next year

implicare *sf* participation

implicit *adj* implied; **condiţie implicită (a unui contract)** = implied condition

import *sn* import; **autorizaţie de import** = import licence; **cota de import** = import quota; **interzicere a importului** = import ban; **taxe de import** = import duty; **taxe suplimentare de import** = import surcharge; *(transport, activități financiar-bancare, etc.)* **importuri invizibile** = invisible imports; **importuri vizibile** = visible imports

importa *vb* to import; **numeroase supermagazine britanice importă vin din România** = many British supermarkets import wine from Romania

important *adj* **(a)** capital; major **(b)** large *sau* considerable *sau* heavy; **investiție importantă** = heavy investment; **pierderi importante** = heavy losses; **acționar important** = major shareholder; **o sumă importantă de bani a fost cheltuită în scopul cercetării** = a considerable amount of money has been spent on research

importanță *sf* importance; **de primă importanță** = (i) most important; (ii) senior; *(post-cheie)* **post de primă importanță** = key post

importator 1 *sm* importer 2 *adj* importing; **țări importatoare de petrol** = oil-importing countries

impozabil *adj* taxable; **venit impozabil** = taxable income

impozit *sn* tax; levy; **impozit direct** = direct tax; **impozit funciar** = property tax; **impozit indirect** = indirect tax; **impozit mediu pe venit** = effective tax rate; **impozit pe avere** = wealth tax; **impozit pe capital** = capital levy; **impozit pe cifra de afaceri** = turnover tax; **impozit pe profiturile societăților (cu răspundere limitată)** = corporation tax; **impozit pe transferul de capital** = capital transfer tax; **impozit pe venit (salariu)** = income tax; **impozit pe vânzări** = sales tax; **impozit perceput de primării** = council tax; **impozit progresiv** = progressive tax; **impozit progresiv pe plus-valoare** = capital gains tax; **impozit regresiv** = regressive tax; **degrevare de impozite** = tax relief;

percepere de impozite = taxation; **profituri înainte de deducerea impozitelor** = pre-tax profits; **scutire de impozite** = tax exemption; **scutit de impozite** = tax-exempt; **a colecta impozite** = to levy; **a impune impozite** *sau* **a percepe impozite** = to impose a tax *sau* to tax; *(în Marea Britanie)* **cod al impozitului pe venit** = tax code; *(în SUA și în Canada)* **impozit federal** = federal tax

impresie *sf* effect

imprimantă *sf* printer; **imprimantă matricială** = dot-matrix printer; **imprimantă laser** = laser printer

impuls *sn* boost

impune *vb* to impose; **a impune taxe pe vânzarea de tutun** = to impose a tax on tobacco; **vânzare impusă** = forced sale

impunere *sf* imposition; **baza de impunere** = tax base; **dublă impunere** = double taxation

inactiv *adj* idle; *(despre situația pieței)* quiet; **bani inactivi** = idle money; **cont bancar inactiv** = dead *sau* dormant account; **perioadă inactivă** = dead season

inaugural *adj* opening

inaugurare *sf* inauguration *sau* opening; **senatorul local a fost invitat la inaugurarea noului complex comercial** = the local MP was invited to the opening of the new shopping mall

incapabil *adj* unable; **este incapabil să-și administreze finanțele singur** = he is unable to deal with his finances on his own

incendiu *sn* fire; **responsabil cu prevenirea incendiilor** = fire safety officer

incintă *sf* **(a)** *(local)* premises; **în incintă** = on the premises **(b)** *(curte)* yard

include *vb* to include; **toate preţurile includ TVA** = all the prices include VAT

inclusiv *adj* inclusive; **preţ inclusiv** *sau* **tarif inclusiv** = all-in price *sau* rate

incompetent *adj* incompetent; **este un director incompetent** = he is an incompetent manager

incompetenţă *sf* incompetence

inconvenient *sn* drawback

independent *adj* **(a)** independent; **comerciant independent** = independent trader; **companie independentă** = independent company **(b)** *(din punct de vedere financiar)* self-supporting; **economie independentă** = self-sufficient economy **(c)** *(computer)* standalone

index *sn* index

indexa *vb* to index-link; **a indexa salariile în raport cu costul de trai** = to link salaries to the cost of living

indexare *sf* indexation; **indexarea salariilor în relaţie cu majorarea preţurilor** = indexation of wage increases

India *sf* India; Notă: capitală: **New Delhi**; monedă: **rupia indiană** = Indian rupee

indian(ă) *s & adj* Indian

indica *vb* to indicate *sau* to show; **a indica pierderi** = to show losses; **cifrele recente au indicat o creştere a preţurilor locuinţelor** = the last figures indicated a rise in house prices

indicator *sn* indicator; **indicator economic** = economic indicator

indicaţie *sf* *(directivă)* guideline

indice *sn* index; **indice al preţurilor** = price index; **indice de dezvoltare** = growth index; *(a la bursa din New York)* **indice Dow Jones** = Dow Jones Index

indigen *adj* indigenous

indigou *sn* carbon paper *sau* carbon; **copie la indigou** = carbon copy

indirect *adj* indirect; **cheltuieli indirecte** = indirect costs; **impozit indirect** = indirect tax; **impunere indirectă** = indirect taxation

individual *adj* **comerciant individual** = sole trader

industrial *adj* industrial; **capacitate industrială** = industrial capacity; **expansiune industrială** = industrial expansion; **platformă industrială** = industrial park

industriaş *sm* industrialist; *(comerciant)* businessman

industrie *sf* industry; **industrie de bază** = basic industry; **industrie extractivă** = extractive industry; **industrie grea** = heavy industry; **industrie incipientă** = infant industry; **industrie uşoară** = light industry

ineficace *adj* inefficient

inerent *adj* **viciu inerent** = in-built defect *sau* inherent vice

inerţie *sf* inertia

inevitabil *adj* automatic; **descalificare inevitabilă** = automatic disqualification; **cheltuieli inevitabile** = unavoidable costs

inferior *adj* **(a)** junior **(b)** *(modest)* poor; **calitate inferioară** = poor quality; **titluri de valoare inferioară** = junk bonds **(c)** inferior; **poziţie inferioară** = back seat

inflaţie *sf* inflation; **a practica o politică de reducere a inflaţiei** = to deflate the economy; **acţiuni de**

contracarare a inflaţiei = anti-inflationary measures; **inflaţie galopantă** = hyperinflation; runaway inflation *sau* galloping inflation; **rata anuală a inflaţiei** = annual rate of inflation; **reducere a inflaţiei** = deflation

inflaţionar *adj* inflationary

inflaţionist *adj* inflationary; **marjă inflaţionistă** = inflationary gap

influenţa *vb* to influence; **a influenţa consumatorii** = to make an impact on consumers; **a influenţa prin mijloace artificiale nivelul preţurilor acţiunilor** = to manipulate share prices

influenţă *sf* influence

informa *vb* **(a)** to advise **(b)** to advertise

informatică *sf* informatics

informaţie *sf* **(a)** piece of information; *(date)* data **(b)** *sfpl* **informaţii** = news; information; **a solicita informaţii** = to inquire; **au cerut informaţii despre conturile cu dobânzi scutite de impozit** = they inquired about the tax free savings accounts; **birou de informaţii** = information bureau **(c)** **prelucrarea informaţiilor pe calculator** = data processing; **recuperarea de informaţii** = information retrieval

infracţiune *sf* offence; **infracţiune fiscală** = tax offence

infrastructură *sf* infrastructure

inginer *sm* engineer; **inginer electronist** = electronics engineer; **inginer de construcţii civile** = civil engineer

inginerie *sf* engineering

iniţial *adj* opening; **ofertă iniţială** = opening bid

iniţiere *sf* induction; **toţi au frecventat cursurile de iniţiere**

înainte de a începe să lucreze = they all attended induction courses before starting work

inopinat *adj* **control inopinat** = snap check *sau* spot check

insera *vb* **a insera anunţuri** = to advertise

insolvabil *adj* insolvent; **a fi declarat insolvabil** = to be declared insolvent; **a fi declarat insolvent** = to be hammered (on Stock Exchange)

insolvabilitate *sf* insolvency

inspecta *vb* to inspect

inspector *sm* **(a)** inspector; **inspector fiscal** = tax inspector *sau* inspector of taxes, *(în SUA)* tax assessor; **inspector financiar** = revenue officer **(b)** *(ofiţer de poliţie)* police inspector

inspecţie *sf* inspection; **a efectua o inspecţie** = to carry out an inspection

instabil *adj* unstable *sau* jumpy; **piaţă instabilă** = jumpy market

institui *vb* to institute

institut *sn* institute; **institut de cercetări** = research institute

instituţie *sf* establishment

instructaj *sn* brief

instrucţiune *sf* instruction; **instrucţiuni de folosire** = handbook *sau* operating manual; **a da instrucţiuni** = to give instructions *sau* to brief

instrui *vb* to train

instrument *sn* **(a)** implement **(b)** *(document legal)* instrument

insultă *sf* affront

integra *vb* **a (se) integra** = to integrate *sau* to incorporate

integrare *sf* integration; **integrare orizontală** = horizontal integration;

integrare verticală = vertical integration

intens *adj* keen

intensiv *adj* intensive; **agricultură intensivă** = intensive farming

intenta *vb* **a intenta proces cuiva** = to bring an action against someone

intenționat *adj* calculated

interdicție *sf* ban

interes *sn* interest; **a-și manisfesta interesul** = to show interest; **interese personale** = vested interests

interesa *vb* to interest

interfață *sf (conexiune)* interface

interimar *adj* caretaker; **guvern interimar** = caretaker government

interior *sn* **(a)** *(telefonic)* extension; **interior 234, vă rog** = can I have extension 234 please? **(b)** inland

intermediar *sm* **(a)** intermediary *sau* middleman **(b)** agency

intern *adj* **(a)** internal; **control financiar intern** = internal audit **(b)** domestic; **piața internă** = home market; **produsele au fost desfăcute pe piața internă** = the goods were sold on the domestic market **(c)** inland

internațional *adj* (i) international; (ii) overseas; **convorbire telefonică internațională** = international call *sau* overseas call

interoga *vb* to question; to challenge; **poliția l-a interogat pe director în legătură cu accidentul de muncă** = the police questioned the manager about the industrial accident

interogare *sf* examination; **interogare suplimentară** = cross-examination

interpret *sm* interpreter

interpreta *vb* to interpret; **el va interpreta pentru președinte la întrunire** = he will interpret for the chairman at the meeting

interstatal *adj* interstate

interurban *adj* inter-city *sau* intercity

intervenție *sf* intervention; **intervenție guvernamentală** = state intervention

intervenționist *adj* interventionist

intervieva *vb* to interview; **omul de afaceri a refuzat să fie intervievat** = the businessman refused to be interviewed

interviu *sn* interview; **a alege candidați la un post pentru interviul final** = to shortlist candidates

interzice *vb* to ban *sau* to bar; **directorul a interzis fumatul în birouri** = the manager banned smoking in offices

interzicere *sf* ban; *(embargou)* embargo; **interzicere a fumatului** = ban on smoking

intra *vb* to enter; **a intra într-o cameră** = to enter a room

intrare *sf* **(a)** entrance *sau* admission *sau* access; **biletul de intrare costă 1000 lei** = the entrance fee is 1000 lei; **prețul biletului de intrare** = entrance fee *sau* admission fee **(b)** **intrare contabilă** = entry in a ledger; **a efectua o intrare (contabilă)** = to post an entry; **a opera intrări contabile** = to enter figures in the books

inunda *vb* **a inunda piața (cu produse)** = to glut (the market)

inutil *adj* useless

inventar *sn (în Marea Britanie)* stock; *(în SUA)* inventory; **a face inventarul** = to take stock; **listă de inventar** = inventory *sau* stocklist

inventaria *vb* to inventory

inventariere *sf* stocktaking

investi *vb* to invest; **a investi într-o afacere** = to put money into a business; **a investi riscant** = to speculate; **a investit jumătate din bani in proprietăţi imobiliare** = he invested half of his money in property

investitor *sm* investor; capitalist; **investitor particular** = private investor

investiţie *sf* investment; **bancă de investiţii** = investment bank; **credit de investiţii** = capital investment loan; **fond de investiţii** = investment fund; **investiţii guvernamentale** = public investment; **investiţii particulare** = private investment; **investiţii pe termen îndelungat** = long-term investments; **a reduce investiţiile** = to disinvest; **societate de investiţii** = unit trust

invita *vb* to ask; **a invita pe cineva la o petrecere** = to ask somebody to a party

invizibil *adj* invisible; *(transport, activităţi financiar-bancare, etc.)* **importuri invizibile** = invisible imports

Iordania *sf* Jordan; Notă: capitală: **Amman;** monedă: **dinar iordanian** = Jordanian dinar

iordanian(ă) *s & adj* Jordanian

ipoteca *vb* to mortgage; **a trebuit să-şi ipotecheze casa pentru a-şi achita datoriile** = to pay off her debts she had to mortgage her house

ipotecă *sf* mortgage

Irak *sm* Iraq; Notă: capitală: **Bagdad** = Baghdad; monedă: **dinar irakian** = Iraqi dinar

irakian(ă) *s & adj* Iraqi

Iran *sm* Iran; Notă: capitală: **Teheran** = Tehran; monedă: **rial iranian** = Iranian rial

iranian(ă) *s & adj* Iranian

Irlanda *sf* Ireland; Notă: capitală: **Dublin;** monedă: **liră irlandeză** = Irish punt *sau* pound

irlandez(ă) *s & adj* Irish

Islanda *sf* Iceland; Notă: capitală: **Reykjavik;** monedă: **coroană islandeză** = Icelandic krona

islandez(ă) **1** *s* Icelander **2** *adj* Icelandic

Italia *sf* Italy; Notă: capitală: **Roma** = Rome; monedă: **liră italiană** = Italian lira

italian(ă) *s & adj* Italian

Îî

îmbarca *vb* a se îmbarca = to board *sau* to embark; **ne-am îmbarcat pe vapor cu câteva minute înainte de plecare** = we embarked a few minutes before departure

îmbunătăţi *vb (a se ameliora)* a se **îmbunătăţi** = to pick up *sau* to upgrade

îmbunătăţire *sf* upgrade; a **îmbunătăţit performanţa calculatorului său adăugând module de RAM (Random Access Memory)** = he upgraded his computer by adding more RAM chips

împacheta *vb* to parcel *sau* to pack; **cărţile au fost împachetate şi expediate ieri** = the books were packed and dispatched yesterday

împachetare *sf* packaging *sau* packing; **hârtie ornamentală de împachetare a cadourilor** = gift-wrapping (paper); **serviciu de împachetare (a cadourilor oferit de unele magazine contra unei mici sume de bani)** = gift-wrapping service *sau* department

împărţi *vb* to divide *sau* to share; to distribute; **a împărţi în acţiuni** = to parcel shares; **a împărţi profiturile** = to share profits; **a împărţi pe din două cu cineva** = to go fifty-fifty with someone

împărţire *sf* distribution

împotriva *adv* against

împotrivi *vb* a se împotrivi = to counter

împrejmui *vb* to enclose

împrejmuire *sau* **îngrădire** *sf* enclosure

împrumut *sn* loan; credit; **împrumut bancar** *sau* **împrumut la bancă** = bank credit *sau* bank loan; **a aranja obţinerea unui împrumut la bancă** = to negotiate a bank loan; **împrumut pe scurtă durată** = short-term loan; **împrumut în condiţii avantajoase** = soft loan; *(ipotecă)* **împrumut pentru cumpărarea unei locuinţe** = mortgage *sau* home loan; **a contracta un împrumut pentru cumpărarea unei locuinţe** = to take out a mortgage (on a home); **împrumut personal** = personal loan; **contract de împrumut** = loan agreement; **persoană sau organizaţie care acordă împrumuturi** = lender *sau* moneylender

împrumuta *vb* (a) *(a da cu împrumut)* to lend *sau* to loan *sau* to advance (money); **banca i-a împrumutat banii după ce i-a analizat cu atenţie situaţia financiară** = the bank lent him the money after having considered his financial status carefully (b) *(a lua cu împrumut)* to borrow; **aş vrea să împrumut nişte bani ca să achit o notă de plată urgentă** = I would like to borrow some money to pay an overdue bill

împuternici *vb* **(a)** to commission *sau* to empower; **a împuternicit un agent să-i vândă acţiunile** = he empowered an agent to sell his shares; **el a fost împuternicit să cerceteze registrele companiei** = he was commissioned to check the company's records **(b)** to delegate

împuternicire *sf* power of attorney

împuternicit *sm* attorney; mandatory

împuţina *vb* **a (se) împuţina** = to decrease; **rezervele noastre s-au împuţinat dramatic** = our reserves have decreased dramatically

înainta *vb* **(a)** *(a avansa)* to advance **(b) a înainta o propunere** = to table a proposal **(c) a înainta spre aprobare** = to submit; **a înainta un proiect spre aprobare** = to submit a project for approval

înainte *adv* ahead; **înainte de** = prior to; **noua linie de asamblare a fost dată în exploatare înainte de termen** = the new production line became operational ahead of schedule; **înainte şi înapoi** = back and forth

înalt *adj* high; **ei produc sisteme muzicale de înaltă fidelitate** = they produce high fidelity systems

înapoi *adv* back; backward; *(a achita)* **a plăti înapoi** = to pay back; **înainte şi înapoi** = back and forth; **a da înapoi** = to back off

înapoia *vb* to return

înapoiat *adj* backward

încadra *vb* **încadra personal** = to staff

încadrare de personal *sf* staffing; **nivele ale încadrării de personal** = staffing levels

încasa *vb* to encash; **a încasa un cec** = to cash a cheque

încasabil *adj* *(despre cecuri, etc.)* encashable

încasări *sfpl* **(a)** takings; **vânzătorul a fost prins furând încasările** = the shop assistant was caught stealing the takings; **registru de încasări** = cash book **(b)** *(din vânzarea biletelor)* box office; **filmul Ziua Independenţei a bătut toate recordurile de încasări în 1996** = the film Independence Day smashed all box office records in 1996

încălca *vb* **(a)** to break *sau* to breach; **a-şi încălca promisiunea** = to go back on one's promise **(b)** to infringe

încălcare *sf* **(a)** breach; **încălcare a contractului** = breach of contract; **încălcare a promisiunii** = breach of promise; **încălcarea contractului de garanţie** = breach of warranty **(b)** infringement; **încălcarea dreptului de autor** = infringement of copyright

încălţăminte *sf* footwear

încărca *vb* **(a)** to load; **a încărca un vapor** *sau* **camion** = to load a ship *sau* lorry; **capacitate utilă de încărcare (a unui camion, etc.)** = commercial load; **capacitate maximă de încărcare** = maximum load; **permis de încărcare** = shipping bill **(b) a încărca exagerat un cont** = to overcharge

încărcat *adj* laden; **navă încărcată la capacitate maximă** = fully-laden ship

încărcătură *sf* shipment; **încărcătura unui vas comercial** = cargo *sau* load; **încărcătură utilă (de marfă sau pasageri)** = payload

începător *sm* apprentice

încerca *vb* to attempt *sau* to try; **a-şi încerca norocul** = to take one's chance

încercare *sf* attempt; **încercarea sa de a deschide o librărie a eşuat** =

his attempt to open a bookshop ended in failure

înceta *vb* to come to a stop *sau* to come to an end; **a înceta activitatea** = to close down; **a înceta lucrul** = to down tools; *(a închide - temporar - o fabrică)* **a înceta producţia** = to shut down

încetare *sf* **încetarea activităţii** = stop; standstill

încheia *vb* **a încheia un acord** = to strike an agreement; **a încheia o afacere avantajoasă** = to strike a bargain; **a încheia un contract financiar** = to negotiate; **a-şi încheia socotelile** = to pay off (debt)

încheiere *sf* end; completion; **de încheiere** = terminal; **încheierea tranzacţiilor la bursă** = close (of day's trading); **încheierea unui contract** = completion of a contract

închide *vb* to close; **închide (temporar) o fabrică** = to shut down; **magazinul este închis duminica** = the store closes on Sundays

închidere *sf* close (of trading); **la închidere, valoarea acţiunilor noastre a scăzut cu 5p (pence)** = at the close, our shares value fell by 5p; **cursul la închidere** = closing price

închiria *vb* **(a)** *(de la cineva)* to lease *sau* to hire *sau* to rent; **compania a închiriat toată clădirea** = the company leased the whole building; **a închiria o maşină** = to hire a car *sau* to lease a car **(b)** *(a afreta)* to charter; **a închiria un vas pentru transport** = to charter a ship **(c)** to let; **a închiria un apartament** = to let a flat; **proprietate (mobilată) de închiriat** = letting **(d)** **a închiria mână de lucru** = to farm out work

închiriere *sf* hire *sau* let; **închiriere de lungă durată (peste 50 de ani)** = long lease; **închiriere de scurtă durată (sub 50 de ani)** = short lease; **închiriere pe termen scurt** = short

let; **închirierea unei maşini** = car hire; **contract de închiriere** = lease; tenancy (agreement); **firmă de închiriere de echipament** = plant-hire firm; **perioadă de închiriere** = tenancy

înclinaţie *sf* propensity; **înclinaţie spre a economisi** = propensity to save

încorpora *vb* **a (se) încorpora** = to incorporate

încredere *sf* trust *sau* confidence *sau* faith; **a avea încredere** = to trust; **omul de afaceri nu prea avea încredere în noul său asociat** = the businessman did not have much confidence in his new partner; **am încredere în banca mea** = I have faith in my bank; **de încredere** = confidential; *(sincer)* bona fide; **demn de încredere** = bankable; dependable; *(solvent)* creditworthy; *(executor)* **persoană de încredere** = fiduciary; **împrumut pe încredere** *sau* **fără garanţii** = fiduciary loan

încredinţa *vb* **(a)** to assign; to charge **(b)** to commit; to entrust; **directorul i-a încredinţat cheile magazinului** = the manager entrusted him with the keys of the shop; **el a încredinţat documentele băncii spre păstrare** = he committed the documents to the bank for safe keeping

încrezător *adj* confident; **ea este încrezătoare că va încheia contractul cu furnizorul** = she is confident she will win the contract with the supplier

încuraja *vb* to stimulate

încuviinţa *vb* to assent

încuviinţare *sf* assent; compliance

îndatora *vb* to oblige

îndatorat *adj* indebted; **vă sunt îndatorat pentru ajutorul acordat** = I am much obliged to you for your help

îndatorire *sf* function *sau* task

îndeplini *vb* to accomplish; to fulfil; to realize *sau* to execute; **a îndeplini un plan** = to realize a plan; **şi-au îndeplinit sarcinile** = they fulfilled their obligations

îndoială *sf* **a pune la îndoială** = to question; **a pune la îndoială competenţa cuiva** = to question somebody's competence

îndoielnic *adj* questionable

îndrepta *vb* to amend; **a se îndrepta spre** = to head for

îndreptăţi *vb* to entitle; **clientul este îndreptăţit să ceară banii înapoi dacă produsul e defect** = the customer is entitled to a refund if the product is defective

îndruma *vb* to direct

îndrumar *sn* directory

înfia *vb* to adopt

înfiinţa *vb* to set up *sau* to establish; **firma a fost înfiinţată acum 100 de ani** = the firm was established 100 years ago

înfrânge *vb* to defeat; **a înfrânge competiţia** = to knock the competition

înfrângere *sf* defeat

îngheţa *vb* to freeze; **a îngheţa salariile** = to freeze wages

îngrădire *sau* **împrejmuire** *sf* enclosure

îngrijitor *sm* caretaker

înjumătăţi *vb* to halve

înlocui *vb* to take over; **Domnul Popescu a înlocuit-o pe Doamna Marin** = Mr Popescu took over from Mrs Marin

înlătura *vb* **a înlătura riscuri financiare prin noi investiţii** = to lay off risks

înmatriculare *sf* *(auto)* **număr de înmatriculare** = registration number

înmâna *vb* **(a)** to consign **(b)** to hand (in)

înregistra *vb* **(a)** *(a nota sau a înregistra operaţiuni contabile)* to record *sau* to enter *sau* to log; **comanda Dvs. a fost înregistrată** = your order has been recorded **(b) a se înregistra la hotel** = to check in at the hotel; **a se a se înregistra la aeroport înaintea zborului** = to check in at the airport (before departure); **trebuie să vă înregistraţi la aeroport cu cel puţin două ore înainte de zbor** = you must check in at least two hours before the time of departure

înregistrare *sf* **(a)** *(notare)* recording; entry **(b)** registration; **certificat de înregistrare** = certificate of registration; **număr de înregistrare** = registration number

înrudit *adj* *(afiliat)* related; affiliated (company)

însărcina *vb* to commission

însoţi *vb* to accompany; **omul de afaceri era însoţit de secretara sa** = the businessman was accompanied by his secretary

înstrăina *vb* to alienate

însuşi *vb* **a-şi însuşi** = to pocket; **din toată suma a plătit un mic comision şi şi-a însuşit restul** = from the total sum he paid a small commission and pocketed the rest

înşela *vb* to defraud; to cheat; **a-şi înşela creditorii** = to defraud one's creditors; **el a fost înşelat de partenerul său şi a pierdut o grămadă de bani** = he was cheated by his partner and lost a lot of money

înşelăciune *sf* *(decepţie)* deceit

înşira *vb* to list

înştiinţare *sf* communication

întări *vb* to consolidate

întâlni *vb* **a (se) întâlni** = to meet; **directorul s-a întâlnit cu reprezentanţii trustului de construcţii** = the manager met the building contractors

întâlnire *sf (de afaceri)* appointment

întâmplare *sf* chance; **la întâmplare** = by chance; at random

întâmplător 1 *adv* by chance 2 *adj* **(a)** *(ocazional)* incidental **(b)** casual; **profit întâmplător** = casual profit **(c)** *(aleatoriu)* random

întârzia *vb* to delay

întârziere *sf* delay; hold-up; **furnizorul şi-a cerut scuze pentru întârzierea livrării bunurilor** = the supplier apologised for the delay in delivering the goods

întreba *vb* to ask; to inquire

întrebare *sf* question; **a pune întrebări** = to query

întrece *vb* to beat; **au fost întrecuţi din nou pe piaţa jucăriilor** = they were beaten again in the toys market; **a întrece la licitaţie oferind cea mai mare sumă** = to outbid someone

întreg *adj* full *sau* complete *sau* total; **muncitor cu normă întreagă** = full-time worker

întreprindere *sf* enterprise *sau* company *sau* firm; *(care implică o doză de risc)* venture; *(fabrică)* works; **întreprindere mică** = small business; **întreprindere în participaţie** = joint venture; **întreprindere particulară** = private enterprise; **întreprindere de stat** = state enterprise

întrerupe *vb* **a întrerupe asocierea într-o afacere** = to dissolve a partnership

întrerupere *sf* stoppage; *(grevă)* **întreruperea lucrului** = stoppage of work

întreţine *vb* **(a)** to entertain **(b)** to keep in good repair *sau* to maintain

întreţinere *sf* maintenance *sau* keeping in good repair; **cheltuieli de întreţinere** = maintenance costs; **contract de întreţinere** = service agreement; **tehnician de întreţinere** = service engineer

întreţinut *sm & adj* dependent

întrevedere *sf* interview

întrunire *sf* meeting

înţelege *vb* **a se înţelege** = to agree; to get along; **ne înţelegem foarte bine** = we get along very well

înţelegere *sf* **(a)** contract *sau* engagement **(b)** agreement; **înţelegere verbală** = gentleman's agreement

învăţătură *sf* knowledge

învoi *vb* **a se învoi (asupra unui târg)** = to bargain

învoială *sf* bargain

învoire *sf* leave; **a cerut acordarea unei învoiri pentru a merge la doctor** = she asked for leave to go to the doctor

Jj

jaf armat *sn* hold-up

Jamaica *sf* Jamaica; Notă: capitală: **Kingston**; monedă: **dolar jamaican** = Jamaican dollar

jamaican(ă) *s & adj* Jamaican

Japonia *sf* Japan; Notă: capitală: **Tokyo**; monedă: **yen japonez** = Japanese yen

japonez(ă) *s & adj* Japanese

jignire *sf* affront

judeca *vb* (a) to assess (b) to judge

judecată *sf* judgement; **a da în judecată** = to bring a case against; **a da în judecată** = to sue *sau* to take legal action; **compania a fost dată în judecată pentru încălcarea contractului** = the company was sued for breach of contract

judecător *sm* judge; **judecător de pace** = magistrate; **judecătorie de pace** = magistrates' court

judecătoresc *adj* judicial; **hotărâre judecătorească** = judge's order; **sentință judecătorească** = judgement

judiciar *adj* **cazier judiciar** = criminal record

jumătate *sf* half; **magazinul are mai mulți cumpărători în a doua jumătate a anului** = the shop is busier in the second half of the year; **rata dobânzilor a fost majorată cu o jumătate de procent** = the interest rates went up by a half per cent; **jumătate de duzină** = half-dozen; **jumătate de normă** = part-time; **lucrează cu o jumătate de normă într-o bancă** = she works part-time in a bank; **lucrător cu jumătate de normă** = part-time worker

jurat *sm* juror; **prim jurat** = foreman (of the jury)

jurământ *sn* oath; **a depune mărturie sub jurământ** = to give evidence under oath

juridic *adj* judicial; **consilier juridic** = legal adviser

jurisdicție *sf* jurisdiction

jurist *sm* lawyer; legal adviser

juriu *sn* jury

jurnal *sn* *(contabilitate)* journal *sau* ledger; **jurnal de bord** = log

just *adj* just; *(echitabil)* fair; **comerț just** = fair trade

justifica *vb* to warrant

Kk

Kenia *sf* Kenya; Notă: capitală:
Nairobi; monedă: **şiling kenian =**
Kenyan shilling

kenian(ă) *s & adj* Kenyan

kilobit *sm* *(1024 de biţi, unitate de
măsură a cantităţii de informaţie stocată de*
un calculator, în memorie sau pe disc)
kilobyte (KB *sau* Kb)

kilogram *sn* kilogram (kg) *sau* kilo

kilometru *sm* kilometre (km)

Kuwait *sm* Kuwait; Notă: monedă:
dinar kuwaitian = Kuwaiti dinar

kuwaitian(ă) *s & adj* Kuwaiti

Ll

ladă *sf* box *sau* case; **ladă de (12) sticle cu vin** = case of wine; **ladă de ambalaj** = packing case; **piesele de schimb au fost expediate în lăzi de lemn** = the spare parts were shipped in wooden boxes

lanţ *sn* chain: **reacţie în lanţ** = chain reaction

Laos *s m* Laos; Notă: capitală: **Vientiane;** monedă: **kip laoţian** = Laotian kip

laoţian(ă) *s & adj* Laotian

lămuri *vb* to clear

lăuda *vb* to boost

lângă *prep* against; **pe lângă** = in addition to

lealitate *sf* faith

lega *vb* to connect

legal 1 *adj* lawful *sau* legal; *(valabil)* valid; **(în mod) legal** = within the law; **sărbătoare legală** = public holiday 2 *adv* legally

legalitate *sf (legitimitate)* legality

legaliza *vb* **(a)** to legalize **(b)** to authenticate; **copie legalizată** = attested copy *sau* certified copy

legaţie *sf* legation

legătură *sf* connection *sau* relation; *(a contacta)* **a ţine legătura** = to contact; **în legătură cu** = in relation to; **a trebuit să vorbească cu directorul de producţie în legătură**

cu noul **program de lucru** = he had to see the production manager in connection with the new working hours

lege *sf* **(a)** law; *(decret)* decree; *(tradiţie)* **lege nescrisă** = common law; **proiect de lege** = bill **(b) legea randamentului descrescând** = Law of Diminishing Returns

legislaţie *sf* legislation; **legislaţia muncii** = labour legislation

legitimaţie *sf* membership card; *(permis)* pass

legitimitate *sf* legality

leneş *adj* idle *sau* lazy

Letonia *sf* Latvia; Notă: capitală: **Riga;** monedă: **lat**

leton(ă) *s & adj* Latvian

leu *sm* leu

Liban *sm* Lebanon; Notă: capitală: **Beirut;** monedă: **liră libaneză** = Lebanese pound

libanez(ă) *s & adj* Lebanese

liber *adj* free; **compania i-a dat mână liberă să reorganizeze atelierul** = the company gave him a free hand to reorganize the workshop; **economie liberă** = free economy; **timp liber** = time off

liberalizare *sf* deregulation

Libia *sf* Libya; Notă: capitală: **Tripoli;** monedă: **dinar libian** = Libyan dinar

libian(ă) *s & adj* Libyan

librar *sm* bookseller

librărie *sf* bookshop

libret *sn* *(carnet de economii)* bankbook *sau* passbook

licenţă *sf* (a) *(autorizaţie)* licence; **licenţă de import** = import licence; **bunuri produse sub licenţă** = goods manufactured under licence; **a acorda o licenţă de exploatare** = to franchise (b) *(patent)* patent

licenţiat *sm* graduate

lichida *vb* (a) to clear; to sell off; **a lichida stocul existent** = to liquidate stock; **toate aceste calculatoare sunt reduse pentru a lichida stocul** = all these computers are reduced to clear (b) *(o întreprindere, afacere)* to wind up; *(un cont)* to close (c) **a lichida proprietăţi sau mijloace fixe** = to realize (a property) (d) *(a plăti)* to redeem; **a lichida o datorie** = to redeem a debt

lichidare *sf* (a) *(încetarea activităţii)* dissolution *sau* winding up (b) liquidation; receivership; **compania se află în lichidare** = the company is in the hands of the receivers (c) closing-down sale (d) *(rambursare)* **lichidarea unei datorii** = paying off (a loan)

licita *vb* to bid; **a licitat împotriva proprietarului de garaj** = he bid against the car dealer

licitaţie *sf* auction *sau* sale; **a întrece la licitaţie** = to overbid; **sală de licitaţii** = sale room; **a vinde la licitaţie** = to auction

lift *sn* lift; *US* elevator

limita *vb* to limit *sau* to restrict; to ration; **a limita cheltuielile** = to keep a check on expenses; **a limita fonduri de investiţie** = to ration investment capital; **a limita importurile** = to restrict imports

limitare *sf* squeeze; **limitarea creditelor oferite de bănci** = credit squeeze; *(deseori impusă de guvern)* **limitarea majorării salariilor** = pay squeeze

limitat *adj* limited

limitativ *adj* restrictive

limită *sf* (a) limit; **limită de vârstă** = age limit (b) *(restricţie)* restriction; **a impune limite pe importuri** = to impose limits on imports (c) *(capăt)* border (d) *(marjă)* margin

lingou *sn* (a) *(de aur sau argint)* ingot; **lingou de aur** = gold ingot (b) bullion

linie *sf* (a) line; **linie de frontieră** = frontier (b) **linie aeriană** = airline; **linie maritimă** = shipping line; *(punct terminus)* **cap de linie** = railhead (c) *(de producţie)* production line; **linie de asamblare** = assembly line (d) *(peron)* platform; **trenul de Braşov va pleca de la linia 10** = the train for Braşov leaves from platform 10

lipsă *sf* (a) lack; *(criză)* scarcity *sau* shortage; **au amânat deschiderea unei noi filiale din cauza lipsei de fonduri** = they postponed the opening of a new branch because of lack of funds (b) *(omisiune)* default

lipsi *vb* to be short of; **a fi lipsit de** = to lack

liră sterlină (£) *sf* 1 liră sterlină = one pound sterling; **o bancnotă de cincizeci de lire** = a fifty-pound note; **o monedă de o liră** = a pound coin; **zonă de influenţă a lirei sterline** = sterling area

listă *sf* (a) *(catalog)* list; **listă de produse şi preţuri** = catalogue; **listă electorală** = electoral register; **listă cuprinzând încărcătura unui vas comercial** = manifest; **listă de**

pasageri = passenger manifest; **listă de preţuri** = price list **(b)** schedule; **listă de lucru** = agenda; **listă cu lucruri de făcut** *sau* **de luat (într-o călătorie)** = checklist

literă *sf (caracter tipografic)* letter; character; **a scrie cu litere majuscule** = to write in capital letters *sau* to print

litigiu *sn* litigation

Lituania *sf* Lithuania; Notă: capitală: **Vilnius**; monedă: **litas lituanian** = Lithuanian litas

lituanian(ă) *s & adj* Lithuanian

livra *vb* to deliver

livrare *sf* delivery; **livrare cu minusuri** = short delivery; **notă de livrare** = delivery note; **termen (dată) de livrare** = delivery time

livră *sf (egală cu 0,45 Kg)* pound (lb); **a vinde legume la livră** = to sell vegetables by the pound

local 1 *sn* premises 2 *adj* local; **administraţia locală** = local authority

locuinţă *sf* accommodation

lojă *sf* box (in theatre); **doi dintre parteneri sau întâlnit în loja particulară a preşedintelui la spectacolul Mizerabilii** = two of the partners met in the chairman's private box at the showing of Les Misérables

lot *sn* pack; **lot de articole** = pack of items

loterie *sf* **(a)** lottery **(b)** *(organizată de obicei în scopuri caritabile)* **loterie cu premii în obiecte** = raffle

lubrifiant *sn* oil

lucra *vb* to work; **a lucra ore suplimentare (plătite dublu)** = to be on double time

lucrare *sf* job; **lucrare terminată** = executed contract; **a efectua diverse lucrări mărunte** = to do odd jobs; **lucrări publice** = public works

lucrător *sm* worker; **lucrător la domiciliu** = homeworker

lucru *sn* **(a)** work *sau* labour; *US* labor; **cantitatea de lucru** = workload; **(şomer) fără lucru** = unemployed *sau* jobless *sau* out of work; *(artizanat)* **lucru la domiciliu** = cottage industry; **lucru în acord** = piece-work; **lucru în curs** = work in progress; **lucru manual** = manual labour; **lucru ocazional** = casual work; **mână de lucru ieftină** = cheap labour; **permis de lucru (pentru străini)** = work permit; **persoană în căutare de lucru** = jobseeker; **săptămână de lucru** = working week **(b)** *(al unei maşini)* **probă de lucru** = test run; **regim de lucru** = run

Lumea a Treia *sf* Third World

lună *sf (calendaristică)* (calendar) month

lusitan(ă) *sau* **portughez(ă)** *s & adj* Portuguese

lux *sn* luxury; **articole de lux** = luxury items

Luxenburg *sm* Luxembourg; Notă: monedă: **franc luxenburghez** = Luxembourg franc

luxenburghez(ă) *s & adj* Luxembourger

Mm

macroeconomie *sf* macro-economics

Madagascar *sm* Madagascar; Notă: capitală: **Antananarivo; monedă: franc malgaş** = Malagasy franc

magazie *sf (antrepozit)* store; *(depozit)* stockroom; **fişă de magazie** = stock control card; **registru de magazie** = stock book

magazin *sn* shop *sau* store; **magazin aparţinând unei reţele de magazine** = chain store; **magazin de articole de menaj** = hardware shop; **magazin de calculatoare** = computer shop; **magazin universal** = department store; **hoţ din magazine** = shoplifter; *(comerciant)* **proprietar de (mic) magazin** = shopkeeper *sau* storekeeper; **reţea de magazine** = chain of stores

magaziner *sau* **magazioner** *sm* warehouseman *sau* storekeeper

maghiar(ă) 1 *s* Hungarian 2 *adj* Hungarian

magistrat *sm (judecător de pace)* magistrate

magnat *sm* magnate *sau* tycoon; **magnat al presei** = media magnate

majora *vb* (a) **a (se) majora** = to increase *sau* to raise; **a majora impozitele** = to raise tax levels; **a majora preţurile** = to put up prices; **a majora artificial preţuri** = to inflate prices; **salariile noastre nu au fost majorate în ultimii doi ani** = we

haven't had a raise for two years **(b) a majora preţul** = to mark up

majorare *sf* **(a)** increase *sau* rise; *(escaladare)* escalation; **majorarea impozitului** = tax increase; **majorarea preţurilor** = price rise; **majorarea salariului** = salary increase **(b) majorare a preţului** = mark-up

majoritate *sf* majority; **în majoritate** = mainly

majusculă *sf* **litere majuscule** = block letters *sau* capital letters; **tasta de (litere) majuscule** = shift key

Malaezia *sf* Malaysia; Notă: capitală: **Kuala Lumpur; monedă: ringgit malaezian** = Malaysian ringgit

malaezian(ă) *s & adj* Malaysian

malgaş(ă) *s & adj* Madagascan

Malta *sf* Malta; Notă: capitală: **Valetta; monedă: liră malteză** = Maltese lira

maltez(ă) *s & adj* Maltese

management *sn (conducere; consiliu de administraţie)* management

managerial *adj* managerial

mandat *sn* **(a)** mandate; warrant **(b)** *(procură)* procuration **(c) mandat poştal** = money order *sau* postal order; mail transfer; **mandat poştal internaţional** = international money order; **mandat poştal telegrafic** =

telegraphic money order; **mandat telegrafic** = cable transfer

manipula *vb* **(a)** to handle; *(a opera)* to operate; **i-a luat trei luni să învețe să manipuleze noul echipament** = it took him three months to learn how to operate the new equipment; **manipulați cu grijă** = handle with care **(b)** to manipulate; to rig; **a manipula piața** = to manipulate the market *sau* to rig the market

manoperă *sf* labour; *US* labor; **cheltuieli de manoperă** = labour charges; **a plătit pentru piesele de schimb și manoperă** = he paid for spare parts and labour

manual 1 *sn (carte tehnică)* manual *sau* handbook 2 **(a)** *adj* manual; **centrală telefonică operată manual de telefoniste** = manual exchange; **lucru manual** = manual labour **(b)** *(lucrat de mână)* handmade

marca *vb (bijuterii)* to hallmark

marcaj *sn* **(a)** *(la bijuterii)* hallmark **(b)** *(pontaj)* tally

marcă *sf* **(a)** *(sortiment)* brand; *(model)* make; **ce marcă este mașina Dvs?** = what make is your car?; **marcă înregistrată** = trade mark **(b)** **marcă germană** = Deutschmark

mare 1 *sf* sea 2 *adj* high; **volum mare de vânzări** = high volume of sales

marfă *sf* **(a)** *(bunuri de consum)* merchandise **(b)** freight **(c)** *(materii prime)* commodity; raw material; **bursă de mărfuri** = commodity market *sau* commodity exchange; **depozit de mărfuri** = goods depot

marginal *adj* marginal; **cheltuieli marginale** = marginal costs

margine *sf* margin

marină *sf* navy *sau* marine; **marină comercială** = merchant marine *sau* merchant navy

maritim *adj* **accident maritim** = marine accident; **asigurare maritimă** = marine insurance; **agent de asigurări maritime** = marine underwriter; **agent maritim de navlosire** = shipping agent; **linie maritimă** *sau* **companie maritimă** = shipping line; **port maritim** = seaport; **pe cale maritimă** = by sea

marjă *sf (limită)* margin; **marjă de profit** = mark-up; **marjă de beneficiu** = profit margin

marketing *sn* marketing; **politică de marketing** = marketing plans

Maroc *sm* Morocco; Notă: capitală: **Rabat**; monedă: **dirham marocan** = Moroccan dirham

marocan(ă) *s & adj* Moroccan

martor *sm (în procese)* deponent

masă *sf* **(a)** weight; **de masă** = large-scale **(b)** table

mașină *sf* **(a)** **mașină de adunat** = adding machine; **mașina de casă** = cash register; **mașină de copiat** = copying machine *sau* photocopier; **mașină de francat** = franking machine **(b)** *(automobil)* car; **cu mașina** = by car; **mașina de serviciu** = company car

mașină-unealtă *sf* machine-tool

material *sn* material; **materiale de construcție** = building materials; **material militar de luptă** = military hardware; **material rulant** = rolling stock

materie *sf* **materii prime** = raw materials; **piața de materii prime** = commodity market *sau* commodity exchange

matinal *adj* early

maxim *adj* maximum; **randament maxim** = peak output

mărfar *sn* goods train

mărgini *vb* to border

mări *vb* **a (se) mări** = to expand

mărire *sf* **mărire de salariu** = rise *sau* raise (in salary); **mărire a profitului și, sau a cifrei de afaceri** = accrual

mărturie *sf (depoziție)* deposition; evidence; **a depune mărturie la tribunal** = to give evidence in court

mărunțiș *sn* loose change *sau* small change

măsura *vb* to measure; **a măsura conținutul unui rezervor de benzină** = to measure the contents of a petrol tank

măsură *sf* measure; **aparat de măsură** = gauge; **croit pe măsură** = made to measure

mână *sf* **(a)** hand; **a da mâna cu cineva** = to shake hands with somebody; **cu mâna** = by hand; **lucrat de mână** = handmade; **mâna a doua** = second-hand; **scris de mână** = (i) handwriting; (ii) handwritten; **nu a putut citi scrisul ei de mână** = he could not read her handwriting **(b) mână de lucru** = labour; **a asigura mână de lucru** = to man

mânui *vb* to handle *sau* to manipulate

mecanic *adj* mechanical; automatic

mecanism *sn (aparat sau dispozitiv)* device

medical *adj* medical; **cabinet medical particular** = doctor's practice; **certificat medical** = medical certificate

medie *sf* average; **a face media** = to average

mediere *sf* conciliation; **comisie de mediere** = conciliation tribunal

mediu **1** *sn (economic sau social)* background **2** *adj* average; **cost mediu** = average cost; **preț mediu** = average price; **stoc mediu** = average stock

megabait *sau* **megabit** *sn (unitate de măsură a capacității de stocare a informației egală cu 1024 kilobiți)* megabyte (Mb *sau* MB)

membru *sm* member; **membru al unui sindicat** = union member; **membru onorific** = honorary member; **calitatea de membru** = membership

memorandum *sn* memo *sau* memorandum

memorizare *sf (stocare de informații pe calculator)* storage; **acest disc (intern) are o capacitate de memorizare de 170 Mb** = this hard disk has a storage capacity of 170 Mb

meniu *sn* menu; **meniu stabilit** *sau* **meniu fix** = set menu

menține *vb* **(a)** to keep *sau* to keep up; **compania încearcă să mențină un nivel scăzut al cheltuielilor** = the company tries to keep the spending down **(b)** *(a fixa)* to peg; **a menține prețurile** = to peg prices **(c)** to maintain; **a menține relații cordiale cu cineva** = to maintain good relations with somebody **(d) a menține o mașină** = to keep a machine in good repair *sau* to maintain a machine **(e) a se menține** = to hold up

mercantil *adj* mercantile

merge *vb* to go; **merge la serviciu cu mașina** = she goes to work by car

merita *vb* to earn; **el nu își merită comisionul** = he does not earn his commission

mesager *sm* courier

mesagerie *sf (coletărie)* parcel post; parcels office; **coletul a fost livrat de către o companie de mesagerie** = the parcel was delivered by a courier company

meseriaş *sm sau* **meşteşugar** *sm* craftsman

meserie *sf (profesiune)* profession

meşteşugar *sm sau* **meseriaş** *sm* craftsman

metal *sn* metal; **metale nepreţioase** = base metals; **a testa puritatea metalelor preţioase** = to assay

metodă *sf (pl)* practices; **metode restrictive** = restrictive practices; **metode lipsite de scrupule** = sharp practice

metodic *adj* methodical; businesslike

metric *adj* **sistem metric** = metric system

metrou *sn (în Marea Britanie)* underground *(în SUA)* subway

metru (m) *sm* metre (m); *US* meter

Mexic *sm* Mexico; Notă: capitală: **Ciudad de Mexico** = Mexico City; monedă: **peso mexican** = Mexican peso

mexican(ă) *s & adj* Mexican

microcalculator *sn* micro *sau* microcomputer

microeconomie *sf* micro-economics

micşora *vb* **a se micşora** = to diminish; **profiturile noastre s-au micşorat considerabil în ultimii doi ani** = our profits have fallen considerably over the past two years

mijloace fixe *snpl* capital assets; **administrarea mijloacelor fixe** = property administration

mijlocitor *sm* go-between

miliardar *sm* billionaire

milimetru (mm) *sm* millimetre (mm)

milion *sn* million

milionar *sm* millionaire

milă *sf (unitate de măsură pentru distanţe egală cu 1,6 km)* mile

mină *sf* mine; **mină de cărbune** = coalmine *sau* pit

mincinos *adj* false; **declaraţie mincinoasă** = false declaration

minicalculator *sn* mainframe; **compania a hotărât înlocuirea minicalculatoarelor cu PC-uri (personal computer)** = the company decided to replace the mainframes with PCs

minier *adj* **concesiune minieră** = mining concession; **industrie minieră** = mining industry

minim *adj* minimum; **profit minim realizat dintr-o investiţie** = marginal return on investment; **salariu minim** = minimum wage; **nevoi minime (de subzistenţă)** = basic needs

minister *sn* government department *sau* ministry **Minister de Finanţe** = Finance Ministry *sau* Ministry of Finance; *(în Marea Britanie)* the Exchequer *sau* the Treasury; **Ministerul de Externe** = the Foreign Office; **Ministerul de Interne** = the Home Office

ministru *sm* minister *sau* Secretary of State; **Ministru de Externe** = Minister of Foreign Affairs; *(în Marea Britanie)* Foreign Secretary; *(în SUA)* Secretary of State; **Ministru de Interne** = Home Secretary; **Prim Ministru** = Prime Minister; **Ministrul de Finanţe** = *(în Marea Britanie)* the Chancellor of the Exchequer; *(în SUA)* Treasury Secretary

minor *adj (neînsemnat)* petty; **cheltuieli minore** = petty expenses; *(fond de piaţă)* **fond pentru cheltuieli minore** = petty cash

minus-valoare *sf* shrinkage

minută *sf (proces verbal)* minutes

miting *sn* assembly *sau* meeting

mitui *vb* to corrupt *sau* to bribe

mită *sf* **(a)** hush money *sau* bribe **(b)** bribery *sau* corruption

mixt *adj* **economie mixtă** = mixed economy

mobil *adj* **(a)** mobile; **forţă de muncă mobilă** = mobile workforce **(b)** moveable; **bunuri mobile** = moveables *sau* personal estate

mobila *vb* to furnish; **cuplul a mobilat apartamentul cu banii împrumutaţi** = the couple used the money from a loan to furnish their flat

mobilă *sf* furniture; **depozit de mobilă** = furniture store

mobilitate *sf* mobility; **mobilitatea forţei de muncă** = mobility of labour

modalitate *sf (fel)* form; **modalităţi diverse de publicitate** = different forms of advertising

moderat *adj* **(a)** reasonable **(b)** conservative; **contabilitate moderată** = conservative accounting

modern *adj* modern; **cel mai modern** = state-of-the-art

moderniza *vb* to update

modernizare *sf* update

modest *adj (inferior)* poor; **rezultate modeste** = poor results

modifica *vb* **a (se) modifica** = to adapt; *(a (se) schimba)* to alter; **cec modificat** = defaced cheque

monedă *sf* **(a)** currency; **monedă controlată** = managed currency; **mondedă convertibilă cu greutate** = soft currency; **monedă naţională** = national currency; **monedă străină** = foreign currency; **a scoate o monedă din uz** = to demonetize **(b)** coin; **am plătit taxiul cu monede de o liră** = I paid the taxi driver in £1 coins; **monedă de 1 penny** = penny coin; **monedă de 10 cenţi** = dime *(în SUA)*; **emitere de monede** = coinage

monetar *adj* monetary; **economie monetară** = monetary economy; **Fondul Monetar Internaţional (FMI)** = International Monetary Fund (IMF); **piaţă monetară** = money market; **politică monetară** = monetary policy; **sistem monetar al unei ţări** = coinage; **sistemul monetar internaţional** = the international monetary system; **unitate monetară** = monetary unit

monetărie *sf* mint

monetiza *vb* to monetize

monopol *sn* monopoly; **monopol absolut** = absolute monopoly; **monopol discriminatoriu** = discriminating monopoly; **monopol fiscal** = fiscal monopoly; **monopol legal** = legal monopoly; **monopol public** = public *sau* state monopoly; **monopolul cumpărătorului** = monopsony

monta *vb* to assemble; **a monta din piese detaşate** = to cannibalize

montaj *sn (asamblare)* assembly; **linie de montaj** = assembly line

mostră *sf* **(a)** *(exemplar)* sample *sau* specimen **(b)** *(model)* pattern

moşie *sf (teren)* estate

moşier *sm (proprietar)* landlord; *(proprietar de teren)* ground landlord

moşteni *vb* to inherit

moştenire *sf* bequest *sau* legacy; **a lăsa moştenire** = to bequeath

moştenitoare *sf* heiress

moştenitor *sm* heir *sau* legatee

motel *sn* motel

motiv *sn* motive *sau* grounds; **are motive serioase să fie nemulţumit** = he has got serious grounds for complaint

moţiune *sf (propunere)* motion; **moţiune abandonată** = dropped motion

Mozambic *sm* Mozambique; Notă: capitală: **Maputo;** monedă: **metical mozambican** = Mozambique metical

mozambican(ă) *s & adj* Mozambiquan

multilateral *adj* multilateral; **comerţ multilateral** = multilateral trade

multinaţional *adj* multinational

mulţumi *vb* **(a)** to satisfy; **directorul este foarte mulţumit de rezultatele echipei** = the manager is very satisfied with the results of the team **(b)** *(exprima gratitudine)* to thank

mulţumire *sf* satisfaction; **mulţumirea clientului** = customer satisfaction

muncă *sf* work; **legislaţia muncii** = labour legislation

munci *vb* to work

muncitor 1 *sm (persoană)* worker *sau* operative; factory hand *sau* man; *(necalificat)* labourer; **muncitor agricol** *sau* **ţăran** = agricultural labourer *sau* farm labourer; **muncitor agricol necalificat** = farmhand; **muncitor ineficient** = inefficient worker *sau* passenger; **muncitor manual** = blue-collar worker *sau* manual labourer; **participarea muncitorilor la beneficii şi luarea deciziilor** = worker participation 2 *adj* industrious

muncitorime *sf* labour

muncă *sf* **(a)** work; **muncă în acord** = task work **(b)** *(lucru)* labour; *US* labor; **accident de muncă** = industrial accident *sau* occupational accident; **conflict de muncă** = industrial dispute *sau* labour dispute; **relaţii de muncă** = industrial relations *sau* labour relations **(c)** *(serviciu)* service; **vechime în muncă** = length of service

munte *sm* mountain; **munte de pietate** = pawnshop; **proprietar al unui munte de pietate** = pawnbroker

muta *vb* **a (se) muta** = to move; to transfer

mutual *adj* mutual; **acord mutual** = mutual agreement; **companie mutuală** = mutual company

Nn

natalitate *sf* birth rate

natural *adj* **(a)** natural; **gaze naturale** = natural gas; **resurse naturale** = natural resources **(b)** *(crud)* **în stare naturală** = raw

naţional *adj* national; **datorie naţională** = national debt; **economie naţională** = national economy; **monedă naţională** = national currency; **la scară naţională** = nationwide; **grevă la scară naţională** = nationwide strike; **publicitate la scară naţională** = national advertising; **venit naţional** = national income

naţionaliza *vb* to nationalize; **guvernul a naţionalizat industria extractivă** = the government nationalized the mining industry

naţionalizare *sf* nationalization

naţionalizat *adj* nationalized *sau* state-controlled

naţiune *sf* nation

navă *sf* ship; **nave comerciale construite după acelaşi model** = sister ships

navetă *sf* **a face naveta** = to commute

navetist *sm* commuter; **2 milioane de navetişti folosesc trenul ca mijloc de transport spre serviciu** = 2 million commuters use the railways to go to work

navlosi *vb* to charter

navlositor *sm* charterer

năzui *vb* to aim

neambalat *adj* loose

neasigurat *adj* uninsured

neaşteptat *adj* unexpected; **profit neaşteptat** = casual profit

neautorizat *adj* unauthorized; **cheltuieli neautorizate** = unauthorized expenditure

necalificat *adj* unqualified; **mână de lucru necalificată** = unskilled work force; **muncitor necalificat** = manual worker

necesita *vb* to require

necesitate *sf* want; requirement

necinstit *adj* fraudulent

neclintit *adj* firm; **în ciuda presiunii atitudinea sa a rămas neclintită** = in spite of the pressure his position was firm

necompletat *adj* blank

neconvertibil *adj* *(despre monedă)* inconvertible (currency)

necotat *adj* **valori necotate** = unlisted securities; **piaţă de valori necotate** = unlisted securities market

nedatat *adj* undated; **banca i-a returnat cecul nedatat şi nesemnat** = the bank returned his undated and unsigned cheque

neeconomic *adj* uneconomic

negarantat *adj* unsecured

negativ *adj* adverse; **balanţă (de plăţi) negativă** = adverse balance (of payments); **sold negativ** = debit balance

neglijenţă *sf* *(în serviciu)* misconduct

negocia *vb* to negotiate; **a negocia un preţ** = to beat down a price; **sindicatul a negociat noile salarii cu conducerea** = the trade union negotiated the new pay package with the management

negociabil *adj* negotiable; *(bancnote, titluri la purtător, etc.)* document **negociabil** = negotiable instrument

negociere *sf* negotiation; **negocierea salariilor** = wage negotiations

negru *sau* **neagră** *adj* black; **bursa neagră** = black market; **listă neagră** = black list

negustor *sm* dealer

neimpozabil *adj* zero-rated; **venit neimpozabil** = non-taxable income

neînsemnat *adj* *(minor)* petty

neloial *adj* unfair; **concurenţă neloială** = unfair competition

neobişnuit *adj* odd; *(de îmbrăcăminte, pantofi, etc.)* **măsuri neobişnuite** = odd sizes

neocupat *adj* vacant; *(într-un hotel)* **camere neocupate** = vacancies

neoficial *adj* unofficial; **(în mod) neoficial** = off the record; **rata de schimb (valutar) neoficială** = unofficial rate of exchange

neonorat *adj* **(a) cec neonorat** = dishonoured cheque **(b)** outstanding; **comandă neonorată** *sau* **comenzi neonorate** = unfulfilled order *sau* outstanding orders

neozeelandez(ă) *s* New Zealander

Nepal *sm* Nepal; Notă: capitală: **Kathmandu**; monedă: **rupia nepaleză** = Nepalese rupee

nepalez(ă) *s & adj* Nepalese

neplătit *adj* *(neachitat)* unpaid *sau* outstanding; **datorii neplătite** = outstanding debts; **facturi neplătite** = unpaid bills

neprelucrat *adj* *(în stare naturală)* raw; **informaţii neprelucrate** = raw data

nepreţuit *adj* priceless

neproductiv *adj* unproductive; **chirie plătită pentru utilaje neproductive** = dead rent; **fonduri neproductive** = idle money; **utilaj neproductiv** = idle machinery

neprofitabil *adj* *(nerentabil)* unprofitable

neputincios *adj* *(despre o lege)* not competent

nerambursabil *adj* irredeemable

nereclamat *sau* **nerevendicat** *adj* unclaimed

nerentabil *adj* *(neprofitabil)* unprofitable

nereuşită *sf* failure

nerevendicat *sau* **nereclamat** *adj* unclaimed; **premiu nerevendicat** = unclaimed prize

net *adj* net *sau* clear; **masă netă** = net weight; **preţ net** = net price; **profit net** = net profit *sau* after-tax profit; **au obţinut un profit net de 1milion lei anul trecut** = they made 1 million lei clear profit last year; **randament net** = net yield; **salariu net** = net salary; **valoare netă** = net worth; **venit net** = net income

nevoie *sf* **a avea nevoie de** = to require; **au nevoie de un expert în**

sisteme de calcul = they require a computer specialist

Nicaragua *sf* Nicaragua; Notă: capitală: **Managua;** monedă: **córdoba nicaraguană** = Nicaraguan córdoba

nicaraguan(ă) *s & adj* Nicaraguan

nişă *sf* niche

nivel *sn* (a) level; **nivel de trai** = standard of living; **nivel înalt** = high-grade; **nivel maxim** = top-grade; **nivel scăzut de investiţii** = low level of investment (b) *(rang)* grade (c) *(normă)* standard

nivela *vb* to grade

nominal *adj* nominal; **acţiuni nominale** = registered shares; **capital nominal** = nominal capital; **valoare nominală** = face value

normal *adj (standard)* regular *sau* standard; *(ordinar)* average

normare *sf* rationing

normă *sf* (a) workload (b) *(cifră de plan)* target figure (c) standard; **norme de producţie** = production standards

Norvegia *sf* Norway; Notă: capitală: **Oslo;** monedă: **coroană norvegiană** = Norwegian krone

norvegian(ă) *s & adj* Norwegian

nota *vb* to note *sau* to write down; to record

notar *sm* notary public

notare *sf* recording

notarial *adj* notarial; **act notarial** = notarial act

notă *sf* (a) *(circulară)* circular; *(aviz)* note (b) **notă de plată** = bill; *(a*

factura) **a trimite o notă de plată** = to bill *sau* to invoice; **notă de credit** *sau* **de stornare** = credit note; **notă de debitare** = debit note

notifica *vb* to notify *sau* to advise

notificare *sf* notificare de numire în post = letter of appointment; **notificare formală în tranzacţii comerciale** = advice

nou *adj* new; **nou-nouţ** = brand-new

Noua Zeelandă *sf* New Zealand; Notă: capitală: **Wellington;** monedă: **dolar neozeelandez** = New Zealand dollar

novice *sm* apprentice

nul *adj* null; void; *(un act, etc)* **a declara nul** = to cancel; **a declara nul şi neavenit** = to declare null and void

număr *sn* (a) *(cantitate)* number (b) *(ediţie)* issue; **a solicitat numărul din aprilie al revistei de informatică** = he asked for the April issue of the computer magazine

nume *sn* name; **numele şi prenumele** = full name

numerar *sn* cash; **achiziţie cu numerar** = cash purchase; **plata unei facturi în numerar** = cash settlement

numerota *vb* to number

numi *vb* to appoint *sau* to nominate; *(a desemna)* **a numi în funcţie** = to designate; **a fost numit şeful echipei de cercetări** = he was nominated head of the research team

numire *sf* denomination; **numire în post** = appointment

Oo

obiect *sn* object; *(de îmbrăcăminte, etc.)* article

obiectiv *sn* *(ţintă)* target; **a fixa obiective** = to set targets

obişnuit **(a)** *(frecvent)* common **(b)** *(firesc)* natural

obliga *vb* to oblige; **scăderea bruscă a volumului vânzărilor a obligat fabrica să reducă producţia** = the sharp fall in sales obliged the factory to reduce production; **contractul ne obligă să finalizăm construcţia podului în doi ani** = the contract obliges us to finish the construction of the bridge in two years

obligatoriu *adj* obligatory; compulsory; *(forţat)* mandatory; **ei au fost anunţaţi că prezenţa la şedinţă era obligatorie** = they were told that their attendance at the meeting was compulsory; **pensionare obligatorie** = mandatory retirement

obligaţie *sf* *(datorie)* obligation; **trustul de construcţii nu şi-a îndeplinit obligaţiile contractuale** = the building company did not fulfil its contractual obligations

obligaţiune *sf* **(a)** *(bon de tezaur)* bond **(b)** debenture; **deţinător de obligaţiuni** = debenture-holder

obstacol *sn* barrier; **obstacole în calea comerţului** = trade barriers

obştesc *adj* public; **proprietate obştească** = public ownership

obţine *vb* to obtain; *(a se califica)* **a obţine un titlu** = to qualify; **a obţinut diploma de inginer** = he has qualified as an engineer; *(a câştiga)* **a obţine net** = to net; **firma a obţinut profituri nete de 5 milioane lei** = the company netted a profit of 5 million lei

ocazie *sf* occasion; **mărfuri de ocazie** = second-hand goods; **a cumpăra ceva de ocazie** = to buy something second-hand

ocazional *adj* *(întâmplător)* incidental; **cheltuieli ocazionale** = incidental expenses; **lucru ocazional** = casual work; **mână de lucru ocazională** = casual labour

ocupa *vb* **a se ocupa de** = to care for; to cater for; *(a avea de a face cu)* to deal with

ocupaţie *sf* **(a)** employment **(b)** *(profesie)* occupation

ocupant *sm* *(al unei locuinţe)* householder

ocupare *sf* occupation; **ocuparea unei clădiri** = occupation of a building

ocupat *adj* **(a)** active **(b)** engaged; **am încercat să-i telefonăm la serviciu dar telefonul lui a sunat ocupat tot timpul** = we tried to ring him at work but the line was engaged all day

oferi *vb* **(a)** *(a propune)* to offer; **din cauză că era un client vechi i s-a**

oferit o tranzacţie în condiţii avantajoase = because he was an established customer he was offered a special deal; **a oferi spre vânzare** = to offer for sale **(b)** to bid

ofertant *sm (persoană sau organizaţie)* tenderer *sau* bidder

ofertă *sf* **(a)** offer; **i s-a făcut o ofertă pe care nu a putut să o refuze** = they made him an offer he could not refuse; **ofertă specială** = premium offer; **legea cererii şi ofertei** = law of supply and demand **(b)** *(de achitarea unui împrumut)* **ofertă în numerar** = tender; **a face o ofertă** = to tender; **a prezenta o ofertă** = to submit a tender; **persoană care acceptă o ofertă** = taker **(c)** bid; **ofertă de preluare** = takeover bid **(d) ofertă combinată** = composite supply; **preţ de ofertă** = supply price

oficial 1 *adj* **(a)** official; **documentele oficiale au fost studiate de către comisia de anchetă** = the official documents were examined by the investigation committee; **ora oficială** = standard time; **schimbul de valută oficial** = the official exchange rate **(b)** formal; **plângere oficială** = formal complaint **2** *adv* **în mod oficial** = (i) formally; (ii) on the record

oficiant *sm* postal clerk

oficiu *sn* office *sau* bureau; **oficiu de calcul** = computer bureau; **oficiu juridic** = legal department; **oficiu poştal** = post office; **oficiul de stare civilă** = register office *sau* registry (office)

ofiţer *sm* **ofiţer de poliţie** = police inspector; **ofiţer cu răspundere pe vas** = ship's officer; **ofiţerul stării civile** = registrar

ofset *sn (printing)* offset

Olanda *sf* Netherlands; Notă: capitală: **Amsterdam;** monedă: **gulden olandez** = Dutch guilder

olandez(ă) *s & adj* Dutch

oligarhie *sf* oligarchy

om-reclamă *sm* sandwich man

omisiune *sf* default

omite *vb* **(a)** to fail; **a omis să declare bunurile prohibitive la vamă** = he failed to declare the prohibited goods at the customs **(b)** to leave out; **a omite plata de dividende** = to pass a dividend

omolog *sm* counterpart *sau* opposite number; **primul ministru britanic s-a întâlnit cu omologul său român** = the British Prime Minister met his Romanian counterpart

onoare *sf* honour; **am onoarea să vă fac cunoştinţă cu partenerul meu de afaceri** = I have the honour of introducing you to my partner

onora *vb* to honour; **un om de afaceri serios trebuie să-şi onoreze promisiunile** = a serious businessman must honour his promises; *(despre cecuri)* **a nu fi onorat** = to bounce; **cecul ei nu a fost onorat** = her cheque has bounced =

onorariu *sn* fee *sau* charge; **onorariul doctorului** = doctor's fee

opera *vb* to operate

operativ *adj* **(a)** active **(b)** operative

operator *sm* operator; **operator calculator** = computer operator; **operator preluare data** = keyboarder *sau* keyboard operator

operaţiune comercială *sf (tranzacţie)* commercial transaction

opinie *sf* opinion; *(părere)* judgement

opri *vb* **(a)** *(a anula)* to call off **(b)** to bar **(c)** to stop; **a (se) opri** = to come to a stop

oprire *sf (încetare)* stop

optim *adj (ideal)* optimum; **condiţii optime pentru vânzare** = optimum conditions for sales

opţional *adj* optional

opţiune *sf (alegere)* option

opune *vb* **a se opune** = to object; **directorul s-a opus clauzei din contract** = the manager objected to the clause in the contract

oral *adj* verbal

orar **1** *sn* timetable; schedule; **potrivit orarului trenul nostru va pleca de la linia 2** = according to the timetable our train leaves from platform 2; **orar de funcţionare** = opening hours **2** *adj* hourly; **tarif orar** = hourly rate

oraş *sn* city

oră *sf* **(a)** hour; **din oră în oră** = hourly; **a fi plătit cu ora** = to be paid by the hour; **muncitor plătit cu ora** = hourly-paid worker; **producţie pe oră** = output per hour; **ore suplimentare** = overtime; **în perioadele de vârf angajaţii sunt încurajaţi să presteze ore suplimentare** = at busy times workers are encouraged to do overtime **(b)** *(în Spania, Franţa, Germania, Polonia, etc.)* **Ora Europei Centrale** = Central European Time; **Ora Europei Occidentale** = Western European Time; *(ora locală în România, Bulgaria, Finlanda, Grecia şi Turcia, două ore în avans faţă de ora Londrei)* **Ora Europei Răsăritene** = Eastern European Time; **ora oficială** = standard time

ordin *sn* **(a)** order; **a da ordine** = to give orders *sau* to command **(b) ordin de plată** = draft; **ordin de plată fixă la intervale regulate** = standing

order; **ordin de plată în lire sterline** = sterling draft

ordinar *adj* **(a)** general; **cheltuieli ordinare** = general expenses **(b)** average

ordinator *sn* computer

ordine *sf* **(a)** order; **fişele de magazie sunt aranjate în ordine alfabetică** = the stock cards are arranged in alphabetical order; **ordine cronologică** = chronological order; **în ordine** = in order; **în ordinea importanţei** = in rank order; **ordine numerică** = numerical order **(b) ordine de zi** = agenda

ordona *vb (a comanda)* to command

ordonanţă *sf (citaţie)* writ

organ *sn (politic)* board

organigramă *sf* organization chart

organiza *vb* **(a)** to run **(b)** to raise

organizare *sf* organization

organizator *sm* organizer

organizaţie *sf* **(a)** organization; **Organizaţia Naţiunilor Unite (ONU)** = United Nations (UN); **organizaţie a patronilor** = employer's organization **(b)** society **(c)** body

Orientul apropiat *sn* Near East

Orientul îndepărtat *sn* Far East

Orientul mijlociu *sn* Middle East

original *adj* original *sau* authentic; real *sau* genuine

origine *sf* origin; **ţară de origine** = country of origin

oscilaţie *sf (fluctuaţie)* swing

ostil *adj (contrar)* adverse

Pp

pachet *sn* **(a)** package *sau* pack; packet *sau* parcel; **pachet de biscuiţi** = packet of biscuits; **pachet de ţigări** = pack of cigarettes **(b) pachet de acţiuni** = block of shares

paginaţie *sf* pagination *sau* layout

pagubă *sf* *(avarie)* damage; **pagubă pricinuită de incendiu** = fire damage

Pakistan *sm* Pakistan; Notă: capitală: **Islamabad**; monedă: **rupia pakistaneză** = Pakistani rupee

pakistanez(ă) *s & adj* Pakistani

Panama *sf* Panama; Notă: capitală: **Ciudad de Panama** = Panama City; monedă: **balboa panameză** = Panamanian balboa

panamez(ă) *s & adj* Panamanian

pană *sf* **a avea o pană** = to break down; **nu au putut ajunge la timp pentru că maşina lor a rămas în pană pe autostradă** = they could not make it in time as their car broke down on the motorway

panou *sn* panel; **panou de expoziţie** = display panel

papetărie *sf* **articole de papetărie** = stationery

Paraguay *sm* Paraguay; Notă: capitală: **Asunción**; monedă: **guaran paraguayan** = Paraguayan guarani

paraguayan(ă) *s & adj* Paraguayan

paraliza *vb* to paralyze; **lipsa de materii prime a paralizat producţia** = the lack of raw materials brought production to a standstill

paralizare *sf* standstill

parc *sn* **(a)** park **(b)** *(totalitatea vehiculelor unei companii)* **parc auto** = fleet of cars

parca *vb* *(maşina)* to park

parcare *sf* car park

paria *vb* to bet; to stake; **a pariat 5.000 lei pe calul ei preferat** = she bet 5,000 lei on her favourite horse; **sumă de bani pariată la curse** = stake

paritate *sf* equivalence; parity; **preţ de paritate** = parity price; **paritatea ratei de schimb** = par of exchange rate

pariu *sn* bet; **agent de pariuri** = bookmaker

parte *sf* **(a)** *(fragment)* part; **fabrica a livrat numai o parte din comandă** = the factory shipped just a part of the consignment; **în parte** = in part **(b)** *(la un contract)* party (to a contract)

partener *sm* associate *sau* partner; **partener activ** *sau* **participant** = active *sau* working partner; **partener comercial** = trading partner

parteneriat *sn* partnership

parter *sn* ground floor

participa *vb* to participate; to take part in

participant *sm* partner

participare *sf* (a) participation; participarea muncitorilor la gestionarea întreprinderii = workers' participation; întreprindere cu participare = joint venture (b) *(cotă)* share; *(capital)* stake; *(deținere de acțiuni)* shareholding

particular *adj* private; bancă particulară = private bank; întreprindere particulară = private enterprise; investitor particular = private investor; sector (economic) particular = private sector; transport particular = private transport; a avea o întrevedere particulară cu cineva = to see someone in private

partid *sn* party; partid politic = political party

parțial *adj* partial *sau* in part; a contribui la plată parțial = to pay the costs in part; comandă parțială = part order; despăgubire parțială = partial compensation; plată parțială = part payment; *(completat cu bani)* schimb parțial = part exchange

pasager *sm* passenger; vas de pasageri = passenger ship; tren de pasageri = passenger train

pasibil *adj* liable (to)

pasionat *adj* keen; el este un pasionat colecționar de artă = he is a keen art collector

pașaport *sn* passport; pașaportul dumneavoastră este expirat = your passport is out of date

patent *sn* patent; oficiu de patente și mărci = patent office

patron *sm* employer; boss

patronaj *sn* organizație importantă sub patronajul căreia se află altele mai mici = umbrella organization

pauper *adj* impecunious

pauză *sf* break; pauză pentru reclame la TV = commercial break; pauză de prânz = lunch break; a lua o pauză = to take a break

pavilion *sn* flag; un vas navigând sub pavilion românesc = a ship sailing under the Romanian flag

pază *sf (protecție)* safeguard

păcăli *vb* to defraud

părăsi *vb* to abandon

părere *sf (opinie)* judgement; a-și exprima părerea asupra unui lucru = to give one's judgement about something

păstra *vb* to keep; păstrează restul = keep the change

păstrare *sf (custodie)* safe-keeping

păsui *vb* to allow

pătrat *adj* square; metru pătrat (m2) = square metre; rădăcină pătrată = square root

pătrime *sf* quarter

păzi *vb (a proteja)* to safeguard

pâine *sf* bread

pârât *sm (acuzat)* defendant

pecuniar *adj* pecuniary

penaliza *vb* to penalize

penalizare *sf* penalty; tarif de penalizare = penalty rates

pensie *sf* pension; superannuation; a ieși la pensie = to retire; fond de pensii = pension fund *sau* superannuation fund; cotizații în fondul de pensii = pension contributions; pensie calculată în funcție de salariu = earnings-related pension; pensie de invaliditate = disability allowance; pensie de limită de vârstă = old age pension *sau* retirement pension; pensie de stat = state pension

pensiona *vb* **a pensiona pe cineva** = to pension someone off

pensionar *sm* pensioner

pentru *prep* pro; **a examina toate argumentele pentru și împotriva** = to consider all pros and cons

percepere *sf (a impozitelor)* levy

perceptor *sm* tax collector

perfecționa *vb (un sistem de calcul, etc.)* to upgrade

periclitate *sf* **spor de periclitate** = danger money

pericol *sn (primejdie)* danger; **pericol de incendiu** = fire hazard; **pericol iminent** = distress; **o navă în pericol (de a se scufunda)** = a ship in distress

periculos *adj (primejdios)* dangerous

periferic *adj* **echipament periferic (pentru calculatoare)** = peripherals

perioadă *sf* term; **perioada minimă de închiriere este de 12 luni** = the minimum term of the lease is 12 months

periodic *sn (publicație)* paper; **periodic profesional** = trade paper

perisabil *adj* perishable; **bunuri perisabile** = perishable goods

perisabilități *sfpl* perishables

permis *sn (legitimație)* pass; *(autorizație)* permit; **permis de conducere** = driving licence; **permis de intrare** = gate pass; **permis de lucru (pentru străini)** = work permit; **permis de lucru acordat imigranților** = green card *(în SUA)*

permisiune *sf* **(a)** consent; **președintele ne-a dat premisiunea să lucrăm împreună în continuare** = the chairman gave his consent to our continuing to work together **(b)** *(aprobare)* sanction

permite *vb* **(a)** to permit *sau* to allow *sau* to authorize; **a-și permite** = to afford; **nu ne putem permite alte reduceri de preț** = we cannot afford further cuts in prices **(b)** to admit

peron *sn* platform

persoană *sf* person *sau* man; **biletul costă 4000 lei de persoană** = the fee is 4,000 per head; **în persoană** = in person; **persoană fictivă** = fictitious person; **persoană fizică** *sau* **juridică** = (legal) person

personal **1** *adj (privat)* private *sau* personal; **directorul folosește mașina personală pentru călătorii în interes de serviciu** = the manager uses his own car for business trips; **calculator personal** = personal computer (PC); **efecte personale** = personal effects; **secretar personal** = personal assistant **2** *sn* staff *sau* personnel; **personal administrativ** = office staff; **șef serviciu personal** = personnel manager

personalitate *sf* character

Peru *sm* Peru; Notă: capitală: **Lima;** monedă: **inti peruvian** = Peruvian inti

peruvian(ă) *s & adj* Peruvian

pescaj *sn (distanța dintre fundul vasului și linia de plutire)* draught

petiționar *sm* applicant

petrodolar *sm* petrodollar

petrol *sn* oil; **țări exportatoare de petrol** = oil-exporting countries; **țări producătoare de petrol** = oil-producing countries

petrolier **1** *sn* tanker **2** *adj* **puț petrolier** = oil well; **sondă petrolieră** = oil rig

piață *sf* **(a)** market; **legumele sunt mai ieftine la piață decât în supermagazinele alimentare** = vegetables are cheaper in the market than in the food stores **(b)** **piață**

externă = foreign market; **piață financiară** = capital market; **piață internă** = domestic market; **piață liberă** = free market; **piață paralelă** = grey market; **piață selectă** = up market; **prețul pieței** = market rate; **cotă din piață** = market share; **economie de piață** = free market economy *sau* free economy; **pe piață** = on sale; **care are căutare pe piață** = saleable **(c) piața de materii prime** = commodity market **(d)** *(scuar)* square

pichet *sn (de greviști)* picket

pierde *vb* to lose; **a pierde clienți** = to lose customers; **a pierde 100.000 lei (într-o tranzacție)** = to be 100,000 lei out of pocket; **banca a pierdut peste un milion de lei din împrumuturi neachitate** = the bank lost over one million lei in bad debts; **și-a pierdut slujba când vânzările au scăzut drastic** = he lost his job when the sales dropped dramatically; *(despre acțiuni, la bursă)* **a-și pierde valoarea** = to fall

pierdere *sf* **(a)** loss; **articol vândut în pierdere cu scopul de a atrage clientela** = loss-leader; **cont de profit și pierderi** = profit and loss account; **pierdere completă** = dead loss; **în pierdere** = (i) at a loss; (ii) out of pocket **(b)** *(risipă)* waste; **pierdere de timp** = waste of time **(c)** wastage; **pierderea de personal prin pesionări și demisii** = natural wastage

piesă *sf* component; **piesă de schimb** = spare part; **a înlocui o piesă** = to replace a part

pintă *sf (unitate de măsură pentru lichide, egală cu 0,568 litri în Marea Britanie și 0,473 litri în Statele Unite)* pint

pirat *sm* pirate; *(copie ilegală)* **copie `pirat' a unei casete video** = a pirate copy of a video

piraterie *sf* piracy

plafon *sn* ceiling; **plafon de salarii** = wage ceiling

plagiat *sn* literary piracy

plagiator *sm* pirate

plan *sn* **(a)** draft; layout **(b)** *(proiect)* plan *sau* proiect; *(program)* schedule; **plan (în caz de) de urgență** = contingency plan *sau* emergency plan; **plan de investiții** = investment plan; **plan de producție** = corporate plan; **plan economic** = economic plan; **a alcătui un plan** = to plan **(c)** budget

planifica *vb* **(a)** to plan; *(a prevedea)* to schedule **(b)** to budget

plasă *sf* bag; **plasă de cumpărături** = shopping bag

plată *sf* payment; paying; *(rambursare)* repayment; *(recompensă)* consideration; **plată anticipată** *sau* **în avans** = advance payment; **plată generată de un contract ilegal** = illegal consideration; **plată integrală** = full payment; **plată în exces** = overpayment; *(mărfuri sau servicii)* **plată în natură** = payments in kind; **plata în numerar** = cash payment; **plata unei facturi în numerar** = cash settlement; **plata la livrare** *sau* **contra ramburs** = cash on delivery; **plata pe loc (în numerar)** = down payment; **plată oferită unui angajat pentru a renunța voluntar la post** = redundancy payment; *(un serviciu, etc.)* **a cere plata pentru** = to charge for; *(șomaj temporar)* **concediu fără plată** = unpaid holiday; **a efectua o plată** = to effect a payment; **stat de plată** = payroll

platformă *sf* **(a)** platform; **platformă petrolieră marină** = oil platform *sau* offshore oil platform **(b)** **platformă industrială** = industrial park

plăti *vb* **(a)** to pay *sau* to settle; *(a achita o notă de plată)* to foot the bill; *(a lichida)* to redeem; **am plătit 75.000 de lire pe această casă** = we paid

£75,000 for this house; **a plăti cu cartea de credit** = to pay by credit card; **a plăti cu cec** = to pay by cheque; **a plăti o datorie** = to settle an account *sau* to pay an account; **a plăti o factură** = to pay a bill; **a plăti în avans** = to pay in advance; **a plăti în numerar** = to pay cash; **a plăti în rate (lunare)** = to pay in instalments; **a consimţit să plătească datoria în 6 rate lunare** = he agreed to pay the debt in 6 monthly payments; **a plăti înapoi** = to pay back; **a nu plăti** = to default on one's payments; **a plăti pe loc** = to pay on demand **(b)** *(a remunera)* to pay *sau* to remunerate; **a fi plătit cu ora** = to be paid by the hour

plătibil *adj* payable; **plătibil în avans** = payable in advance

plătit *adj* **(a)** paid; **plătit în avans** = paid in advance *sau* prepaid; **transport plătit în avans** = prepaid carriage **(b) concediu plătit** = holidays with pay

plătitor *sm* payer

plângere *sf* grievance

pleca *vb* to leave; **trenul va pleca în 15 minute** = the train leaves in 15 minutes

plecare *sf* departure; **avem timp suficient până la plecarea trenului** = we have plenty of time before the departure of the train; **punct de plecare** = point of departure

pledoarie *sf* **pledoarie (a acuzatului)** = plea

plic *sn* envelope; **plic par avion** = airmail envelope

plin *adj* full; **înainte de călătorie a verificat dacă rezervorul maşinii era plin** = before the journey he checked that the tank of his car was full

plonja *vb* *(despre preţuri, etc.)* to plummet *sau* to plunge

plusvaloare *sf* **(a)** increment **(b)** capital gain

plutocraţie *sf* plutocracy

PNB (= Produs Naţional Brut) GNB *sau* Gross National Product

poartă *sf* gate; **îmbarcarea pentru zborul RO 300 se face la poarta numărul 10** = flight RO 300 is boarding at gate 10

pod *sn* bridge; **pod basculă** = weighbridge

pofti *vb* *(a invita)* to ask

pogon *sn* *(masură de suprafaţă anglo-saxonă egală cu 0.405 hectare)* acre

politic *adj* political; **economie politică** = political economy; **partid politic** = political party

politică **(a)** *sf* policy; **politica noastră este să reducem costurile şi să devenim eficienţi** = our policy is to cut the costs and be as efficient as possible; **politică economică** = economic policy; **politică guvernamentală referitoare la importuri** = government policy on imports **(b)** politics

poliţă *sf* policy; **poliţă de asigurări** = insurance policy; **poliţă de asigurări multiplă** = blanket policy; **poliţă provizorie de asigurări** = (i) cover note; (ii) certificate of insurance; **poliţă de asigurări împotriva accidentelor** = accident policy; **poliţă de asigurări împotriva tuturor riscurilor** = comprehensive policy; **a contracta o poliţă de asigurări** = to take out an insurance policy; *(persoană asigurată)* **deţinător al unei poliţe** = policy holder; **a emite o poliţă de asigurări** = to make out a policy

polonez(ă) **1** *s* Pole **2** *adj* Polish

Polonia *sf* Poland; Notă: capitală: **Varşovia** = Warsaw; monedă: **zlot polonez** = Polish zloty

ponta *vb (la poarta întreprinderii)* a **ponta de intrare** *sau* **a ponta de ieşire** = to clock in *sau* clock out

pontaj *sn (marcaj)* tally; **foaie de pontaj** = tally sheet

pontator *sm* tally clerk

port *sn* harbour *sau* the docks; **portul Constanţa** = the port of Constanza; **port autonom** = autonomous port; **port comercial** = commercial port; **port de destinaţie** = final port; **port de escală** = port of call; **port de intrare** = port of entry; **port liber** = free port; *(port scutit de taxe vamale)* **porto franco** = free port; **căpitanul portului** = harbour master; **a face escală la un port** = to call at a port; **a intra în port** = to dock

portar *sm* caretaker

portărel *sm* bailiff

portorican(ă) *s & adj* Puerto Rican

Porto Rico *sm* Puerto Rico; Notă: capitală: **San Juan;** monedă: **dolar american** = US dollar

portuar *adj* **instalaţii portuare** = harbour facilities; **lucrător portuar** = docker; **taxe portuare** = harbour charges *sau* anchorage charges

Portugalia *sf* Portugal; Notă: capitală: **Lisabona** = Lisbon; monedă: **escudo portughez** = Portuguese escudo

portughez(ă) *sau* **lusitan(ă)** *s & adj* Portuguese

poseda *vb* to own; **posedă 10 % din totalul acţiunilor companiei** = he owns 10% of the shares of the company

posesie *sf* possession *sau* ownership; asset

posesor *sm (deţinător)* holder *sau* owner

posibil *adj* potential

posibilitate *sf* facility; **posibilitatea de a obţine credit de maximum 100.000 lei** = credit facility of up to 100,000 lei

post *sn (poziţie)* post; *(slujbă)* job; **post bine plătit** = well paid job; **post vacant** = vacancy; **posturi vacante** = job openings; **notificare de numire în post** = letter of appointment; **a solicita un post de vânzător** = to apply for a post as shop assistant; **titular de post** = office-bearer

post-cheie *sn* key post

postdata *vb* to postdate; **cec postdatat** = postdated cheque

post restant *sn (serviciu)* **post restant** = poste restante

poştal *adj* postal; **carte poştală** = postcard; **căsuţă poştală** = post office box; **cod poştal** = postcode; **cutie poştală** = letterbox *sau* mail box; **mandat poştal** = postal order; **oficiu poştal** = post office; **ştampila poştei** = postmark; **tarif poştal** = postage; **tarif poştal achitat (în avans)** = postage paid

poştă *sf* **(a)** post *sau* mail; **comandă prin poştă** = mail order; **a expedia prin poştă** = to post *sau* to mail; **a pune o scrisoare la poştă** = to put a letter in the mail; **vânzare prin poştă** = mail-order selling **(b)** post office

potenţial **1** *adj (posibil)* potential; **clienţi potenţiali** = potential customers; **piaţă potenţială** = potential market **2** *sn* **(a)** *(resurse)* potential **(b)** **potenţial de câştig** = earning potential

potrivi *vb* **(a)** to fit *sau* to adapt **(b)** **a se potrivi** = to correspond

potrivire *sf* correspondence

potrivit *adj* **(a)** fit **(b)** *(cuvenit)* **la timpul potrivit** = in due course

pozitiv *adj* favourable; **balanţă de comerţ pozitivă** = favourable balance of payments

poziţie *sf* (a) *(post)* post; *(funcţie)* function (b) *(situaţie)* **poziţie actuală** = state of affairs

practic *adj* (a) businesslike (b) constructive; **propunere practică** = constructive proposal

practicant *sm* trainee

practică *sf noun* practice; **practici comerciale** = trade practices; **practici industriale** = industrial practices

prăbuşi *vb* **a se prăbuşi** = to collapse

prăbuşire *sf* collapse

preaviz *sn* notice; **şi-a părăsit slujba fără a prezenta cuvenitul preaviz de o lună de zile** = she left her job without giving the required one month's notice

precis *adj* *(exact sau corect)* exact *sau* accurate

predominant *adj* prevailing; **criză economică predominantă** = prevailing economic depression; **preţuri predominante (ridicate)** = prevailing prices

preferat *adj* *(privilegiat)* preferred

preferenţial *adj* preferential; **dobândă preferenţială** = prime rate; **listă preferenţială** = shortlist; **plăţi preferenţiale** = preferential payments; **tarif preferenţial** = preferential tariff; **tratament preferenţial** = preferential treatment

preferinţă *sf* choice

prefix *sn* prefix; **prefix telefonic** = dialling code

pregăti *vb* to fix; **a pregăti un buget** = to fix a budget

pregătire profesională *sf* (a) *(experienţă)* background (b) *(ucenicie)* training

prejudicia *vb* to damage *sau* to prejudice

prejudiciu *sn* prejudice

prelua *vb* to take over; **a prelua conducerea unei companii; a achiziţiona o companie** = to take over a company

preluare *sf* takeover; **ofertă de preluare** = takeover bid

prelucra *vb* to process; **a prelucra materii prime** = to process raw materials

prelucrare *sf* **prelucrarea de date pe calculator** = data processing

prelungi *vb* to extend; **a prelungi (reînnoi) un contract** = to extend a contract

prelungire *sf* extension

premeditare *sf* premeditation *sau* calculation

premiu *sn* award; prize

presă *sf* press; **comunicat de presă** = press release; **presa naţională** = the national press

preselecţie *sf* *(listă preferenţială)* shortlist

presupune *vb* to believe

preşedinte *sm* (a) chairman; *(fotoliu prezidenţial)* **postul de preşedinte** = chair *sau* post of chairman (b) **preşedintele unei întreprinderi** = chief executive; *(în SUA)* **preşedintele ţării** = chief executive

preţ *sn* price *sau* tariff; rate; **achiziţie la un preţ avantajos** = bargain buy; **preţ competitiv** = competitive price *sau* keen price; **preţ convenit** = agreed price; **preţ cu amănuntul** = (i) all-in rate; (ii) retail price; **preţ de catalog** =

list price; **preţ de cost** = cost price; **preţ de fabrică** = factory price; **preţ de vânzare** = selling price; **preţ fixat de producător** = administered price; **preţ inclusiv** = all-in price; **preţ întreg** = full rate; **preţ maximal** = price ceiling; **preţ mediu** = average price; **preţ minim acceptabil (la o licitaţie)** = reserve price; **preţ minim de vânzare recomandat de producător** = Manufacturer's recommended price (MRP); **preţ net** = net price; **preţ real** = actual price; **preţ redus** = reduced rate *sau* bargain price; **preţul curent** = the going rate; **preţul pieţei** = the market rate; **preţul ţiţeiului brut a crescut** = the price of crude oil has increased; **preţuri fixe** = set prices; **preţuri oficiale** = scheduled prices; **determinarea preţurilor** *sau* **referitor la preţuri** = pricing; **indice de preţuri cu amănuntul** = retail price index; **listă de preţuri** = price list; **politică de preţuri** = pricing policy; **a reduce preţurile** = to cut prices; **regimul preţurilor** = pricing system; **războiul preţurilor** = price war; **a stabili preţul** = to price **(b)** value

preţios *adj* valuable; **informaţii preţioase** = valuable information

prevăzut *adj* projected

prevedea *vb* **(a)** to forecast **(b)** to schedule

prevedere *sf (clauză)* clause

preveni *vb* to anticipate

preventiv *adj* preventive; **măsuri preventive** = preventive measures; **a lua măsuri de prevenire a incendiilor, furtului, fraudei** = to take preventive measures against fire, theft, fraud

previziune *sf* **(a)** *(prognoză)* forecast **(b)** calculation **(c)** *(pl)* expectations

prezent *sn* present

prezenta *vb* to present *sau* to produce *sau* to submit; **a prezenta documente** = to produce documents; **a prezenta un cont** *sau* **o factură** = to render an account; **a prezenta o factură spre aprobare** = to present a bill for acceptance

prezentare *sf* demonstration

prezida *vb* to chair; **prezidează şedinţa** = he is chairing the meeting

prezidiu *sn* chair

prim *adj* **(a)** primary; **materii prime** = raw materials; primary *sau* basic commodities **(b) Prim Ministru** = Prime Minister **(c) primul curs (la bursă)** = opening price

primar 1 *adj* **industrie primară (de bază)** = primary industry 2 *sm* mayor

primă *sf* **(a)** *(recompensă financiară)* bonus; **primă de merit** = merit bonus; **plata de prime stimulente** = incentive payment; **primă stimulativă** = incentive bonus; **primă specială acordată unui salariat la angajare** = golden hello; **primă de fidelitate acordată salariaţilor** = golden handcuffs **(b)** premium; **primă de asigurări** = insurance premium; **primă de risc** = risk premium **(c)** subsidy; **primă de export** = export subsidy *sau* bounty

primejdie *sf* danger

primejdios *adj* dangerous

primejdui *vb* *(a compromite)* to compromise; **lipsa de fonduri poate primejdui proiectul în totalitate** = the lack of funds might compromise the whole project

primi *vb* to receive *sau* to get; **a primit comanda prin poştă trei zile după ce a plătit** = he received his mail order within three days of payment; **a primit o scrisoare de la directorul băncii sale** = he got a letter from his bank manager;

vânzătorul credea că vor mai primi imprimante = the shop assistant thought that they would get more computer printers in

primire *sf* receipt; **aviz de primire** = advice of delivery; **chitanţă de primire** = delivery receipt; **a confirma primirea plăţii** = to acknowledge receipt of payment; **a semna de primirea bunurilor** = to receipt

primitor *sm* receiver

principal *adj* principal *sau* main; *(de primă importanţă)* senior; *(fundamental)* prime; **contabilitatea se află în clădirea principală** = the accounts department is situated in the main building; **asociat principal** = senior partner

principiu *sn* principle; **principiul impozitării după posibilităţile contribuabilor** = ability-to-pay principle; **acord de principiu** = agreement in principle; **în principiu** = in principle

prioritate *sf* priority; **a acorda prioritate** = to give priority; **a avea prioritate** = to have priority

privat *adj* private; **proprietate privată** = private property

privatiza *vb* to privatize *sau* to denationalize

privatizare *sf* privatization *sau* denationalization

privilegiat *adj* preferred; **acţiuni privilegiate** = preference shares; **creditor privilegiat** = preferred creditor

priză *sf* power point

proba *vb* to sample

probabilitate *sf* chance; **probabilitatea de succes în noua sa afacere este de 50 %** = there is a 50% chance that he will succeed in his new business

probă *sf* test; **perioadă de probă** = trial period *sau* qualifying period

problemă *sf* **(a)** *(chestiune)* problem *sau* question *sau* issue; **a ridica o problemă într-o şedinţă** = to raise a question in a meeting; **problemă actuală** = current problem **(b)** query

procedeu *sn* process; **procedee de fabricaţie** = industrial processes

procentaj *sn* percentage; rate; **procentaj de scont** = percentage discount *sau* mark-down; **procentaj fix** = flat rate; **creştere a procentajului** = percentage increase

proces **(a)** *(procedeu)* process **(b)** lawsuit *sau* suit; case *sau* action; **a intenta proces** = to take legal action; **a intenta proces cuiva** = to bring an action against someone

proces verbal *sn* *(minută)* minutes; **preşedintele a cerut procesul verbal al şedinţei precedente** = the chairman asked for the last meeting's minutes

procesare *sf* *(prelucrare)* processing

procesor *sn* processor

procură *sf* procuration; *(autorizaţie)* warrant; *(delegaţie)* proxy

producător *sm* maker *sau* producer

produce *vb* **(a)** *(a fabrica)* to produce *sau* to make *sau* to manufacture; to develop; **firma produce monitoare pentru calculatoare** = the company manufactures computer monitors; **a produce în serie** = to mass produce **(b)** to create

producere *sf* *(fabricaţie)* making

productiv *adj* *(eficient)* productive

productivitate *sf* productivity; *(randament)* output; **primă de productivitate** = output bonus

producţie *sf* **(a)** production; **producţie de serie** = mass production; **cost de producţie** = production cost; **linie de producţie** = production line; **plan de producţie** = corporate plan; **ritm de producţie** = production rate; **a mări ritmul de producţie** = to speed up production; **secţie de producţie** = factory unit **(b)** output *sau* outturn; **a mări producţia cu 5%** = to increase output by 5%; **producţie brută** = gross output; **producţie netă** = net output; **producţie pe oră** = output per hour

produs *sn* **(a)** product; commodity; **produs de bază** = basic product; basic commodity; **produs final** = end product; *(subprodus)* **produs secundar** = byproduct **(b)** produce; **produse agricole** = farm produce **(c) produs naţional brut (PNB)** = gross national product (GNP)

profesa *vb (a practica o profesie)* to exercise (a profession)

profesie *sau* **profesiune** *sf* profession; career *sau* occupation; **de profesie medic** = doctor by profession; **ea a ales contabilitatea drept profesie** = she chose accounting as her career; **a practica o profesie** *sau* **a profesa** = to exercise a profession

profesional *adj (de muncă)* occupational; **riscuri profesionale** = occupational hazards

profit *sn (beneficiu)* **(a)** profit; **profit brut** = gross profit *sau* pre-tax profit; **profit după deducerea impozitelor** = after-tax profit; **profit neaşteptat** = windfall profit; **profit net** = after-tax profit *sau* net profit; **profit procentual** = percentage profit; **200,000 lei în profit** = 200.000 lei in profit; **a înregistra profituri** = to show a profit; **a obţine profituri** = to make a profit; **a obţine un profit de 40.000 lei** = to make a 40,000 lei profit *sau* to be 40,000 lei in pocket; **obţinere de profituri excesive** = profiteering; **contul de profit şi piederi** = profit

and loss account; **a menţine o afacere în profit** = to keep a company afloat **(b)** interest *sau* yield; proceeds; **profit din investiţii** = return on investment; **profit net** = net yield; **profituri din vânzare** = the proceeds of a sale **(c)** surplus; **profituri dobândite prin creşterea dobânzilor** = acquired surplus **(d)** advantage

profita *vb* to profit

profitabil *adj* **(a)** profitable *sau* profit-making; **afacere profitabilă** = paying business **(b)** gainful; **ocupaţie profitabilă** = gainful occupation

prognoză *sf* forecast; **prognoză meteorologică** = weather forecast

program *sn* **(a)** programme *sau* schedule *sau* timetable; plan; **program de activităţi** = schedule of events; **program de dezvoltare** = development programme **(b)** program; *(software)* software; **program de calculator** = computer program; **program de contabilitate pe calculator** = accounting program

programa *vb* to program; **a programa un calculator** = to program a computer

programabil *adj* programmable

programare *sf* programming; **limbaj de programare** = programming language

programator *sm* programmer

progresa *vb* to advance; *(a merge bine)* to get on

proiect *sn* project *sau* plan; **proiect de dezvoltare** = developing project; **schiţă de proiect** = draft project

proiecta *vb* **(a)** to design; **noul complex a fost proiectat în întregime pe calculator** = the new complex was designed entirely on the computer **(b)** to draft

proiectant *sm* designer

proiectare *sf* design; **proiectare asistată de calculator** = Computer Aided Design (CAD); **proiectare industrială** = industrial design

proiectat *adj* projected

promisiune *sf* commitment; **promisiune solemnă** = undertaking

promite *vb* to promise *sau* to undertake

promova *vb* (a) to promote; **a fost promovat contabil şef** = he was promoted to chief accountant (b) *(în funcţie)* to upgrade (c) *(a spijini)* to back

promovare *sf* promotion *sau* advancement

proporţie *sf* ratio

proprietar *sm* owner *sau* proprietor; *(moşier)* landlord; **bunurile furate au fost înapoiate proprietarului** = the stolen goods were returned to the owner; **proprietarul unei locuinţe** = homeowner; **proprietar de magazin** = shopkeeper; **propietar de teren** = ground landlord

proprietate *sf* property; *(fonduri)* asset; *(calitatea de proprietar)* ownership; **proprietate comună** = common ownership; **proprietate de stat** = state ownership; public property; **aceasta este proprietatea statului** = this property belongs to the state; *(teren)* **proprietate funciară** = land; **proprietate particulară** *sau* **proprietate privată** = private property

proprietăreasă *sf* proprietress; *(moşier)* landlady

propriu *adj (personal)* own

propune *vb* to propose; **a propune un amendament** = to propose an amendment

propunere *sf* proposal; *(moţiune)* motion; **a înainta o propunere** = to put forward a proposal; **a refuza o** propunere = to turn down a proposal; **a prezenta o propunere** = to table a motion (b) *(a oferi)* to offer

prospera *vb* to boom; **afacerea a prosperat în anii '80** = the business boomed during the 1980s

prosperitate *sf* wealth

protecţie *sf* care *(pază)* safeguard

protecţionism *sn* protectionism

proteja *vb* (a) to protect *sau* to safeguard; **a proteja interesele clienţilor** = to safeguard the interests of the customers (b) to cover; **a fi protejat pe deplin de poliţa de asigurări** = to be fully covered

provenienţă *sf* origin; **software de provenienţă americană** = software of American origin

provizional *adj* **dividend provizional** = interim dividend

provizoriu *adj (temporar în funcţie)* acting; **preşedintele provizoriu îndeplineşte funcţiile preşedintelui până o altă persoană este aleasă** = the acting chairman is carrying out the duties of chairman until a new person is elected

provoca *vb* to challenge

provocare *sf* challenge

prudent *adj* conservative; **preziceri prudente** = conservative estimates

public 1 *sn* public; **relaţii cu publicul** = public relations (PR) 2 *adj* public; **investiţie publică** = government investment; **lucrări publice** = public works; **opinie publică** = public opinion; **sector public (al economiei)** = public sector

publica *vb* to publish; **a publica o carte** = to publish a book

publicaţie *sf (periodic)* publication *sau* newspaper; *(buletin informativ)* **publicaţie periodică** = journal

publicitar *adj* promotional; **agenţie publicitară** = publicity bureau; **campanie publicitară** = publicity campaign; **material publicitar** = publicity matter; **spaţiu publicitar alocat într-o publicaţie** = advertising space

publicitate *sf* publicity *sau* advertising; **de publicitate** = advertising *sau* promotional; **agenţie de publicitate** = advertising agency; **buget alocat pentru publicitate** = advertising budget; **material de publicitate** = promotional material; **mica publicitate** = want ads

punct *sn* point; *(fund)* **punct minim** = bottom; **a atinge punctul minim** = to bottom out; *(vânzările acoperă cheltuielile, fără profit realizat)* **punct mort** = break-even point; **punct terminus** = destination

punctualitate *sf* time-keeping

pune *vb* to put; *(obligaţiuni, etc.)* **a pune în circulaţie** = to issue; **a pune**

în practică = to implement; **a pune în vigoare** = to put into force

pungă *sf* bag

punte *sf (de comandă a unui vas)* bridge

purta *vb* to bear; **documentul poartă semnatură sa** = the document bears his signature

purtător *sm* bearer; **bunurile au fost înmânate purtătorului scrisorii** = the goods were handed to the bearer of the letter; **cec la purtător** = cheque to bearer *sau* bearer cheque

puşculiţă *sf* piggy bank

putere *sf* force *sau* power; **putere de cumpărare** = buying power; **putere executivă** = executive power

puţ *sn (mină de cărbune)* pit

puţin *adj* few; **am primit foarte puţine comenzi săptămâna trecută** = we received very few orders last week

Qq

quart *sn (măsură de 1,136 litri)* quart

Rr

rabat *sn (reducere)* rebate; *(scont)* discount; **rabat comercial** = trade discount

radiogramă *sf* radio telegram

ramburs *sn* refund; **ramburs total** = full refund; **contra ramburs** = carriage forward; cash on delivery

rambursa *vb* **(a)** to refund **(b)** *(a achita)* to repay *sau* to pay back

rambursabil *adj* **(a)** repayable; **un împrumut rambursabil în 3 ani** = a loan repayable over 3 years **(b)** refundable; **garanţie rambursabilă** = refundable deposit **(c)** *(care poate fi amortizat)* redeemable

rambursare *sf* **(a)** *(plată)* repayment; payoff; payback; **modalităţi de rambursare** = terms and conditions of repayment; **perioadă de rambursare** = repayment period; **rambursarea unui împrumut** = refunding of a loan; *(într-un contract de împrumut)* **clauza rambursării** = payback clause **(b)** *(amortizare)* redemption

rampă *sf* ramp; **rampă de încărcare** = loading ramp

ramură *sf* branch

randament *sn* **(a)** *(producţie)* output **(b)** *(rentabilitate)* yield **(c)** efficiency; **randament industrial** = industrial efficiency; **randament tehnic al unui utilaj** = technical efficiency

rang *sn* grade *sau* rank

rapid *adj* quick *sau* rapid; **redresare rapidă** = quick recovery

raport *sn* *(proporţie)* ratio; **raportul dintre succes şi eşec** = ratio of success to failure

rată *sf* **(a)** instalment; **rată lunară** = monthly instalment; **a achitat plata maşinii în 24 de rate lunare** = he paid for the car in 24 monthly instalments **(b)** *(curs)* rate; **rate de bază ale dobânzilor bancare** = bank base rate; **rata dobânzilor** = interest rate; **rata de scont** = discount rate

ratifica *vb* to ratify *sau* to sanction; **bugetul de cheltuieli a fost ratificat de consiliul de administraţie** = the expenditure budget was sanctioned by the board

ratificare *sf* ratification

raţie *sf* ration

raţionaliza *vb* **(a)** to ration **(b)** to rationalize

raţionalizare *sf* **(a)** *(normare)* rationing **(b)** rationalization

rămâne *vb* **a rămâne în urmă** = to fall behind

rămânere *sf* **rămânere în urmă (cu lucrul)** = backlog

răspundere *sf* liability; **a-şi asuma răspunderea pentru ceva** = to accept liability for something; **răspundere limitată** = limited liability; **societate**

cu răspundere limitată = limited liability company

răspuns *sn* answer; feedback

răspunzător *adj* liable for

răsturna *vb* **a (se) răsturna** = to keel over *sau* to capsize

război *sn* war; **război al preţurilor** = price war

rând *sn* queue

reacţie *sf* **(a)** reaction; **reacţie în lanţ** = chain reaction **(b)** *(feedback)* feedback

reacţiona *vb* to react

real *adj* real *sau* actual; **preţ real** = actual price; **salariu real** = real wages; **venit real** = real income

realiza *vb* **(a)** *(a-şi da seama)* to realize; **a realizat că nu va putea plăti următoarea rată** = he realized that he could not meet the next instalment **(b)** to carry out *sau* to accomplish

recensământ *sn* census

recepţie *sf* **(a)** reception **(b)** reception desk

recepţioner *sm* reception clerk

recesiune *sf* recession

rechiziţie *sf* **(a)** requisition; **rechiziţie de materiale** = materials requisition **(b)** **document oficial de rechiziţie** = requisition (order)

recicla *vb* **(a)** *(cadre)* to retrain **(b)** *(resurse)* to recycle

reciclare *sf* **reciclare profesională** = retraining; **curs de reciclare** = refresher course; **50 din angajaţii noştri au fost trimişi la un curs de reciclare** = 50 of our staff were sent on a refresher course

recipient *sn* container

recipisă *sf* *(chitanţă)* receipt; **recipisă de expediere** = certificate of posting

reciproc *adj* reciprocal *sau* mutual; **acord reciproc de reducere a taxelor vamale** = reciprocal trade agreement

reciprocitate *sf* reciprocity

reclamant *sm* plaintiff

reclamaţie *sf* complaint; **clientul doreşte să facă reclamaţie în legătură cu produsul cumpărat** = the customer wants to make a complaint about the product he had bought; **condică de sugestii şi reclamaţii** = complaints book

reclamă *sf* *(publicitate)* advertising *sau* publicity; advertisement *sau* promotion; **a face reclamă** = to advertise *sau* to promote *sau* to publicize; **reclamă comercială la TV** = TV commercial

recomanda *vb* to advise

recomandare *sf* *(caracterizare, atestat)* testimonial

recompensă *sf* **(a)** *(plată)* payment *sau* consideration; **recompensă pecuniară** = payback **(b)** *(primă)* bonus; *(stimulent pecuniar)* bounty

reconstrucţie *sf* reconstruction; **reconstrucţie economică** = economic reconstruction

recruta *vb* to recruit

recunoaşte *vb* **(a)** *(a admite)* to admit *sau* to acknowledge; **contabilul şi-a recunoscut necinstea** = the accountant admitted he had been dishonest **(b)** to appreciate; **străduinţele sale erau recunoscute** = his efforts were appreciated

recunoaştere *sf* **(a)** admission *sau* acknowledgement **(b)** appreciation

recupera *vb* (a) to get back *sau* to recover; **şi-au recuperat banii după ce l-au dat în judecată pe furnizor** = they recovered their money after taking the supplier to court (b) to reclaim; **a recupera teren arabil** = to reclaim land

recuperabil *adj* recoverable

recuperare *sf* recovery

recurs *sn* (a) recourse (b) appeal; *(a contesta o decizie)* **a face recurs** = to appeal against a decision; **a face recurs împotriva unei hotărâri judecătoreşti** = to have recourse to the courts

redacta *vb* to edit

redactor *sm* sub-editor

redactor-şef *sm* editor

redresa *vb* (a) **a se redresa** = to salvage (b) to recover; **economia a început să se redreseze după o perioadă de recesiune accentuată** = after a period of deep recession the economy started to recover

redresare *sf* recovery; **redresare economică** = economic recovery; **redresare rapidă** = rapid *sau* quick recovery

reduce *vb* (a) *(a diminua)* to reduce *sau* to cut; *(a scurta)* to shorten; **a reduce cheltuielile** = to reduce expenditure; **a reduce impozitele** = to reduce taxes; **a reduce perioada de rambursare a datoriilor** = to shorten credit terms; **a reduce preţurile** = to cut prices; **a vinde la preţuri reduse** = to sell at giveaway prices; **preţ redus** = bargain price *sau* knockdown price; **a reduce sever** = to slash; **a reduce producţia drastic** = to slash output; **a reduce preţuri substanţial** = to slash prices (b) to deduct (c) **a (se) reduce** = to fall (away); **comenzile s-au redus anul acesta** = orders have fallen away this year

reducere *sf* (a) reduction *sau* rebate; **a oferi o reducere de 15%** = to offer a rebate of 15% *sau* a 15% rebate (b) reduction *sau* cut; **reducere de preţ** = price reduction *sau* markdown; **reducere de personal** = job cuts; **reducerea personalului** = staff reduction; **reduceri de preţuri** = cuts in price *sau* price cuts (c) abatement *sau* relief; **reducere a impozitului** = tax abatement *sau* tax rebate *sau* tax relief

reeşalonare *sf* rescheduling; **acord de reeşalonare a datoriilor** = rescheduling agreement

reevalua *vb* (a) to revalue (b) to reassess

reevaluare *sf* revaluation; **reevaluare mijloacelor fixe şi investiţiilor** = revaluation of assets

reexporta *vb* to re-export

reexportare *sf* re-export

reface *vb* **a (se) reface** = to recover

refacere *sf* recovery

referi *vb* **a se referi** = to apply

refuza *vb* (a) to refuse *sau* to decline; **invitaţia a fost refuzată politicos** = the invitation was politely declined; **omul de afaceri a refuzat interviul** = the businessman refused to be interviewed; **compania a refuzat orice implicare în tranzacţie** = the company declined to become involved in the deal (b) to boycott

regie *sf* administration; **în regie** = state-managed

registratură *sf* mail room

registru *sn* register; *(manual sau computerizat)* **registru contabil** = ledger; **registru contabil al unei companii** = a company's books; **registru de facturi** = bought ledger; **registru de încasări** = cash book; **registru de vânzări** = sales ledger; **shareholders' register** = lista acţionarilor; **a nota în registru** = to register; **a nota într-un registru convorbirile telefonice** = to log phone calls; **a opera o intrare în registru** = to enter something in a register; **după confirmarea rezervării, omul de afaceri a semnat în registrul hotelului** = after his reservation was confirmed, the businessman checked into the hotel

regiune *sf* district

regla *vb* to regulate

reglementare *sf (dispoziţie)* regulation

regula *vb* to regulate

regulat *adj* regular; **zbor regulat** = regular flight

regulă *sf* **(a)** law *sau* rule; **a aplica o regulă** = to apply a rule **(b) reguli procedurale** = standing order

reintroduce *vb (a recupera)* **a reintroduce în circuitul productiv** = to reclaim

reînnoi *vb* **(a)** to renew; **a reînnoi o poliţă de asigurare** = to renew an insurance policy; **a reînnoi un abonament** = to renew a subscription **(b) a reînnoi o comandă** = to reorder

relaţie *sf* **(a)** *(cunoştinţă)* connection **(b)** *(pl)* **relaţii** = relations; **relaţii cu publicul** = public relations *sau* PR; **relaţii de muncă** = industrial relations

remite *vb* to remit

remorca *vb* to haul; *(un vas, etc.)* to tow

remorcare *sf* hauling *sau* towage

remorcă *sf* trailer

remunera *vb* to remunerate

remuneraţie *sf (salariu)* remuneration

renovare *sf* redevelopment; **renovare urbanistică** = urban redevelopment

rentabil *adj* profit-making *sau* profitable; paying

rentabilitate *sf* profitability; yield

rentă *sf* **(a)** annuity **(b)** rent; **rentă funciară** = land rent

rentier *sm* annuitant; person of independent means

renumit *adj (de bună reputaţie)* old-established

renunţa *vb* to abandon; **a renunţat la ideea de a investi într-o altă afacere** = he abandoned the idea of investing in another business; **a renunţa la o despăgubire** = to waive damages

renunţare *sf* renunciation; **renunţarea de bună voie la slujbă** = voluntary redundancy; **clauză de renunţare** = waiver (clause); **scrisoare de renunţare** = letter of renunciation

repara *vb* to fix *sau* to service; **am chemat tehnicianul să îmi repare maşina de scris** = I called the repairman to fix my typewriter

reparaţie *sf* repair *sau* maintenance; **centru de reparaţii** = service centre

repartiza *vb* **(a)** *(a trasa)* to distribute *sau* to divide **(b)** to assign *sau* to allocate

repartizare *sf* **(a)** distribution; **repartizarea investiţiilor publice** = distribution of public investment **(b)** assignment

repercusiune *sf* knock-on effect

reprezenta *vb* to represent; **îşi reprezintă firma în Londra** = he represents his firm in London

reprezentant *sm* representative; **reprezentant comercial** = representative *sau* rep *sau* salesman; **I-am trimis pe reprezentantul nostru să discute contractul de**

vânzare = we sent our representative to discuss the sales contract

reprezentare *sf* representation; **cheltuieli de reprezentare** = entertainment allowance

reprezentativ *adj* representative

repudia *vb (a rezilia)* to repudiate

respecta *vb (o lege, etc.)* to comply (with); **a respecta o hotărâre judecătorească** = to comply with a court order

respinge *vb* to defeat; **noul proiect de lege a fost respins în parlament** = the new bill was defeated in parliament

respingere *sf* veto

responsabil 1 *adj* liable for *sau* responsible 2 *s* **responsabil cu prevenirea incendiilor** = fire safety officer

responsabilitate *sf* responsibility; liability *sau* charge

rest *sn* (a) remainder (b) change; **vânzătorul i-a dat restul în monede de £1** = the shop assistant gave him the change in £1 coins (c) *(pl)* **resturi** = junk; scrap

restanţă *sf* arrears; backlog; **a plăti restanţele** = to pay off arrears of debt; **restanţă de salariu** = back pay

restanţier *sm* slow payer; **a fi restanţier** = to be in arrears *sau* to fall behind with payments

restaurare *sf* reconstruction

restituire *sf* (a) restitution (b) *(retragere)* **restituire (la bancă)** *sau* **operaţiune de restituire** = withdrawal

restrânge *vb* to restrict

restrictiv *adj* restrictive *sau* limiting; **clauză restrictivă (a unui contract)** = limiting clause; **piaţă restrictivă** = captive market; **practici comerciale restrictive** = restrictive trade practices

restricţie *sf* restriction *sau* restraint *sau* squeeze; **restricţii la importuri** = restraints on imports; **restricţii ale schimburilor comerciale** = restraint of trade

restructurare *sf* *(reducerea personalului)* staff reductions

resursă *sf* (a) energy; **nu are resurse să ducă la bun sfârşit ceea ce a început** = he hasn't got the energy to finish what he has started (b) resources; **resurse financiare** = financial resources; **resurse naturale** = natural resources; **resurse umane** = human resources; **resurse umane nefolosite** = a pool of unemployed labour (c) *(potenţial)* potential

retrage *vb* (a) *(a scoate)* to draw; **a retrage bani de la bancă** = to withdraw; **a retrage din circulaţie** = to call in (b) **a se retrage** = to back off; **a se retrage din afaceri** = to retire *sau* to get out of the rat race

retragere *sf* *(operaţiune de restituire)* withdrawal

retroactiv *adj* retroactive; **impozit retroactiv** = back duty

retrograda *vb* to downgrade

retrospectiv *adj* *&* *adv* retrospective(ly); **a valida retrospectiv** = to backdate

reţea *sf* (a) network; **reţea de calculatoare** = computer network; **reţea de distribuţie** = distribution network (b) **reţea de magazine** = chain of stores

reţine *vb* *(din salariu)* to keep back (money)

reţinere *sf* **reţineri pe salariu** = stoppage (from pay)

reuşi *vb* to manage to; **au reuşit să mărească productivitatea muncii prin instalarea de echipament nou** = they managed to increase productivity by installing new equipment

revânzare *sf* resale

revendicare *sf* claim

revistă *sf* magazine *sau* review; **revistă de informatică** = computer magazine; **revistă de modă** = fashion magazine

revizie *sf* *(contabilă)* audit; **efectuarea reviziei mijloacelor fixe (de către un revizor)** = verification of assets; **a efectua o revizie contabilă** = to audit

revizor *sm* **(a) revizor contabil** = auditor **(b)** *(asigurări)* adjuster

revizui *vb* to review

revoca *vb* **(a)** to countermand **(b)** to rescind

rezerva *vb* to book *sau* to reserve; **a rezerva o masă la restaurant** = to book a table at a restaurant; **a rezerva un bilet de tren** = to make a train reservation; *(la avion sau tren sau la teatru)* **a rezerva un loc** = to book a seat

rezervare *sf* booking *sau* reservation; **taxă de rezervare** = booking fee

rezervă *sf* reserve; **fond de rezervă** = standby fund; **fonduri de rezervă** = reserve funds; buffer stocks; **rezerve bancare** = bank reserves; **rezerve de exploatare** = operating reserve; **rezerve în aur** = gold reserves; **raportul dintre rezerve şi moneda în circulaţie** = reserve ratio

reziduu *sn* **rezidduri industriale** = waste; **rezidduri nucleare (radioactive)** = nuclear waste

rezilia *vb* to repudiate; *(a anula)* to rescind; **a rezilia un contract** = to rescind a contract; to repudiate an agreement

rezista *vb* to hold on

rezonabil *adj* reasonable; **preţuri rezonabile** = reasonable prices

rezultat *sn* effect

ridica *vb* **(a)** to collect; **au ridicat bunurile când au plătit** = they collected the goods when they paid **(b)** *(a totaliza)* **a se ridica la** = to amount to

ridicat *adj* high; **dobânzi ridicate** = high interest; **preţuri ridicate** = high prices

ridicata *sf* **cu ridicata** = wholesale *sau* in bulk; **achiziţii cu ridicata** = bulk purchase; **comerţ cu ridicata** = wholesale trade; **preţ cu ridicata** = wholesale price; **a vinde cu ridicata** = to sell in bulk *sau* to sell wholesale; **vânzare cu ridicata** = wholesale selling

riguros *adj* calculated

risc *sn* risk *sau* hazard; **risc care poate fi asigurat** = insurable risk; **risc calculat** = calculated risk; **risc financiar** = financial risk

risca *vb* to risk *sau* to run a risk; *(a specula)* **a risca în afaceri** = to venture **(b)** to stake; **a riscat totul convingându-l să-şi urmeze studiile** = she staked everything on convincing him to continue his studies

riscant *adj* risky

risipi *vb* to waste

risipă *sf* waste; **risipă de resurse financiare** = waste of money

ritm *sn* rate; **ritm de vânzare** = rate of sales

rival *sm* rival *(în afaceri)* competitor

rivaliza *vb* to compete

robotică *sf* robotics

român, românesc, română, românească *adj* Romanian

român(că) *sm(f)* Romanian

România *sf* Romania; Notă: capitală: **Bucureşti** = Bucharest; monedă: **leu** = leu

rotaţie *sf* turnover; **rotaţia cadrelor** = turnover of staff

rotund *adj* circular

Ruanda *(Urundi) sf* Rwanda; Notă: capitală: **Kigali;** monedă: **franc ruandez** = Rwandan franc

ruandez(ă) *s & adj* Rwandan

rubrică *sf* column; **el citeşte rubrica de informaţii financiare în fiecare dimineaţă** = he reads the City column every morning; **rubrica `cumpărări'** = want ads

ruga *vb* **(a)** to ask; **roagă-l să aducă ultimul raport** = ask him to fetch the latest report **(b) a se ruga de cineva** = to appeal to someone

rugăminte *sf* appeal

ruina *vb* to ruin; *(a distruge financiar)* **competiţia dură l-a ruinat** = the tough competition broke him

rulant *adj* **material rulant** = rolling stock

rulment *sn (capitaluri circulante)* **fonduri de rulment** = working capital *sau* quick assets

rulotă *sf* trailer

rus(ă) *sau* **rusesc, rusească** *s & adj* Russian

Rusia *sf* Russia; Notă: capitală: **Moscova** = Moscow; monedă: **rublă** = rouble

Ss

sac *sn* sack; **a vinde legume în saci** = to sell vegetables by the sack

salariat 1 *adj* salaried 2 *sm* wage-earner; employee; *(pe statul de plată)* payee

salariu *sn* salary *sau* pay *sau* wage; earnings; *(remunerație)* remuneration; **salariu brut** = gross salary *sau* gross wage; **salariu de bază** = basic pay *sau* basic wage; **salariu mediu** = average wage; **salariu minim** = minimum wage; **salariu minim garantat** = guaranteed minimum wage; **salariu net** = net salary *sau* net wage; take-home pay; **chitanță de salariu** = pay slip; **compensație pentru pierderea de salariu** = compensation for loss of earnings; `a îngheța' salariile *sau* a nu acorda măriri de salariu** = to freeze wages; **înghețarea salariilor** = wage freeze; **majorarea salariului** = pay rise *sau* salary increase; **salariile noastre nu au fost majorate în ultimi doi ani** = we haven't had a pay rise for two years; **negocierea salariilor** = wage negotiations; **plafon de salarii** = wage ceiling; **popriri pe salariu** = salary deductions; **restanță de salariu** = back pay; **i s-a spus că salariul ei va fi revizuit după 6 luni** = she was told that they would review her salary after 6 months; **scala salariilor** = salary scales *sau* wage brackets; **ziua de salariu** = pay day

salarizare *sf* wages; payment of salary; **salarizare în acord** = incentive wage; **nivele de salarizare** = wage levels

sală *sf* **sală de ședințe** *sau* **conferințe** = conference room

salon *sn* **salon de prezentare** = showroom

salva *vb* to salvage; **a salva încărcătura de pe o epavă** = to salvage cargo from a wreck

Salvador *sm* El Salvador; Notă: capitală: **San Salvador;** monedă: **colón salvadorian** = Salvadorian colón

salvadorian(ă) *s & adj* Salvadorian

salvare *sf (operațiune de salvare)* salvage; *(plătită de un armator echipei de salvare)* **primă de salvare** = salvage money; **vas de salvare** = salvage vessel

sancționa *vb* (a) to penalize; **a fost sancționat pentru neândeplinirea sarcinilor de serviciu** = he was penalized for failing to perform his basic duties (b) to authorize

sancțiune *sf* sanction; **sancțiuni economice** = economic sanctions

sarcină *sf* directive; *(datorie)* assignment; **sarcină de muncă** = task

satisface *vb* to satisfy; **a satisface o cerere** = to satisfy a demand; **a satisface cererea pentru** = to satisfy the demand for *sau* to keep up with the demand for; **a satisface cerințele cuiva** = to meet someone's demands

satisfacţie *sf* satisfaction

satura *vb* to saturate; **a satura piaţa** = to saturate the market; **piaţa aparatelor de fotografiat este saturată** = the market for cameras is saturated

saturaţie *sf* saturation; glut; **punct de saturaţie** = saturation point

sălta *vb* to jump; **preţul acţiunilor a săltat brusc** = share prices rose sharply

sănătate *sf* health; **a se pensiona pe motive de sănătate** = to retire for medical reasons; **certificat de sănătate** = doctor's certificate *sau* medical certificate

săptămână *adj* week; **săptămână de lucru** = working week; **două săptămâni** = fortnight; **bunurile dumneavoastră vor fi livrate în două săptămâni** = your goods will be delivered in a fortnight

sărac *adj* poor *sau* impecunious; indigent; **extrem de sărac** = poverty-stricken

sărăcie *sf* poverty

sărbătoare *sf* **sărbătoare legală** *sau* **sărbătoare oficială** = bank holiday *sau* public holiday; legal holiday

scală *sf* scale; **scală mobilă (de valori)** = sliding scale; **scală mobilă a tarifelor** = sliding scale of charges

scară *sf* **(a)** *(gamă)* scale; **pe scară mare** = on a large scale **(b)** bracket; **scara salariilor** = salary scales *sau* wage brackets

scădea *vb* **(a)** *(a coborî)* to fall *sau* to decrease *sau* to decline *sau* to ease; **comenzile au scăzut trimestrul trecut** = orders have declined over the last quarter; **a scădea brusc** = to sink; **a scădea din nou** = to fall back; **după o creştere vertiginoasă preţurile au scăzut din nou** = after a steep rise prices fell back; **a scădea rapid** = to

plummet *sau* to plunge **(b)** *(a deduce)* to deduct

scădere *sf* decrease *sau* decline *sau* fall; **scăderea preţului petrolului** = fall in the price of oil; **scăderea valorii acţiunilor** = decline in the value of shares *(a preţurilor)* **scădere bruscă** = collapse *sau* slump; **în scădere** = on the decrease

scăpare *sf* mistake *sau* slip-up

scăzut *adj* poor; **nivel scăzut** = low level

schimb *sn* **(a)** *(transfer)* exchange; **schimb de contracte** = exchange of contracts; *(completat cu bani)* **schimb parţial** = part exchange; **piesă de schimb** = spare part **(b)** **schimb valutar** = exchange *sau* exchange rate; **controlul schimbului valutar** = exchange control

schimba *vb* **(a)** to exchange; **a schimba bani** = to change (money); **a trebuit să schimbe maşina nouă cu una mai modestă datorită greutăţilor financiare** = due to financial hardship he had to exchange his new car for a cheaper one; **a schimbat dolarii în lire sterline** = he exchanged dollars for pounds; **aş dori să schimb £100 în lei** = I would like to change £100 into lei; *(despre bunuri sau bani)* **a schimba proprietarul** = to change hands **(b) a (se) schimba** = to change

schimbare *sf* change; *(de strategie)* shift; **schimbarea rutei de către o navă** = deviation

schiţa *vb* to draft *sau* to draw up; **a schiţa un contract** = to draft a contract; **a schiţa un itinerar** = to draw up an itinerary

schiţă *sf* **(a)** design **(b)** draft; **directorul a studiat schiţa raportului său** = the manager examined the draft of his report

scoate *vb* to draw; *(a efectua o restituire)* **a scoate bani de la bancă =** to withdraw money from the bank

scont *sn (rabat)* discount; **furnizorul oferă un scont generos pentru achiziții en gros =** the supplier offers a generous discount on bulk purchases; **scont de bază =** basic discount; **rata de scont =** discount rate; **valoare de scont =** discounted value

sconta *vb (o cambie)* to discount

scop *sn* aim *sau* goal *sau* end *sau* object; **scopul său este să câștige cât mai mulți bani =** his aim is to make more money; **scopul său e să deschidă un studio de înregistrări =** his goal is to open a recording studio; **scopul pentru care compania a fost înființată =** the object of the company

scrie *vb* to write; **a scrie scrisori =** to correspond

scris *sn* writing; **în scris =** in writing *sau* on paper; **confirmare în scris =** letter of acknowledgement

scrisoare *sf* (a) letter; **scrisoare de confirmare =** letter of acknowledgement; **scrisoare de renunțare =** letter of renunciation; **scrisoare par avion =** airmail letter (b) *(fraht)* **scrisoare de trăsură =** waybill

scuar *sn (piață)* square

scufunda *vb* **a (se) scufunda =** to sink; **vasul a fost scufundat de o furtună violentă =** the ship sank *sau* was sunk in a violent storm

scump *adj (costisitor)* expensive *sau* dear; **bani scumpi =** dear money; **acest calculator este mai scump decât ne-am așteptat =** this computer is dearer than we expected; **foarte scump =** very expensive

scurge *vb* **a se scurge =** to drain

scurgere *sf* drain; **scurgere de capital =** flight of capital; **scurgere de capital în afara țării =** outflow of capital *sau* flight of capital; **scurgerea de capital afară din țară =** drain of capital

scurt *adj* short *sau* brief; **scurtă durată =** short-term; **împrumut pe scurtă durată =** short-term loan; **zbor de scurtă durată =** short-haul flight

scurta *vb* to shorten

scuti *vb* to exempt

scutire *sf* (a) exemption; **scutire de impozite =** tax-exemption (b) *(reducere)* rebate; **scutire de taxe parțială pentru familii cu copii =** child's allowance

scutit *adj* exempt; **scutit de impozite =** tax-exempt

sechestra *vb* to sequester

sechestrare *sf* sequestration

sechestru *sn (dreptul de a confisca bunurile datornicilor până sumele datorate sunt achitate)* lien

secret 1 *sn* confidence; **în secret =** in confidence 2 *adj* hidden; **fonduri secrete =** hidden assets

secretar *sm* secretary; **secretarul companiei =** company secretary; *(autoritatea supremă într-o organizație internațională)* **Secretar General =** secretary-general

secretară *sf* secretary

sector *sn* (a) sector; **sector economic =** economic sector; **sector (economic) particular =** private sector; **sector public =** public sector (b) district; **șef de sector =** area manager *sau* district manager

secție *sf* (a) *(departament)* division; *(unitate)* unit; **secție de export =** export department; **secție de marketing =** marketing division; **secție de producție =** production division *sau* production unit; *(linie)* production line; **şef de secţie** = head of department **(b)** *(atelier)* workshop

secundar *adj* **(a)** secondary; **industrie secundară** = secondary industry; *(subprodus)* **produs secundar** = byproduct **(b)** subsidiary

securitate *sf (siguranţă)* safety

sediu *sn* premises; **sediu central** = head office *sau* headquarters; **sediu comercial** = commercial premises

seif *sn* **(a)** strongbox *sau* safe; **în fiecare seară directorul pune banii şi cecurile în seif** = every night the manager puts the cash and the cheques into the safe **(b)** *(tezaur la o bancă)* strongroom

select *adj* exclusive; **club select** = exclusive club

selecţionare *sf* picking; **selecţionare de articole pentru o comandă** = order picking

semestrial *adj & adv* half-yearly

semestru *sn* half-year

semicalificat *adj* semi-skilled; **muncitor semicalificat** = semi-skilled worker

semna *vb* to sign; **a uitat să semneze cecul** = he forgot to sign the cheque; **a semna un contract de muncă** = to sign a contract of employment *sau* to sign on

semnala *vb* to point out; **a semnalat faptul că productivitatea va scădea fără introducerea de echipament nou** = he pointed out that without new equipment productivity would suffer

semnaliza *vb* to flag

semnatar *sm* signatory; **semnatari ai unui tratat internaţional** = signatories of an international treaty

semnătură *sf* signature

Senegal *sm* Senegal; Notă: capitală: **Dakar;** monedă: **franc CFA** = CFA franc

senegalez(ă) *s & adj* Senegalese

separat *adj* different

serie *sf* series; *(de masă)* **de serie** = large-scale; **producţie de serie** = large-scale production *sau* mass production; **a produce în serie** = to mass-produce

servi *vb* **a (de) servi** = to serve; **a servi un client** = to serve a customer

service *sn* service; **service post-vânzare** *sau* **service în garanţie** = after-sales service; **industria serviciilor** = service industry *sau* tertiary industry

serviciu *sn* **(a)** service; **serviciu personal** = personnel department; **a presta servicii** = to service **(b)** *(muncă)* work; **în interes de serviciu** = on business; **merge la serviciu cu trenul** = he goes to work by train; **pierderea serviciului** = redundancy **(c)** *(slujbă)* employment; **atribuţii de serviciu** = job description

servietă *sf* briefcase

servitor *sm* servant; **a lucra ca servitor** = to be in service

set *sn* set

sezon *sn* season; **sezon de vârf** = busy season; **sezon mort** = low season; **sezon turistic** = tourist season

sezonier *adj* **(a)** seasonal; **şomaj sezonier** = seasonal unemployment **(b)** **lucrător sezonier** = casual worker; **post sezonier** = casual vacancy

sfat *sn* counsel

sfătui *vb* to counsel *sau* to advise; **a nu se sfătui cu nimeni** = not to take advice from anyone

sfârşi *vb* **a se sfârşi** = to end *sau* to close

sfârşit *sf* end *sau* close; **sfârşit de lună** = month end; **sfârşitul contractului** = end of contract

sfert *sn* quarter; *(monedă de 25 de cenţi)* **un sfert de dolar** = quarter; **in sfert de litru (250 ml)** = a quarter of a litre; **aştept de un sfert de oră** = I have been waiting for a quarter of an hour

sigila *vb (un plic, pachet, etc.)* to seal

sigilat *adj* **plic sigilat** = sealed envelope

sigiliu *sn (ştampilă)* seal *sau* stamp; **sigiliul companiei** = company's seal *sau* common seal

sigur *adj* safe *sau* secure; **investiţie sigură** = safe *sau* secure investment

siguranţă *sf* safety *sau* security; **coeficient de siguranţă** = safety margin; **a lua măsuri de siguranţă** = to take safety measures; **în siguranţă** = safe

sili *vb* to force

siloz *sn* silo

simbol *sn* token

simbolic *adj* nominal; **sumă simbolică percepută** = nominal charge

simplu *adj (de bază)* basic

sincer *adj & adv* sincere; bona fide

sinceritate *sf (bună credinţă)* bona fides

sindicalism *sn* unionism

sindicalist *sm* unionist

sindicat *sn* union; **sindicat al meşteşugarilor** = craft union; **sindicat patronal** = trade association; **sindicat profesional** = trade union; *(în SUA)* labor union; **membrii (de rând) ai unui sindicat** = rank and file; **muncitori afiliaţi la un sindicat** = organized labour

Siria *sf* Syria; Notă: capitală: **Damasc** = Damascus; monedă: **liră siriană** = Syrian pound

sirian(ă) *s & adj* Syrian

sistem *sn* system; **inginer de sistem (de calcul)** = systems analyst

situaţie *sf* **(a)** state of affairs **(b)** status; **situaţie financiară** = financial status

slăbi *vb* to depress

slăbire *sf* decline

slovac(ă) *s & adj* Slovakian

Slovacia *sf* Slovakia; Notă: capitală: **Bratislava;** monedă: **coroană** = koruna

sloven(ă) *s & adj* Slovenian

Slovenia *sf* Slovenia; Notă: capitală: **Ljubljana;** monedă: **tolar**

slujbă *sf* **(a)** job; **500 de persoane şi-au pierdut slujba** = 500 people lost their jobs *sau* 500 jobs got the axe **(b)** *(serviciu)* employment

social *adj* social; **asigurări sociale** = social security; **asistenţă socială** = welfare; **a trăi din ajutorul social** = to live on social security payments; **bilanţ social** = social report; **bunăstare socială** = social welfare; **cheltuieli sociale** = social costs; **legislaţie socială** = social legislation

societate *sf* **(a)** *(asociere)* partnership; *(întreprindere)* company; **societate imobiliară** = building society; **societate anonimă** = public company; **societate comercială** = trading company *sau* general partnership; **societate cu răspundere limitată (SRL)** = limited company; **societate pe acţiuni** = joint-stock company; **societate în comandită, cu răspundere limitată** = limited partnership **(b)** society; **societate de consum** = consumer society; **societate mondenă** = high society

socoteală *sf* account

socoti *vb* to calculate

software *sn (programe de pentru calculator)* software

sold *sn* **(a)** balance; **sold bancar =** bank balance; **sold de casă =** cash balance **(b)** sale **(c)** *(pl)* **solduri =** seconds

solicita *vb* to ask (for); to apply for; to command *sau* to demand; *(a necesita)* to require; *(a cere)* to request; **a solicita ajutor =** to apply for help; **datorită calificărilor sale el a putut să solicite ferm o mărire de salariu =** due to his qualifications, he could command a pay rise

solicitant *sm (petiţionar)* applicant

solicitare *sf (cerere în scris)* application

solvabil *adj* solvent

solvabilitate *sf* solvency

solvent *adj (demn de încredere)* creditworthy

soma *vb* to call on; **banca l-a somat să îşi achite datoria =** the bank called on him to pay his debt

Somalia *sf* Somalia; Notă: capitală: **Mogadishu;** monedă: **şiling somalez =** Somali shilling

somalez(ă) *s & adj* Somali

somaţie *sf* **(a)** call **(b)** **somaţie de plată =** demand; **somaţie finală de plată =** final demand

sonda *vb* **a sonda opinia publică =** to poll

sondaj *sn (colectare de mostre)* sampling; **sondaj de opinie =** opinion poll

sondă *sf* oil rig

sortiment *sn* **(a)** range *sau* choice; **magazinul local avea un sortiment redus de mărfuri =** the local shop had a limited choice of goods **(b)**

(marcă) brand; **sortiment local (vândut în regiunea în care este produs) =** local brand (sold in the region where it is manufactured)

sosire *sf* arrival

Spania *sf* Spain; Notă: capitală: **Madrid;** monedă: **peseta spaniolă =** Spanish peseta

spaniol(ă) *s & adj* Spanish

spărgător de gheaţă *sn (vas)* icebreaker

spărtură *sf* breach

special *adj* particular; **această imprimantă cu cerneală funcţionează numai cu un tip special de hârtie =** this ink jet printer works with a particular type of paper; **depuneri speciale (de sume mari) =** special deposits; **în special =** in particular *sau* mainly; **compania este interesată în special în desfacerea produselor sale peste hotare =** the company is interested mainly in selling its products abroad

specialist *sm* expert *sau* specialist

specializare *sf* specialization

specific *adj (reprezentativ)* representative

specimen *sn* specimen; **specimen de semnătură =** specimen signature

spectacol *sn* show

specula *vb* to venture; **a specula la bursă =** to speculate on the stock exchange

speculant *sm* speculator; profiteer; *(escroc)* racketeer; **speculant la bursă =** stag

speculativ *adj* speculative

speculaţie *sf* speculation; **capital de speculaţie =** venture capital; **a face speculaţii la bursă =** to speculate on the stock exchange

speculă *sf* a plăti preţuri de speculă = to pay black market prices; (preţ de) speculă = rip-off

spionaj *sn* espionage; spionaj economic = industrial espionage

spirală *sf* spiral; spirala inflaţiei = inflationary spiral; spirala preţurilor şi salariilor = wage-price spiral

sponsor *sm* sponsor *sau* backer; echipa de fotbal locală a găsit un sponsor pentru noul campionat = the local football team found a sponsor for the new season

spori *vb* (a) to accumulate *sau* to add to (b) to rise

sprijini *vb* (a promova) to back; planul este sprijinit de acţionarii importanţi = the plan is backed by the senior shareholders

sprijinire *sf* (valorizare) valorization

stabil *adj* constant; preţurile sunt stabile deocamdată = the prices are constant for the time being

stabili *vb* (a) (a fixa) to set *sau* to establish; to settle (b) (a judeca sau a evalua) to assess

stabilit *adj* set; meniu stabilit = set menu

stabilitate *sf* stability; stabilitatea preţurilor = price stability

stabiliza *vb* (despre preţuri, etc.) a (se) stabiliza = to level off

stabilizare *sf* stabilization; fond de stabilizare = stabilization fund

stabilizator *sm* stabilizer

stagiar *sm* graduate trainee

stagnant *adj* (inactiv) stagnant *sau* quiet; economie stagnantă = stagnant economy

stagnare *sf* (depresiune) stagnare (a afacerilor) = depression; stagnare economică combinată cu inflaţie şi

rată ridicată a şomajului = stagflation

stand *sn* rack; stand expoziţional = display rack

standard 1 *sn* standard 2 *adj* standard; tarif standard = standard charges

standardizare *sf* standardization

stare *sf* state; stare de funcţionare = working order; oficiul de stare civilă = registry (office)

stat *sn* (a) (ţară) state; stat al bunăstării sociale = welfare state; bancă de stat = state bank; (naţionalizat) controlat de stat = state-controlled; funcţionar de stat = public servant; întreprindere de stat = state enterprise; planificare de stat = state planning; proprietate de stat = public property; sector de stat = public sector (b) stat de plată = payroll ledger

Statele Unite ale Americii (SUA) *sfpl* United States of America (USA); Notă: capitală: **Washington;** monedă: **dolar american** = US dollar

statistic *adj* statistical; analiză statistică = statistical analysis

statistică *sf* statistics

statistician *sm* (a) statistician (b) actuary

staţie *sf* staţie de autobuz = bus stop; staţie de benzină = service station

steag *sn* (drapel) flag

stenodactilograf(ă) *sm(f)* shorthand typist

stenograf(ă) *sm(f)* stenographer

stenografie *sf* shorthand

steward *sm* steward

stewardesă *sf* stewardess; airline hostess

stimula *vb* *(a încuraja)* to stimulate; **a stimula comerţul cu ţările Europei de Est** = to stimulate trade with the eastern European countries

stimulare *sf* boost

stimulent *sm* inducement

stivuitor *sn* forklift truck

stoc *sn* stock; *(în SUA)* inventory; **avem o gamă largă de încălţăminte în stoc** = we have a large selection of footwear in stock; **stocuri în exces** = overstocks; **stocuri tampon** = buffer stocks

stoca *vb* to stock

stocare *sf* *(acumulare de stoc de rezervă)* stockpiling; **stocare de informaţii pe calculator** = storage

străin 1 *adj* (a) overseas; offshore; **bancă străină** = overseas bank; **şi-a transferat toţi banii într-o bancă străină** = he transferred all his money to an offshore bank; **fonduri depuse în bănci străine** = offshore funds (b) foreign; **monedă străină** = foreign currency 2 *sm* foreigner

străinătate *sf* overseas; **din străinătate** = overseas *sau* abroad; **în străinătate** = abroad

strânge *vb* (a) to rake in (b) squeeze; **a strânge profituri (deseori, indiferent de mijloace)** = to squeeze profits (c) to raise; **a strânge fonduri pentru o societate caritabilă** = to raise funds for a charity (d) **a strânge provizii** = to store

strica *vb* to damage

stricăciune *sf* damage; *(accident)* breakdown

structură *sf* pattern; **structură a comerţului** = trade pattern; **structură a preţurilor** = pattern of prices

studia *vb* *(a cerceta)* to research; to study

studiu *sn* research; **studiul comportamentului consumatorilor** = consumer research; **în studiu** = under consideration

subaltern *s & adj* subordinate; junior

subarenda *vb* to sublet *sau* to sublease

subarendare *sf* sublet *sau* sublease

subdezvoltat *adj* underdeveloped; backward; **economie subdezvoltată** = backward economy; **ţări subdezvoltate** = underdeveloped countries

subînchiria *vb* to sublet *sau* to sublease; **a subînchiriat o cameră într-un apartament spaţios** = he subleased a room in a big flat

subînchiriere *sf* sublease; **contract de subînchiriere** = subtenancy

subînţeles *adj* implied

subordonat *sm & adj* dependent

subproducţie *sf* underproduction

subprodus *sn* byproduct

subsidiar *adj* subsidiary; *(sucursală)* **companie subsidiară** = subsidiary company

subvenţie *sf* *sau* **subvenţionare** *sf* subvention *sau* subsidy; grant; **subvenţie guvernamentală** = government grant; **subvenţionare de către guvern** = public subsidy; **subvenţionarea monedei naţionale** = currency backing

subvenţiona *vb* to subsidize; **guvernul subvenţionează industria grea** = the government subsidizes heavy industry

subzistenţă *sf* subsistence; **nivel minim de subzistenţă** = poverty line

sucursală *sf* branch *sau* branch office; subsidiary company; **sucursală a unei firme** = satellite office

sudafrican(ă) *s & adj* South African

Sudan *sm* Sudan; Notă: capitală: **Khartum;** monedă: **liră sudaneză** = Sudanese pound

sudanez(ă) *s & adj* Sudanese

suedez(ă) 1 *adj* Swedish 2 *s* Swede

Suedia *sf* Sweden; Notă: capitală: **Stockholm;** monedă: **coronă suedeză** = Swedish krona

sugera *vb* to indicate

sumar *sn* summary

sumă *sf* (a) *(adunare)* addition (b) *(total)* sum *sau* amount *sau* total; **sumă asigurată** = sum insured; **sumă de bani plătită în întregime** = lump sum (c) fund

supermagazin *sn* superstore *sau* megastore; **supermagazin aflat în afara orașului** = hypermarket

supliment *sn* **supliment de călătorie** = excess fare

suplimentar *adj* excess; **profit suplimentar** = excess profit

suport *sn* *(financiar)* backing

suporta *vb* to bear; **camionul nu va suporta această sarcină** = the lorry will not bear this load

supraestima *vb* to overvalue

supraevalua *vb* to overvalue

supraevaluat *adj* overrated

supraîncărca *vb* to overcharge

suprima *vb* to delete *sau* to cross out; **fondurile destinate proiectului au fost suprimate total** = the funds for the project were cut to nil

supune *vb* **a supune atenției (într-o ședință)** = to table; **a supune discuției** = to lay on the table

supus *sm* servant

surplus *sn* excess *sau* surplus; **surplus de cereale** = wheat surplus; **surplus economic** = economic surplus

sursă *sf* source; channel; **sursă de venit** = source of income; **veniturile din toate sursele trebuie declarate autorităților fiscale** = income from all sources must be declared to the tax authorities; **ziarul a obținut relatările din diverse surse** = the newspaper got its reports through various channels

suspendare *sf* stoppage

susține *vb* to declare; **ea susținea că era nevinovată** = she declared she was innocent

sută 1 *adj & noun* hundred; **o sută de dolari** = one hundred dollars 2 *sf* **la sută** = per cent (%); **comisionul nostru este de 10 la sută (10 %)** = our commission is 10 %; **în Marea Britanie rata actuală TVA este de 17.5 la sută (%)** = in Britain the current VAT rate is 17.5 per cent (%)

Șș

șalupă *sf* motor boat; tender

șansă *sf* chance

șantaj *sn* blackmail

șantaja *vb* to blackmail

șantier *sn* **șantier de construcții** = building site; **șantier naval** = shipyard

ședință *sf* meeting; **ședință de consiliu** = management meeting

șef *sm* head *sau* leader; *(patron)* boss; **conducerea dorea să discute cu șeful grupului de acțiune** = the management wanted to talk to the leader of the pressure group; **șef de birou** = chief clerk; **șef de birou personal** = personnel manager; **șef de echipă** = foreman; **șef de secție** = head of department; **cine este șeful?** = who is in charge?

șefă *sf* **șefă de echipă** = forewoman

șeptel *sn* cattle *sau* livestock

șoma *vb* to be out of a job

șomaj *sn* unemployment; **șomaj voluntar** = voluntary redundancy; **șomaj sezonier** = seasonal unemployment; **ajutor de șomaj** = unemployment benefit

șomer *adj* unemployed; **este șomer de mai bine de șase luni** = he has been out of work for more than six months; **șomerii** = the unemployed *sau* the jobless

ștampilă *sf* stamp; **ștampilă de cauciuc** = rubber stamp

ști *vb* to know

știre *sf* news; **buletin de știri** = news (report)

Tt

tabel *sn* table

tacit *adj* tacit *sau* implied; **aprobare tacită** = tacit approval; **contract tacit** = implied contract

tactică *sf (politică)* policy; strategy

tagmă *sf* guild

talon *sn* counterfoil

Tanzania *sf* Tanzania; Notă: capitală: **Dodoma**; monedă: **şiling tanzanian** = Tanzanian shilling

tanzanian(ă) *s & adj* Tanzanian

tarabă *sf* booth; market stall

tarif *sn* tariff *sau* charge *sau* rate; **care este tariful pentru curăţarea unui palton?** = what is the charge for cleaning a coat?; **tarif protecţionist** = protective tariff; **tarif inclusiv** = all-in rate; **tarif pe oră** = time rate; **tarif biletului de călătorie** = fare; **tarif întreg** = full fare; **tarif punitiv** = retaliatory tariff; **tarif redus pentru energia electrică** = off-peak tariff *sau* off-peak rate

tarifar *adj* **politică tarifară** = tariff barriers

tastatură *sf* keyboard

taxă *sf* **(a)** tax *sau* levy; **taxa asupra valorii adăugate (TVA)** = value added tax (VAT); **taxe pe import** = import levy; **a impune taxe** = to tax *sau* to levy; **impunere a unei taxe** = taxation; **sumă din salariu scutită de taxe** = personal allowance **(b)** fee *sau* tariff; **taxă de magazinaj** = storage (charge); **taxă vamală** = customs tariff

taxi *sn* taxi *sau* cab; **costul călătoriei cu taxiul** = taxi fare

tărăgănare *sf* delay

târg *sn* **(a)** *(expoziţie)* fair **(b)** *(centru comercial)* emporium **(c)** *(piaţă)* market

tehnic *adj* **compartiment tehnic** = engineering department; **ştiinţe tehnice aplicate** = technology

tehnician *sm* engineer; **tehnician de întreţinere** = service engineer

tehnocraţie *sf* technocracy

tehnologie *sf* technology

tejghea *sf* counter; **pe sub tejghea** = under the counter

telecomunicaţii *sfpl* telecommunications; **satelit de telecomunicaţii** = telecommunications satellite; **reţea de telecomunicaţii** = telecommunications network

telefon *sn* telephone *sau* phone; **telefon public** = pay phone; **telefon portabil** *sau* **telefon mobil** = portable phone *sau* mobile phone; **carte de telefon** = telephone directory *sau* directory *sau* phone book; **număr de telefon** = telephone number *sau* phone number; **a căuta un număr în cartea de telefon** = to look up a number in the telephone directory; **a forma un număr de telefon** = to dial (a number); **a comanda prin telefon** =

to order by telephone *sau* by phone; **a rezerva o masă la restaurant prin telefon** = to book a table by telephone by phone; **vânzări prin telefon** = telesales

telefona *vb* to telephone *sau* to phone *sau* to call *sau* to ring; **a telefonat ca să anuleze comada** = she rang to cancel the order; **a telefona gratuit** = to call freephone; *(în SUA)* to call toll free

telefonic *adj* **centrală telefonică** = telephone exchange; **comandă telefonică** = telephone order; **convorbire telefonică** = call *sau* telephone call *sau* phone call; **după convorbirea telefonică el s-a decis să cumpere mai multe acţiuni** = after the telephone call he decided to buy more shares; **prefix telefonic** = dialling code

telefonist(ă) *s* telephonist; operator

telegraf *sn* telegraph

telegrafia *vb* to telegraph *sau* to send a telegram

telegrafic *adj* telegraphic; **mandat telegrafic** = telegraphic transfer

telegramă *sf* telegram; *(transmisă prin cablu)* cablegram; **a trimite o telegramă** = to send a telegram *sau* to telegraph; **telegramă prin cablu** = cable; **a transmite o telegramă prin cablu** = to cable

teleimprimatoare *sf* teleprinter

televiziune *sf* **televiziune prin cablu** = cable television

telex *sn* telex; **mesaj prin telex** = a telex

temei *sn* *(motiv)* ground

temporar *adj* **(a) temporar în funcţie** = acting **(b)** *(sezonier)* **post temporar** = casual vacancy; **şomaj temporar** = seasonal unemployment

tendinţă *sf* propensity

tentativă *sf* attempt

teoretic *adj* theoretical; **profit teoretic** = paper profit

teorie *sf* theory; *(pe hârtie)* **în teorie** = in theory *sau* on paper

teren *sn* ground; land; estate; **propietar de teren** = ground landlord

teritorial *adj* territorial; **ape teritoriale** = territorial waters

termen *sn* **(a)** *(perioadă)* term; **termen limită de terminare (a unei lucrări, etc)** = deadline; **a termina o lucrare înainte de termen** = to finish a project ahead of schedule **(b)** **depunere pe termen** = term deposit; **(pe) termen lung** = long-term; **investiţii pe termen lung** = long-term investment; **împrumut pe termen lung** = long-term loan; **(pe) termen scurt** = short-term **(c)** *(condiţie)* terms; **termeni ai contractului de vânzare** = conditions of sale

termina *vb* to complete; **construcţia a fost terminată înainte de sfârşitul anului** = the building was completed before the end of the year; **a termina treaba** = to knock off

terminal *sm* **(a)** *(aerogară)* **terminal aerian** = air terminal; **terminal maritim** = ocean terminal **(b) terminal de calculator** = computer terminal

terminus *sn* terminus; *(cap de linie)* railhead; **punct terminus** = terminal

testa *vb* *(puritatea metalelor preţioase)* to assay

testament *sn* will

textil *adj* textile; **baloturi de materiale textile** = piece goods

tezaur *sn* **(a)** vault *sau* strongroom **(b)** treasury; **bonuri de tezaur** = treasury bonds

Thailanda *sf* Thailand; Notă: capitală: **Bangkok;** monedă: **baht thailandez** = Thai baht

thailandez(ă) *s & adj* Thai

tichet *sn* ticket; **tichet de îmbarcare** = boarding card

timbru *sn* **(a) timbru poştal** = postage stamp; **a aplica timbre pe o trimitere poştală** = to stamp; **a cumpărat trei timbre de £2** = he bought three £2 stamps **(b) timbru fiscal** = stamp duty

timp *sm* time; **timp mort** = idle time

timpuriu *adj* early

tipar *sn* **(a)** pattern; **colecţie de tipare (de croit)** = pattern book **(b)** print

tipări *vb* to print

tipăritură *sf* print

tipografic *adj* **atelier tipografic** = printing works

tipografie *sf* printer; printing works; **manuscrisul era gata pentru a fi trimis la tipografie** = the manuscript was ready to be sent to the printer

titlu *sn* *(acţiune)* share; *(obligaţiune)* bond; **titlu de acţiuni** = share certificate; **titlu de participare** = equity paper; **titlu la purtător** = bearer bond

titluri *snpl* stock *sau* securities; **titluri negociabile** = negotiable paper; **titluri de stat** = consolidated annuities *sau* consols; **titluri (acţiuni) de stat** = government securities; **titluri foarte sigure (emise de stat)** = gilt-edged-securities

titular *sm* *(de post)* holder (of a post)

tocmeală *sf* bargaining; negotiation

tocmi *vb* **a se tocmi** = to bargain; *(exagerat)* to haggle; **a se tocmi la preţ** = to haggle over the price; **cele două părţi s-au tocmit la preţ** = the two parties bargained about the prices

Togo *sm* Togo; Notă: capital **Lomé;** monedă: **franc CFA** = CFA franc

togolez(ă) *s & adj* Togolese

tombolă *sf* raffle

tonaj *sn* tonnage; **tonaj brut** = gross tonnage

tonă *sf* *(1000 kg)* tonne; *(1016.05 kg)* **tona britanică** = long ton *sau* British ton; *(907 kg)* **tonă nordamericană** = short ton

total **1** *sn* *(sumă)* total *sau* amount *sau* sum; **total general** = grand total **2** *adj* total; *(general)* general; **cantitatea totală** *sau* **suma totală** = total amount; **cost total** = total cost; **pierderi totale** = total loss; **3** *adv* completely

totaliza *vb* to amount to *sau* to total

tradiţie *sf* *(lege nescrisă)* common law

traducător *sm* translator

traduce *vb* **(a)** to translate **(b)** to interpret

trafic *sn* **(a)** *(circulaţie)* traffic; **am ajuns târziu din cauza traficului intens de camioane de tonaj pe autostradă** = we arrived late because of the heavy lorry traffic on the motorway **(b) trafic ilegal de mărfuri** = contraband

trafica *vb* to traffic

trage *vb* to haul

tragere *sf* haul

transatlantic *sn* liner

transborda *vb* to transfer

transbordare *sf* transfer; **serviciu de transbordare** = transfer service

transfer *sn* (a) transfer; exchange; **transfer bancar =** (i) bank transfer; (ii) remittance; **transfer electronic (de fonduri) =** electronic transfer; **acord de transfer =** transfer agreement; **plăţi prin transfer =** transfer payments (b) assignment *sau* transfer

transfera *vb* to transfer *sau* to assign; **a rugat să fie transferat în altă secţie =** he asked to be transferred to a different department; **a transfera proprietăţi** *sau* **bunuri =** to transfer *sau* to alienate (property)

transferabil *adj* transferable; alienable

translator *sm* *(interpret)* interpreter

transmite *vb* *(a emite)* to network; **a transmite un program de televiziune tuturor receptoarelor din reţea =** to network a television programme

transport *sn* (a) transport; **transport aerian =** air transport; **transport de mărfuri =** freight *sau* haulage; **transport pe cale ferată =** rail freight *sau* rail transport; **companie de transport =** carrier; **compania de transport este răspunzătoare de securitatea bunurilor transportate =** the carrier is accountable for the safety of the goods transported; **mijloc de transport =** means of transport; **transport în comun** *sau* **public =** public transport; **transport particular =** private transport (b) consignment; **acesta este ultimul transport pe acest trimestru =** this is the last consignment for this quarter (c) carriage *sau* transport (costs); **transport plătit =** carriage paid; **cheltuieli de transport =** transport costs *sau* haulage costs (d) *(circulaţie)* traffic

transporta *vb* to transport *sau* to carry; **a transporta bunuri =** to transport goods *sau* to freight;

camioanele lor transportă bunuri în toată Europa = their lorries haul goods all over Europe

tranzacţie *sf* deal; **tranzacţie comercială =** transaction *sau* deal; **tranzacţie globală =** package deal; **a încheia o tranzacţie =** to make a deal *sau* to set up a deal

tranzit *sn* transit; **în tranzit =** in transit; **bunuri deteriorate în tranzit =** goods damaged in transit; **viză de tranzit =** transit visa

tranziţie *sf* transition

trasa *vb* (a) *(pe hartă)* to chart (b) *(a repartiza)* to assign

trata *vb* to deal with

tratat *sn* *(internaţional)* treaty

trată *sf* bill of exchange

treabă *sf* (a) business; **cu treabă =** on business; **a se apuca de treabă =** to get down to business (b) job

tren *sn* train; **tren de pasageri =** passenger train; **tren de marfă =** freight train *sau* goods train; **a călători cu trenul =** to travel by rail

treptat 1 *adj* gradual; **redresare treptată a economiei =** gradual recovery of the economy 2 *adv* gradually

tribunal *sn* law court

trimestrial 1 *adj* quarterly; **factură trimestrială =** quarterly bill; **plată trimestrială (regulată) =** quarterage; **revistă cu apariţie trimestrială =** quarterly 2 *adv* quarterly

trimestru *sn* quarter; **plătim chiria la sfârşitul fiecărui trimestru =** we pay the rent at the end of each quarter

trimis *sm* delegate

trimite *vb* *(a expedia)* to send; to consign; **a trimite plata prin poştă =** to send payment by post; **a trimite un**

cec pentru o plată = to remit by cheque; **a trimite o scrisoare recomandată cu valoare declarată** = to register a letter

trimitere *sf* dispatch; dispatching; **trimitere poştală cu valoare declarată** = registered post; **trimitere poştală recomandată** = recorded delivery

trişor *sm (escroc)* cheat; **unul din jucătorii de cărţi s-a dovedit a fi trişor** = one of the card players was found to be a cheat

troc *sn* barter

trust *sn* trust; **trust de investiţii** = investment company

trusă *sf* set; **trusă de scule** = set of tools

Tunisia *sf* Tunisia; Notă: capitală: **Tunis;** monedă: **dinar tunisian** = Tunisian dinar

tunisian(ă) *s & adj* Tunisian

tură *sf* shift; **tura de noapte** = night shift; **tură de schimb** = relief shift; **munca în ture** = shift work

turc(ă) **1** *s* Turk **2** *adj* Turkish

turcesc, turcească *adj* Turkish

Turcia *sf* Turkey; Notă: capitală: **Ankara;** monedă: **liră turcească** = Turkish lira

turism *sn* tourism; **agenţie de turism** = tour operator

turist *sn* tourist

turistic *adj* **birou de informaţii turistice** = tourist bureau; **clasă turistică** = tourist class *sau* economy class

tutore *sm* guardian

Țț

țară *sf* nation *sau* state; **țară de origine** = country of origin

țel *sn* aim *sau* goal *sau* end

țesătorie *sf* mill; **țesătorie de bumbac** = cotton mill

ține *vb* **(a)** to hold; **a-și ține cuvântul dat** = to keep one's promise **(b)** to belong

țintă *sf* target

ținti *vb* to aim at *sau* to target

țiței *sn* oil *sau* petroleum; **țiței brut** = crude oil *sau* crude petroleum

Uu

ucenic *sm* trainee; apprentice

ucenicie *sf* training; apprenticeship

Ucrainia *sf* Ukraine; Notă: capitală: **Kiev**; monedă: **karbovanets**

ucrainian(ă) *s & adj* Ukrainian

UE = UNIUNEA EUROPEANA

Uganda *sf* Uganda; Notă: capitală: **Kampala**; monedă: **şiling ugandez** = Ugandan shilling

ugandez(ă) *s & adj* Ugandan

ulaj *sn* ullage

ulei *sn* *(de gătit)* (cooking) oil; **importăm ulei de măsline din Grecia** = we import olive oil from Greece

ultim *adj* final; **ultima rată (de plată)** = final instalment

uncie *sf* *(măsură de greutate egală cu 28 de grame)* ounce

unealtă *sf* implement

ungar(ă) *sau* **maghiar(ă)** *adj* Hungarian

Ungaria *sf* Hungary; Notă: capitală: **Budapesta** = Budapest; monedă: **forint**

ungur *sau* **unguroaică** *sau* **maghiar(ă)** *s* Hungarian

uni *vb* to associate; to combine; to connect; **şi-au unit eforturile ca să scoată afacerea din impas** = they combined their efforts in pulling the business out of trouble

unic *adj* *(exclusiv)* sole; **tranzacţie unică** = one-off deal

unilateral *adj* unilateral; **contract unilateral** = unilateral contract

unire *sf* union

unit *adj* corporate *sau* joint; **Statele Unite ale Americii (SUA)** = United States of America (USA)

unitar *adj* **cost unitar** = unit cost; **preţ unitar** = unit price

unitate *sf* (a) unit; **unitate de măsură** = unit of measure; **unitate monetară** = monetary unit (b) *(secţie)* unit; **unitate comercială** = business unit (c) item

Uniunea Europeană (UE) *sf* European Union (EU)

universal *adj* universal; general; **magazin universal** = general store; **unealtă universală** = general-purpose tool

urgenţă *sf* emergency

urmă *sf* **în urmă** = back; **a rămâne în urmă** = to fall behind; **în cele din urmă** = finally; **în cele din urmă l-am convins să se ralieze proiectului nostru** = we finally convinced him to join our project

Uruguay *sm* Uruguay; Notă: capitală: **Montevideo**; monedă: **peso uruguayan** = Uruguayan peso

uruguayan(ă) *s & adj* Uruguayan

uşor *adj* light; **industria uşoară** = light industry

util *adj* useful

utila *vb* to equip; **atelierul a fost utilat cu un strung nou** = the workshop was equipped with a new lathe

utilaj *sn* equipment; **utilaj greu** = heavy equipment

utiliza *vb* to use *sau* to utilize; **pentru tipărirea broşurilor utilizăm o imprimantă laser** = we use a laser printer for printing brochures

utilizare *sf* use *sau* usage *sau* utilization

utilizator *sm* user

uza *vb* **a (se) uza** = to erode

uzină *sf* factory *sau* plant; **uzină chimică** = chemical plant; **uzină de automobile** = car factory

uzufruct *sn* usufruct

uzufructar *sm* beneficial owner

uzufructuar *sm* user

uzură *sf* (*fizică*) wear and tear; obsolescence; **uzură a utilajelor** = deterioration; **uzură morală a echipamentului, maşinii, etc** = external deterioration *sau* obsolescence; **uzură planificată** = built-in obsolescence

Vv

vacant *adj* vacant; **post vacant** = vacancy; **posturi vacante** = job openings; **a aflat de postul vacant în ziarul local** = she found out about the vacancy in the local newspaper

vacanţă *sf* holiday *sau* vacation

vagon *sn* wagon; **vagon cisternă** = tanker; **vagon de dormit** = sleeping-car

vagonaj *sn* wagonage

valabil *adj* valid; **bilet valabil** = valid ticket; **paşaport valabil** = valid passport; **a fi valabil** = to be valid *sau* to run; **poliţa Dvs de asigurări este valabilă un an de zile** = your insurance policy runs for one year

valid *adj* valid

valida *vb* to validate

valoare *sf* (a) value; **valoare adaugată** = added value; **valoare comercială** = market value; **valoare nominală** = (i) intrinsic value *sau* face value; (ii) denomination; **bani cu valoare nominală redusă** = money in small denominations; **a stabili valoarea nominală a monedei** = to monetize; **valoare de răscumpărare a unei poliţe de asigurări** = cash surrender value; **valoare de scont** = discounted value; **valoare reziduală** = scrap value; **lucruri de valoare** = valuables; **aproape toate lucrurile sale de valoare au fost distruse de incendiu** = most of his valuables were destroyed in the fire; **a pierde din**

valoare = to depreciate; **majoritatea mijloacelor fixe ale companiei şi-au pierdut din valoare** = most of the company's fixed assets have depreciated; **a reduce valoarea mijloacelor fixe** = to write down (b) *(sumă sau total)* amount

valori *sfpl* (a) *(titluri)* securities; **valori de prim ordin (sigure)** *sau* **valori foarte sigure (emise de stat)** = gilt-edged securities (b) paper; **valori acceptate de bănci** = bankable paper

valorificare *sf (a resurselor naturale)* **grad de valorificare** = yield

valorizare *sf* valorization

valoros *adj* valuable; **foarte valoros** = priceless

valutar *adj* **schimb valutar** = foreign exchange

valută *sf* currency *sau* foreign currencies; **valută convertibilă** = hard currency; **valută neconvertibilă** = inconvertible currency *sau* soft currency

vamal *adj* **certificat vamal (de bunuri)** = clearance certificate; **depozit vamal** = bonded warehouse; **formalităţi vamale de expediţie** = customs clearance; **tarife vamale** = customs tariffs; **taxă vamală** = customs duty; **taxă vamală combinată** = compound duty; **taxe vamale preferenţiale** = preferential duty

vamă *sf* customs; **a trece bunuri prin vamă** = to clear goods through customs; **bunuri depozitate în vamă** = goods held in bond

vameş *sm* customs officer

vandabil *adj* saleable

vapor *sn* ship

varia *vb* to vary; to range

variabil *adj* variable; **buget variabil** = variable budget; **costuri variabile** = variable costs; **factor variabil** = variable factor

varietate *sf* variety

vas *sn* ship; **vas comercial** = ship *sau* cargo boat *sau* cargo ship; **proprietar de vase de transport de mărfuri** = ship owner

vărsat *adj* loose; **a vinde zahăr vărsat** = to sell loose sugar

vânzare *sf* (a) sale; **vânzare forţată de împrejurări nefavorabile** = distress sale; **vânzare forţată de o hotărâre judecătorească** = winding-up sale; **vânzare impusă** = forced sale; **vânzare particulară** = private sale; **vânzare pe scală mică** = goods sold over the counter; **vânzare la preţ redus** = sale (at a low price); **de vânzare** = for sale; **act de vânzare** = bill of sale; **personal de vânzări** = sales force; **în vânzare** = on sale; **a oferi o casă spre vânzare** = to put a house up for sale (b) selling; **vânzare directă** = direct selling; **vânzare prin poştă** *sau* **din catalog** = mail-order selling; **vânzare cu ridicata** = wholesale selling; **preţ de vânzare** = selling price (c) sell; **vânzare forţată** *sau* **sub presiune** = hard sell; **vânzări pe piaţa internă** = domestic sales; **vânzări peste hotare** = overseas sales; **impozit pe vânzări** = sales tax; **volum de vânzări** = sales volume

vânzătoare *sf* saleswoman; *(magazin)* saleslady *sau* sales clerk *sau* shop assistant

vânzător *sm* salesman; *(magazin)* sales clerk *sau* shop assistant; *(al unei proprietăţi)* seller; vendor; **vânzător ambulant** = hawker *sau* street vendor; **vânzător de ziare şi reviste** = newsagent

vârf *sn* peak; **perioadă de vârf** = peak period; **în afara orelor de vârf** = off-peak

vecinătate *sf* neighbourhood

vehicul *sn* vehicle; **vehicul de tonaj greu** = heavy goods vehicle (HGV)

Venezuela *sf* Venezuela; Notă: capitală: **Caracas**; monedă: **bolivar venezuelan** = Venezuelan bolivar

venezuelan(ă) *s & adj* Venezuelan

veni *vb* to arrive

venit *sn* income *sau* revenue; **venit anual** = annual income; *(provenit din salariu)* **venit câştigat** = earned income; **venit constant** = regular income; **venit disponibil** = disposable income; **venit fix** = fixed income; **venit mediu** = average revenue; **venit naţional** = national income; **venit net** = net income; **venit pe cap de locuitor** = per capita income; **venit provenit din dobânzi** = unearned income; *(teorie economică)* **efectul venitului** = income effect; **impozit pe venit** = income tax

verbal *adj* verbal; **comandă verbală** = verbal order; **înţelegere verbală** = verbal agreement

verifica *vb* to control; *(a bifa)* to check *sau* to verify; **el a verificat bunurile livrate şi a semnat de primire** = he checked the consignment and signed for the goods delivered; **registrul contabil este verificat lunar** = the books are checked monthly

vertical *adj* vertical; **integrarea verticală a industriei** = vertical integration of industry

vertiginos *adj & adv (despre preţuri)*
a creşte vertiginos = to rocket

veto *sn* veto; **drept de veto** = right of veto

viabil *adj* viable

viabilitate *sf* (a) viability (b) feasibility; **studiu atent al viabilităţii unui produs proiectat** = feasibility study

video-casetă *sf* videocassette; videotape

Vietnam *sm* Vietnam; Notă: capitală: **Hanoi** monedă: **dong** **vietnamez** = Vietnamese dong

vietnamez(ă) *s & adj* Vietnamese

vigoare *sf* **în vigoare** = actual; **a fi în vigoare** = to be in force; **a intra în vigoare** = to come into operation *sau* to become operative *sau* to operate; **noile reguli vor intra în vigoare la începutul anului financiar** = the new rules will operate from the beginning of the financial year; **a pune în vigoare** = to enforce; **punere în vigoare** = enforcement; **a rămâne în vigoare** = to remain in effect

vină *sf* fault; **a recunoscut că era vina lui** = he admitted it was his fault

vinde *vb* to sell; *(a comercializa)* to market; **se vinde la preţul de 4.000 lei bucata** = they sell at 4,000 lei each; **nu vindem articole de papetărie** = we do not handle *sau* sell stationery; **a vinde cu ridicata** *sau* **în vrac** = to sell in bulk; **a vinde în pierdere** = to sell at a loss; **a vinde mai ieftin decât competiţia** = to undersell; **a vinde mai mult decât competiţia** = to outsell; **a vinde sub valoarea reală** = to undersell; **acest model de** automobil japonez se vinde numai în America = this Japanese make of car is being marketed only in America; **articol care se vinde bine** = good seller; **articol care se vinde foarte bine** = best-seller *sau* money-spinner; **acest articol nu se vinde prea bine** = this item does not sell well; **articole care nu se vând** = unsold items; **arta de a vinde** = salesmanship

vinovat *adj* guilty; **tribunalul l-a găsit vinovat de falsificare de bancnote** = the court found him guilty of forging banknotes

violare *sf* breach; infringement

viza *vb* to target; **a viza o anume piaţă de desfacere** = to target a market

viză *sf* visa; **viză de intrare** = entry visa; **viză turistică** = tourist visa; **formular de viză** = visa application form

vizibil *adj* visible; **importuri vizibile** = visible imports

vizitator *sm* caller

vocaţie *sf* calling

voiaj *sn* travel; **agenţie de voiaj** = travel agency

voiajor *adj* **comis voiajor** = sales rep *sau* commercial traveller

volum *sn* capacity

vot *sn* vote; **vot de încredere** = vote of confidence; **a obţine voturi** = to poll; **a obţinut 500 de voturi** = he polled 500 votes

vota *vb* to vote; to poll

votant *sm* voter

Zz

Zair *sm* Zaire; Notă: capitală: **Kinshasa;** monedă: **zair =** zaïre

zairez(ă) *s & adj* Zairean

Zambia *sf* Zambia; Notă: capitală: **Lusaka;** monedă: **kwacha zambian =** Zambian kwacha

zambian(ă) *s & adj* Zambian

zbor *sn* flight *sau* long-haul flight; **zbor regulat =** scheduled flight; **zborul RO 393 de la Bucureşti va ateriza pe aeroportul Stansted în 15 minute =** flight RO 393 from Bucharest will land at Stansted airport in 15 minutes

zero *sn* *(cifra)* zero *sau* nought; *(nimic)* nil

zi *sf* date; **la zi =** up to date; **a aduce la zi =** to post up

ziar *sn* newspaper; **ziar cotidian =** daily paper; **ziar cotidian de seară =** evening paper

zilnic 1 *adj* daily 2 *adv* daily

zonă *sf* **zonă (pietonală) comercială =** shopping precinct; **zonă industrială =** industrial estate

English-Romanian

Englez-Român

Aa

abandon *verb* **(a)** *(leave)* a abandona *or* a părăsi **(b)** *(give up)* a renunţa; **he abandoned the idea of investing in another business** = a renunţat la ideea de a investi într-o altă afacere

abandonment *noun* abandonare *f;* renunţarea la proprietate în favoarea altei părţi; **abandonment of goods in customs** = abandonarea mărfurilor în vamă

abatement *noun* reducere *f or* diminuare *f;* **tax abatement** = reducere a impozitului

ability-to-pay principle *noun* principiul *n* impozitării după posibilităţile contribuabilor

abroad **1** *adjective* din străinătate **2** *adverb* în străinătate *or* peste tot

absent *adjective* absent (de la locul de muncă sau o întrunire); **we could not start the meeting as the chairman was absent** = nu am putut începe şedinţa pentru că preşedintele era absent

absentee *noun* persoană *f* care absentează (nemotivat)

absenteeism *noun* absenteism *n* (termen denumind totalitatea absenţelor nemotivate)

absolute monopoly *noun* monopol *n* absolut (situaţia teoretică în care un singur producător controlează în totalitate piaţa de desfacere)

absorption *noun* absorbţie *f*

accept *verb* **(a)** a accepta *or* a fi de acord; **to accept the conditions of a contract** = a accepta (şi respecta) condiţiile unui contract **(b)** *(regard favourably)* a consimţi

acceptance *noun* acceptare *f;* **bank acceptance** = acceptare bancară; **partial acceptance** = acceptare parţială

acceptor *noun* persoană *f* care acceptă o factură sau notă de plată asumându-şi responsabilitatea de a plăti

access *noun* intrare *f or* cale *f* de acces; **access to a market** = dreptul *n* şi, sau abilitatea *f* de a desface legal produse pe piaţă

accession to estate *noun* preluarea *f* unei proprietăţi ca urmare a actului de vânzare-cumpărare sau de succesiune

accommodation *noun* **(a)** cazare *f* **(b)** *(lodgings)* locuinţă *f* **(c)** *(compromise)* compromis *n;* **to reach an accommodation with creditors** = a ajunge la un compromis cu creditorii

accompany *verb* **(a)** a însoţi *or* a acompania; **the businessman was accompanied by his secretary** = omul de afaceri era însoţit de secretara sa **(b)** *(escort)* a escorta

accomplish *verb* **(a)** a îndeplini *or* a realiza **(b)** *(fulfil)* a desăvârşi

account *noun* **(a)** cont *n;* **bank account** = cont bancar; **current account** = cont curent; **deposit account** = cont de depozit; **expense account** = cont curent de cheltuieli; **profit and loss account** =

contul de profit şi pierderi; **savings account** = cont de economii; **to settle an account** or **to pay an account** = a plăti o datorie **(b)** *(balance sheet)* socoteală *f* or bilanţ *n;* **accounts department** = contabilitate *f;* **accounts manager** = contabil-şef *m;* **accounts payable** = bani *mpl* datoraţi de o firmă *or* de plătit; **accounts receivable** = bani datoraţi unei firme *or* de primit

accountancy *noun* contabilitate *f*

accountant *noun* contabil *m*

accounting *noun* contabilitate *f;* **accounting period** = exerciţiu *n* financiar; **accounting system** = sistem *n* contabil (manual sau computerizat)

accounts clerk *noun* funcţionar *m* comercial

accrual *noun* creştere *f* (continuă) *or* mărire *f* a profitului şi, sau a cifrei de afaceri

accumulate *verb* **(a)** a (se) acumula **(b)** *(grow substantially)* a creşte *or* a spori

accurate *adjective* precis *or* exact

acknowledge *verb* **(a)** *(confirm the receipt of goods)* a confirma (primirea bunurilor, plăţii, etc.) **(b)** *(admit)* a recunoaşte *or* a admite

acknowledgement *noun* **(a)** recunoaştere *f* **(b)** *(confirmation)* confirmare *f;* **letter of acknowledgement** = scrisoare *f* de confirmare (de primire, etc.)

acquire *verb* a cumpăra *or* a achiziţiona; **the property was acquired by an unknown buyer** = proprietatea a fost achiziţionată de un cumpărător anonim

acquisition *noun* **(a)** *(something acquired)* achiziţie *f* **(b)** *(the fact of acquiring)* achiziţionare *f or* faptul *n* de a cumpăra ceva util

acquit *verb* **(a)** *(pay a debt)* a (se) achita de o datorie **(b)** *(discharge)* a ierta (o datorie)

acre *noun* pogon *n* (ă măsură de suprafaţă anglo-saxonă egală cu 0,405 hectare)

act **1** *verb* **(a)** *(do something)* a acţiona **(b)** *(work)* a funcţiona (ca interpret, etc.) **2** *noun* **(a)** *(deed)* faptă *f* **(b)** *(bill* or *document)* act *n or* document *n* legal

acting *adjective* temporar în funcţie *or* provizoriu; **the acting chairman is carrying out the duties of chairman until a new person is elected** = preşedintele interim îndeplineşte funcţiile preşedintelui până o altă persoană este aleasă

act in law *noun* întocmirea unui act oficial (contract *or* testament, etc.)

action *noun* **(a)** *(action)* acţiune *f* or faptă *f* **(b)** proces *n* civil *or* proces penal *or* acţiune legală; **to bring an action against someone** = a intenta proces cuiva

active *adjective* **(a)** *(diligent)* activ *or* ocupat **(b)** *(working)* operativ *or* care funcţionează **(c)** participant; **active partner** = partener *m* care lucrează efectiv în companie; **active balance** = balanţă activă (de comerţ *or* de plăţi, etc.); **active money** = bani activi *or* folosiţi în vânzări-cumpărări, care aduc profit

actual *adjective* **(a)** actual *or* în vigoare **(b)** real; **actual price** = preţ real **(c)** *(existing now)* curent

actuary *noun* statistician *m or* expert *m* în calcularea riscurilor financiare

adapt *verb* **(a)** a (se) adapta **(b)** *(adjust)* a (se) potrivi **(c)** *(alter)* a (se) modifica

add *verb* **(a)** a aduna; **to add up** = a aduna (o coloană de cifre, etc.) **(b) to add to** = a spori

added value *noun* valoare *f* adaugată

addition *noun* **(a)** *(person or thing added)* adăugare *f or* adaos *n* **(b)** sumă *f or* adunare *f;* **in addition to** = pe lângă; în plus

address 1 *noun* **(a)** adresă *f or* locaţie *f* **(b)** *(speech)* alocuţiune *f or* cuvânt *n* 2 *verb (write or speak to)* a (se) adresa (unui grup, etc.)

addressee *noun* destinatar *m*

adjudicate *verb (in a dispute)* a arbitra

adjudication order *noun* ordin *n* (judecătoresc) de declarare a falimentului

adjuster *noun* revizor *m* contabil (asigurări)

administer *verb* a administra; **administered price** = preţ *n* fixat de producător

administration *noun* **(a)** *(management)* administraţie *f* **(b)** administrare *f;* **property administration** = administrarea proprietăţilor *or* mijloacelor fixe

administrative *adjective* administrativ

administrator *noun* administrator *m*

admission *noun* **(a)** intrare *f;* **admission fee** = preţul biletului de intrare **(b)** *(acknowledgement)* admitere *f or* recunoaştere *f*

admit *verb* **(a)** a admite **(b)** *(allow)* a permite **(c)** a recunoaşte; **the accountant admitted he had been dishonest** = contabilul şi-a recunoscut necinstea

adopt *verb* **(a)** a adopta; **the board of directors adopted the new proposal** = consiliul directorilor a adoptat noua propunere **(b)** *(a child)* a înfia

advance 1 *verb* **(a)** a avansa *or* a înainta **(b)** *(make progress)* a progresa **(c)** *(pay before it is due)* a plăti în avans **(d)** *(lend money)* a împrumuta bani 2 *noun* avans *n;* **in advance** = în avans 3 *adjective* anticipat *or* în avans; **advance payment** = plată anticipată *or* în avans

advancement *noun* avansare *f or* promovare *f*

advantage *noun* **(a)** avantaj *n or* circumstanţă *f* favorabilă **(b)** *(profit)* beneficiu *n or* profit *n*

adverse *adjective* **(a)** advers **(b)** contrar *or* ostil **(c)** negativ; **adverse balance (of payments)** = balanţă (de plăţi) negativă

advertise *verb* **(a)** a face reclamă **(b)** *(an official statement)* a anunţa *or* a informa **(c)** *(in a newspaper)* a insera anunţuri

advertisement *noun* **(a)** anunţ *n* public **(b)** reclamă *f*

advertising 1 *noun* publicitate *f or* reclamă *f* 2 *adjective* de publicitate; **advertising agency** = agenţie de publicitate; **advertising budget** = buget alocat pentru publicitate

advice *noun* notificare *f* oficială în tranzacţii comerciale; **advice note** = aviz de expediţie; **advice of delivery** = aviz de primire; **debit advice** = aviz de debit

advise *verb* **(a)** a sfătui **(b)** *(recommend)* a recomanda **(c)** *(notify)* a informa *or* a notifica

adviser *noun* **(a)** consilier *m* **(b)** **legal adviser** = jurist *m* **(c)** *US* consultant *m*

affair *noun* **(a)** afacere *f* **(b)** *(concern)* grijă *f*

affect *verb* a afecta; **the tax increase will not affect our company** = majorarea impozitelor nu va afecta compania noastră

affiliate *verb* a (se) ataşa *or* a (se) afilia; **affiliated company** = companie afiliată

affirm *verb* **(a)** a afirma **(b)** *(announce)* a declara

affirmation *noun* **(a)** afirmaţie *f* **(b)** *(statement)* declaraţie *f*

affluence *noun* bogăție *f or* belșug *n*

affluent *adjective* bogat

afford *verb* **(a)** a oferi **(b)** a-și permite; **we cannot afford further cuts in prices** = nu ne putem permite alte reduceri de preț

affront *noun* insultă *f or* jignire *f*

Afghan *noun & adjective* afgan(ă)

Afghanistan *noun* Afganistan *m* NOTE: capital: **Kabul;** currency: **afghani** = afgan *m*

afloat *adverb* *(of a business)* fără datorii; **to keep a company afloat** = a menține o afacere în profit

after-hours trading *noun* operațiuni *fpl* de bursă după ora oficială de închidere

after-sales service *noun* service post-vânzare *or* service în garanție

after-tax profit *noun* profit *n* net

aftermath *noun* consecințe *fpl or* efect *n*

against *adverb* **(a)** împotriva *or* contra **(b)** lângă

agency *noun* **(a)** agenție *f;* **employment agency** = agenție de plasare; **travel agency** = agenție de voiaj *or* agenție turistică **(b)** intermediar *m*

agenda *noun* **(a)** *(list of issues to be considered at a meeting)* ordine *f* de zi **(b)** listă *f* de lucru

agent *noun* **(a)** agent *m;* **employment agent** = agent de plasare; **estate agent** = agent imobiliar; **insurance agent** = agent de asigurări **(b)** *(force or effect)* factor *m*

agree *verb* **(a)** a fi de acord; **the two companies agreed on the safety issue** = cele două companii au căzut de acord privitor la capitolul siguranță; **agreed price** = preț convenit **(b)** *(be in harmony)* a se înțelege

agreement *noun* **(a)** înțelegere *f* **(b)** acord *n or* aranjament *n;* **clearing agreement** = acord de clearing; **rescheduling agreement** = acord de reeșalonare a datoriilor; **transfer agreement** = acord de transfer **(c)** contract *m* în scris sau verbal; **loan agreement** = contract de împrumut; **tenancy agreement** = contract de închiriere

agriculture *noun* agricultură *f*

ahead *adverb* **(a)** înainte; **the new production line became operational ahead of schedule** = noua linie de asamblare a fost dată în exploatare înainte de termen **(b)** mai devreme

aid 1 *noun (financial)* ajutor *n* financiar 2 *verb* a ajuta

aim 1 *verb* **(a)** a ținti **(b)** *(seek to achieve)* a năzui 2 *noun* țel *n or* scop *n;* **his aim is to make more money** = scopul său este să câștige cât mai mulți bani

air-conditioned *adjective* (echipat) cu aer condiționat

air freight *noun* transport *n* de mărfuri pe calea aerului

airfreight *verb* a expedia pe calea aerului

airline *noun* linie *f* aeriană; companie *f* de transport aerian

airmail 1 *noun* par avion; **the package sent by airmail reached its destination in only four days** = coletul trimis par avion a ajuns la destinație în numai patru zile 2 *verb* a expedia par avion

airport *noun* aeroport *n;* **we will land at Bucharest-Otopeni Airport at 1.55 pm** = vom ateriza la aeroportul București-Otopeni la ora 1.55

airtight *adjective* etanș *or* ermetic

Albania *noun* Albania *f* NOTE: capital: **Tirana;** currency: **Albanian lek** = lek *m* albanez

Albanian *noun & adjective* albanez(ă)

Algeria *noun* Algeria *f* NOTE: capital: **Algiers** = Alger; currency: **Algerian dinar** = dinar *m* algerian

Algerian *noun & adjective* algerian(ă)

alienable *adjective* transferabil

alienate *verb* **(a)** a transfera proprietăţi *or* bunuri **(b)** a înstrăina

all-in price *noun* preţ *n* inclusiv; **all-in rate** = preţ cu amănuntul *or* tarif inclusiv

allocate *verb* **(a)** a aloca; **to allocate funds for research** = a aloca fonduri pentru cercetare **(b)** a repartiza

allocation *noun* alocaţie *f*

allotment *noun* alocare *f*; **share allotment** = alocare de acţiuni

allout strike *noun* grevă *f* generală

allow *verb* **(a)** a permite **(b)** a păsui; **to allow a debtor more time to pay** = a acorda unui debitor răgaz de a plăti

allowance *noun* **(a)** alocaţie *f* **(b)** pensie *f*; **disability allowance** = pensie de invaliditate

alphabetical order *noun* ordine *f* alfabetică

alter *verb* a (se) schimba *or* a (se) modifica

alternate *verb* a alterna

alternative **1** *adjective* alternativ **2** *noun* alternativă *f*

ambassador *noun* ambasador *m*

amend *verb* **(a)** *(a law)* a amenda (o lege) **(b)** a corecta *or* a îndrepta

America *noun* **United States of America (USA)** = Statele Unite ale Americii (SUA)

American *noun & adjective* american(ă); **American dollar** = dolar american

amortize *verb* **(a)** a amortiza; **the investment cost is to be amortized over 10 years** = costul investiţiei ar trebui amortizat în 10 ani **(b)** a achita un împrumut

amount **1** *noun* valoare *f*; sumă *f or* total *n* **2** *verb* **to amount to** = a se ridica la *or* a totaliza

analyse *verb* a analiza *or* a examina; **to analyse an account** = a analiza un cont

analysis *noun* **(a)** analiză *f* **(b)** rezultatul *n* unei analize; **comparative analysis** = analiză comparativă; **dynamic analysis** = analiză dinamică; **static analysis** = analiză statică

analyst *noun* analist *m*

anchorage *noun* **(a)** ancorare *f or* ancoraj *n* **(b)** port *n*; **anchorage charges** = taxe portuare

Andorra *noun* Andora *f* NOTE: capital: **Andorra la Vella**; currencies: **French franc** = franc *m* francez, **Spanish peseta** = peseta *f* spaniolă

Andorran *noun & adjective* andoran(ă)

Angola *noun* Angola *f* NOTE: capital: **Luanda**; currency: **kwanza**

Angolan *noun & adjective* angolan(ă)

annual *adjective* anual; **annual accounts** = revizie contabilă anuală; **annual cost** = cost anual; **annual general meeting (AGM)** = adunare generală anuală; **annual report** = raport anual

annul *verb* a anula; **the contract was annulled by both parties** = contractul a fost anulat de ambele părţi

annuity *noun* rentă *f*

answer *noun* răspuns *n*

anticipate *verb* **(a)** a anticipa *or* a se aştepta; **we anticipated a delay of two weeks in delivering the order** = ne aşteptam la o întârziere de două săptămâni pentru livrarea comenzii; **anticipated profit** = profit anticipat **(b)** a preveni

antidumping laws *noun* legi *fpl* antidumping

antiinflation measures *noun* acţiuni *fpl* de contracarare a inflaţiei

appeal 1 *noun* **(a)** *(legal)* apel *n or* recurs *n;* **to make an appeal** = a face apel **(b)** *(request)* cerere *f or* rugăminte *f* 2 *verb* **(a) to appeal against a decision** = a face recurs *or* a contesta o decizie **(b)** a se ruga de cineva

applicant *noun* solicitant *m or* petiţionar *m*

application *noun* cerere *f* în scris; solicitare *f;* **you have to make an application to the bank in order to get a loan** = ca să obţineţi un împrumut, trebuie să faceţi cerere la bancă; **application form** = formular *n* de cerere

applied *adjective* aplicat; **applied economics** = economie *f* aplicată

apply *verb* **(a)** a face cerere; **he applied for a loan but was refused** = a făcut cerere de împrumut dar a fost refuzată **(b)** *(ask for)* a solicita; **to apply for help** = a solicita ajutor **(c)** a aplica; **to apply a rule** = a aplica o regulă **(d)** *(affect)* a se referi

appoint *verb* **(a)** a numi *or* a desemna (într-o funcţie *or* post) **(b)** *(prescribe)* a prescrie **(c)** *(decide on)* a decide

appointment *noun* **(a)** *(arrangement to meet at a specifc time and place)* locul *n* şi ora *f* stabilite pentru o consultaţie *or* un interviu, etc. **(b)** *(vacancy)* post *n* vacant **(c)** *(to a job)* numire *f* în post **(d)** *(meeting)* întâlnire *f* (de afaceri)

appraise *verb* **(a)** a aprecia **(b)** *(value)* a evalua

appraiser *noun* specialist *m* în evaluări *or* evaluator *m*

appreciate *verb* **(a)** a aprecia; **customers always appreciate getting a good discount** = clienţii apreciază rabatul comercial întotdeauna **(b)** a recunoaşte; **his efforts were appreciated** = strǎduinţele sale erau recunoscute

apprentice *noun* **(a)** ucenic *m* **(b)** începător *m or* novice *m*

apprenticeship *noun* ucenicie *f*

approve *verb* a aproba

approval *noun* aprobare *f;* **tacit approval** = aprobare tacită

area *noun* sector *n;* **area manager** = şef *m* de sector

Argentina *noun* Argentina *f* NOTE: capital: **Buenos Aires**; currency: **Argentinian peso** = peso argentinian

Argentinian *noun & adjective* argentinian(ă)

arrears *noun* restanţe *fpl;* **to be in arrears** = a fi restanţier, în urmă cu plata (ratelor); **to pay off arrears of debt** = a plăti restanţele

arrival *noun* **(a)** sosire *f* **(b)** destinaţie *f;* **arrival station** = staţie *f* de destinaţie **(c)** nou venit *m*

arrive *verb* **(a)** a sosi *or* a ajunge la destinaţie **(b)** a veni

article *noun* **(a)** articol *n* **(b)** *(item of clothing)* obiect *n* (de îmbrăcăminte, etc.)

ask *verb* **(a)** a întreba **(b)** a cere *or* a ruga; **ask him to fetch the latest report** = roagă-l să aducă ultimul raport; **asking price** = curs cerut **(c)** *(ask for)* a solicita **(d)** a pofti *or* a invita; **to ask somebody to a party** = a invita pe cineva la o petrecere

assay *verb* a testa puritatea metalelor preţioase

assemble *verb* **(a)** a aduna **(b)** a asambla

assembly *noun* **(a)** *(gathering)* adunare *f* **(b)** miting *n* **(c)** asamblare *f or* montaj *n;* **assembly line** = linie de montaj

assent 1 *noun* încuviinţare *f* 2 *verb* a încuviinţa

assess *verb* a judeca *or* a evalua; a stabili; **to assess the value of a property** = a evalua valoarea unei proprietăţi

asset *noun* **(a)** proprietate *f or* fonduri *n;* **capital assets** = mijloace *npl* fixe; **current assets** = activ *n* curent; **net assets** = active *npl* nete **(b)** *(wealth)* posesiuni *or* avere

assign *verb* **(a)** *(to give a job)* a repartiza; a trasa (sarcini, etc.) **(b)** *(allot)* a încredinţa **(c)** *(transfer formally)* a transfera

assignee *noun* cesionar *m*

assignment *noun* **(a)** *(allotment)* repartizare *f* **(b)** *(task)* sarcină *f or* datorie *f* **(c)** cesiune *f* **(d)** *(legal transfer)* transfer *n*

assist *verb* **(a)** a ajuta **(b)** *(be present or take part)* a participa

assistant *noun* **(a)** *(helper)* ajutor *n* **(b)** *(subordinate)* asistent *m*

associate 1 *noun* asociat *m or* partener *m;* **asocciate company** = companie afiliată 2 *verb* **(a)** a asocia *or* a uni **(b)** *(become partner)* a deveni asociat

association *noun* asociaţie *f or* grup *n*

assurance *noun* asigurare *f;* **assurance company** = companie de asigurări

assure *verb* **(a)** a (se) asigura **(b)** *(convince)* a convinge (prin cuvinte)

attach *verb* a ataşa *or* a anexa; **he attached photocopies of the documents** = a anexat fotocópii ale documentelor

attaché *noun* ataşat *m;* **commercial attaché** = ataşat comercial

attempt 1 *verb* a încerca 2 *noun* încercare *f;* tentativă *f;* **his attempt to open a bookshop ended in failure** = încercarea sa de a deschide o librărie a eşuat

attest *verb* *(certify the validity of)* a certifica; a autentifica

attested copy *noun* copie *f* legalizată

attorney *noun* **(a)** agent *m or* împuternicit *m;* **power of attorney** = împuternicire *f* **(b)** *US* avocat *m*

auction 1 *noun* licitaţie *f* 2 *verb* a vinde la licitaţie

audit 1 *noun* revizie *f* (contabilă) 2 *verb* a efectua o revizie contabilă

auditor *noun* revizor *m* contabil

austerity *noun* austeritate *f;* **austerity budget** = buget *n* de austeritate

Australia *noun* Australia *f* NOTE: capital: **Canberra;** currency: **Australian dollar** = dolar australian

Australian *noun* & *adjective* australian(ă)

Austria *noun* Austria *f* NOTE: capital: **Vienna** = Viena; currency: **Austrian schilling** = şiling austriac

Austrian *noun* & *adjective* austriac(ă)

authentic *adjective* **(a)** autentic **(b)** original

authenticate *verb* **(a)** a autentifica *or* a legaliza **(b)** a dovedi

authority *noun* autoritate *f*

authorize *verb* **(a)** a autoriza **(b)** a permite **(c)** a sancţiona

autocrat *noun* conducător *m* absolut

autofinancing *noun* autofinanţare *f*

automate *verb* a automatiza

automatic *adjective* **(a)** automatic **(b)** mecanic **(c)** inevitabil; **automatic disqualification** = descalificare inevitabilă

automation *noun* automatizare *f*

available *adjective* disponibil; **the invoices are not available for checking** = facturile nu sunt disponibile pentru verificare

average 1 *noun* medie *f* 2 *adjective* **(a)** normal *or* ordinar **(b)** mediu; **average**

cost = cost mediu; **average price** = preț mediu; **average stock** = stoc mediu **3** *verb* a face media

avoid *verb* **(a)** a evita; **he tries to avoid buying expensive equipment** = el încearcă să evite cumpărarea de echipament costisitor **(b)** *(quash)* a casa (o sentință)

avoirdupois *noun* sistem *n* anglo-saxon de măsurare a greutății

award **1** *noun* **(a)** premiu *n* **(b)** *(judicial decision)* hotărâre *f* judecătorească **2** *verb* **(a)** *(give as a prize)* a acorda (un premiu, etc.) **(b) to award damages** = a acorda despăgubiri

away *adverb* departe; **he is away from the office at the moment** = el nu este în birou acum

axe **1** *noun* topor *n;* **500 jobs got the axe** = 500 de persoane și-au pierdut slujba **2** *verb* a concedia

Bb

back 1 *noun* verso; **the clauses of the contract were printed on the back of the document** = clauzele contractului se aflau pe verso 2 *adverb* **(a)** în spate *or* în urmă; **back and forth** = înainte şi înapoi **(b)** înapoi; **to pay back** = a plăti înapoi *or* a achita; **the loan must be paid back within 24 months** = împrumutul trebuie achitat în 2 ani 3 *verb* **(a)** a promova *or* a spijini; **the plan is backed by the senior shareholders** = planul e sprijinit de acţionarii importanţi **(b) to back off** = a se retrage *or* a da înapoi 4 *adjective* **back seat** = poziţie inferioară *or* înjositoare

backdate *verb* **(a)** a antedata **(b)** a valida retrospectiv

back duty *noun* impozit *n* retroactiv

backer *noun* sponsor *m*

background *noun* **(a)** pregătire *f* profesională *or* experienţă *f*; **his background in the microelectronics industry allowed him to get a well paid job** = datorită experienţei sale în microelectronică el a dobândit un post bine plătit **(b)** mediu *n or* cadru *n* (economic *or* social)

backing *noun* suport *n or* ajutor *n* (financiar); **currency backing** = subvenţionarea *f* monedei naţionale

backlog *noun* restanţe *fpl or* rămâneri *fpl* în urmă (cu lucrul)

backward 1 *adjective* înapoiat *or* subdezvoltat; **backward economy** = economie subdezvoltată 2 *adverb* (also **backwards**) înapoi

bad debt *noun* datorie *f* care nu va fi achitată

bag *noun* pungă *f or* plasă *f*; **shopping bag** = plasă de cumpărături

baggage *noun* bagaj *n*

Bahamas, The *noun* Insulele Bahamas *fpl* NOTE: capital: **Nassau;** currency: **Bahamian dollar** = dolar *m* bahamez

Bahamian *noun & adjective* bahamez(ă)

bail 1 *noun* cauţiune *f* 2 *verb* a elibera pe cauţiune

bailiff *noun* **(a)** *(officer of a court)* portărel *m* **(b)** *(agent of a landlord)* arendaş *m* (în Marea Britanie)

balance 1 *noun* **(a)** balanţă *f*; **balance of payments** = balanţă de plăţi **(b) balance sheet** = bilanţ *n*; **balance sheet analysis** = analiza *f* bilanţului **(c)** sold *n*; **bank balance** = sold bancar; **cash balance** = sold de casă **(d)** *(device for weighing)* cântar *n* 2 *verb* a echilibra; **balanced growth** = creştere *f* echilibrată

ban 1 *noun* interdicţie *f or* interezicere *f*; **ban on smoking** = interzicere a fumatului 2 *verb* a interzice; **the manager banned smoking in offices** = directorul a interzis fumatul în birouri

Banca d'Italia Banca Naţională Italiană *f*

Bangladesh *noun* Bangladeş NOTE: capital: **Dhaka** = Dacca; currency: **taka**

Bangladeshi *adjective & noun* bangladeş(ă)

bank 1 *noun* (a) bancă *f or* instituţie *f* financiară; **bank account** = cont *n* bancar; **bank base rate** = rate *fpl* de bază ale dobânzilor bancare; **bank book** = carnet *n* de depuneri; **bank charges** = costuri *fpl* bancare; **bank manager** = director *m* de bancă; **bank reserves** = rezerve *fpl* bancare; **High Street bank** = bancă comercială; **Romanian Foreign Trade Bank** = Banca Română de Comerţ Exterior; **savings bank** = casă *f* de economii (b) **piggy bank** = puşculiţă *f* (c) **data bank** = bancă de date 2 *verb* (a) a depune *or* a depozita bunuri sau bani la bancă (b) a ţine banii în bancă *or* a avea cont în bancă; **he banks with Barclays (Bank)** = are un cont la banca Barclays

bankable *adjective* (a) acceptat de bancă; **bankable paper** = valori acceptate de bănci (b) demn de încredere

banker *noun* bancher *m*

bank holiday *noun* sărbătoare *f* legală

banking *noun* (a) operaţii *fpl* bancare (b) finanţe *fpl*

banknote *noun* bancnotă *f;* **the banknotes proved to be forged** = bancnotele s-au dovedit a fi false

Bank of England Banca Angliei *f*

bankrupt 1 *noun* falit *m* 2 *adjective* falit *or* care a dat faliment; **he was declared bankrupt** = el a fost declarat falit

bankruptcy *noun* faliment *n*

Banque de France Banca Franceză *f*

bar 1 *noun* (a) bar *n;* **after the meeting they went to the hotel bar** = după şedinţă s-au dus la barul hotelului (b) coloană *f* (de grafic) 2 *verb* (a) a opri (b) a bara *or* a interzice

bargain 1 *noun* (a) tocmeală *f* (b) învoială *f or* acord *n* (c) chilipir *n;* afacere *f* favorabilă; **bargain price** = preţ *n* redus; **to strike a bargain** = a cumpăra ieftin; a încheia o afacere avantajoasă (d) tranzacţie *f* 2 *verb* (a) a se tocmi; **the two parties bargained about the prices** = cele două părţi sau tocmit la preţ (b) a se învoi (asupra unui târg)

bargain for *verb* a se aştepta la

bargain on *verb* a se baza pe *or* a se bizui pe

barge *noun* şlep *n or* şalandă *f*

barrel *noun* (a) *(cylindrical container)* butoi *n* (b) *(measure of capacity)* baril *m;* **the owners of the restaurant imported 10 barrels of red wine from Romania** = patronii restaurantului au importat 10 barili de vin din România

barrier *noun* (a) barieră *n* (b) obstacol *n;* **trade barriers** = obstacole în calea comerţului

barrister *noun* avocat *m*

barter *noun* troc *n;* comerţ *n* de schimb

base 1 *noun* bază *f* 2 *adjective* ieftin *or* fără valoare; **base metals** = metale nepreţioase 3 *verb* a (se) baza; **his marketing ideas were based on speculation** = ideile sale de marketing se bazau pe speculaţii

BASIC (= Beginner's All-purpose Symbolic Instructions Code) BASIC, limbaj simplu de programare a calculatoarelor

basic *adjective* (a) fundamental (b) esenţial (c) simplu *or* de bază; **basic pay** = salariu *n* de bază (d) **basic needs** = nevoi *fpl* minime (de subzistenţă)

basket *noun* coş *n;* **shopping basket** = coş de cumpărături

bear 1 *verb* **(a)** a purta; **the document bears his signature** = documentul poartă semnătura sa **(b)** a suporta; **the lorry will not bear this load** = camionul nu va suporta această sarcină **(c)** a specula la bursă **(d)** a genera o reducere a prețurilor (la bursă) 2 *noun* baissier

bearer *noun* **(a)** purtător *m;* **the goods were handed to the bearer of the letter** = bunurile au fost înmânate purtătorului scrisorii; **cheque to bearer** *or* **bearer cheque** = cec *n* la purtător **(b)** cărăuș *m*

beat *verb* **(a)** a întrece; **they were beaten again in the toys market** = au fost întrecuți din nou pe piața jucăriilor **(b) to beat down a price** = a negocia un preț

beforehand *adverb* în avans *or* anticipat

Belgian *noun & adjective* belgian (ă)

Belgium *noun* Belgia *f* NOTE: capital: **Brussels** = Bruxelles; currency: **Belgian franc** = franc *m* belgian

believe *verb* **(a)** a crede *or* a gândi; **he believes he was rushed into signing the contract** = el crede că a fost forțat să semneze contractul **(b)** a presupune

belong *verb* **(a)** a aparține; **this property belongs to the state** = aceasta este proprietatea statului **(b)** a ține

beneficial owner *noun* deținător *m* de drept (al unei proprietăți); uzufructar *m*

benefit 1 *noun* **(a)** beneficiu *n* **(b)** favoare *f;* **the interest rates were to his benefit** = rata dobânzilor era în favoarea lui **(c)** ajutor *n* (de stat); **sickness benefit** = indemnizație *f* de concediu medical; **unemployment benefit** = ajutor de șomaj 2 *verb* a beneficia; **everyone on low incomes will benefit from the new measures** = toată lumea cu un venit mic va beneficia de pe urma noilor măsuri

bequeath *verb* a lăsa moștenire

bequest *noun* moștenire *f*

bespoke *adjective* de comandă

best seller *noun* articol care se vinde foarte bine

bet 1 *verb* a paria; **she bet £15 on her favourite horse** = a pariat £15 pe calul ei preferat 2 *noun* pariu *n*

bid 1 *verb* **(a)** a licita; **he bid against the car dealer** = a licitat împotriva proprietarului de garaj **(b)** a oferi 2 *noun* *(offer to buy)* ofertă *f*

bidder *noun* ofertant *m*

bill 1 *noun* **(a)** *(written statement for goods supplied)* notă *f* de plată **(b)** poliță *f* **(c)** *(a draft of a proposed law)* proiect *n* de lege **(d)** certificat *n;* **bill of health** = certificat de sănătate **(e)** act *n;* **bill of sale** = act de vânzare **(f) bill of exchange** = cambie *f* *or* trată *f* 2 *verb* a trimite o notă de plată *or* a factura

billion *noun* miliard *n*

billionaire *noun* miliardar *m*

birth rate *noun* natalitate *f*

black 1 *adjective* **(a)** negru *or* neagră **(b) black list** = listă neagră **(c) black market** = bursa neagră 2 *verb* a boicota un produs

blackleg *noun* spărgător *m* de grevă

blacklist *verb* a boicota un produs

blackmail 1 *noun* șantaj *n* 2 *verb* a șantaja

black money *noun* bani *mpl* obținuți din afaceri dubioase sau ilegale

blank 1 *adjective* **(a)** necompletat **(b)** în alb; **blank cheque** = cec în alb 2 *noun* *(space to be filled in a form)* spațiu *n* gol (într-un formular)

blanket policy *noun* poliță *f* de asigurări multiplă

bloc *noun* **(a)** bloc *n* *or* grup *n* de țări cu interese comune **(b)** *(group of* *people)* grup de persoane cu interese comune

block 1 *noun* **(a)** *(block of shares)* pachet *n* de acţiuni în aceaşi companie **(b)** *(block of flats)* bloc *n* de locuinţe **(c)** *(block letters)* litere *fpl* majuscule **2** *verb* a bloca

blockade *noun* blocadă *f* maritimă; **blockade runner** = spărgător *m* de blocadă

blue collar worker *noun* muncitor *m* manual

board 1 *noun* **(a)** bord *n;* **on board a ship** = la bordul unei nave **(b)** consiliu *n;* **board of directors** = consiliul de administraţie; **board meeting** = şedinţă *f* de consiliu **(c)** *(group of people who administer)* comisie *f or* comitet *n;* **advisory board** = comisie consultativă **2** *verb* a se îmbarca; **boarding card** = tichet *n* de îmbarcare

body *noun* **(a)** organizaţie *f* **(b)** grup *n;* **governing body** = grup conducător **(c)** organ *n* (politic)

bogus *adjective* fals; **bogus company** = companie fantomă

Bolivia *noun* Bolivia *f* NOTE: capital: **La Paz;** currency: **Bolivian peso** = peso bolivian

Bolivian *noun & adjective* bolivian(ă)

bona fide *adverb & adjective (Latin)* sincer *or* de încredere

bona fides *noun (Latin)* sinceritate *f or* bună credinţă *f*

bona vacantia *noun (Latin)* bunuri fără un proprietar evident

bond *noun* **(a)** *(debt of company or government)* titlu *n or* obligaţiune *f;* bon *n* de tezaur; **bearer bond** = titlu la purtător **(b)** **goods held in bond** = bunuri *npl* depozitate în vamă

bonded warehouse *noun* depozit *n* vamal

bonus *noun* primă *f or* recompensă *f* financiară *or* gratificaţie *f;* **bonus share** = acţiune *f* gratuită *or* titlu *n* gratuit; **incentive bonus** = primă stimulativă; **insurance bonus** = primă de asigurări; **merit bonus** = primă de merit

book 1 *noun* **(a)** carte *f* **(b)** a **company's books** = registru *n* contabil al unei companii **2** *verb* **(a)** a înregistra operaţiuni contabile **(b)** a rezerva; **to book a table at a restaurant** = a rezerva o masă la restaurant; **to book a seat** = a rezerva un loc (la avion *or* tren sau la teatru)

booking *noun* rezervare *f;* **booking fee** = taxă *f* de rezervare; **booking office** = casă *f* de bilete

bookkeeper *noun* contabil *m*

bookkeeping *noun* contabilitate *f*

booklet *noun* broşură *f;* **we picked this trip from the booklet issued by the travel agent** = am ales această excursie din broşura publicată de agenţia de voiaj

bookmaker *noun* agent *m* de pariuri (la meciuri *or* curse de cai *or* ogari, etc.)

bookseller *noun* librar *m*

bookshop *noun* librărie *f*

boom 1 *noun* boom *or* avânt *n* economic *or* dezvoltare *f* **2** *verb* **(a)** a prospera; **the business boomed during the 1980s** = afacerea a prosperat în anii '80 **(b)** a creşte (despre preţul acţiunilor)

boost 1 *noun* impuls *n or* stimulare *f* **2** *verb* a creşte forţat

booth *noun* **(a)** tarabă *f* **(b)** **telephone booth** = cabină *f* telefonică

border 1 *noun* **(a)** graniţă *f or* frontieră *f;* **the company's products are sold across the border** = produsele companiei sunt vândute peste hotare; **border line** = linie *f* de frontieră **(b)** capăt *n or* limită *f* **2** *verb* a mărgini

borrow *verb* a lua bani cu împrumut; **I would like to borrow some money to pay an overdue bill** = aş vrea să împrumut nişte bani ca să achit o notă de plată urgentă

boss *noun* şef *m or* conducător *m;* patron *m*

bottom 1 *noun* fund *n or* punct *n* minim 2 *verb* (a) a atinge fundul (despre un vas) (b) **to bottom out** = a atinge punctul minim

bought ledger *noun* registru *n* de facturi

bounce *verb* (despre cecuri) a nu fi onorat; **her cheque has bounced (it has been returned unpaid)** = cecul ei nu a fost onorat (a fost returnat neplătit)

bounty *noun* (a) *(reward)* recompensă *f* (b) *(incentive)* gratificaţie *f;* primă *f* (de export)

box *noun* (a) cutie *f* (b) ladă *f;* **the spare parts were shipped in wooden boxes** = piesele de schimb au fost expediate în lăzi de lemn (c) lojă *f;* **two of the partners met in the chairman's private box at the showing of Les Misérables** = doi dintre parteneri sau întâlnit în loja particulară a preşedintelui la spectacolul Mizerabilii (d) **letter box** = cutie poştală (e) **P.O. Box** = căsuţă *f* poştală

box office *noun* (a) casă *f* de bilete (b) încasări *fpl* (din vânzarea biletelor); **the film Independence Day smashed all box office records in 1996** = filmul Ziua Independenţei a bătut toate recordurile de încasări în 1996

boycott 1 *verb* (a) a boicota (b) a refuza 2 *noun* boicot *n*

bracket *noun* scară *f;* **wage brackets** = scara salariilor

branch 1 *noun* (a) ramură *f* (b) filială *f or* sucursală *f;* **this bank has 200 branches throughout the country** = această bancă are 200 de filiale în ţară 2 *verb* **to branch out** = a se extinde

brand 1 *noun* (a) marcă *f or* sortiment *n;* **local brand (sold in the region where it is manufactured)** = sortiment local (vândut în regiunea în care este produs) (b) etichetă 2 *verb* a eticheta

brand-new *adjective* nou-nouţ

Brazil *noun* Brazilia *f* NOTE: capital: **Brasilia;** currency: **real**

Brazilian *noun & adjective* brazilian(ă)

breach 1 *noun* (a) încălcare *f or* violare *f;* **breach of contract** = încălcare a contractului; **breach of promise** = încălcare a promisiunii; **breach of warranty** = încălcarea contractului de garanţie (b) breşă *f or* spărtură *f;* **to step into the breach** = a sări în ajutor 2 *verb* a încălca

bread *noun* (a) pâine *f* (b) *(earnings)* câştig *n*

breadline *noun* limita *f* subzistenţei; **to be on the breadline** = a fi foarte sărac, la limita subzistenţei

breadwinner *noun* persoană *f* care îşi câştigă existenţa muncind

break 1 *noun* (a) micşorarea *f* preţului acţiunilor la bursă (b) **commercial break** = pauză *f* pentru reclame la TV (c) pauză *f;* **lunch break** = pauză de prânz; **to take a break** = a lua o pauză 2 *verb* (a) a ruina financiar pe cineva; **the tough competition broke him** = competiţia dură l-a ruinat (b) *(breach)* a încălca

break down *verb* (a) a defalca (b) a avea o pană; **they could not make it in time as their car broke down on the motorway** = nu au putut ajunge la timp pentru că maşina lor a rămas în pană pe autostradă

breakdown *noun* (a) defalcare *f or* detaliere *f;* **the auditor asked for a breakdown of the expenses** = revizorul a cerut un raport detaliat al cheltuielilor (b) stricăciune *f;* accident *n*

break up *verb* **(a)** *(of ship)* a (se) face bucăţi (despre o navă); **the wrecked ship broke up on the coral reef** = epava eşuată pe reciful de corali s-a făcut bucăţi **(b)** a dezmembra

bribe *verb* **1** *noun* **(a)** mită *f* **(b)** corupţie *f* **2** *verb* a mitui

bribery *noun* mită *f*

bridge *noun* **(a)** *(bridge of a ship)* punte *f* de comandă a unui vas **(b)** pod *n*

brief **1** *noun* **(a)** dosar *n* **(b)** *(instructions)* instructaj *n* **2** *adjective* scurt **3** *verb* a da instrucţiuni

briefcase *noun* servietă *f*

British *noun* & *adjective* britanic(ă)

broker *noun* **(a)** agent *m* **(b)** agent comercial **(c)** **(stock)broker** = broker *m* *or* agent de schimb

budget **1** *noun* **(a)** buget *n;* **balanced budget** = buget echilibrat; **budget estimate** = estimaţie *f* bugetară; **draft budget** = proiect *n* de buget; **military budget** = buget militar; **ordinary budget** = buget general **(b)** plan *n* **2** *verb* **(a)** *(plan)* a planifica **(b)** a repartiza din buget

buffer stocks *noun* stocuri *npl* tampon; rezerve *fpl*

build *verb* **(a)** a construi **(b)** *(create)* a crea

building *noun* **(a)** construcţie *f;* **building site** = şantier *n* de construcţii **(b)** clădire *f*

building society *noun* **(a)** societate *f* de credite pentru construirea de locuinţe **(b)** societate imobiliară **(c)** casă de economii

Bulgaria *noun* Bulgaria *f* NOTE: capital: **Sofia**; currency: **lev** = leva *f*

Bulgarian *noun* & *adjective* bulgar(ă)

bulk *noun* cantitate *f;* **bulk purchase** = achiziţii *fpl* en gros *or* cu ridicata; **to sell in bulk** = a vinde cu ridicata

bullion *noun* lingou *n* (de aur sau argint)

Bundesbank Banca Federală Germană

burden *noun* **(a)** datorie *f;* **the burden of the contract** = datoria *f* faţă de contract **(b)** cheltuieli *fpl* generale *or* indirecte (chirie *or* impozite, etc.)

bureau *noun* **(a)** birou *n* **(b)** oficiu *n;* **bureau de change** = agenţie *f* de schimb valutar **(c)** departament *n*

bureaucracy *noun* birocraţie *f*

business *noun* **(a)** afaceri *fpl;* **he came up with a new business proposition** = el a propus o nouă afacere **(b)** comerţ *n* **(c)** treabă *f;* **on business** = cu treabă *or* în interes de serviciu; **to get down to business** = a se apuca de treabă

businesslike *adjective* **(a)** practic **(b)** metodic

businessman *noun* om *m* de afaceri; industriaş *m;* comerciant *m*

businesswoman *noun* femeie *f* de afaceri

buy **1** *verb* a cumpăra; **to buy a property for £80,000** = a cumpăra o casă în valoare de £80.000; **to buy out** = a cumpăra o afacere în întregime; **to buy over** = a mitui **2** *noun* **(a)** achiziţie *f;* **bargain buy** = chilipir *n;* achiziţie la un preţ avantajos **(b)** **best buy** = cel mai bun produs de cumpărat

buying power *noun* putere *f* de cumpărare

buy up *verb* **(a)** a cumpăra tot; a cumpara masiv **(b)** a acapara

byproduct *noun* produs *n* secundar *or* subprodus *n*

Cc

cab *noun* taxi *n*

cabinet *noun* guvern *n;* **cabinet meeting** = şedinţă *f* de guvern

cable **1** *noun* **(a)** cablu *n;* **cable television** = televiziune *f* prin cablu **(b)** telegramă *f* prin cablu (transoceanic); **cable transfer** = mandat *n* telegrafic **2** *verb* a transmite o telegramă prin cablu

cablegram *noun* telegramă *f* *or* cablogramă (transmisă prin cablu)

cabotage *noun* pescuit *n* dea lungul coastei

CAD (= Computer Aided Design) proiectare *f* asistată de calculator

calculate *verb* **(a)** a calcula *or* a socoti **(b)** *(plan)* a plănui **(c) to calculate on** = a se baza pe

calculated *adjective* **(a)** calculat *or* riguros; **calculated risk** = risc *n* calculat **(b)** *(intended)* intenţionat

calculation *noun* **(a)** calculare *f;* **to base one's calculations on** = a se baza pe **(b)** *(premeditation)* premeditare *f* **(c)** *(forecast)* previziune *f*

calculator *noun* calculator *n* electronic (de buzunar); maşină de adunat

calculus *noun* calcul *n*

calendar *noun* calendar *n;* **calendar month** = lună *f* calendaristică; **calendar year** = an *m* calendaristic

call **1** *noun* **(a)** chemare *f* *or* apel *n* **(b)** somaţie *f* **(c)** convorbire *f* telefonică;

after the telephone call he decided to buy more shares = după convorbirea telefonică el s-a decis să cumpere mai multe acţiuni; **callbox** = cabină *f* telefonică **2** *verb* **(a)** a chema **(b)** *(make a telephone call)* a telefona **(c)** *(bid)* a licita **(d)** a face o escală; **the ship calls at Constanţa** = vaporul va face escală la Constanţa

call in *verb* a retrage din circulaţie

call off *verb* a opri *or* a anula

call on *verb* a soma; **the bank called on him to pay his debt** = banca l-a somat să îşi achite datoria

caller *noun* vizitator *m*

calling *noun* vocaţie *f*

Cambodia *noun* Cambodgia *f* NOTE: capital: **Phnom Penh**; currency: **riel**

Cambodian *noun & adjective* cambodgian(ă)

Cameroon *noun* Camerun *m* NOTE: capital: **Yaoundé**; currency: **CFA franc** = franc *m* CFA

Cameroonian *noun & adjective* camerunez(ă)

campaign *noun* campanie *f;* **economy campaign** = campanie de economisire; **sales campaign** = campanie de creştere a vânzărilor

Canada *noun* Canada *f* NOTE: capital: **Ottawa**; currency: **Canadian dollar** = dolar *m* canadian

Canadian *noun & adjective* canadian(ă)

cancel *verb* **(a)** a declara nul (un act, etc) **(b)** a anula; **he phoned to cancel his order** = el a telefonat să anuleze comanda

cancellation *noun* **(a)** anulare *f;* **cancellation of a booking** = anularea unei rezervări **(b)** contramandare *f*

candidate *noun* candidat *m;* **the candidates for the post of director had to take a stiff examination** = candidaţii la postul de director au susţinut un examen riguros

cannibalize *verb* a monta din piese detaşate

capacity *noun* **(a)** capacitate *f;* **deadweight capacity of a ship** = capacitatea deadweight (de încărcare) a unei nave; **installed capacity** = capacitate instalată **(b)** volum *n*

capital **1** *noun* **(a)** capitală *f;* **Bucharest is the capital of Romania** = Bucureşti este capitala României **(b)** *(money)* capital *n;* **active capital** = capital lichid *or* bani gheaţă; **capital equipment** = capital fix; **capital expenditures** = cheltuieli *fpl* de capital; **capital gains tax** = impozit *n* progresiv pe avere; **capital transfer tax** = impozit pe transferul de capital; **dead capital** = capital neproductiv *or* neinvestit; **flight of capital** = scurgere *f* de capital (peste hotare); **reserve capital** = capital de rezervă; **working capital** = capital operativ **(c)** *(letter)* literă *f* majusculă **2** *adjective* important

capitalism *noun* capitalism *n*

capitalist *noun* **(a)** capitalist *m* **(b)** adept *m* al sistemului economic capitalist

capsize *vb* a (se) răsturna

captain *noun* căpitan *m* de vas (comercial sau de pasageri)

captive market *noun* piaţă *f* captivă *or* restrictivă

capture **1** *verb* a captura *or* a acapara; **to capture 20% of the market** = a acapara 20% din piaţă **2** *noun* *(thing or person captured)* captură *f*

car *noun* **(a)** maşină *f or* automobil *n;* **by car** = cu maşina; **car park** = parcare *f;* **company car** = maşina de serviciu; **private car** = autoturism *n* personal

carat *noun* **(a)** carat *n* (unitate *f* de măsurare a purităţii aurului); **24 carat gold** = aur de 24 de carate *or* pur **(b)** unitate de măsurare a greutăţii diamantelor; **5 carat diamond ring** = inel *n* cu diamant de 5 carate

carbon *noun* indigou *n;* **carbon copy** = copie *f* la indigou

card *noun* **(a)** *(business card)* carte *f* de vizită **(b)** **membership card** = legitimaţie *f* **(c)** **credit card** = carte de credit **(d)** cartelă *f* **(e)** **filing card** = fişă *f*

cardholder *noun* deţinător *m* al unei cărţi de credit *or* titular *m*

care **1** *noun* **(a)** *(worry)* grijă *f* **(b)** *(caution)* atenţie *f* **(c)** *(protection)* protecţie *f* **2** *verb* **(a)** *(take care of)* a avea grijă de **(b)** a se ocupa de

career *noun* **(a)** carieră *f;* **he had a remarkable career in teaching** = el a avut o carieră remarcabilă ca profesor **(b)** profesie *f;* **she chose accounting as her career** = ea a ales contabilitatea drept profesie

care of (C/O) *(on address)* în grija (adresă pe plic); **Mr Jones care of (C/O) Mr Scott** = Domnului Jones în grija Domnului Scott

caretaker **1** *noun* **(a)** portar *m* **(b)** îngrijitor *m* **2** *adjective* interimar *or* provizoriu; **caretaker government** = guvern *n* interimar

cargo *noun* încărcătură *f;* **air cargo** = bunuri *npl* transportate pe calea aerului

cargo boat *noun* cargobot *n* or vas *n* comercial

carriage *noun* transport *n;* **carriage forward** = contra ramburs; **carriage paid** = transport plătit

carrier *noun* (a) companie *f* de transport; **the carrier is accountable for the safety of the goods transported** = compania de transport este răspunzătoare de securitatea bunurilor transportate (b) **bulk carrier** = cargobot *n*

carry *verb* (a) a transporta (b) **to carry out** = a executa *or* a realiza

cartel *noun* cartel *n* or grup *n* de producători; **international cartel** = cartel internaţional

case *noun* (a) ladă *f;* **case of wine** = ladă de (12) sticle cu vin; **packing case** = ladă de ambalaj (b) *(state of affairs)* caz *n* (c) *(suit for trial)* proces; **to bring a case against** = a da în judecată

cash 1 *noun* bani *mpl* (gheaţă) *or* numerar; **cash advance** = avans *n* în bani gheaţă; **cash balance** = sold *n* de casă; **cash desk** = casă *f;* **cash flow** = circulaţia *f* banilor; **cash in hand** = bani în mână, disponibili *npl* pe loc; **cash on delivery** = plata *f* la livrare *or* contra ramburs; **cash offer** = ofertă *f* în bani peşin; **cash purchase** = achiziţie *f* cu numerar; **cash register** = maşina *f* de casă (care înregistrează încasările); **cash settlement** = plata unei facturi în numerar; **cash voucher** = bon *f* de casă; **to pay in cash** = a plăti cu bani peşin; **ready cash** = bani avuţi la îndemână 2 *verb* **to cash a cheque** = a încasa un cec

cash book *noun* registru *n* de încasări

cashier *noun* casier *n*

casual *adjective* întâmplător; **casual labour** = mână *f* de lucru ocazională; **casual profit** = profit *n* întâmplător *or* neaşteptat; **casual vacancy** = post *n* temporar *or* sezonier; **casual work** = lucru *f* ocazional; **casual worker** = lucrător *m* sezonier

catalogue *noun* listă *f* de produse şi preţuri; catalog *n*

catastrophe *noun* catastrofă *f* or accident *n* natural sau provocat; **that insurance company recognizes the following types of catastrophe: earthquakes, flood and storms** = acea companie de asigurări recunoaşte următoarele tipuri de catastrofă; cutremure, inundaţii şi furtuni violente

category *noun* categorie *f* or clasă *f;* **they only sell computers in the 80486 category** = ei vând calculatoare numai din clasa procesorului 80486

cater for *verb* a se ocupa de

cattle *noun* bovine *fpl;* şeptel *n*

cede *verb* a ceda (proprietăţi)

ceiling *noun* plafon *n;* **price ceiling** = preţ *n* maximal; **wage ceiling** = plafon de salarii

Celsius *noun* **today the temperature will reach 10° Celsius** = temperatura va atinge 10° celsius azi

census *noun* recensământ *n*

cent *noun* sută *f;* **per cent** = la sută; **in Britain the current VAT rate is 17.5 per cent (%)** = în Marea Britanie rata actuală TVA este de 17.5 la sută (%)

centimetre (cm) *noun* centimetru *m* (cm)

central bank *noun* bancă *f* centrală (de stat)

Central European Time *noun (one hour ahead of GMT)* Ora *f* Europei Centrale (în Spania, Franţa, Germania, Polonia, etc.)

centralize *verb* (a) a centraliza; **centralized economy** = economie *f* centralizată (b) *(concentrate administration)* a concentra

centralization *noun* (a) centralizare *f* (b) concentrare *f*

certificate *noun* **(a) share certifiate** = titlu *n* de acţiuni **(b)** certificat *n;* **birth certificate** = certificat de naştere; **doctor's certificate** or **medical certificate** = certificat de sănătate; **marriage certificate** = certificat de căsătorie; **certificate of deposit** = chitanţă *f* de depunere *or* depozitare; **certificate of insurance** = poliţă *f* (provizorie) de asigurări; **certificate of posting** = recipisă *f* de expediere **certificate of registry** = certificat de naţionalitate a unei nave

certify *verb* **(a)** a certifica **(b)** *(declare by certificate)* a dovedi *or* a atesta *(in Britain)* **certified accountant** = contabil *m* atestat *or* calificat (în Marea Britanie); **certified copy** = copie *f* legalizată

cession *noun* cedarea *f* proprietăţii creditorilor

chain *noun* lanţ *n* or ciclu *n;* **chain free property** = casă *f* de vânzare vacantă; **chain reaction** = reacţie *f* în lanţ; **chain of stores** = reţea *f* de magazine; **chain store** = magazin *n* aparţinând unei reţele de magazine

chair 1 *noun* **(a)** fotoliu *n* (prezidenţial) *or* postul *n* de preşedinte **(b)** prezidiu *n* 2 *verb* a prezida; **he is chairing the meeting** = prezidează şedinţa; **the manager chairs the meeting** = directorul conduce şedinţa

chairman *noun* preşedinte *m*

challenge 1 *noun* **(a)** confruntare *f* **(b)** provocare *f* 2 *verb* **(a)** a provoca **(b)** a interoga

Chamber of Commerce *noun* Cameră *f* de Comerţ

chance *noun* **(a)** şansă *f;* **to take one's chance** = a-şi încerca norocul **(b)** întâmplare *f;* **by chance** = întâmplător *or* la întâmplare **(c)** probabilitate *f;* **there is a 50 % chance that he will succeed in his new business** = probabilitatea de succes în noua sa afacere este de 50 %

Chancellor of the Exchequer *noun* Ministrul *m* de Finanţe (în Marea Britanie)

change 1 *noun* rest *n;* **the shop assistant gave him the change in £1 coins** = vânzătorul i-a dat restul în monede de £1; **small change** = mărunţiş *n* 2 *verb* a schimba; **I would like to change £100 into lei** = aş dori să schimb £100 în lei; **to change hands** = a schimba proprietarul (despre bunuri sau bani)

channel *noun* **(a)** canal *n* **(b)** cale *f;* **to go through the official channels** = a merge pe căi oficiale **(c)** sursă *f;* **the newspaper got its reports through various channels** = ziarul a obţinut relatările din diverse surse

The (English) Channel *noun* Canalul *n* Mânecii; **Channel Tunnel** = tunel *n* feroviar sub Canalul Mânecii care leagă Marea Britanie de Franţa

character *noun* **(a)** caracter *n* or personalitate *f* **(b)** caracter *n* or literă *f;* **Chinese characters** = caractere chinezeşti

charge 1 *noun* **(a)** responsabilitate *f;* **who is in charge?** = cine este şeful? **(b)** cost *n* or tarif *n;* **what is the charge for cleaning a coat ?** = care este tariful pentru curăţarea unui palton?; **admission charge** = costul biletului (de intrare); **charge account** = cont *n* deschis **(c)** acuzaţie *f;* **they face a charge for shoplifting** = ei riscă acuzaţia de furt din magazin **(d)** onorariu *n* 2 *verb* **(a)** a încredinţa **(b) to charge for** = a cere plata pentru (un serviciu, etc.)

chart 1 *noun* **(a)** hartă *f;* **Admiralty chart** = hartă marină oficială a Amiralităţii (în Marea Britanie) **(b)** grafic *n* or diagramă *f;* **flow chart** = diagramă; **organization chart** = organigramă *f;* **sales chart** = grafic de vânzări 2 *verb* a trasa (pe hartă)

charter 1 *noun* **(a)** cartă *f* or document *n* **(b) charter flight** = cursă *f* charter; **charter party** = charter party or contract *n* de navlosire **2** *verb* **(a)** a închiria; a navlosi *or* a afreta; **to charter a ship** = a închiria un vas pentru transport **(b)** *(in Britain)* **chartered accountant** = contabil *m;* atestat *or* calificat (în Marea Britanie)

charterer *noun* navlositor *m*

cheap *adjective* **(a)** ieftin; **cheap labour** = mână *f* de lucru ieftină; **this computer is cheaper by mail order** = acest calculator este mai ieftin comandat prin poştă **(b)** de calitate inferioară; **these shoes are cheap and ugly** = aceşti pantofi sunt de calitate inferioară şi urâţi

cheat **1** *verb* **(a)** a înşela; **he was cheated by his partner and lost a lot of money** = el a fost înşelat de partenerul său şi a pierdut o grămadă de bani **(b)** a decepţiona **2** *noun* escroc *m* or trişor *m;* **one of the card players was found to be a cheat** = unul din jucătorii de cărţi s-a dovedit a fi trişor

check **1** *noun* **(a)** control *n;* **to keep a check on expenses** = a limita cheltuielile **(b)** *US* cec **2** *verb* a verifica *or* a bifa; **the books are checked monthly** = registrul contabil este verificat lunar; **he checked the consignment and signed for the goods delivered** = el a verificat bunurile livrate şi a semnat de primire

check in *verb* **(a)** a se înregistra la hotel; **after the reservation was confirmed, the businessman checked in** = după confirmarea rezervării, omul de afaceri a semnat în registrul hotelului **(b)** a se înregistra la aeroport înaintea zborului; **you must check in at least two hours before the time of departure** = trebuie să vă înregistraţi la aeroport cu cel puţin două ore înainte de zbor

checklist *noun* listă *f* cu lucruri de făcut *or* de luat (într-o călătorie)

check out *verb* a plăti şi părăsi hotelul

checkout *noun* casă *f* unde se plăteşte pentru bunurile cumpărate (în supermagazin)

check with *verb* a corespunde; a fi în concordanţă cu

cheque *noun* cec *n;* **this store accepts cash and cheques only** = acest magazin acceptă numai bani şi cecuri; **cheque account** = cont *n* curent personal; **cheque book** = carnet *n* de cecuri; **cheque card** = carte *f* de acoperire a cecului (cu specimen de semnătură); **crossed cheque** = cec barat; **to write a cheque** *or* **to make out a cheque** = a completa un cec

chief executive *noun* **(a)** *GB* preşedintele *m* unei întreprinderi *or* autoritatea supremă într-un trust *or* concern, etc. **(b)** *US* preşedintele ţării

child's allowance *noun* scutire *f* de taxe parţială pentru familii cu copii

child benefit *noun* alocaţie *f* de stat

Chile *noun* Chile *f* NOTE: capital: **Santiago (de Chile)** currency: **Chilean peso** = peso *m* chilian

Chilean *noun & adjective* chilian(ă)

China *noun* China *f* NOTE: capital: **Beijing** currency: **yuan**

Chinese **1** *noun* chinez(ă) **2** *adjective* chinezesc *or* chinezească

choice *noun* **(a)** alegere *f;* **by choice** = pe alese **(b)** preferinţă *f* **(c)** sortiment *n;* **the local shop had a limited choice of goods** = magazinul local avea un sortiment redus de mărfuri

choose *verb* a alege; **the customers could choose from a good range of products** = clienţii au putut alege dintr-o gamă largă de sortimente

chronological order *noun* ordine *f* cronologică

circular **1** *noun* circulară *f* or notă *f;* **the company sent out a circular offering free delivery to all established customers** = compania a trimis o circulară oferind livrare gratuită tuturor clienţilor fideli **2** *adjective* circular *or* rotund

circulate *verb* a circula

circulation *noun* circulaţie *f;* **to put money into circulation** = a pune bani în circulaţie

city *noun* oraş *n;* **the City** = centrul financiar al Londrei; **intercity** = interurban

civil *adjective* civil; **civil action** = acţiune *f* civilă; **to bring a civil action** = a se constitui parte civilă (în procese); **civil engineering** = construcţii *fpl* civile; **civil law** = drept *n* civil; **civil servant** = funcţionar *m* de stat; **all the civil servants got a rise of 3% last month** = luna trecută toţi funcţionarii de stat au primit o mărire de salariu de 3%

claim **1** *noun* **(a)** revendicare *f* **(b)** drept *n;* **he has no claim to this land** = nu are drept legal asupra acestui teren; **insurance claim** = cerere *f* de despăgubiri a persoanei asigurate; **to settle a claim** = a conveni asupra plăţii unei despăgubiri **2** *verb* **to claim damages** = a cere despăgubiri

claimant *noun* persoană *f* asigurată care cere despăgubiri companiei de asigurări; reclamant *m*

class *noun* clasă *f;* **economy class or tourist class** = clasa turistică; **first class ticket** = bilet *n* clasa întâia

classify *verb* a clasifica; **classified advertisements** = anunţuri *npl* la mica publicitate

clause *noun* clauză *f* or prevedere *f;* **one of the contract's clauses forbids strikes** = una din clauzele contractului interzice grevele

clear **1** *adjective* **(a)** clar *or* evident; **it was clear that house prices would rise again** = era evident că preţul locuinţelor va creşte din nou **(b)** curat; **clear conscience** = conştiinţă curată **(c)** net; **they made £100,000 clear profit last year** = au obţinut un profit net de £100.000 anul trecut **2** *verb* **(a)** a clarifica *or* a lămuri; **the businessman's**

speech cleared the doubts = discursul omului de afaceri a clarificat orice dubiu; **cleared cheque** = cec clarificat **(b)** a lichida; **all these computers are reduced to clear** = toate aceste calculatoare sunt reduse pentru a lichida stocul **(c) to clear goods through customs** = a trece bunuri prin vamă **(d)** a acoperi *or* a amortiza (costuri *or* cheltuieli); **his venture was a disaster as he did not even clear his expenses** = afacerea lui a fost un eşec total de vreme ce el nu şi-a acoperit nici măcar cheltuielile

clearance *noun* **customs clearance** = formalităţi *fpl* vamale de expediţie; **clearance certificate** = certificat *n* vamal (de bunuri)

clerical *adjective* funcţionăresc; administrativ; **clerical worker** = funcţionar *m*

clerk *noun* funcţionar *m;* **bank clerk** = funcţionar de bancă; **chief clerk** = şef *m* de birou; **filing clerk** = arhivar *m;* **justices' clerk** = grefier *f;* **sales clerk** = vânzător *m*

client *noun* cumpărător *m* or client *m;* **the shop tries to keep its clients happy** = magazinul încearcă să-şi menţină cumpărătorii mulţumiţi

clientele *noun* clientelă *f*

cloakroom *noun* garderobă *f*

clock *verb* a cronometra timpul de lucru; **to clock in** or **clock out** = a ponta de intrare *or* a ponta de ieşire (la poarta întreprinderii)

close **1** *noun* **(a)** încheierea tranzacţiilor la Bursă; **at the close, our shares value fell by 5p** = la închidere, valoarea acţiunilor noastre a scăzut cu 5p (pence) **(b)** sfârşit **2** *verb* **(a)** a închide; **the store closes on Sundays** = magazinul e închis duminica; **to close down** = a da faliment *or* a înceta activitatea **(b)** a sfârşi **(c)** *(an account)* a lichida (un cont)

closing down sale *noun* lichidare *f*

closing price *noun* cursul *n* la închidere (la Bursă)

COBOL (= Common Business Oriented Language) COBOL, limbaj de programare a calculatoarelor (în domeniul finanţelor)

code 1 *noun* **(a)** cod *n;* **dialling code =** prefix *n* telefonic; **post code =** cod poştal **(b)** *(set of rules)* codice *n* **(c) tax code =** cod al impozitului pe venit (în Marea Britanie) **(d)** cifru *n* 2 *verb* a cifra

coin *noun* monedă *f;* **I paid the taxi driver in £1 coins =** am plătit taxiul cu monede de o liră

coinage *noun* **(a)** *(act of coining)* fabricare de monede **(b)** *(system of coins in use in a country)* sistem *n;* monetar al unei ţări

collaborate *verb* a colabora; **the computer manufacturer collaborated with the software company on a new machine =** fabrica de calculatoare a colaborat cu compania de software în realizarea unui nou calculator

collapse 1 *noun* **(a)** prăbuşire *f;* colaps *n* **(b)** cădere *f;* **the collapse of the totalitarian regimes in Eastern Europe offers the foreign investors new business prospects =** căderea regimurilor totalitariste în Europa de Est oferă oamenilor de afaceri străini noi posibilităţi de investiţii 2 *verb* **(a)** a cădea **(b)** a se prăbuşi *or* a eşua; **his business collapsed owing thousands of pounds =** întreprinderea sa a eşuat datorând mii de lire

colleague *noun* coleg *n*

collect *verb* **(a)** a colecta **(b)** a ridica *or* a lua; **they collected the goods when they paid =** au ridicat bunurile când au plătit

collective 1 *adjective* colectiv; **the new product was the result of collective work =** noul produs a fost rezultatul muncii colective 2 *noun* colectiv *n or* grup *n;*

collective farm = cooperativă *f* agricolă de producţie

collectivism *noun* colectivism *n*

collector *noun* **(a) tax collector =** perceptor *m* **(b)** colecţionar *m*

college *noun* **(a)** colegiu *n* **(b)** facultate *f;* **commercial college =** facultate de comerţ *or* academie *f* de comerţ

Colombia *noun* Columbia NOTE: capital: **Bogotá;** currency: **Colombian peso =** peso *m* columbian

Colombian *noun* & *adjective* columbian(ă)

colonialism *noun* colonialism *n*

column *noun* **(a)** coloană *f* (de cifre); **to add up a column of figures =** a aduna o coloană de cifre **(b)** rubrică *f;* **he reads the City column every morning =** el citeşte rubrica de informaţii financiare în fiecare dimineaţă

combination *noun* **(a)** combinaţie *f* **(b)** *(sequence of numbers or letters)* cifru *n;* **combination lock =** închizătoare *f* cu cifru

combine 1 *noun* **(a)** cartel *n* **(b)** asociaţie *f* 2 *verb* **(a)** a combina **(b)** a asocia *or* a uni; **they combined their efforts in pulling the business out of trouble =** şi-au unit eforturile ca să scoată afacerea din impas

command 1 *verb* **(a)** a comanda *or* a ordona **(b)** a solicita; **due to his qualifications, he could command a pay rise =** datorită calificărilor sale el a putut să solicite ferm o mărire de salariu 2 *adjective* **command economy =** economie *f* de comandă

commerce *noun* **(a)** comerţ *n* **(b)** comerţ (subiect de studiu în academiile comerciale)

commercial 1 *adjective* comercial; **commercial aircraft =** aeronavă *f* de transport de mărfuri; **commercial port =** port *n* comercial; **commercial traveller =**

comis *m* voiajor 2 *noun* reclamă *f* comercială la TV

commercialization *noun* comercializare *f*

commercialize *verb* a comercializa

commission 1 *noun* (a) autorizaţie *f* (b) comisie *f* or comitet *n;* the government set up a commission to investigate the corruption allegations = guvernul a înfiinţat o comisie de investigare a acuzaţiilor de corupţie (c) comision *n;* banker's commission = comision bancar; insurance commission = comision de asigurări 2 *verb* (a) a împuternici *or* a autoriza; he was commissioned to check the company's records = el a fost împuternicit să cerceteze registrele companiei (b) a însărcina

commit *verb* (a) *(bind oneself)* a se obliga (să) (b) a încredinţa; he committed the documents to the bank for safe keeping = el a încredinţat documentele băncii spre păstrare

committee *noun* comitet *n;* member of a committee = membru *m* al unui comitet

commitment *noun* (a) angajament *n* (b) promisiune *f*

commodity *noun* (a) bunuri *npl* or produse *npl;* basic commodities = produse de bază; staple commodities = bunuri necesare (b) marfă *f* or materii *fpl* prime; commodity market = piaţa *f* de materii prime (c) articole *npl* (de comerţ)

common *adjective* (a) comun (b) obişnuit *or* frecvent; common mistake = greşeală *f* frecventă; common law = tradiţie *f* or lege *f* nescrisă; common seal = ştampila *f* or sigiliul *n* companiei

communicate *verb* a comunica; he communicated very successfully with his customers = el comunica cu succes cu clienţii săi

communication *noun* comunicare *f* or înştiinţare *f*

communism *noun* comunism *n*

communist *noun* & *adjective* comunist (m)

commute *verb* a face naveta

commuter *noun* navetist *m* 2 million commuters use the railways to go to work = 2 milioane de navetişti folosesc trenul ca mijloc de transport spre serviciu

company *noun* companie *f* or societate *f* or întreprindere *f;* he has been working in this company for 30 years = lucrează în această companie de 30 de ani; most companies are keen to cut production costs = majoritatea companiilor caută să reducă costurile de producţie; company secretary = secretarul *m* companiei; investment company = trust *n* de investiţii; limited company = societate cu răspundere limitată; subsidiary company = companie subsidiară; trading company = societate comercială

compensate *verb* a (se) compensa; last year's loss was partly compensated for by the increase in orders this year = pierderile de anul trecut au fost compensate parţial de creşterea comenzilor de anul acesta

compensation *noun* (a) compensaţie *f;* he received £1000 in compensation for the loss of commission = a primit o compensaţie de £1000 pentru pierderile de comision (b) despăgubire *f;* he sued his former employer for compensation = l-a dat în judecată pe fostul patron pentru despăgubiri

compete *verb* (a) a concura *or* a face concurenţă; we can now compete with other companies on the audio systems market = acum putem şi noi face concurenţă celorlalte companii pe piaţa sistemelor audio (b) a rivaliza

competence *noun* competenţă *f;* **the financial adviser proved his competence by offering various ways of saving money** = consultantul financiar şi-a dovedit competenţa oferind numeroase căi de economisire

competent *adjective* competent *(in law)* **not competent** = (despre o lege) neputincios

competition *noun* competiţie *f or* concurenţă *f;* **fair competition** = competiţie loială; **healthy competition** = concurenţă sănătoasă *or* constructivă; **unfair competition** = concurenţă neloială

competitive *adjective* competitiv; **competitive market** = piaţă *f* competitivă *or* de concurenţă; **competitive price** = preţ *n* competitiv

competitor *noun* concurenţă *f or* rival *m* în afaceri; **we will beat our competitors with these low prices** = vom înfrînge concurenţa cu aceste preţuri reduse

complaint *noun* reclamaţie *f;* **the customer wants to make a complaint about the product he had bought** = clientul doreşte să facă reclamaţie în legătură cu produsul cumpărat; **complaints book** = condică *f* de sugestii şi reclamaţii

complete **1** *adjective* complet *or* întreg **2** *verb* **(a)** a completa **(b)** a termina; **the building was completed before the end of the year** = construcţia a fost terminată înainte de sfârşitul anului.

completely *adverb* complet *or* total

completion *noun* **(a)** completare *f;* **please send your application upon completion** = vă rugăm să expediaţi cererea după completare **(b)** încheiere *f;* **completion of a contract** = încheierea unui contract

complex **1** *noun* complex *n;* **industrial complex** = complex industrial **2** *adjective* complex *or* complicat

compliance *noun* **(a)** încuviinţare *f* **(b)** conformitate *f;* **in compliance with your request** = în conformitate cu rugămintea dumneavoastră; ascultând de cererea dumneavoastră

comply *verb* **(a)** a respecta (o lege, etc.); **to comply with a court order** = a respecta o hotărâre judecătorească **(b)** *(act in accordance)* a se conforma

component *noun* component *n or* piesă *f;* **the processor is the most important component of a computer** = procesorul este cel mai important component al unui calculator

compromise **1** *noun* **(a)** compromis *n* **(b)** concesie *f;* **to reach a compromise** = a ajunge la un compromis *or* aranjament **2** *verb* **(a)** *(settle a dispute)* a face un compromis **(b)** *(bring into disrepute or danger)* a compromite; a primejdui; **the lack of funds might compromise the whole project** = lipsa de fonduri poate primejdui proiectul în totalitate

compute *verb* a calcula

computer *noun* calculator *n or* ordinator *n;* **computer bureau** = oficiu *n* (centru) de calcul; **computer operator** = operator *m* (de) calculator; **computer specialist** = expert *m* în sisteme de calcul

computerize *verb* a computeriza

concession *noun* **(a)** concesie *f;* **to make a concession** = a ceda **(b)** concesiune *f;* **mineral concession** = concesiune de exploatare a minereurilor

conciliation *noun* conciliere *f or* mediere *f;* **conciliation tribunal** = comisie *f* de mediere

condition *noun* condiţie *f;* **conditions of employment** = condiţii ale contractului de muncă; **conditions of sale** = termeni *mpl* ai contractului de vânzare; **implied condition** = condiţie implicită *or* subînţeleasă

conditional *adjective* (a) condiţional (b) condiţionat; **conditional acceptance** = acceptare *f* condiţionată (a bunurilor, etc.); **conditional offer** = ofertă *f* condiţionată

conduct *verb* a conduce; **the manager conducts the meeting** = directorul conduce şedinţa

conference *noun* conferinţă *f*; **conference room** = sală *f* de şedinţe *or* conferinţe; **press conference** = conferinţă de presă

confidence *noun* (a) încredere *f*; **the businessman did not have much confidence in his new partner** = omul de afaceri nu prea avea încredere în noul său asociat (b) secret *n*; **in confidence** = în secret

confident 1 *noun* confident *m* 2 *adjective* confident *or* încrezător; **she is confident she will win the contract with the supplier** = ea este încrezătoare că va încheia contractul cu furnizorul

confidential *adjective* (a) confidenţial; **please remember that what we discussed is strictly confidential** = vă rog să ţineţi minte că tot ce am discutat este strict confidenţial (b) de încredere

confirm *verb* a confirma; **he was asked to confirm his telephone order in writing** = i s-a cerut să confirme în scris comanda telefonică; **to confirm a booking** = a confirma o rezervare

confirmation *noun* confirmare *f*; **letter of confirmation** = scrisoare *f* de confirmare

confirmed *adjective* confirmat; **confirmed irrevocable credit** = credit *n* confirmat irevocabil

Congo *noun* Congo *m* NOTE: capital: **Brazzaville**; currency: **CFA franc** = franc *m* CFA

Congolese *noun & adjective* congolez(ă)

connect *verb* (a) a lega (b) a uni

connection *noun* (a) legătură *f*; **he had to see the production manager in connection with the new working hours** = a trebuit să vorbească cu directorul de producţie în legătură cu noul program de lucru (b) relaţie *f or* cunoştinţă *f*; **he managed to obtain the appointment through a connection** = a reuşit să obţină audienţa printr-o cunoştinţă (c) conexiune *f*

consent 1 *verb* consimţi 2 *noun* consimţământ *n or* permisiune *f*; **the chairman gave his consent to our continuing to work together** = preşedintele ne-a dat premisiunea să lucrăm împreună în continuare

conservative 1 *noun* conservator *m* 2 *adjective* (a) conservator (b) prudent; **conservative estimates** = preziceri *fpl* prudente (c) moderat; **conservative accounting** = contabilitate *f* moderată

consider *verb* (a) a considera; **I consider your suggestions very useful** = consider sugestiile Dvs. foarte folositoare (b) a chibzui *or* a cântări; **to consider an offer** = a chibzui asupra unei oferte; **all things considered** = ţinând seama de toate

consideration *noun* (a) *(payment)* plată *f or* recompensă *f*; **illegal consideration** = plată generată de un contract ilegal (b) **under consideration** = în studiu (c) *(careful thought)* chibzuială *f or* judecată *f*

considerable *adjective* important *or* considerabil; **a considerable amount of money has been spent on research** = o sumă importantă de bani a fost cheltuită în scopul cercetării

consign *verb* (a) a trimite *or* a expedia; **the goods were consigned two days ago** = bunurile au fost expediate acum două zile (b) a înmâna

consignee *noun* destinatar *m*

consignment *noun* (a) transport *n*; **this is the last consignment for this quarter** = acesta este ultimul transport

pe acest trimestru **(b)** expediere *f* **(c)**
consignment note = conosament *n*

consolidate *verb* **(a)** a întări **(b)**
(make stronger) a consolida **(c)** a grupa;
consolidated annuities or consols = titluri
de stat

consolidation *noun* consolidare *f*

consortium *noun* consorţiu *n*

constant **1** *noun* constantă *f* **2**
adjective constant *or* stabil; **the prices
are constant for the time being** =
preţurile sunt stabile deocamdată

construct *verb* a construi; **the new
underground line was constructed by a
consortium of British and French
companies** = noua linie de metrou a
fost construită de un consorţiu de
companii britanice şi franceze

construction *noun* construcţie *f;*
construction company = antrepriză *f* de
construcţii; **the building was under
construction when they bought one of
the flats** = clădirea se afla în construcţie
când au cumpărat unul din
apartamente

constructive *adjective* constructiv *or*
practic; **constructive proposal** =
propunere *f* practică

consul *noun* consul *m*

consular *adjective* consular

consulate *noun* consulat *n*

consult *verb* **(a)** a consulta; **he will not
make any decision until he has consulted
his closest associate** = el nu va lua o
hotărâre până când nu se va consulta
cu asociatul său cel mai apropiat **(b)**
(take into account, consider) a cântări

consultant *noun* **(a)** asesor *m* **(b)**
consilier *m*

consumables *plural noun* materiale
npl consumabile

consume *verb* a consuma

consumer *noun* consumator *m* *(in the
economical sense)* **consumer demand** =

cerere *f* (teorie economică); **consumer
durables** = bunuri *npl* de folosinţă
îndelungată; **consumer goods** = bunuri
de consum; **consumer group** = grup *n*
de consumatori; **consumer research** =
studiul *n* comportamentului
consumatorilor; **consumer's surplus** =
profitul *n* consumatorului

consumption *noun* consum *n* *or*
consumaţie *f*

contact **1** *noun* **(a)** contact *n* **(b)**
cunoştinţă *f;* **he has many contacts in
the publishing business** = are multe
cunoştinţe în lumea editurilor de carte
2 *verb* a contacta *or* a ţine legătura; **to
contact someone by phone** = a contacta
pe cineva la telefon; a telefona

contain *verb* a conţine; **this box
contains the video recorder together
with leads and instructions** = această
cutie conţine aparatul video, cabluri şi
instrucţiuni de folosire

container *noun* **(a)** recipient *n* **(b)**
container *n;* **container traffic** =
transportul *n* de mărfuri în containere

contents *noun* **(a)** conţinut *n;*
contents of a file = conţinut al unui
dosar **(b)** *(in a book)* cuprins *n* *or* tablă *f*
de materii (într-o carte)

contraband *noun* contrabandă *f* *or*
trafic *n* ilegal de mărfuri

contract **1** *noun* **(a)** contract *n;*
bilateral contract = contract bilateral;
consensual contract = contract verbal;
formal contract = contract oficial; **illegal
contract** = contract ilegal; **moneylending
contract** = contract de împrumut;
unilateral contract = contract unilateral
(b) *(agreement)* înţelegere *f* *or* acord *n* **2**
verb a contracta

contractor *noun* antreprenor *m;*
building contractor = antrepriză *f* de
construcţii *or* companie *f* de contrucţii

contribute *verb* **(a)** a contribui; **they
found a sponsor to contribute to the cost
of research** = ei au găsit un sponsor

care să contribuie la acoperirea costurilor de cerecetare **(b)** a cotiza

control 1 *noun* **(a)** control *n* **(b) quality control** = control (tehnic) de calitate **(c) stock control** = inventar *n;* **stock control card** = fişă *f* de magazie **2** *verb* a controla *or* a verifica

convertibility *noun* convertibilitate *f*

convertible currency *noun* monedă *f or* valută *f* convertibilă

cooperative *noun* cooperativă *f;* **agricultural cooperative** = cooperativă agricolă de producţie; **consumer's cooperative** = cooperativă de consum; **credit cooperative** = casă *f* de ajutor reciproc

co-owner *noun* coproprietar *m*

copier *noun* maşină *f* de copiat *or* copiator *m*

copy 1 *noun* copie *f* 2 *verb* a copia

copyright 1 *noun* drept *n* de autor **2** *verb* a-şi asuma drepturi de autor **3** *adjective* protejat de dreptul de autor

corporate *adjective* **(a)** asociat **(b)** unit; **corporate image** = imagine *f* publică a unei întreprinderi; **corporate plan** = plan *n* de producţie **(c)** corporativ

corporation *noun* **(a)** corporaţie *f;* **corporation tax** = impozit *n* pe profiturile societăţilor cu răspundere limitată; **finance corporation** = societate financiară **(b)** *US* societate (anonimă)

correct 1 *adj* corect 2 *verb* a corecta

correspond *verb* **(a)** *(write letters)* a corespunda *or* a scrie scrisori **(b)** *(be similar)* a corespunde *or* a se potrivi

correspondence *noun* **(a)** corespondenţă *f;* **his first task is to open the correspondence every morning** = prima lui îndatorire este deschiderea corespondenţei în fiecare dimineaţă. **(b)** potrivire

corrupt *verb* **(a)** a corupe **(b)** *(bribe)* a mitui

corruption *noun* **(a)** corupţie *f* **(b)** *(bribe)* mită *f*

cost 1 *noun* cost *n or* cheltuieli *fpl;* **administrative costs** = cheltuieli administrative; **annual cost** = cost anual; **average cost** = preţ *n* mediu; **average unit cost** = cost mediu unitar; **cost price** = preţ de cost; **fixed costs** = cheltuieli fixe; **joint costs** = cheltuieli comune; **marginal costs** = cheltuieli marginale; **overall costs** = cheltuieli globale; **production cost** = cost de producţie; **selling cost** = cost de desfacere **2** *verb* a costa

Costa Rica *noun* Costa Rica *f* NOTE: capital: **San José**; currency: **colón**

Costa Rican *noun & adjective* costarican(ă)

cottage industry *noun* lucru *n* la domiciliu *or* artizanat *n*

council *noun* consiliu *n;* **council tax** = impozit *n* perceput de primării; **town council** = consiliu municipal

counsel 1 *noun* **(a)** avocat *m* **(b)** *(advice)* sfat *n;* **to keep one's own counsel** = a nu se sfătui cu nimeni **2** *verb* a sfătui

counter 1 *noun* tejghea *f;* **goods sold over the counter** = vânzare pe scală mică; **under the counter** = pe sub tejghea *or* ilegal **2** *verb* a se împotrivi

counterbid *noun* contraofertă *f*

counterfeit 1 *noun* **(a)** *(forgery)* fals *n* **(b)** *(imitation)* imitaţie *f* **2** *adjective* *(forged)* fals *or* contrafăcut **3** *verb* a falsifica bani

counterfoil *noun* talon *n;* cotor *n* (de chitanţe, carnet de cecuri, etc.)

counterinflationary *adjective* antiinflaţionar

countermand *verb* a contramanda; a revoca

counteroffer *noun* contraofertă *f*

counterpart *noun* omolog *m or* corespondent *m;* **the British Prime Minister met his Romanian counterpart** = primul ministru britanic s-a întâlnit cu omologul său român

courier *noun* **(a)** curier *m* **(b)** mesager *m;* **the parcel was delivered by a courier company** = coletul a fost livrat de către o companie de mesagerie

cover 1 *noun* **(a)** acoperire *f* **(b)** garanţie *f;* **cover note** = poliţă *f* provizorie de asigurări; **full cover** = asigurare *f* totală 2 *verb* **(a)** a acoperi **(b)** a proteja; **to be fully covered** = a fi protejat pe deplin de poliţa de asigurări

craftsman *noun* meseriaş *m or* meşteşugar *m*

craft union *noun* sindicat *n* al meşteşugarilor

create *verb* **(a)** a crea; **the project created 100 new jobs** = proiectul a creat 100 noi locuri de muncă **(b)** a produce

credit 1 *noun* **(a)** credit *n or* împrumut *n;* **bank credit** = împrumut la bancă; **credit card** = carte *f* de credit; **credit limit** = limită *f* a creditului; **credit note** = notă *f* de stornare; **fixed credit** = credit fix; **open credit** = credit deschis *or* nelimitat **(b)** **letter of credit** = acreditiv *n* 2 *verb* **(a)** a acorda credit **(b)** a credita

creditor *noun* creditor *m*

creditworthy *adjective* demn de încredere; solvent

crew *noun* echipaj *n*

Croatia *noun* Croaţia *f* NOTE: capital: **Zagreb;** currency: **dinar**

Croatian *noun & adjective* croat(ă)

Cuba *noun* Cuba *f* NOTE: capital: **Havana;** currency: **Cuban peso** = peso *m* cubanez

Cuban *noun & adjective* cubanez(ă)

currency *noun* **(a)** *(coinage)* monedă *f* **(b)** valută *f;* **foreign currency** = valută *or* monedă străină; **hard currency** = valută convertibilă *or* forte; **inconvertible currency** = valută neconvertibilă; **managed currency** = monedă controlată; **national currency** = monedă naţională **(c)** devize *fpl*

current *adjective* curent *or* actual; **current account** = cont *n* curent; current price = preţ *n* actual

customer *noun* client *m;* **customer satisfaction** = mulţumirea *f* clientului; **regular customer** = client vechi *or* al casei

customs *noun* vamă *f;* **customs officer** = vameş *m;* **customs tariffs** = tarife *npl* vamale

cut 1 *noun* reducere *f;* **cuts in price** = reduceri de preţuri; **job cuts** = reduceri de personal 2 *verb* a reduce; **to cut prices** = a reduce preţurile

cycle *noun* ciclu *n;* **business cycle** = ciclu economic

Cypriot *noun & adjective* cipriot(ă)

Cyprus *noun* Cipru NOTE: capital: **Nicosia;** currency: **Cyprus pound** = liră *f* cipriotă

Czech *noun & adjective* ceh(ă)

Czech Republic *noun* Republica Cehă *f* NOTE: capital: **Prague** = Praga; currency: **Czech koruna** = coroană *f* cehă

Dd

daily 1 *adjective* zilnic *or* cotidian; **daily newspaper** = (ziar) cotidian *n* 2 *adverb* zilnic *or* în fiecare zi; **I read a newspaper daily** = citesc un ziar în fiecare zi

damage 1 *noun* pagubă *f or* stricăciune *f;* avarie *f;* **damage claim** = cerere *f* de despăgubiri pentru pierderi parţiale; **fire damage** = pagubă *f* pricinuită de incendiu (b) daune *fpl or* despăgubiri *fpl;* **to claim money in damages** = a pretinde bani drept despăgubiri; **compensatory damages** = despăgubiri compensatorii 2 *verb* (a) a strica (b) *(inflict damage on)* a prejudicia

Dane *noun* danez(ă)

danger *noun* primejdie *f or* pericol *n;* **danger money** = spor *n* de periclitate

dangerous *adjective* primejdios *or* periculos

Danish *adjective* danez

data *noun* date *fpl or* informaţie *f;* **data bank** = bancă *f* de date; **data processing** = prelucrarea informaţiilor pe calculator

date 1 *noun* (a) dată *f;* **all the documents received through the post are stamped with the day's date** = toate documentele primite prin poştă sunt ştampilate cu data respectivă; **out of date** = depăşit *or* demodat; **up to date** = actual *or* la zi (b) *(day of the month)* zi *f* 2 *verb* a data *or* a pune data (pe un

document, etc); **he forgot to date the cheque** = a uitat să pună data pe cec

dead account *noun* cont *n* bancar inactiv *or* colector *n*

deadline *noun* termen *n* limită de terminare a unei lucrări, etc

deadlock *noun* impas *n;* **the negotiations have reached a deadlock** = negocierile sunt în impas

dead loss *noun* pierdere *f* completă

dead rent *noun* chirie *f* plătită pentru utilaje neproductive

dead season *noun* sezon *n* mort *or* perioadă *f* inactivă

deadweight *noun* capacitatea *f* totală de încărcare a navei

deal 1 *noun* (a) **a great deal** *or* **a good deal** = cantitate *f* (considerabilă) (b) *(business arrangement)* afacere *f or* tranzacţie *f;* **to set up a deal** = a încheia o tranzacţie (c) acord *n;* **the two parts signed the deal** = cele două părţi au semnat acordul 2 *verb* **to deal with** = a avea de a face cu *or* a trata; a se ocupa cu

dealer *noun* negustor *m or* comerciant *m*

dear *adjective* scump *or* costisitor; **this computer is dearer than we expected** = acest calculator este mai scump decât ne-am aşteptat

dear money *noun* bani *mpl* scumpi *or* când dobânzile sunt ridicate

debenture *noun* obligaţiune *f;* **debenture-holder** = deţinător *m* de obligaţiuni

debit 1 *noun* **(a)** debit *n;* **debit balance** = sold *n* negativ; **debit note** = notă *f* de debitare **(b)** **debit account** = cont *n* debitor 2 *verb* a debita; **to debit an account** = a debita un cont

debt *noun* datorie *f;* **to be in debt** = a datora (bani); **debt amortization** = achitarea *f* datoriei; **debt-collecting agency** = agenţie *f* de colectare a datoriilor; **debt of honour** = datorie de onoare; **debt servicing** = plătirea *f* de dobânzi pentru o datorie; **external debt** = datorie externă; **floating debt** = datorie flotantă (pe termen lung); **national debt** = datorie naţionlă; **permanent debt** = datorie permanentă; **public debt** = datorie publică; **to run into debt** = a se îngloda în datorii; **temporary debt** = datorie temporară

debtor *noun* debitor *m;* datornic *m;* **debtor economic sector** = sector *n* economic debitor; **debtor nation** = naţiune debitoare

deceit *noun* înşelăciune *f or* decepţie *f*

decentralization *noun* descentralizare *f*

decide *verb* a decide *or* a hotărî; **he decided to try a new strategy for attracting customers** = s-a hotărât să încerce o nouă stratagemă de atragere a clienţilor

decision *noun* **(a)** decizie *f or* hotărâre *f;* **to reach a decision** = a ajunge la o hotărâre **(b)** *(conclusion, resolution)* concluzie *f*

declaration *noun* declaraţie *f;* **declaration of bankruptcy** = declararea *f* falimentului

declare *verb* **(a)** a declara; **at the customs they said they had nothing to declare** = la vamă au spus că nu aveau nimic să declare **(b)** a susţine; **she declared she was innocent** = ea susţinea că era nevinovată

declared value *noun* valoare *f* declarată (la vamă)

decline 1 *noun* **(a)** declin *n or* scădere *f;* **decline in the value of shares** = scăderea valorii acţiunilor **(b)** *(loss of strength)* slăbire *f or* diminuare *f* **(c)** *(decay)* decădere *f* 2 *verb* **(a)** a declina *or* a refuza; **the company declined to become involved in the deal** = compania a refuzat orice implicare în tranzacţie; **the invitation was politely declined** = invitaţia a fost refuzată politicos **(b)** a scădea; **orders have declined over the last quarter** = comenzile au scăzut trimestrul trecut.

decrease 1 *noun* scădere *f or* diminuare *f;* **on the decrease** = în scădere 2 *verb* **(a)** *(become smaller)* a scădea **(b)** a (se) împuţina; **our reserves have decreased dramatically** = rezervele noastre s-au împuţinat dramatic

decree 1 *noun* decret *f or* lege *f;* **to rule by decree** = a guverna prin decrete 2 *verb* a decreta

deduct *verb* a scădea *or* a reduce; a deduce; **to deduct a sum for expenses** = a deduce o sumă pentru cheltuieli

deed *noun* **(a)** contract *n* **(b)** act *n or* document *n* legal (acord în scris, semnat şi parafat de ambele părţi); **deed of transfer** = act de transferare a acţiunilor; **notarial deed** = act notarial

deface *verb* a deteriora; **defaced coins or notes** = monede *fpl* sau bancnote deteriorate; **defaced cheque** = cec *n* contrafăcut *or* modificat

defalcation *noun* **(a)** furt *n* de bunuri (de către custode) **(b)** deturnare *f* de fonduri

default 1 *noun* **(a)** *(failure)* eşec *n* **(b)** *(lack)* lipsă *f or* omisiune *f* 2 *verb* a nu plăti; **to default on one's payments** = a nu plăti *or* a se eschiva să plătească

defeat 1 *noun* (a) înfrângere *f* (b) eşec *n;* **eventually he had to admit defeat** = în cele din urmă el a trebuit să-şi recunoască eşecul 2 *verb* (a) a înfrânge (b) a respinge; **the new bill was defeated in parliament** = noul proiect de lege a fost respins în parlament

defendant *noun* acuzat *m;* pârât *m*

deficit *noun* deficit *n;* **the company has a £10,000 deficit** = compania are un deficit de 10.000 de lire; **balance of payments deficit** = defict al balanţei de plăţi; **deficit spending** = deficit bugetar

deflate *verb* **to deflate the economy** = a practica o politică de reducere a inflaţiei

deflation *noun* reducere *f* a inflaţiei

defraud *verb* a înşela *or* a păcăli; **to defraud one's creditors** = a-şi înşela creditorii

defray *verb* a plăti (în locul cuiva); a acoperi cheltuieli; **his boss told him that they would defray his expenses** = şeful lui i-a spus că îi va plăti cheltuielile

delay 1 *noun* întârziere *f or* tărăgănare *f;* **the supplier apologised for the delay in delivering the goods** = furnizorul şi-a cerut scuze pentru întârzierea livrării bunurilor 2 *verb* a întârzia

delegate 1 *noun* delegat *m or* trimis *m* 2 *verb* a delega *or* a împuternici

deliver *verb* a livra; **delivered price** = preţ *n* cu amănuntul

delivery *noun* livrare *f;* **delivery note** = notă *f* de livrare; **delivery receipt** = chitanţă *f* de primire; **delivery time** = termen *n* (dată) de livrare

demand 1 *noun* (a) cerere *f;* **composite demand** = cerere diversificată; **demand curve** = curba *f* (structura) cererii; **demand-led inflation** = inflaţie *f* generată de cerere excesivă; **elastic demand** = cerere flexibilă; **excess demand** = cerere excesivă a unui produs pe piaţă (b) somaţie *f* de plată;

final demand = somaţie finală de plată; **payment on demand** = cerere de plată pe loc 2 *verb* (a) *(ask)* a cere (b) a solicita

democracy *noun* democraţie *f*

demography *noun* demografie *f*

demonetize *verb* a demonetiza *or* a scoate o monedă din circulaţie

demonstrate *verb* a demonstra

demonstration *noun* (a) *(political)* demonstraţie *f* (b) demonstrare *f or* prezentare *f*

denationalize *verb* a denaţionaliza *or* a privatiza; **the government will denationalize the public transport sector** = guvernul va denaţionaliza sectorul transportului în comun

denationalization *noun* denaţionalizare *f or* privatizare *f*

Denmark *noun* Danemarca *f* NOTE: capital: **Copenhagen** = Copenhaga; currency: **Danish krone** = coroană *f* daneză

denomination *noun* (a) *(specific name)* nume *n;* numire *f* (b) *(class, category)* categorie *f* (c) valoare *f* nominală; **money in small denominations** = bani cu valoare nominală redusă

department *noun* (a) *(government department)* departament *n or* minister *n* (b) secţie *f;* **export department** = secţie de export; **head of department** = şef *m* de secţie *or* de serviciu; **legal department** = oficiu *n* juridic; **personnel department** = serviciu *n* personal (c) **department store** = magazin *n* universal

departure *noun* plecare *f;* **point of departure** = punct *n* de plecare; **we have plenty of time before the departure of the train** = avem timp suficient până la plecarea trenului

depend *verb* a depinde; **we depend on the supplier to deliver the raw materials in time** = depindem de capacitatea furnizorului de a livra materia primă la timp

dependable *adjective* demn de încredere

dependent 1 *adjective* întreţinut; dependent 2 *noun* subordonat *m*

deponent *noun* deponent *m;* martor *m* în procese

deposit 1 *noun* (a) depunere *f;* depozit *n;* **deposit account** = cont *n* de depozit; **deposit slip** = foaie *f* de depunere; **fixed deposit** = depunere pe termen (b) garanţie *f or* acont *n;* **the terms of sale are 10% deposit and 12 monthly payments of £35** = condiţiile de vânzare sunt: 10 % acont şi 12 rate lunare de £35 2 *verb* a depune (bani la bancă)

deposition *noun* depoziţie *f;* mărturie *f*

depositor *noun* depunător *m*

depot *noun* (a) depozit *n;* **goods depot** = depozit de mărfuri (b) depou *n;* **bus depot** = garaj *n* de autobuze; **train depot** = depou feroviar

depreciate *verb* (a) a amortiza; **the cost of the investment is to be depreciated over 10 years** = costul investiţiei ar trebui amortizat în 10 ani (b) a (se) deprecia *or* a pierde din valoare; **most of the company's fixed assets have depreciated** = majoritatea mijloacelor fixe ale companiei şi-au pierdut din valoare

depreciation *noun* amortizare *f* a fondurilor fixe; **depreciation rate** = coeficient de amortizare; **straight-line depreciation** = amortizare uniformă

depress *verb* (a) *(reduce activity)* a diminua (activitatea economică) (b) a slăbi

depressed *adjective* deprimat; **depressed market** = piaţă *f* în criză, când oferta este mai mare decât cererea

depression *noun* criză *f* economică *or* depresiune *f;* stagnare *f* (a afacerilor)

deputy *noun* (a) adjunct *m;* **deputy manager** = director *m* adjunct (b) *(parliamentary representative - in France, Romania, etc.)* deputat *m*

deregulation *noun* liberalizare *f*

design 1 *noun* (a) desen *n;* schiţă *f* (b) proiectare *f;* **industrial design** = proiectare industrială 2 *verb* (a) a desena (b) a proiecta; **the new complex was designed entirely on the computer** = noul complex a fost proiectat în întregime pe calculator

designer *noun* (a) desenator *m* (b) proiectant *m*

designate 1 *verb* *(appoint to an office)* a desemna *or* a numi în funcţie 2 *adjective* *(appointed to an office)* numit în funcţie *or* titular de post

desk *noun* (a) *(office furniture)* birou *n;* **he sat down at his desk and began working** = s-a aşezat la birou şi a început să lucreze; **I need a new desk with more drawers** = am nevoie de un birou nou cu mai multe sertare (b) *(counter)* ghişeu *n* (c) *(cash desk)* casă *f* într-un magazin; **he paid for the goods at the desk** = a plătit pentru cumpărături la casă

desktop *noun* (a) suprafaţă *f* utilă de lucru a unui birou (b) care poate fi aşezat pe birou (un PC, o imprimantă, etc); **desktop publishing program** = software de editare şi tipărire de text cu ajutorul unui calculator şi al unei imprimante laser

destination *noun* destinaţie *f or* punct *n* terminus

detail 1 *noun* detaliu *n or* amănunt *n;* **you will find all the details in our latest catalogue** = veţi afla toate amănuntele în ultimul nostru catalog 2 *verb* a detalia *or* a descrie în amănunt; **he was asked to detail his plan** = i s-a cerut să descrie în amănunt planul său

deterioration *noun* **(a)** *(of food)* deteriorarea *f* calității produselor (alimentare) **(b)** uzură *f* a utilajelor; **due to advanced deterioration, the building had to be demolished and replaced by a new one** = datorită degradării avansate, clădirea a trebuit să fie demolată și înlocuită cu una nouă; **physical or internal deterioration** = degradare *f* fizică; **external deterioration or obsolescence** = uzură morală a echipamentului, mașinii, etc

determine *verb* **(a)** *(estabilish precisely)* a determina **(b)** a definitiva; **to determine the conditions of a contract** = a definitiva un contract

determined *adjective* hotărât *or* decis; **they were determined to finish the work before the end of the year** = erau deciși să termine treaba înainte de sfârșitul anului

Deutschmark *noun* marca *f* germană

devalue *verb* a (se) devaloriza

devaluation *noun* devalorizare *f*

develop *verb* **(a)** a (se) dezvolta **(b)** *(plan and produce)* a produce *or* a fabrica; **to develop a new product** = a fabrica un produs nou

developing countries *noun* țări *fpl* în curs de dezvoltare

development *noun* dezvoltare *f*; **development aid** = ajutor *n* de dezvoltare; **development areas** = arii *fpl* de dezvoltare (unde guvernul intervine pentru atragerea de noi activități industriale); **economic development** = dezvoltare economică; **industrial development** = dezvoltare industrială

deviation *noun* **(a)** deviere *f or* abatere *f* **(b)** schimbarea *f* rutei de către o navă

device *noun* **(a)** aparat *n or* dispozitiv *n;* mecanism *n* **(b)** plan *n;* **to leave somebody to his own devices** = a lăsa pe cineva să se descurce singur

diagram *noun* grafic *n or* diagramă *f*

dial 1 *noun* cadran *n* 2 *verb* a forma un număr de telefon

dialling code *noun* prefix *n* telefonic

diary *noun* agendă *f;* **desk diary** = agendă de birou

dictate *verb* a dicta; **to dictate a letter to a secretary** = a dicta o scrisoare unei secretare

dictating machine *noun* dictafon *n;* casetofon *n*

differ *verb* a se deosebi; a diferi

difference *noun* **(a)** deosebire *f;* **what is the difference between the two offers?** = care e deosebirea dintre cele două oferte? **(b)** diferență *f;* **price difference** = diferență de prețuri **(c)** *(disagreement)* dezacord *n*

different *adjective* **(a)** diferit **(b)** separat

differential *adjective* diferențial; **differential pay** = salarizare *f* diferențială; **differential prices** = prețuri *npl* diferențiale

differentiation *noun* diversificare *f* a produselor

difficult *adjective* dificil *or* greu de îndeplinit; **difficult task** = sarcină *f* dificilă

difficulty *noun* **(a)** dificultate *f* **(b)** piedică *f;* **they had a lot of difficulty opening a branch in the Far East** = au întâmpinat multe piedici încercând să deschidă o reprezentanță în Orientul îndepărtat

dilapidations *noun* lucruri pe care chiriașul trebuie să le repare la încheierea contractului de închiriere

dime *noun* US *(informal)* monedă *f* de 10 cenți

diminish *verb* **(a)** a descrește *or* a se micșora; **our profits have diminished considerably over the past two years** =

profiturile noastre s-au micșorat considerabil în ultimii doi ani; **Law of Diminishing Returns** = legea randamentului descrescând **(b)** a diminua *or* a atenua

direct 1 *verb* a îndruma *or* a dirija; a conduce; **he directs our operations in London** = el conduce filiala noastră din Londra 2 *adjective* direct; **direct action** = acțiune *f* directă; **direct cost** = cheltuieli *fpl* directe; **direct debit payment** = plata *f* prin debitarea directă a contului curent personal; **direct sale** = vânzare *f* directă 3 *adverb* direct; **to sell direct** = a vinde direct

directive *noun* directivă *f or* sarcină *f*

director *noun* director *f;* **board of directors** = consiliul *n* de administrație; **managing director** = director general

directory *noun* **(a)** ghid *m or* îndrumar *n* **(b)** carte *f* de telefon; **to look up a number in the telephone directory** = a căuta un număr în cartea de telefon

disclose *verb* **(a)** a dezvălui **(b)** a divulga; **banks should not disclose any details about a customer's accounts** = băncile nu ar trebui să divulge detalii privind conturile clienților lor

discount 1 *noun* scont *n or* rabat *n;* **the supplier offers a generous discount on bulk purchases** = furnizorul oferă un scont generos pentru achiziții en gros; **basic discount** = scont de bază; **discount rate** = rata de scont 2 *verb* **(a)** a deconta **(b)** a sconta (o cambie); **discounted value** = valoare *f* de scont

discretion *noun* **(a)** discreție *f;* **this job requires discretion and tact** = această afacere reclamă discreție și tact **(b)** *(freedom to act and think)* discernământ *n*

discretionary spending *noun* cheltuire *f* nechibzuită

discrimination *noun* discriminare *f or* tratare *f* diferențială

dishonour *verb* **(a)** a dezonora **(b)** a nu plăti; **to dishonour a bill** = a nu plăti o notă de plată; **dishonoured cheque** = cec *n* neonorat

disintegration *noun* dezintegrare *f or* împrăștiere *f*

disinvest *verb* *(reduce investment)* a reduce investițiile

disk *noun* disc *n;* **floppy disk** = disc floppy *or* dischetă *f;* **hard disk** = hard disc (disc intern într-un calculator)

dismiss *verb* a da afară *or* a concedia; **she was dismissed for being impolite to customers** = ea a fost concediată pentru lipsă de politețe față de clienți

dismissal *noun* concediere *f;* **unfair dismissal** = concediere pe nedrept

dispatch 1 *verb* a expedia; **the goods have been packed and dispatched** = bunurile au fost ambalate și expediate 2 *noun* expediere *f or* trimitere *f;* **dispatch department** = expediție *f;* **dispatch note** = notă *f* de expediție

dispatching *noun* expediere *f or* trimitere *f*

disposable income *noun* venit *n* disponibil

dispute 1 *noun* **(a)** *(quarrel)* ceartă *f* **(b)** *(debate)* dezbatere *f* **(c)** conflict *n;* **industrial dispute** = conflict de muncă 2 *verb* *(debate, argue)* a dezbate

dis-saving *noun* economii *fpl* negative

dissolution *noun* **(a)** *(disintegration)* dizolvare *f* **(b)** încetarea *f* activității; lichidare *f*

dissolve *verb* **(a)** a dizolva **(b)** a desface; **to dissolve a partnership** = a întrerupe asocierea într-o afacere

distrain *verb* a confisca (bunuri)

distress *noun* **(a)** confiscare *f* de bunuri (ca urmare a unei hotărâri judecătorești) **(b)** dificultate *f or* pericol *n* iminent; **a ship in distress** = o navă în pericol (de a se scufunda)

distress sale *noun* vânzare *f* forţată de împrejurări nefavorabile

distribute *verb* **(a)** a distribui; **new catalogues were distributed to all our important customers** = cataloagele noi au fost distribuite tuturor clienţilor noştri importanţi **(b)** a împărţi **(c)** a repartiza

distribution *noun* **(a)** distribuţie *f*; **distribution channels** = reţea *f* de distribuţie; **distribution costs** = cheltuieli de distribuţie; **Theory of Distribution** = teoria *f* distribuţiei **(b)** împărţire *f* **(c)** repartizare *f*; **distribution of public investment** = repartizarea investiţiilor publice

distributor *noun* distribuitor *m*

district *noun* **(a)** regiune *f* **(b)** sector *n*; **district manager** = şef *m* de sector **(c)** district *n*; **commercial district** = centru *n* comercial

divide *verb* **(a)** a împărţi **(b)** a repartiza

dividend *noun* **(a)** deîmpărţit *n* **(b)** dividend *n*; **accumulated dividend** = dividend acumulat *or* neplătit la timp; **interim dividend** = dividend intermediar

division *noun* **(a)** departament *n or* secţie *f*; **marketing division** = departamentul de marketing; **production division** = secţie de producţie **(b)** diviziune *f*

dock 1 *noun* doc *n*; **the docks** = port *n*; **loading dock** = doc de încărcare 2 *verb* a intra în port; **the cargo boat was expected to dock at 10.00 hours** = cargoul era aşteptat să sosească la ora 10

docker *noun* docher *m or* lucrător *m* portuar

document *noun* act *n or* document *n*; **legal document** = document oficial

documentary *adjective* documentar

documentation *noun* **(a)** documentare *f* **(b)** documentaţie *f*; **after studying the documentation he wrote his report** = după ce a studiat documentaţia a întocmit raportul

domestic *adjective* **(a)** casnic; **domestic appliances** = aparate *npl* de uz casnic **(b)** intern; **the goods were sold on the domestic market** = produsele au fost desfăcute pe piaţa internă

donor *noun* donator *m*

dot-matrix printer *noun* imprimantă *f* matricială

double 1 *adjective* dublu; **to be on double time** = a lucra ore suplimentare (plătite dublu); **double figures** = număr *n* din două cifre (de la 10 la 99); **double taxation** = impunere dublă 2 *verb* a (se) dubla; **the number of customers has almost doubled over the past year** = numărul clienţilor aproape s-a dublat în cursul anului trecut

Dow Jones Index *noun* indice *m* Dow Jones la bursa din New York

down *adverb* jos *(immediate payment)* **cash down** *or* **money down** = banii jos *or* plata pe loc

downgrade *verb* **(a)** a (se) degrada **(b)** a retrograda

downmarket *adjective* de calitate modestă (despre comerţ, desfacere, servicii, etc.)

down time *noun* timp *m* mort

down tools *verb* **(a)** a înceta lucrul **(b)** a refuza să lucreze

downtown *noun & adverb* centrul oraşului

downturn *noun* scădere *f* a preţurilor, cantităţii, etc

dozen *noun* duzină *f*

draft 1 *noun* **(a)** *(banking)* ordin *n* de plată; **sterling draft** = ordin de plată în lire sterline **(b)** schiţă *f;* **the manager examined the draft of his report** = directorul a studiat schiţa raportului său **(c)** plan *n* **2** *verb* **(a)** a schiţa; **to draft a contract** = a schiţa un contract **(b)** a proiecta

drain **1** *noun* scurgere *f;* **brain drain** = exodul *n* intelectualilor peste graniţă; **drain of capital** = scurgerea de capital afară din ţară **2** *verb* a se scurge

draught *noun* pescaj *n* (distanţa dintre fundul vasului şi linia de plutire)

draw **1** *verb* **(a)** a atrage; **to draw someone's attention** = a atrage atenţia cuiva **(b)** a retrage *or* a scoate; **to draw money** = a scoate bani de la bancă; a efectua o restituire **(c) to draw a cheque** = a completa un cec **2** *noun* retragere *f or* restituire *f* (la bancă)

draw up *verb* a schiţa; **to draw up an itinerary** = a schiţa un itinerar

drawback *noun* dezavantaj *n or* inconvenient *n*

drawing account *noun* cont *n* curent

drive **1** *noun* **(a)** **economy drive** = campanie *f* de reducere a costurilor **(b)** energie *f or* ambiţie *f* **2** *verb* a conduce *or* a dirija *or* a forţa; **to drive a**

hard bargain = a forţa un contract dezavantajos; **to drive prices up or down** = a dirija nivelul preţurilor

due **1** *adjective* **(a)** *(owed, outstanding)* datorat **(b)** *(expected to arrive)* aşteptat; **the next shipment is due in two days** = următoarea livrare este aşteptată în două zile **(c)** cuvenit *or* potrivit; **in due course** = la timpul potrivit; **with due care** = cu grija cuvenită

duplicate *adj* duplicat; **in duplicate** = în două exemplare *or* în duplicat

durable goods *noun* bunuri *npl* de folosinţă îndelungată

Dutch **1** *noun* olandez(ă) **2** *adjective* olandez(ă)

Dutch auction *noun* licitaţie *f* la care se coboară preţul până se găseşte un cumpărător

duty *noun* **(a)** datorie *f* **(b) compound duty** = taxă *f* vamală combinată; **customs duty** = taxă vamală; **preferential duty** = taxe vamale preferenţiale

duty-free *adjective* scutit de taxe (vamale); **duty-free shop** = magazin *n* duty-free

Ee

early 1 *adjective* **(a)** timpuriu **(b)** matinal *(in Britain)* **early closing day** = o zi pe săptămână în care unele magazine închid la prânz (în Marea Britanie) **2** *adverb* devreme *or* curând

earmark *verb* a aloca (fonduri)

earn *verb* **(a)** a câştiga (prin muncă); **they earn £200 a week** = ei câştigă 200 de lire pe săptămână **(b)** a merita; **he does not earn his commission** = el nu îşi merită comisionul **(c)** a aduce dobânzi; **this account earns him a decent interest** = acest cont îi aduce o dobândă rezonabilă

earning capacity *or* **earning power** *noun* capacitate *f* de câştig

earning potential *noun* potenţial *n* de câştig

earning rate *noun* rata *f* profitului unei companii

earnings *plural noun* **(a)** salariu *n;* **compensation for loss of earnings** = compensaţie *f* pentru pierderea de salariu **(b)** câştig *n*

ease *verb* a scădea; **prices have eased in the last month** = preţurile au scăzut în ultima lună

Eastern European Time *noun* *(local time in Romania, Bulgaria, Finland, Greece and Turkey, two hours ahead of GMT)*Ora *f* Europei Răsăritene (ora locală în România, Bulgaria, Finlanda, Grecia şi Turcia, două ore în avans faţă de ora Londrei)

EC (= European Community) CEE (Comunitatea Economică Europeană)

economic *adjective* economic; **economic development** = dezvoltare economică; **economic geography** = geografie economică; **economic growth** = creştere *or* dezvoltare economică; **economic indicator** = indicator economic; **economic planning** = planificare economică; **economic policy** = politică economică; **economic sanction** = sancţiune economică; **economic system** = sistem economic; **economic theory** = teorie economică; **economic trends** = tendinţe economice; **economic warfare** = conflict economic

economical *adjective* **(a)** *(sparing)* econom **(b)** economic(os); **economical fuel consumption** = consum economic de carburanţi

economics *plural noun* **(a)** *(the science of the production and distribution of wealth)* ştiinţe *fpl* economice *or* economie *f* **(b)** economie *f* politică

economist *noun* economist *m*

economize *verb* a economisi; **to economize on raw materials** = a economisi materii prime

economy *noun* **(a)** *(careful use)* economie *f* *or* chibzuială *f* **(b)** economie; **black economy** = bursa neagră *or* comerţ ilicit; **capitalist economy** = economie capitalistă; **the country is trying to rebuild its economy after the collapse of the communist**

regime = după prăbuşirea regimului comunist ţara încearcă să îşi reconstruiască economia

Ecuador *noun* Ecuador *m* NOTE: capital: **Quito**; currency: **sucre**

Ecuadorian *noun & adjective* ecuadorian(ă)

edit *verb* **(a)** *(text)* a prepara **(b)** *(book)* a edita **(c)** *(newspaper)* a redacta

editor *noun* redactor-şef *m*

editorial 1 *adjective* editorial 2 *noun* editorial *n or* articol *n* de fond; **his main job is writing editorials for the Sunday edition of the newspaper** = sarcina sa principală este redactarea unui editorial pentru ediţia duminicală a ziarului

EEC (= European Economic Community) CEE (Comunitatea Economică Europeană)

effect 1 *noun* **(a)** rezultat *n* **(b)** efect *n;* **the effect of the rise in interest rates could not be foreseen immediately** = efectul majorării ratei dobânzilor nu putea fi prevăzut imediat; **to remain in effect** = a rămâne în vigoare **(c) effects** = echipament *n;* bunuri *npl* personale mobile **(d)** impresie *f* 2 *verb* **(a)** a efectua *or* a face; **to effect a compromise** = a face un compromis; **to effect a payment** = a efectua o plată **(b)** a produce

effective *adjective* efectiv *or* concret; **effective demand** = cerere concretă; **effective tax rate** = impozit *n* mediu pe venit

efficiency *noun* **(a)** eficienţă *f;* **economic efficiency** = eficienţă economică **(b)** randament *n;* **industrial efficiency** = randament industrial; **technical efficiency** = randament tehnic al unui utilaj

efficient *adjective* **(a)** eficace *or* eficient; **efficient system** = sistem eficient **(b)** capabil; **efficient worker** = lucrător capabil

Egypt *noun* Egipt *m* NOTE: capital: **Cairo**; currency: **Egyptian pound** = liră *f* egipteană

Egyptian *noun & adjective* egiptean(ă)

elasticity *noun* elasticitate *or* flexibilitate; **elasticity of demand** = flexibilitatea cererii; **elasticity of supply** = flexibilitatea ofertei

elect 1 *verb* **(a)** a alege (prin vot); **to elect the chairman of a society** = a alege un preşedinte al unei societăţi **(b)** a (se) decide; **he elected to open a branch in London** = s-a decis să înfiinţeze o filială la Londra 2 *adjective* **president-elect** = preşedinte *m* ales

election *noun* alegere *f;* **general election** = alegeri generale

electoral register *noun* listă *f* electorală

electronic *adjective* electronic; **electronic funds transfer** = transfer electronic de fonduri (modalitate modernă de plată în magazine unde cumpărătorul plăteşte cu cartea de credit sau de debit în loc de cec sau bani peşin)

electronics *plural noun* electronică *f;* **electronics engineer** = inginer *m* electronist

element *noun* **(a)** element *n* **(b)** aspect *n;* **they studied carefully all the elements of the agreement** = au studiat cu atenţie toate aspectele înţelegerii **(c)** component *n*

elevator *noun* **(a)** stivuitor *n or* electrocar *n;* elevator *n* **(b)** *US* lift *n or* ascensor *n*

eligible *adjective* eligibil; **he was eligible for a university grant** = avea dreptul la bursă de studii universitare

El Salvador *noun* Salvador *m* NOTE: capital: **San Salvador**; currency: **Salvadorian colón** = colón salvadorian

embargo 1 *noun* interzicere *f or* embargou *n;* **to be under an embargo** =

a fi interzis **2** *verb* a pune embargou asupra

embark *verb* a se îmbarca; **we embarked a few minutes before departure** = ne-am îmbarcat pe vapor câteva minute înainte de plecare

embassy *noun* ambasadă *f*

embezzle *verb* a delapida

embezzlement *noun* delapidare *f*

emergency *noun* **(a)** *(extremity)* urgenţă *f* **(b)** *(danger)* pericol *n* **(c)** **state of emergency** = stare *f* de necesitate

emerging countries *noun* ţări *fpl* în curs de dezvoltare

emigrant *noun* emigrant *m*

emigrate *verb* a emigra

emigration *noun* emigrare *f*

employ *verb* **(a)** a angaja; **as the business grew the company employed more staff** = odată cu creşterea cifrei de afaceri compania a angajat personal nou **(b)** *(use up)* a folosi

employed 1 *adjective* angajat *or* activ **2** *noun* oameni *mpl* ai muncii, angajaţi

employee *noun* salariat *m or* angajat *m*

employer *noun* patron *m*

employment *noun* **(a)** angajare *f;* **employment agency** = agenţie *f* de plasare; **employment contract** = contract *n* de angajare; **full-time employment** = angajare cu normă întreagă **(b)** *(profession, occupation)* ocupaţie *f* **(c)** *(job)* slujbă *f or* serviciu *n*

emporium *noun* centru *n* comercial; piaţă *f or* târg *n*

empower *verb* **(a)** a împuternici; **he empowered an agent to sell his shares** = a împuternicit un agent să-i vândă acţiunile **(b)** a autoriza

empties *plural noun* lăzi *fpl* de ambalaj refolosibile

encash *verb* a încasa; **to encash a cheque** = a încasa un cec

encashable *adjective* (despre cecuri, etc.) încasabil, care poate fi transformat în bani lichizi

enclose *verb* **(a)** a pune în plic; a anexa; **I enclose a copy of the agreement as requested** = veţi găsi în plic o copie a contractului conform cu cererea dumneavoastră **(b)** a împrejmui

enclosure *noun* **(a)** conţinut *n* (într-un plic, scrisoare, etc.) **(b)** îngrădire *f;* împrejmuire *f*

end 1 *noun* **(a)** sfârşit *n or* încheiere *f;* **to come to an end** = a înceta; **end of contract** = sfârşitul contractului; **end product** = produs final; **to make ends meet** = a supravieţui de la un salariu la altul, a se descurca cu dificultate; **month end** = sfârşit de lună **(b)** *(objective, goal)* scop *n or* ţel *n* **2** *verb* a se sfârşi

endorse *verb* **(a)** a confirma; **to endorse a cheque** = a confirma prin semnătură un cec **(b)** a andosa **(c)** a gira

endorsement *noun* **(a)** gir *n* **(b)** *(authorization)* aprobare *f* **(c)** andosare *f;* **blank endorsement** = andosare în alb; **procuration endorsement** = andosare prin procură

energetic *adjective* **(a)** energetic *or* plin de vitalitate **(b)** activ

energy *noun* **(a)** forţă *f or* resurse *fpl;* **he hasn't got the energy to finish what he has started** = nu are resurse să ducă la bun sfârşit ceea ce a început **(b)** energie *f;* **the company is trying to save energy** = compania încearcă să economisească energia (electrică)

energy saving 1 *noun* factor *n* de economisire a energiei **2** *adjective* economic(os); **energy-saving measures** = măsuri *f* de economisire a energiei

enforce *verb* **(a)** a aplica; **to enforce the terms of an agreement** = a aplica condiţiile unei înţelegeri; **to enforce a law** = a aplica o lege **(b)** *(apply)* a pune în vigoare

enforcement *noun* **(a)** aplicare *f* **(b)** punere *f* în vigoare

engage *verb* **(a)** a angaja; **they engaged a computer expert to set up a computer network** = ei au angajat un inginer de sistem pentru a pune la punct reţeaua de calculatoare **(b)** a obliga; **the contract engages us to finish the construction of the bridge in two years** = contractul ne obligă să finalizăm construcţia podului în doi ani

engaged *adjective* ocupat; **we tried to ring him at work but the line was engaged all day** = am încercat să-i telefonăm la serviciu dar telefonul lui a sunat ocupat tot timpul

engagement *noun* angajament *n;* acord *n;* înţelegere *n;* **to break an engagement** = a încălca un acord

engineer *noun* inginer *m;* tehnician *m;* **civil engineer** = inginer de construcţii civile; **electronics engineer** = inginer electronist

engineering *noun* inginerie *f;* **specialist in civil engineering** = expert *m* în construcţii civile; **engineering department** = compartiment tehnic

England *noun* Anglia *f* NOTE: capital: **London** = Londra; currency: **pound sterling (£)** = liră sterlină (£)

English *noun & adjective* englez(ă)

enter *verb* **(a)** a intra; **to enter a room** = a intra într-o cameră **(b) to enter figures in the books** = a opera intrări contabile **(c)** a înregistra

enterprise *noun* întreprindere *f;* **private enterprise** = întreprindere particulară; **state enterprise** = întreprindere de stat

entertain *verb* **(a)** a acorda atenţie **(b)** *(a guest)* a întreţine

entertainment account *noun* cont *n* de protocol

entertainment allowance *noun* cheltuieli *fpl* de reprezentare

entitle *verb* a îndreptăţi; **the customer is entitled to a refund if the product is defective** = clientul este îndreptăţit să ceară banii înapoi dacă produsul este defect

entrance *noun* **(a)** intrare *f* **(b)** acces *n* **(c) entrance fee** = preţul *n* biletului de intrare; **the entrance fee is £10** = costul biletului de intrare este £10

entrepreneur *noun* antreprenor *m*

entrust *verb* a încredinţa; **the manager entrusted him with the keys of the shop** = directorul i-a încredinţat cheile magazinului

entry *noun* **(a)** înregistrare *f* **(b) entry in a ledger** = intrare contabilă **(c) entry visa** = viză de intrare

envelope *noun* plic *n;* **airmail envelope** = plic par avion

equal **1** *adjective* egal; **to be equal to** = a fi în stare să; **equal opportunities** = şanse egale (pentru toţi); **equal pay** = sistem just (nedescriminatoriu) de salarizare **2** *verb* a egala *or* a fi egal cu

equalize *verb* **(a)** a egaliza **(b)** a compensa; **to equalize dividends** = a compensa dividende

equilibrium *noun* echilibru *n;* **equilibrium amount** = sumă *f* de echilibru; **equilibrium price** = preţ *n* de echilibru; **partial equilibrium** = echilibru parţial

equip *verb* **(a)** a dota; **the office was equipped with powerful computers** = biroul era dotat cu calculatoare puternice **(b)** a utila; **the workshop was equipped with a new lathe** = atelierul a fost utilat cu un strung nou

equipment *noun* **(a)** echipament *n or* accesorii *npl;* **equipment leasing** = închiriere *f* de echipament; **office**

equipment = accesorii de birou **(b)** utilaj *n;* **heavy equipment** = utilaj greu

equities *plural noun* acţiuni *fpl* obişnuite (la bursă)

equity *noun* **(a)** beneficiu *n;* participarea *f* la beneficii **(b)** **shareholders' equity** = capital al acţionarilor **(c) equity paper** = titlu *n* de participare

equivalence *noun* paritate *f;* echivalenţă *f*

equivalent 1 *adjective* echivalent; **to be equivalent to** = a fi echivalent *or* egal cu 2 *noun* echivalent *n;* **one pint is the equivalent of 0.568 litre** = o pintă este echivalentul a 0,568 litri

erode *verb* a (se) eroda *or* a (se) uza

erosion *noun* eroziune *f;* **soil erosion** = eroziunea solului

error *noun* greşeală *f or* eroare *f;* **by error** = din greşeală; **printing error** = greşeală de tipar; **to make an error** = a face o greşeală *or* a greşi

escalate *verb* a creşte *or* a escalada

escalation *noun* majorare *f or* escaladare *f;* **escalation of prices** = escaladare a preţurilor

escalator clause *noun* clauza *f* tarifului progresiv

escape clause *noun* clauză *f* de eschivare

escrow *noun* sumă *f* de bani sau altă valoare reţinută ca garanţie

espionage *noun* spionaj *n;* **industrial espionage** = spionaj economic

essential *adj* esenţial

establish *verb* **(a)** a stabili **(b)** a înfiinţa; **the firm was established 100 years ago** = firma a fost înfiinţată acum 100 de ani

establishment *noun* instituţie *f or* firmă *f*

estate *noun* **(a)** moşie *f or* teren *n* **(b)** bunuri *npl* imobiliare; **estate agency** = agenţie imobiliară; **estate agent** = agent imobiliar **(c)** zonă *f or* cartier *n;* **housing estate** = cartier rezidenţial; **industrial estate** = zonă industrială

estimate 1 *verb* **(a)** *(judge)* a aprecia **(b)** *(assess)* a evalua 2 *noun* **(a)** calcul *n;* **rough estimate** = calcul aproximativ **(b)** deviz *n* **(c)** evaluare *f;* **estimate of costs** = evaluare a cheltuielii

estimation *noun* apreciere *f;* estimare *f*

Estonia *noun* Estonia *f* NOTE: capital: **Tallinn;** currency: **krona**

Estonian *noun & adjective* estonian(ă)

Ethiopia *noun* Etiopia *f* NOTE: capital: **Addis Ababa** = Addis Abeba; currency: **Ethiopian birr** = birr etiopian

Ethiopian *noun & adjective* etiopian(ă)

Eurobond *noun* euroobligaţiune *f* (emisă pe o europiaţă)

Eurocheque *noun* eurocec *n*

Euromarket *noun* europiaţă *f*

Europe *noun* Europa *f*

European *adjective & noun* european; **European countries** = ţări europeane; **European Community (EC)** = Comunitatea Economică Europeană (CEE); **European Union (EU)** = Uniunea *f* Europeană

evade *verb* **(a)** *(avoid paying)* a evita (o plată, etc.) **(b)** *(dodge)* a se sustrage de la

evasion *noun* **(a)** evitare *f* **(b)** evaziune *f* (fiscală); **he was found guilty of tax evasion** = a fost găsit vinovat de evaziune fiscală

evidence *noun* dovadă *f;* mărturie *f;* **to give evidence in court** = a depune mărturie în instanţă judecătorească

exact 1 *adjective* precis *or* exact *or* corect 2 *verb* a cere; **to exact payment from debtors** = a cere datorilor să plătească

exaction *noun* somație *f* de plată

examination *noun* (a) cercetare *f or* examen *n* (b) examinare *f;* expertiză *f;* **the customs official continued their examination of the suspect lorry** = vameşul a continuat examinarea camionului suspect (c) interogare *f;* **cross-examination** = interogare suplimentară

examine *verb* (a) a cerceta (b) a examina; **the customer examined the car thoroughly before buying it** = clientul a examinat minuţios maşina înainte de a o cumpăra

except 1 *preposition* (a) fără (b) cu excepţia; **all goods and services are subject to VAT except books, newspapers and children's clothes** = toate bunurile de consum şi serviciile sunt supuse TVA cu excepţia cărţilor, ziarelor şi articolelor de îmbrăcăminte pentru copii 2 *verb* a excepta

excess 1 *noun* (a) exces *n* (b) surplus *n* 2 *adjective* (a) suplimentar; **excess profit** = profit suplimentar (b) depăşit; **excess capacity** = capacitate depăşită (c) **excess fare** = supliment *n* de călătorie

exchange 1 *noun* (a) schimb *n;* transfer *n;* **exchange of contracts** = schimb de contracte; **part exchange** = schimb parţial (b) schimb valutar; **exchange control** = controlul *n* schimbului valutar; **exchange rate** = schimb valutar (c) **the Stock Exchange** = Bursa *f* (d) **telephone exchange** = centrală telefonică 2 *verb* (a) a schimba; **due to financial hardship he had to exchange his new car for a cheaper one** = a trebuit să schimbe maşina nouă cu una mai modestă datorită greutăţilor financiare (b) a schimba bani; **he exchanged dollars for**

pounds = a schimbat dolarii în lire sterline

Exchequer (the) *noun* *GB* Ministerul *n* de Finanţe (în Marea Britanie); **the Chancellor of the Exchequer** = Ministrul de Finanţe

excise 1 *noun* impozit *n* pe cifra de afaceri 2 *verb* a impune impozite

exclude *verb* a exclude; **the prices quoted exclude VAT** = preţurile citate exclud TVA

exclusive *adjective* (a) exclusiv; **exclusive sales agreement** = contract de vânzare exclusiv (b) select; **exclusive club** = club select *or* exclusivist

execute *verb* (a) a executa *or* a îndeplini; **to execute an order** = a executa un ordin (b) *(enforce)* a pune în vigoare (o lege, etc.)

executive 1 *noun* (a) director *m* (b) consiliu executiv 2 *adjective* (a) executiv (b) eficace

executor *noun* *(of a will)* executor *m* al unui testament

exempt 1 *adjective* scutit; **tax-exempt** = scutit de impozite 2 *verb* a scuti

exemption *noun* scutire *f;* **tax-exemption** = scutire de impozite

exhibit 1 *noun* exponat *n;* **their exhibits were highly praised** = exponatele lor au fost foarte apreciate 2 *verb* a (se) expune

exhibition *noun* expoziţie *f*

exorbitant *adj* exorbitant

expand *verb* (a) a (se) mări (b) a (se) extinde (c) a (se) dezvolta; **the economy is expanding at a constant rate** = economia se dezvoltă într-un ritm constant

expansion *noun* (a) dezvoltare *f;* **expansion of foreign trade** = dezvoltarea comerţului exterior (b) expansiune *f*

expectations *plural noun* previziuni *fpl*

expenditure *noun* cheltuieli *fpl;* **capital expenditure** = cheltuieli de capital; **productive expenditure** = bani cheltuiți de stat pentru construirea de drumuri, clădiri, etc

expense *noun* cheltuială *f;* **expense account** = cont *n* curent de cheltuieli; **they stayed at the hotel at the company's expense** = au stat la hotel pe cheltuiala companiei; **incidental expenses** = cheltuieli ocazionale; **overhead expenses** = cheltuieli de întreținere; **preliminary expenses** = cheltuieli de constituire *or* preliminarii; **travelling expenses** = cheltuieli de călătorie

expensive *adjective* scump *or* costisitor; **the new computer network proved to be more expensive than they had expected** = o nouă rețea de calculatoare s-a dovedit a fi mai costisitoare decât s-au așteptat

experience *noun* experiență *f;* **we have a lot of experience in selling books** = avem o experiență bogată în domeniul vânzării de carte

expert *noun* expert *m or* specialist *m;* **he asked the advice of a financial expert** = a cerut sfatul unui expert financiar

expertise *noun* expertiză *f;* **financial expertise** = expertiză financiară

expiration *noun* expirare *f;* **expiration of an insurance policy** = expirarea unei polițe de asigurări

expire *verb* a expira; **his insurance policy will expire in three months** = polița lui de asigurări va expira în trei luni

export **1** *noun* export *n;* **export bounty** = subvenții *fpl* la export; **export licence** = licență *f* de export; **export quota** = cotă *f* de export; **goods for export** = bunuri de export **2** *verb* a exporta; **we export machinery and import foodstuffs** = exportăm utilaje și importăm materii prime pentru industria alimentară

exporter *noun* exportator *m*

extend *verb* a extinde *or* a prelungi; **to extend a contract** = a prelungi (reînnoi) un contract

extension *noun* **(a)** prelungire *f;* extensie *f* **(b)** interior *n* (telefonic); **can I have extension 234 please?** = interior 234, vă rog

extraordinary *adj* extraordinar

Ff

face value *noun* valoare *f* nominală

facility *noun* (a) facilitate *f* or posibilitate *f*; **credit facility of up to £1000** = posibilitatea de a obţine credit de maximum £1000; **overdraft facility** = facilitate de descoperit (b) **facilities** = condiţii favorabile

facsimile *noun* (a) facsimil *n* (b) facsimil *n* (fax) (aparat de transmitere a documentelor prin linia telefonică)

factor *noun* (a) element *n* (b) factor *n*; **cyclic factor** = factor ciclic; **cost factor** = factor de cost; **deciding factor** = factor decisiv; **factors of production** = factori de producţie

factoring *noun* factoring *n* (finanţare similară creditului)

factory *noun* fabrică *f* or uzină *f*; **car factory** = uzină de automobile; **factory hand** = muncitor *m*; **factory price** = preţ *n* de fabrică; **factory unit** = secţie *f* de producţie; **shoe factory** = fabrică de încălţăminte

Fahrenheit scală de măsurare a temperaturii, apa îngheaţă la 32° şi fierbe la 212°

fail 1 *verb* (a) a eşua; **his effort to set up his own business failed** = eforturile sale de a întemeia o afacere au eşuat (b) a omite; **he failed to declare the prohibited goods at the customs** = a omis să declare bunurile prohibitive la vamă (c) a dezamăgi; **his partner failed him** = partenerul său l-a dezamăgit (d) a da faliment; **his venture failed after struggling for two years** = întreprinderea lui a dat faliment după doi ani de eforturi zadarnice 2 *noun* **without fail** = sigur

failure *noun* (a) eşec *n* or nereuşită *f* (b) *(bankruptcy)* faliment *n*

fair 1 *noun* expoziţie *f* or târg *n*; **our representative goes to the Frankfurt Book Fair every year** = reprezentantul nostru merge la Expoziţia de Carte din Frankfurt în fiecare an; **trade fair** = expoziţie comercială 2 *adjective* just or echitabil; **fair deal** = tranzacţie echitabilă; **fair dealings** = practici comerciale corecte; **fair price** = preţ corect; **fair trade** = comerţ just

faith *noun* (a) încredere *f*; **I have faith in my bank** = am încredere în banca mea (b) cinste or lealitate (c) **in good faith** = cu bună credinţă

fall 1 *noun* (a) cădere *f* (b) scădere *f*; **fall in the price of oil** = scăderea preţului petrolului 2 *verb* (a) a cădea (b) a scădea or a coborî; **the prices are falling** = preţurile scad (continuu); **our profits have fallen considerably over the past two years** = profiturile noastre s-au micşorat considerabil în ultimii doi ani

fall away *verb* a descreşte or a (se) reduce; **orders have fallen away this year** = comenzile s-au redus anul acesta

fall back *verb* (despre preţuri) a scădea din nou; **after a steep rise prices fell back** = după o creştere vertiginoasă preţurile au scăzut din nou

fall behind *verb* a rămâne în urmă *or* a fi restanţier; **she fell behind with her loan repayments** = ea a rămas în urmă cu ratele la împrumut

false *adjective* **(a)** greşit; **false calculation** = calcul greşit **(b)** fals; **false alarm** = alarmă falsă **(c) false bottom** = fund dublu (al unei valize) **(d)** mincinos; **false declaration** = declaraţie mincinoasă

falsify *verb* a falsifica

falsification *noun* falsificare *f;* **falsification of accounts** = falsificarea de conturi

fancy *adjective* **(a)** fantezist; **fancy goods** = bunuri *or* articole fanteziste (care atrag clienţi prin insolit) **(b)** foarte scump *or* exorbitant; **fancy prices** = preţuri exorbitante

fare *noun* ·**(a)** bilet *n* **(b)** tarif *n or* costul *n* biletului de călătorie; **full fare** = tarif întreg; **return fare** = costul biletului de călătorie dus şi întors; **single fare** = costul biletului de călătorie pentru dus; **taxi fare** = costul călătoriei cu taxiul

Far East *noun* Orientul îndepărtat

farm 1 *verb* **(a)** a cultiva **(b) to farm out work** = a închiria mână de lucru 2 *noun* fermă *f*

farmer *noun* fermier *m*

farmhand *noun* muncitor *m* agricol necalificat

fault *noun* **(a)** vină *f;* **he admitted it was his fault** = a recunoscut că era vina lui **(b)** defect *n;* **mechanical fault** = defect mecanic

faulty *adjective* defectuos; **the technician was called to replace the faulty power cable** = tehnicianul a fost chemat să schimbe cablul de alimentare defectuos

favour *noun* **(a)** favoare *f;* **all members of the board are in favour of taking on more staff for the Christmas season** = toţi membrii consiliului de administraţie sunt în favoarea angajării de personal sezonier pentru perioada de Crăciun; **to ask for a favour** = a cere o favoare **(b)** avantaj *n*

favourable *adjective* pozitiv; **favourable balance of payments** = balanţă de plăţi pozitivă

fax 1 *noun* facsimil *n or* fax *n* 2 *verb* a transmite prin fax

feasibility *noun* fezabilitate *f or* viabilitate *f;* **feasibility study** = studiu *n* atent al viabilităţii unui produs proiectat

federal *adjective* federal; **Federal Reserve System** = Sistemul Federal al Resurselor, sistem bancar american, format din 12 bănci

federation *noun* federaţie *f or* asociaţie *f;* **federation of trade unions** = asociaţie de sindicate

fee *noun* **(a)** onorariu *n;* **doctor's fee** = onorariul doctorului **(b)** taxă *f* **(c) entrance fee** = preţ *n* al biletului de intrare

feedback *noun* feedback *n or* reacţie *f;* răspuns *n*

ferry 1 *noun* bac *n or* feribot *n;* **we took the ferry from Dover** = am luat bacul de la Dover 2 *verb* a traversa cu bacul

few *adjective* **(a)** puţini *or* puţine; **we received very few orders last week** = am primit foarte puţine comenzi săptămâna trecută **(b)** nu prea mulţi; **few people trusted him as manager** = nu prea mulţi aveau încredere în el ca director

fictitious *adjective* fictiv; **fictitious assets** = fonduri fictive; **fictitious person** = persoană juridică

fiduciary *noun* **(a)** executor *m or* persoană *f* de încredere **(b) fiduciary loan** = împrumut *n* pe încredere *or* fără garanţii

fifty-fifty *adjective & adverb* în părţi egale; **to go fifty-fifty with someone** = a împărţi pe din două cu cineva

figure 1 *noun* cifră *f;* **sales figures** = cifra de vânzări; **six figure sum** = sumă cu şase cifre (peste 100.000); **to work out the figures** = a calcula 2 *verb* **to figure out** = a calcula; a estima

file 1 *noun* **(a)** dosar *n;* **he was asked to fetch last year's sales file** = i s-a cerut să aducă dosarul cu vânzările pe anul trecut **(b)** arhivă *f* **(c)** *(computer)* fişier *n* 2 *verb* a clasa documente la dosar *or* a clasa dosare în arhivă

filing clerk *noun* arhivar *m*

Filipino *noun & adjective* filipinez(ă)

final *adjective* final *or* ultim; **final demand** = cerere finală de plată; **final instalment** = ultima rată (de plată); **final port** = port *n* de destinaţie

finally *adverb* în cele din urmă; **we finally convinced him to join our project** = în cele din urmă l-am convins să se ralieze proiectului nostru

finance 1 *noun* **(a)** finanţe *fpl;* **finance house** = societate financiară **(b)** **finances** = bani *mpl or* fonduri *npl* 2 *verb* a finanţa; **the private sector will finance the construction of the new underground line** = sectorul particular va finanţa construirea noii linii de metrou

financial *adjective* financiar; **financial adviser** = consilier financiar; **financial assistance** = ajutor financiar; **financial crisis** = criză financiară; **financial period** = exerciţiu financiar; **financial position** = situaţie financiară; **financial resources** = resurse financiare; **Financial Times (Stock Exchange) Index** = Indice la bursa londoneză iniţiat de cotianul `Financial Times'; **financial year** = an financiar

financially *adverb* (din punct de vedere) financiar

financier *noun* om *m* de afaceri

fine 1 *noun* amendă *f;* **the insurance company was asked to pay a £50,000 fine** = compania de asigurări a fost somată să plătească o amendă de £50.000 2 *verb* a amenda

Finland *noun* Finlanda *f* NOTE: capital: **Helsinki;** currency: **markka** = marcă *f*

Finn *noun* finlandez(ă)

Finnish *adjective* finlandez(ă)

fire safety officer *noun* responsabil *m* cu prevenirea incendiilor

firm 1 *noun* firmă *f or* întreprindere *f* comercială 2 *adjective* **(a)** ferm; **firm offer** = ofertă fermă **(b)** neclintit; **in spite of the pressure his position was firm** = în ciuda presiunii atitudinea sa a rămas neclintită

first class *noun* clasa *f* întâia (cea mai comfortabilă în călătorii cu trenul, avionul, etc.)

first-class *adjective* de prima calitate; **first-class hotel** = hotel categoria lux

fiscal *adjective* fiscal; **fiscal policy** = politică fiscală; **fiscal year** = an fiscal

fit 1 *verb* **(a)** *(suit)* a potrivi **(b)** *(match)* a corespunde 2 *adjective* **(a)** *(suitable)* potrivit **(b)** *(able)* capabil *or* apt

fit in *verb* a găsi timp pentru; **the manager fitted me in between two meetings** = directorul şi-a găsit timp să mă primească între două şedinţe

fit out *verb* a echipa; **they fitted out the workshop** = au echipat atelierul

fittings *plural noun* accesorii *npl or* garnituri *fpl*

fix *verb* **(a)** a fixa; **to fix a meeting** = a fixa data unei şedinţe **(b)** *(arrange)* a aranja **(c)** a repara; **I called the repairman to fix my typewriter** = am chemat tehnicianul să îmi repare maşina de scris **(d)** a pregăti; **to fix a budget** = a pregăti un buget

fixed *adjective* **(a)** fix; **fixed assets** = mijloace fixe; **fixed charges** = tarife fixe; **fixed cost** = cheltuieli fixe; **fixed exchange rate** = schimb valutar fix **(b)** aranjat (deseori, în culise)

fixtures *plural noun* instalaţii *fpl*

flag **1** *noun* **(a)** steag *n or* drapel *n* **(b)** pavilion *n;* **a ship sailing under the Romanian flag** = un vas navigând sub pavilion românesc **2** *verb* a semnaliza

flat rate *noun* procentaj *n* fix

flea market *noun* piaţă *f* de vechituri *or* talcioc *n*

fleet *noun* **(a)** *(flotilla)* flotă *f* maritimă **(b)** **fleet (of cars)** = parc *n* auto *or* totalitatea vehiculelor unei companii; **fleet car** = autoturismul *n* companiei

flexible *adjective* **(a)** flexibil *or* elastic; **flexible budget** = buget flexibil; **flexible tariffs** = sistem tarifar flexibil **(b)** *(adjustable)* adaptabil

flexitime *noun* program *n* de lucru flexibil

flier *noun* **(a)** foaie *f* volantă **(b)** **high flier** = persoană ambiţioasă

flight *noun* **(a)** zbor *n;* **flight RO 393 from Bucharest will land at Stansted airport in 15 minutes** = zborul RO 393 de la Bucureşti va ateriza pe aeroportul Stansted în 15 minute **(b)** fugă *f* (de răspundere) **(c)** **flight of capital** = scurgerea *f* de capital în afara ţării

float **1** *noun* **(a)** sumă *f* de bani păstrată într-un cont de economii (pentru dobânzi) **(b)** sumă *f* de bani aflată în casă la deschiderea magazinului **2** *verb* **to float a company** = a procura capital prin emiterea de acţiuni

floor *noun* **(a)** podea *f;* **floor space** = arie *f* productivă într-o clădire **(b)** *(lowest point)* **wages floor** = salariu *n* minim **(c)** *(in building)* etaj *n;* **the accounts department is on the 3rd floor** = contabilitatea se află la etajul trei

flow **1** *noun* **(a)** curent *n* **(b)** **flow chart** = diagramă *f* **(c)** circulaţie *f;* **cash flow** = circulaţia *f* banilor

folder *noun* dosar *n;* **he put the documents in a folder** = a pus actele într-un dosar

food *noun* alimente *npl;* hrană *f*

foodstuffs *noun* materii *fpl* prime pentru industria alimentară

foot *verb* **to foot the bill** = a plăti *or* a achita (o notă de plată)

footwear *noun* încălţăminte *f*

force **1** *noun* **(a)** forţă *f or* putere *f;* **to be in force** = a fi în vigoare; **force of public opinion** = forţa opiniei publice **(b)** energie *f* **2** *verb* a forţa *or* a sili; **the company was forced to pay a substantial fine** = compania a fost forţată să plătească o amendă substanţială; **forced sale** = vânzare *f* impusă

forecast **1** *noun* **(a)** previziune *f or* prognoză *f;* **weather forecast** = prognoză meteorologică **(b)** estimare *f;* **forecast of expenses** = estimare a cheltuielilor **2** *verb* **(a)** a prevedea **(b)** a estima

foreign *adjective* **(a)** străin **(b)** extern **(c)** exterior; **foreign currency** = valută *f or* devize *fpl;* **foreign exchange** = schimb *n* valutar; **Foreign Secretary** = Ministru *m* de Externe; **foreign trade** = comerţ *n* exterior

foreigner *noun* străin *f*

foreman *noun* **(a)** şef *m* de echipă **(b)** prim jurat *m*

forewoman *noun* şefă *f* de echipă

forge *verb* a falsifica; **to forge a signature** = a falsifica o semnătura

forgery *noun* **(a)** falsificare *f* **(b)** fals *n*

forklift truck *noun* electrocar *n or* stivuitor *n*

form **1** *noun* **(a)** formular *n;* **to fill in a form** = a completa un formular **(b)** formă *f* **(c)** fel *n or* modalitate *f;*

different forms of advertising = modalități diverse de publicitate **2** *verb* a forma *or* a crea

formal *adjective* **(a)** oficial; **formal complaint** = plângere oficială **(b)** formal

formality *noun* formalitate *f;* **customs formalities** = formalități vamale

formally *adverb* (în mod) oficial

former *adjective* **(a)** fost; **the former managing director retired 5 months ago** = fostul director general a ieșit la pensie acum 5 luni **(b)** anterior

fortnight *noun* două săptămâni *fpl;* **your goods will be delivered in a fortnight** = bunurile dumneavoastră vor fi livrate în două săptămâni

fortnightly *adverb & adjective* bilunar; **in Romania, employees are paid fortnightly** = în România salariații sunt plătiți bilunar

fraction *noun* **(a)** *(mathematics)* fracție *f* **(b)** *(small piece)* fracțiune *f*

France *noun* Franța *f* NOTE: capital: **Paris;** currency: **French franc** = franc francez

franchise **1** *noun* franșiză *f;* concesionare *f* **2** *verb* a acorda o licență de exploatare

frank *verb* a franca; **franking machine** = mașină *f* de francat

fraud *noun* fraudă *f;* **to gain profits by fraud** = a obține profituri prin fraudă

fraudulent *adjective* fraudulent *or* necinstit; **fraudulent misrepresentation** = dezinformare frauduloasă

free *adjective* **(a)** liber; **the company gave him a free hand to reorganize the workshop** = compania i-a dat mână liberă să reorganizeze atelierul; **free competition** = competiție deschisă; **free economy** = economie liberă *or* de piață; **free port** = porto franco *or* port *n* scutit de taxe vamale **(b)** gratis *or* gratuit; **free delivery** = livrare gratuită; **free**

sample = exemplar gratuit; **the catalogue is free** = catalogul este gratuit

freehold *noun* dreptul *n* de a deține o proprietate funciară .

freephone *or* **freefone** *noun* serviciu *n* telefonic gratuit; **to call freephone** = a telefona gratuit (servicii speciale cu prefix 0800 în Marea Britanie)

freeze *verb* a îngheța *or* a bloca; **to freeze credits** = a bloca accesul la credite; **to freeze wages** = a îngheța salariile *or* a nu acorda măriri de salariu

freight **1** *noun* **(a)** marfă *f;* **freight train** = tren *n* de marfă *or* mărfar **(b)** transport *n* de mărfuri **2** *verb* a transporta bunuri

freighter *noun* vas *n* comercial; avion *n* de transport comercial

French *adjective* francez(ă)

Frenchman *noun* francez

Frenchwoman *noun* franțuzoaică

frontier *noun* graniță *f or* frontieră *f*

fulfil *verb* a îndeplini **they fulfilled their obligations** = și-au îndeplinit sarcinile

full *adjective* **(a)** plin; **before the journey he checked that the tank of his car was full** = înainte de călătorie a verificat dacă rezervorul mașinii era plin **(b)** întreg; **full name** = numele și prenumele; **full rate** = preț întreg (fără scont); **full-time worker** = muncitor cu normă întreagă

function **1** *noun* **(a)** funcție *f or* poziție *f* **(b)** îndatorire *f;* **her main function is to supervise the work in the office** = datoria ei de bază este să supravegheze activitatea din birou **2** *verb* a funcționa; **this printer does not function properly** = această imprimantă nu funcționează corespunzător

functionary *noun* funcționar *m* oficial

fund 1 *noun* **(a)** fond *n* *or* sumă *f* de bani; **contingency fund** = fond de rezervă; **the International Monetary Fund (IMF)** = Fondul Monetar Internaţional (F.M.I) **(b) funds** = fonduri *npl* *or* resurse *fpl;* **the firm lacks the necessary funds to open another branch** = compania nu are fondurile suficiente pentru deschiderea unei alte filiale 2 *verb* a furniza fonduri

furnish *verb* **(a)** a mobila; **the couple used the money from a loan to furnish their flat** = cuplul a mobilat apartamentul cu banii împrumutaţi **(b)** a aproviziona

furniture *noun* mobilă *f;* **furniture store** = depozit *n* de mobilă

futures *plural noun* acţiuni *fpl* pe termen (care urmează să fie valorificate la o dată ulterioară)

Gg

Gabon *noun* Gabon *m* NOTE: capital: **Libreville;** currency: **CFA franc** = franc CFA

Gabonese *noun & adjective* gabonez(ă)

gain 1 *verb* (a) a câştiga (b) a dobândi; **to gain experience** = a dobândi experienţă 2 *noun* (a) câştig (b) creştere (în valoare); **capital gain** = plusvaloare *f;* **capital gains tax** = impozit *n* pe plusvaloare (c) **gains** = profit *n*

gainful *adjective* profitabil; **gainful occupation** = ocupaţie profitabilă

gallon *noun* galon *n* (unitate de măsurare a lichidelor egală cu 4,54 litri în Marea Britanie şi 3,78 litri în SUA)

galloping inflation *noun* inflaţie *f* galopantă

gate *noun* (a) poartă *f;* **flight RO 300 is boarding at gate 10** = îmbarcarea pentru zborul RO 300 se face la poarta numărul 10 (b) spectatori *mpl;* **gate money** = preţul *n* biletului la stadion; **record gate** = record *n* de încasări *or* participare

gauge 1 *verb (assess)* a aprecia 2 *noun* (a) *(pattern)* etalon *n* (b) *(meter)* aparat *n* de măsură

general *adjective* (a) ordinar; **general expenses** = cheltuieli ordinare (b) general *or* total; **general average** = medie generală; **general election** = alegeri generale; **general manager** = director general; **general-purpose tool** = unealtă universală; **general store** = magazin universal; **general strike** = grevă generală

gentleman's agreement *noun* înţelegere *f* verbală

genuine *adjective* original

German *noun & adjective* german(ă)

Germany *noun* Germania *f;* **Federal Republic of Germany** = Republica Federală a Germaniei NOTE: capital: **Bonn;** currency: **Deutschmark (DM)** = marcă germană (DM)

get *verb* (a) a primi; **he got a letter from his bank manager** = a primit o scrisoare de la directorul băncii sale; **the shop assistant thought that they would get more computer printers in** = vânzătorul credea că vor mai primi imprimante (b) a câştiga (muncind); **an accountant may get $40,000 a year** = un contabil poate câştiga 40.000 $ pe an

get across *verb* a se face înţeles *or* a face să înţeleagă

get along *verb* a se înţelege; **we get along very well** = ne înţelegem foarte bine

get back *verb* a recupera

get on *verb* (a) a se descurca (b) a merge bine *or* a progresa

get round *verb* a evita; **he could not get round the traffic jam on the motorway** = nu a putut să evite traficul intens de pe autostradă

get through *verb* a comunica (la telefon)

Ghana *noun* Ghana *f* NOTE: capital: **Accra**; currency: **Ghanaian cedi** = cedi ghanez

Ghanaian *noun & adjective* ghanez(ă)

gift *noun* cadou *n or* dar *n*

gift-wrapping *noun* (a) hârtie *f* ornamentală de împachetare a cadourilor (b) serviciu *n* de împachetare (a cadourilor oferit de unele magazine contra unei mici sume de bani)

gilt-edged-securities *noun* titluri *npl or* valori *fpl* foarte sigure (emise de stat)

giro *noun* **giro cheque** = cec *n* poştal

giveaway 1 *noun* obiect *n* oferit gratuit, condiţionat de achiziţionarea altui articol 2 *adjective* redus; **to sell at giveaway prices** = a vinde la preţuri reduse

glut *noun* (a) abundenţă *f* (b) *(saturation)* saturaţie *f* 2 *verb* a inunda piaţa (cu produse)

GNB (= Gross National Product) PNB (Produs Naţional Brut)

go 1 *verb* (a) a merge; **she goes to work by car** = merge la serviciu cu maşina (b) a se duce; **he goes to the head office every week** = se duce la centrală în fiecare săptămână (c) **to go back on one's promise** = a-şi încălca promisiunea (d) **to go under** = a da faliment

go-ahead 1 *noun* autorizaţie *f* 2 *adjective* (a) energetic *or* dinamic (b) *(enterprising)* întreprinzător

go-between *noun* mijlocitor *m or* agent *m*

goal *noun* ţel *n or* scop *n*; **his goal is to open a recording studio** = scopul său este să deschidă un studio de înregistrări

going rate *noun* preţ *n* curent

gold *noun* aur *n;* **to deal in gold** = a face comerţ cu aur; **gold bars** = lingouri *npl* de aur; **gold coins** = monede *fpl* de aur; **gold reserves** = rezerve în aur

gold-mine *noun* (a) mină *f* de aur (b) *(property that brings much profit)* orice proprietate *f* care aduce un profit bun

golden hello *noun* primă *f* specială acordată unui salariat la angajare

golden handcuffs *noun* primă *f* de fidelitate acordată salariaţilor

gold-field *noun* bazin *f* aurifer

good *adjective* bun *or* de calitate; **good faith** = bună credinţă; **£200 to the good** = £200 în profit

goods *plural noun* (a) bunuri *npl or* mărfuri *npl;* articole *npl;* **consumer goods** = bunuri de consum; **goods and chattels** = bunuri personale; **goods in transit** = bunuri în tranzit; **household goods** = articole de uz casnic; **luxury goods** = articole de lux (b) **goods depot** = depozit *n* de mărfuri; **goods train** = mărfar *n*

govern *verb* a guverna *or* a conduce

government *noun* guvern *n or* administraţie *f;* **government investment** = investiţie publică; **government securities** = titluri *npl* (acţiuni) de stat; **local government** = administraţia locală

governmental *adjective* guvernamental

grade 1 *noun* rang *n or* grad *n;* nivel *n;* **high-grade** = nivel înalt; **top-grade** = nivel maxim; **top-grade petrol** = benzină *f* `super', cu cifră octanică ridicată 2 *verb* (a) a nivela (b) a clasifica

gradual *adjective* (a) gradat (b) treptat; **gradual recovery of the economy** = redresare treptată a economiei

gradually *adverb* treptat

graduate *noun* absolvent *m;* licenţiat *m;* **graduate trainee** = stagiar

gram or **gramme** *noun* gram *n* (1000 g = 1Kg)

grant 1 *noun* **(a)** bursă *f;* **student's grant** = bursă de studii **(b)** subvenţie *f;* **government grant** = subvenţie guvernamentală 2 *verb* **(a)** a acorda; **to grant a loan** = a acorda un împrumut **(b)** a aloca

graph *noun* grafic *n;* **graph paper** = hârtie *f* milimetrică

gratuity *noun* **(a)** bacşiş *n;* **he was told off for accepting gratuities** = a fost admonestat pentru primirea de bacşiş **(b)** gratificaţie *f*

Great Britain *noun* Marea Britanie *f* NOTE: capital: **London** = Londra; currency: **pound sterling (£)** = liră sterlină (£)

Greece *noun* Grecia *f* NOTE: capital: **Athens** = Atena; currency: **drachma** = drahmă *f*

Greek 1 *noun* **(a)** grec or greacă or elen(ă) **(b)** *(language)* limba greacă 2 *adjective* grec(esc), grecească; elen(ă)

greenback *noun* US *(informal) (American currency)* dolarul *m* american *(paper money)* bancnotă

green card *noun* **(a)** cartea *f* verde, (certificat *n* de asigurare auto pe timpul călătoriilor în străinătate) **(b)** US permis *n* de lucru acordat imigranţilor

Green Paper *noun* document *n* oficial (emis de guvernul britanic) referitor la un proiect de lege

green pound *noun* valoare *f* a lirei sterline folosită în calcularea preţurilor şi subvenţiilor agricole

grievance *noun* plângere *f*

gross 1 *noun* măsură *f* de 12 duzini 2 *adjective* brut; **gross margin** = beneficiu brut; **gross profit** = profit brut; **gross salary** = salariu brut; **gross national product (GNP)** = produs naţional brut (PNB) 3 *verb* a obţine beneficii brute

ground *noun* **(a)** teren *n;* **ground floor** = parter *n;* **ground landlord** = moşier or propietar *m* de teren; **ground rent** = rentă *f* funciară **(b)** *(plural)* motiv *n* or temei *n;* **he has got serious grounds for complaint** = are motive serioase să fie nemulţumit

group 1 *noun* **(a)** *(of people)* grup *n* **(b)** *(of businesses)* grup or concern *n* industrial 2 *verb* a (se) grupa

grow *verb* **(a)** a creşte; **the company's sales have grown a great deal since the arrival of the new managing director** = deverul companiei a crescut considerabil decând un nou director general a fost angajat **(b)** *(develop)* a se dezvolta **(c)** *(cultivate)* a cultiva; **they grow their own vegetables in the back garden** = ei cultivă legume în grădina din spatele casei

growth *noun* **(a)** creştere *f* **(b)** dezvoltare *f;* **economic growth** = dezvoltare economică; **growth industry** = industrie cu potenţial rapid de dezvoltare; **growth rate** = rata dezvoltării

guarantee 1 *noun* garanţie *f;* **with this TV set you get a twelve-month guarantee** = pentru acest televizor aveţi garanţie de un an de zile; **guarantee certificate** = certificat *n* de garanţie 2 *verb* a garanta; **to guarantee a debt** = a garanta plata unei datorii

guaranteed minimum wage *noun* salariu *n* minim garantat

guaranteed prices *noun* preţuri *npl* agricole minime garantate

guarantor *noun* girant *m* or garant *m*

Guatemala *noun* Guatemala *f* NOTE: capital: **Guatemala City** = Ciudad de Guatemala; currency: **Guatemalan quetzal** = quetzal guatemalez

Guatemalan *noun & adjective* guatemalez(ă)

guardian *noun* tutore *m*

guide *noun* (a) ghid *m* (b) călăuză *f*

guideline *noun* directivă *f;* indicaţie *f;* **to follow the government guidelines** = a aplica directivele guvernamentale

guild *noun* (a) corporaţie *f* (b) breaslă *f or* tagmă *f;* **craft guild** = breasla meşteşugarilor

guilty *adjective* vinovat; **the court found him guilty of forging banknotes** = tribunalul l-a găsit vinovat de falsificare de bancnote

Guyana *noun* Guyana *f* NOTE: capital: **Cayenne;** currency: **Guyana dollar** = dolar *m* guyanez

Guyanese *noun & adjective* guyanez(ă)

Hh

haggle *verb* a se tocmi (exagerat); **to haggle over the price** = a se tocmi la preţ

Haiti *noun* Haiti *m* NOTE: capital: **Port-au-Prince**; currency: **Haitian gourde** = gourd haitian

Haitian *adjective & noun* haitian(ă)

half 1 *noun* jumătate *f;* **the shop is busier in the second half of the year** = magazinul are mai mulţi cumpărători în a doua jumătate a anului; **half-dozen** = jumătate de duzină *or* şase 2 *adjective* jumătate; **the interest rates went up by a half per cent** = rata dobânzilor a fost majorată cu o jumătate de procent

half-year *noun* semestru *n*

half-yearly *adjective & adverb* semestrial

hallmark 1 *noun* (a) marcaj *n* (la bijuterii) (b) marcă *f* 2 *verb* a marca (bijuterii)

halve *verb* a înjumătăţi

hammer *noun* (a) ciocan *n* (b) ciocănel *n* (la licitaţii); **to go under the hammer** = a fi vândut la licitaţie publică

hammered *adjective* *(on Stock Exchange)* **to be hammered** = a fi declarat insolvabil (la Bursă)

hand 1 *noun* (a) mână *f;* **by hand** = cu mâna; **second-hand** = mâna a doua; **to shake hands with somebody** = a da mâna cu cineva (b) *(worker)* muncitor *m or* angajat *m;* **the company took on**

200 hands = compania a angajat 200 de muncitori 2 *verb* a înmâna

handbill *noun* afiş *n* publicitar

handbook *noun* manual *n or* instrucţiuni *fpl* de folosire

hand in *verb* *(deliver by hand)* a înmâna

handle *verb* (a) a mânui (b) a vinde; **we do not handle stationery** = nu vindem articole de papetărie (c) a manipula; `**handle with care**' = ´manipulaţi cu grijă´

handling charges *noun* cheltuieli *fpl* de expediţie

hand luggage *noun* bagaj *n* de mână

handmade *adjective* manual *or* lucrat de mână

handout *noun* (a) donaţie *f* (b) *(free gift)* cadou *n*

handover *noun* (a) (perioadă de) tranziţie *f* (b) *(surrender possession of)* dare *f* în primire

hand over *verb* a da în primire

handwriting *noun* scris *n* de mână; **he could not read her handwriting** = nu a putut citi scrisul ei de mână

handwritten *adjective* scris de mână

harbour *noun* port *n;* **harbour charges** = taxe *fpl* portuare; **harbour facilities** = instalaţii *fpl* portuare; **harbour master** = căpitanul *m* portului

hard *adjective* **hard sell** = vânzare forţată *or* sub presiune; **hard disk** = hard disk (disc intern rigid, flosit la stocarea de informaţii pe calculator)

hard cash *noun* bani *mpl* gheaţă

hard currency *noun* valută *f* convertibilă

hardware *noun* (a) fierărie *f;* **hardware shop** = magazin *n* de articole de menaj (b) **computer hardware** = hardware (suport *n* fizic al calculatorului); componente *npl* fizice în arhitectura calculatorului (c) **military hardware** = material *n* militar de luptă

haul 1 *noun* (a) distanţă *f;* **long-haul flight** = zbor *n* (b) tragere *f* (c) remorcare *f* 2 *verb* (a) *(draw)* a trage (b) *(tow)* a remorca (c) a transporta; **their lorries haul goods all over Europe** = camioanele lor transportă bunuri în toată Europa

haulage *noun* (a) transport *n* de mărfuri (b) **haulage costs** = cheltuieli *fpl* de transport

hawker *noun* vânzător *m* ambulant

hazard *noun* (a) pericol *n;* **fire hazard** = pericol de incendiu (b) risc *n*

head 1 *noun* (a) şef *m;* **head of department** = şef de secţie (b) **head office** = centrală *f or* sediu *n* (c) persoană sau animal numărat; **the fee is £2 per head** = biletul costă 2 lire de persoană 2 *verb* (a) a conduce; **he heads the delegation** = conduce delegaţia (b) **head for** = a se îndrepta spre

headed paper *noun* hârtie *f* cu antetul companiei

headquarters *plural noun* sediu *n or* centrală *f*

headword *noun* cuvânt-titlu *n* (în dicţionar)

health *noun* sănătate *f*

heavy *adjective* (a) important; **heavy investment** = investiţie importantă; **heavy losses** = pierderi grele *or* importante (b) greu; **heavy goods vehicle (HGV)** = vehicul *n* de tonaj greu; **heavy industry** = industria grea

heir *noun* moştenitor *m*

heiress *noun* moştenitoare *f*

heliport *noun* heliport *n* (loc *n* de aterizare, decolare pentru helicoptere)

help 1 *noun* ajutor *n;* **financial help** = ajutor financiar 2 *verb* a ajuta; **the bank loan helped him to start his own business** = împrumutul de la bancă l-a ajutat să înfiinţeze propria sa întreprindere

HGV (heavy goods vehicle) *noun* vehicul *n* de tonaj greu

hidden *adjective* ascuns *or* secret; **hidden assets** = fonduri secrete; **hidden damage** = avarie ascunsă a unei nave

high *adjective* (a) înalt; **they produce high fidelity systems** = ei produc sisteme muzicale de înaltă fidelitate (b) ridicat; **high interest** = dobânzi *fpl* ridicate; **high prices** = preţuri *npl* ridicate (c) mare; **high volume of sales** = volum *n* mare de vânzări

hire 1 *noun* închiriere *f;* **car hire** = închirierea unei maşini 2 *verb* (a) a angaja; **the firm hires extra staff for the busy season** = firma angajează personal sezonier în perioadele de vârf (b) a închiria; **to hire a car** = a închiria o maşină

hire out *verb* a da cu chirie

hire purchase *noun* achiziţie *f* cu plata în rate

hold 1 *verb* (a) a ţine (b) a deţine; **the chairman holds 50% of the shares in his company** = preşedintele deţine 50% din acţiunile companiei sale

hold back *verb* a se abţine

holder *noun* deţinător *m or* posesor *m;* **debenture-holder** = deţinător de obligaţiuni

holding company *noun* societate *f* anonimă deţinătoare de acţiuni

hold on *verb* a rezista

hold up *verb* a se menţine

hold-up *noun* (a) jaf *n* armat (b) *(in a traffic jam)* întârziere *f*

holiday *noun* vacanţă *f or* concediu *n;* **bank holiday** = sărbătoare *f* legală; **holiday entitlement** = numărul *n* de zile de concediu la care un lucrător are dreptul; **holiday pay** = banii *mpl* de concediu

homegrown *adjective* autohton *or* indigen; **homegrown industry** = industrie autohtonă

home market *noun* piaţa *f* internă

homeowner *noun* proprietarul *m* unei locuinţe

homeworker *noun* lucrător *m* la domiciliu

honour 1 *verb* (a) a onora; **a serious businessman must honour his promises** = un om de afaceri serios trebuie să-şi onoreze promisiunile (b) a plăti; **to honour a bill** = a plăti o factură 2 *noun* onoare *f;* **I have the honour of introducing you to my partner** = am onoarea să vă fac cunoştinţă cu partenerul meu de afaceri

horizontal integration *noun* integrare *f* orizontală

hotel *noun* hotel *n;* **hotel bill** = nota *f* de plată a camerei la hotel; **hotel manager** = director *m* de hotel

hostess *noun* gazdă *f;* **airline hostess** = stewardesă *f*

hour *noun* oră *f;* **to be paid by the hour** = a fi plătit cu ora; **output per hour** = producţie pe oră

hourly 1 *adverb* din oră în oră; **hourly-paid worker** = muncitor plătit cu ora 2 *adjective* orar; **hourly rate** = tarif orar

house *noun* casă *f or* imobil *n;* **house property** = proprietate imobiliară; **house agent** = agent imobiliar

householder *noun* ocupant *m* al unei locuinţe (proprietar sau chiriaş)

House of Commons *noun* Camera *f* Comunelor (cameră inferioară a Parlamentului Britanic)

House of Lords *noun* Camera *f* Lorzilor (cameră superioară a Parlamentului Britanic)

hundred *adjective & noun* sută *f;* **one hundred dollars** = o sută de dolari

Hungarian 1 *noun* ungur *or* unguroaică *or* maghiar(ă) 2 *adjective* ungar(ă) *or* maghiar(ă)

Hungary *noun* Ungaria *f* NOTE: capital: **Budapest** = Budapesta; currency: **forint**

hush money *noun* mită *f*

hyperinflation *noun* inflaţie *f* galopantă

hypermarket *noun* supermagazin *n* aflat în afara oraşului

Ii

icebreaker *noun* spărgător *n* de gheaţă (vas)

Iceland *noun* Islanda *f* NOTE: capital: **Reykjavik**; currency: **Icelandic krona** = coroană islandeză

Icelandic *noun & adjective* islandez(ă)

ideal *adjective* ideal

idle *adjective* (a) leneş (b) inactiv; **idle machinery** = utilaj *n* neproductiv; **idle money** = bani *mpl* inactivi *or* fonduri *npl* neproductive; **idle time** = timp *m* mort

illegal *adjective* ilegal

illegality *noun* ilegalitate *f*

illicit *adjective* ilicit; **illicit gain** = câştig ilicit; **illicit trading** = comerţ ilicit

image *noun* imagine *f;* **corporate image** = imagine publică (a unei întreprinderi)

imbalance *noun* dezechilibru *n*

IMF (= International Monetary Fund) Fondul Monetar Internaţional (FMI)

immigrant *noun* imigrant *m*

immobilize *verb* *(capital)* a imobiliza *or* a transforma capital lichid în mijloace fixe

immovable 1 *adjective* imobil 2 *noun* proprietate *f* imobiliară

impact *noun* impact *n* *or* efect *n;* **to make an impact on consumers** = a influenţa consumatorii (prin campanii publicitare)

impecunious *adjective* pauper *or* sărac

imperfect *adjective* imperfect *or* cu defecte (despre un produs, etc.); **the bookshop returned the imperfect copies to the publisher** = librăria a returnat editurii exemplarele (de carte) imperfecte

imperialism *noun* imperialism *n*

implement 1 *noun* instrument *n* *or* unealtă *f* 2 *verb* a implementa *or* a pune în practică; **the new plan will be implemented next year** = planul va fi implementat anul viitor

implied *adjective* implicit *or* subînţeles; tacit; **implied condition** = condiţie implicită (a unui contract); **implied contract** = contract tacit

import 1 *noun* (a) import *n;* **import ban** = interzicere *f* a importului; **import duty** = taxe *fpl* de import; **import licence** = autorizaţie *f* de import; **import quota** = cota *f* de import; **import surcharge** = taxe *fpl* suplimentare de import (b) **imports** = importuri *npl* *or* totalitatea bunurilor importante; **invisible imports** = importuri invizibile (constituite din servicii ca transport, activităţi financiar-bancare, etc.); **visible imports** = importuri vizibile *or* propriu-zise 2 *verb* a importa; **many British supermarkets import wine from Romania** = numeroase supermagazine britanice importă vin din România

importer *noun* importator *m*

importing *adjective* importator; **oil-importing countries** = ţări importatoare de petrol

impose *verb* a impune; **to impose a tax on tobacco** = a impune taxe pe vânzarea de tutun

imposition *noun* impunere *f*

impound *verb* a confisca; **the customs officials impounded the smuggler's goods** = vameşii au confiscat marfa contrabandistului

impounding *noun* confiscare *f*

incentive *noun* primă *f* stimulativă; **incentive payment** = plata *f* de prime stimulente; **staff incentives** = bonificaţii *fpl* de stimulare a productivităţii acordate personalului

incidental *adjective* întâmplător *or* ocazional; **incidental expenses** = cheltuieli *fpl* ocazionale

include *verb* a include; **all the prices include VAT** = toate preţurile includ TVA

inclusive *adjective* inclusiv

income *noun* venit *n;* **annual income** = venit anual; **disposable income** = venit disponibil; **earned income** = venit câştigat (provenit din salariu); **fixed income** = venit fix; **income effect** = efectul *n* venitului (teorie economică); **income tax** = impozit *n* pe venit; **national income** = venit naţional; **net income** = venit net; **per capita income** = venit pe cap de locuitor; **unearned income** = venit provenit din dobânzi sau dividende)

incompetence *noun* incompetenţă *f*

incompetent *adjective* incompetent; **he is an incompetent manager** = este un director incompetent

incorporate *verb* **(a)** a (se) încorpora **(b)** *(integrate)* a (se) integra **(c)** a forma şi înregistra o companie; **a company incorporated in the USA** = o companie înfiinţată în SUA

increase 1 *noun* creştere *f or* majorare *f;* **capital increase** = creştere a capitalului; **salary increase** = majorarea salariului; **tax increase** = majorarea impozitului 2 *verb* a creşte *or* a (se) majora; **last year our profits increased substantially** = profiturile noastre au crescut substanţial anul trecut

increment *noun* plusvaloare *f;* creştere *f*

indebted *adjective* îndatorat; dator

indebtedness *noun* sumă *f* datorată; datorie *f*

indemnity *noun* **(a)** *(compensation for loss)* compensaţie *f* **(b)** garanţie *f;* **letter of indemnity** = document *n* care garantează despăgubirea în caz de pierderi

indent 1 *noun* comandă *f* de import 2 *verb* **to indent for something** = a face o comandă; **the printing shop indented for ink and paper** = tipografia a făcut comandă de hârtie şi cerneală

independent *adjective* independent; **independent company** = companie *f* de sine stătătoare, independentă; **independent means** = sursă *f* de venit, cum ar fi rentă, dobânzi, etc.; **a person of independent means** = rentier *m;* **independent trader** = comerciant *m* independent

index *noun* **(a)** indice *n;* **Dow Jones Index** = indice Dow Jones (la bursa din New York); **growth index** = indice de desvoltare; **price index** = indice al preţurilor **(b)** *(in a book)* index *n*

indexation *noun* indexare *f;* **indexation of wage increases** = indexarea salariilor în relaţie cu majorarea preţurilor

index-linked *adjective* corelat; ajustat; **index-linked pensions** = pensii corelate cu majorarea preţurilor

India *noun* India *f* NOTE: capital: **New Delhi;** currency: **Indian rupee** = rupia indiană

Indian *adjective & noun* indian(ă)

indicate *verb* **(a)** a indica; **the last figures indicated a rise in house prices** = cifrele recente au indicat o creştere a preţurilor locuinţelor **(b)** *(suggest)* a sugera

indicator *noun* indicator *n;* **economic indicator** = indicator economic

indictment *noun* (act de) acuzare *f;* acuzaţie *f*

indigenous *adjective* indigen *or* autohton; **indigenous product** = produs autohton

indigent *adjective* sărac

indirect *adjective* indirect; **indirect costs** = cheltuieli indirecte; **indirect tax** = impozit indirect; **indirect taxation** = impunere indirectă

inducement *noun* stimulent *m*

induction *noun* iniţiere *f;* **they all attended induction courses before starting work** = toţi au frecventat cursurile de iniţiere înainte de a începe să lucreze

industrial *adjective* **(a)** industrial; **industrial accident** = accident *n* de muncă; **industrial capacity** = capacitate *f* industrială; **industrial dispute** = conflict *n* de muncă; **industrial expansion** = expansiune *f* industrială; **industrial park** = platformă *f* industrială **(b) industrial relations** = relaţii *fpl* de muncă

industrialist *noun* industriaş *m*

industrious *adjective* muncitor *or* harnic

industry *noun* industrie *f;* **basic industry** = industrie de bază (cum ar fi industria grea, cea constructoare de maşini, etc.); **extractive industry** = industrie extractivă; **heavy industry** = industrie grea; **infant industry** = industrie incipientă; **light industry** = industrie uşoară

inefficient *adjective* ineficace

inelastic demand *noun* cerere *f* lipsită de elasticitate

inertia *noun* inerţie *f*

inexpensive *adjective* **(a)** ieftin **(b)** economic

inflate *verb* **to inflate prices** = a majora artificial preţuri

inflation *noun* inflaţie *f;* **annual rate of inflation** = rata *f* anuală a inflaţiei

inflationary *adjective* inflaţionar; **inflationary gap** = marjă inflaţionistă

influence **1** *noun* influenţă *f* **2** *verb* a influenţa; **to influence consumers** = a influenţa consumatorii

information *noun* informaţii *fpl;* **a piece of information** = informaţie *f;* **information bureau** = birou *n* de informaţii; **information retrieval** = recuperarea *f* de informaţii

informatics *noun* informatică *f*

infrastructure *noun* infrastructură *f*

infringe *verb* a încălca

infringement *noun* încălcare *f or* violare *f;* **infringement of copyright** = încălcarea dreptului de autor

ingot *noun* lingou *n;* **gold ingot** = lingou de aur

inherent vice *noun* viciu *n* ascuns *or* inerent

inherit *verb* a moşteni

injunction *noun* hotărâre *f* judecătorească

inland *adjective* **(a)** intern **(b)** interior; **the Inland Revenue** = Fiscul (în Marea Britanie)

inquire *verb* **(a)** a întreba **(b)** a solicita informaţii; **they inquired about the tax free savings accounts** = au cerut informaţii despre conturile cu dobânzi scutite de impozit **(c) to inquire into** = a ancheta

inquiry *noun* **(a)** *(research)* cercetare *f* **(b)** anchetă *f;* **an official inquiry into how the funds were used** = o anchetă oficială prvitoare la modul în care fondurile au fost folosite

insolvency *noun* insolvabilitate *f*

insolvent *adjective* insolvabil *or* falit; **to be declared insolvent** = a fi declarat insolvabil

inspect *verb* a inspecta

inspection *noun* inspecţie *f;* control *n;* **to carry out an inspection** = a efectua o inspecţie

inspector *noun* **(a)** inspector *m* **(b)** *(police officer)* inspector *or* ofiţer *m* de poliţie **(c)** controlor *m*

instalment *noun* rată *f;* **US installment plan** = achiziţii *fpl* cu plata în rate; **monthly instalment** = rată lunară; **he paid for the car in 24 monthly instalments** = a achitat plata maşinii în 24 de rate lunare

institute **1** *noun* institut *n;* **research institute** = institut de cercetări **2** *verb* a institui

instruction *noun* instruţiune *f;* **to give instructions** = a da instrucţiuni

instrument *noun* instrument *n;* document *n* legal

insurance *noun* **(a)** asigurare *f* **(b)** asigurări *fpl;* **insurance agent** = agent *m* de asigurări; **insurance company** = companie *f* de asigurări; **car insurance** *or* **motor insurance** = poliţă *f* de asigurări auto; **insurance policy** = poliţă de asigurare

insure *verb* **(a)** a asigura **(b)** a încheia o poliţă de asigurări

insured *noun* **the insured** = persoană *f* asigurată

insurer *noun* companie *f* de asigurări

integrate *verb* a (se) integra

integration *noun* integrare *f;* **horizontal integration** = integrare orizontală; **vertical integration** = integrare verticală

intensive *adjective* intensiv; **intensive farming** = agricultură intensivă

inter-city *adjective* interurban

interest **1** *noun* **(a)** interes *n;* **to show interest** = a-şi manisfesta interesul; **interest group** = grup de persoane cu interese comune **(b)** dobândă *f;* **back interest** = dobândă retroactivă; **compound interest** = dobânzi compuse; **interest charge** = dobândă negativă; **interest earned** = dobânzi creditoare; **interest-free loan** = împrumut *n* fără dobânzi percepute; **interest rate** = rata *f* dobânzii; **net interest** = dobândă netă; **penalty interest** = dobândă de întârziere; **this account pays 4.5% interest** = acest cont oferă dobândă de 4,5% **(c)** profit **2** *verb* a interesa

interface **1** *noun* interfaţă *f;* conexiune *f* **2** *verb* a conecta

interim dividend *noun* dividend *n* provizional

intermediary *noun* intermediar *m*

internal *adjective* intern; **internal audit** = control *n* financiar intern

international *adjective* internaţional; **International Monetary Fund (IMF)** = Fondul *n;* Monetar Internaţional (FMI); **international call** = convorbire telefonică internaţională

interpret *verb* a traduce *or* a interpreta; **he will interpret for the chairman at the meeting** = el va interpreta pentru preşedinte la întrunire

interpreter *noun* translator *m or* interpret *m*

interstate *adjective* interstatal

intervention *noun* intervenţie *f;* **state intervention** = intervenţie guvernamentală

interventionist   *adjective*
intervenţionist

interview 1 *noun* **(a)** interviu *n* **(b)** *(meeting)* întrevedere *f* 2 *verb* a intervieva; **the businessman refused to be interviewed** = omul de afaceri a refuzat să fie intervievat

in transit *phrase* în tranzit (despre mărfuri, etc.)

intrinsic value *noun* valoare *f* intrinsecă

inventory 1 *noun* **(a)** *GB* inventar *n* **(b)** *US* stoc *n* 2 *verb* a inventaria

invest *verb* a investi; **he invested half of his money in property** = a investit jumătate din bani in proprietăţi imobiliare

investment *noun* investiţii *fpl;* **capital investment loan** = credit *n* de investiţii; **investment bank** = bancă *f* de investiţii; **investment fund** = fond *n* de investiţii; **long-term investment** = investiţii pe termen îndelungat; **private investment** = investiţii particulare; **public investment** = investiţii guvernamentale

investor *noun* investitor *m;* **private investor** = investitor particular

invoice 1 *noun* factură *f* 2 *verb* a factura

invoicing *noun* facturare *f;* **invoicing department** = birou *n* de facturare

Iran *noun* Iran *m* NOTE: capital: **Tehran** = Teheran; currency: **Iranian rial** = rial iranian

Iranian *noun & adjective* iranian(ă)

Iraq *noun* Irak *m* NOTE: capital: **Baghdad** = Bagdad; currency: **Iraqi dinar** = dinar irakian

Iraqi *noun & adjective* irakian(ă)

Ireland *noun* Irlanda *f* NOTE: capital: **Dublin;** currency: **Irish punt** or **pound** = liră irlandeză

Irish *noun & adjective* irlandez(ă)

irredeemable *adjective* **(a)** nerambursabil **(b)** care nu poate fi amortizat (despre investiţii)

issue 1 *noun* **(a)** emisie *f* **(b)** emitere *f;* **issue price** = preţ *n* de emitere **(c)** ediţie *f* or număr *n;* **he asked for the April issue of the computer magazine** = a solicitat numărul din aprilie al revistei de informatică **(d)** problemă *f* or chestiune *f;* **current issue** = problemă actuală 2 *verb* a emite or a pune în circulaţie (obligaţiuni, etc.)

Italian *noun & adjective* italian(ă)

Italy *noun* Italia *f* NOTE: capital: **Rome** = Roma; currency: **Italian lira** = liră italiană

item *noun* **(a)** articol *n* **(b)** unitate *f*

itemize *verb* a amănunţi or a detalia; **itemized invoice** = factură *f* detaliată

Jj

Jamaica *noun* Jamaica *f* NOTE: capital: **Kingston;** currency: **Jamaican dollar** = dolar jamaican

Jamaican *noun & adjective* jamaican(ă)

Japan *noun* Japonia *f* NOTE: capital: Tokyo; currency: **Japanese yen** = yen japonez

Japanese *noun & adjective* japonez(ă)

jettison *verb* a arunca încărcătura peste bord

job *noun* **(a)** treabă *f or* lucrare *f;* **to do odd jobs** = a efectua diverse lucrări mărunte; **odd-job-man** = angajat *m* fără atribuţii precise, folosit pentru efectuarea de diverse lucrări **(b)** slujbă *f or* post *n;* **to apply for a job** = a face cerere de angajare; **500 people lost their jobs** = 500 de persoane şi-au pierdut slujba; **to be out of a job** = a şoma; **job centre** = birou *n* de plasare; **job description** = atribuţii *fpl* de serviciu; **to look for a job** = a căuta de lucru; **well-paid job** = post bine plătit

jobber *noun* **(a)** *(formerly Stock Exchange)* agent *m* de bursă **(b)** *US* angrosist *m*

jobless *adjective* fără lucru; **the jobless** = şomerii *mpl*

jobseeker *noun* persoană *f* în căutare de lucru

joint *adjective* **(a)** comun; **joint account** = cont comun; **joint owner** = coproprietar *m;* **joint ownership** = proprietate *f* comună; **joint-stock bank** = bancă *f* comercială (pe acţiuni); **joint venture** = întreprindere *f* cu participare **(b)** *(joined together)* unit

jointly *adverb* în comun

Jordan *noun* Iordania *f* NOTE: capital: **Amman;** currency: **Jordanian dinar** = dinar iordanian

Jordanian *noun & adjective* iordanian(ă)

journal *noun* **(a)** *(accounts book)* jurnal *n* (contabil) **(b)** publicaţie *f* periodică *or* buletin *n* informativ

journey *noun* călătorie *f;* **journey order** = comandă *f* luată pe durata vizitei unui reprezentant al unei firme

judge **1** *noun* judecător *m;* **judge's order** = hotărâre *f* judecătorească **2** *verb* **(a)** *(law)* a judeca **(b)** *(consider)* a considera

judgement *noun* **(a)** *(sentence)* sentinţă *f* judecătorească **(b)** *(opinion)* părere *f or* opinie *f;* **to give one's judgement about something** = a-şi exprima părerea asupra unui lucru

judicial *adjective* **(a)** judecătoresc **(b)** juridic

jump *verb* **(a)** a sălta; **share prices jumped** = preţul acţiunilor a săltat brusc **(b)** a se grăbi; **to jump at an offer** = a se grăbi să accepte o ofertă

jumpy *adjective* instabil; **jumpy market** = piaţă instabilă

junior 1 *noun* subaltern *m;* **office junior** = funcţionar *m or* conţopist *m* 2 *adjective* inferior

junk *noun* (a) resturi *npl* (b) fleacuri *npl;* **junk bonds** = titluri *npl* de valoare inferioară; **junk mail** = corespondenţă *f;* care conţine broşuri publicitare

jurisdiction *noun* jurisdicţie *f*

jury *noun* juriu *n*

just *adjective* drept *or* just

Kk

K *abbreviation* o mie; **he earns in excess of £35K a year** = câştigă peste £35.000 pe an

keel 1 *noun* chilă *f* 2 *verb* **to keel over** = a (se) răsturna

keen *adjective* **(a)** acut *or* intens; **keen competition** = competiţie *f;* ardentă *or* intensă **(b)** pasionat; **he is a keen art collector** = el este un pasionat colecţionar de artă **(c) keen price** = preţ *n;* competitiv

keep *verb* **(a)** a administra o afacere; **to keep a shop** = a administra un magazin (pentru realizarea de profituri) **(b) to keep one's promise** = a-şi ţine cuvântul dat **(c)** a păstra; **keep the change** = păstrează restul **(d)** a menţine; **the company tries to keep the spending down** = compania încearcă să menţină un nivel scăzut al cheltuielilor

keep back *verb* **(a)** *(decline to disclose)* a ascunde **(b)** *(retain)* a reţine (din salariu)

keeping *noun* **(a)** păstrare *f;* **safe keeping** = custodie *f* **(b)** *(in good repair)* întreţinere *f*

keep on *verb* a continua; **they kept on working in spite of the fact that they were worn out** = au continuat să lucreze în ciuda faptului că erau epuizaţi

keep up *verb* **(a)** a menţine **(b)** a satisface; **to keep up with demand** = a satisface cererea

Kenya *noun* Kenia *f* NOTE: capital: **Nairobi;** currency: **Kenyan shilling** = şiling kenian

Kenyan *noun & adjective* kenian(ă)

key *noun* cheie *f;* **key factor** = factor *n;* cheie; **key money** = arvună *f or* avans *n;* **key post** = post-cheie *or* de primă importanţă

keyboard *noun* tastatură *f*

keyboarder *noun* operator *m* preluare data

keyboarding *noun* introducerea *f* de date în calculator prin intermediul tastaturii

kickback *noun* comision *n* ilegal; mită *f* oferită oficialilor pentru ajutor financiar

killing *noun* câştig *n* neaşteptat; **to make a killing** = a specula şi câştiga (la bursă)

kilo (kg) *noun* kilogram *n*

kilobyte (KB *or* **Kb)** *noun* kilobit *m* (= 1024 de biţi, unitate de măsură a cantităţii de informaţie stocată de un calculator, în memorie sau pe disc)

kilogram (kg) *noun* kilogram *n*

kilometre (km) *noun* kilometru *m*

kiosk *noun* chioşc *n;* **newspaper kiosk** = chioşc de ziare; **telephone kiosk** = cabină *f* telefonică

kite *noun* **to fly a kite** = a lansa o propunere în scopul atragerii atenţiei clienţilor potenţiali

knock *verb* (a) ciocăni (la uşă) (b) **to knock the competition** = a înfrânge competiţia

knockdown prices *noun* preţuri *npl* reduse

knock off *verb* (a) *(finish work)* a termina treaba (b) *(reduce the price of)* a reduce din preţ

knock-on effect *noun* repercusiune *f;* efect *n* secundar

know *verb* (a) a şti (b) a cunoaşte; **he knows his trade** = îşi cunoaşte meseria

know-how *noun* cunoştinţe *fpl* ştiinţifice, tehnice; abilitatea *f* de a cunoaşte ceva în mod deosebit; expertiză

knowledge *noun* (a) cunoaştere *f* (b) cunoştinţe *fpl or* învăţătură *f;* **basic knowledge** = cunoştinţe elementare

Korea *noun* Republica Coreea *m* NOTE: capital: **Seoul** = Seul: currency: **Korean won** = won corean

Korean *noun & adjective* corean(ă)

Kuwait *noun* Kuwait *m* NOTE: currency: **Kuwaiti dinar** = dinar kuwaitian

Kuwaiti *noun & adjective* kuwaitian(ă)

Ll

label 1 *noun* etichetă *f* 2 *verb* a eticheta

labour *or US* **labor** *noun* **(a)** muncă *f or* lucru *n;* **labour charges** = cheltuieli *fpl* de manoperă; **labour dispute** = conflict *n* de muncă; **labour legislation** = legislaţia *f* muncii; **labour relations** = relaţii *fpl* de muncă **(b)** *(in USA)* **labor union** = sindicat *n* (în SUA) **(c)** mână *f* de lucru *or* muncitorime *f;* **cheap labour** = mână de lucru ieftină; **manual labour** = lucru manual **(d)** manoperă *f;* **he paid for spare parts and labour** = a plătit pentru piesele de schimb şi manoperă

labourer *noun* muncitor *m* (necalificat); **agricultural or farm labourer** = muncitor agricol *or* ţăran

lack 1 *noun* lipsă *f or* carenţă *f;* **they postponed the opening of a new branch because of lack of funds** = au amânat deschiderea unei noi filiale din cauza lipsei de fonduri 2 *verb* a fi lipsit de *or* a nu avea

laden *adjective* încărcat; **fully-laden ship** = navă *f* încărcată la capacitate maximă

lame duck *noun* companie *f* ineficientă care nu poate supravieţui fără ajutor guvernamental

land 1 *noun* teren *n or* proprietate *f* funciară; **land reform** = reformă *f* agrară; **land register** = cadastru *n* 2 *verb* **(a)** a debarca **(b)** a descărca; **to land goods at a port** = a descărca bunuri în port **(c)** *(of a plane)* a ateriza

landing *noun* **(a)** *(plane)* aterizare *f* **(b)** *(passengers)* debarcare *f;* **landing card** = talon de debarcare

landlady *noun* proprietăreasă *f;* deţinătoare *f* de teren

landlord *noun* proprietar *m;* moşier *m*

Laos *noun* Laos NOTE: capital: **Vientiane;** currency: **Laotian kip** = kip laoţian

Laotian *noun & adjective* laoţian(ă)

lapsed insurance policy *noun* poliţă de asigurări expirată care nu a fost reînnoită

large-scale *adjective* de serie *or* de masă; **large-scale production** = producţie *f* de serie

Latvia *noun* Letonia *f* NOTE: capital: **Riga;** currency: **lat**

Latvian *noun & adjective* leton(ă)

law *noun* **(a)** *(legislation)* lege *f;* **within the law** = (în mod) legal **(b)** drept *n;* **civil law** = drept civil; **criminal law** = drept penal; **law court** = tribunal *n* **(c)** *(regulation)* regulă *f*

lawful *adjective* legal

lawsuit *noun* proces *n or* acţiune *f* civilă

lawyer *noun* **(a)** avocat *m* **(b)** jurist *m*

lay off *verb* **(a)** a concedia temporar; **because of a sharp drop in sales the shop had to lay off two assistants** = datorită scăderii bruşte a vânzărilor magazinul a trebuit să concedieze temporar doi vânzători **(b) to lay off risks** = a înlătura riscuri financiare prin noi investiţii

lay out *verb* **(a)** *(expose to view)* a expune **(b) to lay out money** = a cheltui bani conform unui plan bine stabilit (în investiţii)

layout *noun* **(a)** *(of a building)* plan *n* **(b)** *(of printed matter)* tehnoredactare *f;* paginaţie *f*

leader (a) *(share)* acţiuni *fpl* sau titluri *npl* principale (la bursă) **(b)** conducător *m or* şef *m; the management wanted to talk to the leader of the pressure group* = conducerea dorea să discute cu şeful grupului de acţiune **(c)** *(product)* articol *n or* produs *n* de primă importanţă

lease 1 *noun* **(a)** contract *n* de închiriere; **long lease** = închiriere de lungă durată (peste 50 de ani); **short lease** = închiriere de scurtă durată (sub 50 de ani); **sublease** = subînchiriere *f* **(b)** concesiune *f* 2 *verb* **(a)** *(from someone)* a închiria (de la cineva); **to lease a car** = a închiria o maşină; **the company leased the whole building** = compania a închiriat toată clădirea **(b)** *(to someone)* a concesiona (cuiva)

leave 1 *noun* **(a)** concediu *n; he is entitled to an annual leave of 25 days* = are dreptul la un concediu anual de 25 de zile; **sick leave** = concediu medical **(b)** învoire *f; she asked for leave to go to the doctor* = a cerut acordarea unei învoiri pentru a merge la doctor **2** *verb* **(a)** a pleca; **the train leaves in 15 minutes** = trenul va pleca în 15 minute **(b)** a abandona; **he left his job in London when he was offered a good position with a firm in Scotland** = şi-a abandonat slujba din Londra când i s-a oferit un post avantajos la o firmă din Scoţia

leave out *verb* a omite

Lebanese *noun & adjective* libanez(ă)

Lebanon *noun* Liban *m* NOTE: capital: **Beirut;** currency: **Lebanese pound** = liră libaneză

ledger *noun* registru *n* contabil (manual sau computerizat); **bought ledger** = registru de facturi; **payroll ledger** = stat *n* de plată; **sales ledger** = registru de vînzări

legacy *noun* moştenire *f*

legal *adjective* legal; **to take legal action** = a intenta proces *or* a da în judecată; **legal adviser** = consilier *m* juridic; **legal claim** = drept legitim; US **legal holiday** = sărbătoare *f* oficială

legality *noun* legalitate *f;* legitimitate *f*

legalize *verb* a legaliza

legally *adverb* legal

legatee *noun* moştenitor *m*

legation *noun* legaţie *f*

legislation *noun* legislaţie *f;* **labour legislation** = legislaţia muncii

lend *verb* a da cu împrumut; **the bank lent him the money after having considered his financial status carefully** = banca i-a împrumutat banii după ce i-a analizat cu atenţie situaţia financiară

lender *noun* persoană *f* sau organizaţie *f* care acordă împrumuturi

let 1 *verb* **(a)** *(of landlord)* a închiria; **to let a flat** = a închiria un apartament **(b)** a arenda **2** *noun* închiriere *f;* **short let** = închiriere pe termen scurt

letter *noun* **(a)** scrisoare *f;* **airmail letter** = scrisoare par avion; **circular letter** = circulară *f;* **letter of acknowledgement** = confirmare *f* în scris; **letter of appointment** = notificare *f* de numire în post; **letter of renunciation** = scrisoare de renunţare **(b)** *(printed character)* literă *f or* caracter *n* tipografic; **to write in capital letters** = a scrie cu litere majuscule

letter of credit (L/C) *noun* acreditiv *n*

letterhead *noun* antet *n*

letting *noun* proprietate *f* (mobilată) de închiriat

level 1 *noun* nivel; **low level of investment** = nivel scăzut de investiții 2 *verb* **to level off** = a (se) stabiliza (despre prețuri, etc.)

levy 1 *noun* **(a)** percepere *f* (a impozitelor) **(b)** impozit *n* *or* taxe *fpl;* **capital levy** = impozit pe capital; **import levy** = taxe *fpl* pe import 2 *verb* **(a)** a impune taxe **(b)** a colecta impozite

liability *noun* **(a)** responsabilitate *f or* răspundere *f;* **to accept liability for something** = a-și asuma răspunderea pentru ceva; **limited liability** = răspundere limitată; **limited liability company** = societate *f* cu răspundere limitată **(b) liabilities** = datorii *fpl*

liable *adjective* **(a) liable for** = răspunzător; responsabil **(b) liable to** = pasibil de

libel 1 *noun* calomnie *f;* **action for libel** = acțiune civilă pentru calomniere 2 *verb* a calomnia

Libya *noun* Libia *f* NOTE: capital: **Tripoli;** currency: **Libyan dinar** = dinar libian

Libyan *noun & adjective* libian(ă)

licence *noun* **(a)** autorizație *f or* licență *f;* **import licence** = licență de import; **liquor licence** = autorizație de comercializare a băuturilor alcoolice; **off licence** = magazin de băuturi alcoolice **(b) driving licence** = permis *n* de conducere **(c) goods manufactured under licence** = bunuri produse sub licență

license *verb* a autoriza

lien *noun* sechestru *n* (dreptul de a confisca bunurile datornicilor până sumele datorate sunt achitate)

life expectancy *noun* rata *f* longevității

lifeless *adjective (stock market)* lipsit de viață (situație în care doar foarte puține tranzacții sunt încheiate)

lift *noun* ascensor *n*

light *adjective* **(a)** *(of a lorry, ship, etc.)* gol *or* fără încărcătură **(b)** ușor; **light industry** = industria ușoară

lighter *noun* șlep *n*

lighthouse *noun* far *n*

limit 1 *noun* limită *f;* **age limit** = limită de vârstă; **to impose limits on imports** = a impune limite pe importuri; **weight limit** = greutate *f* maximă admisă 2 *verb* a limita

limited *adjective* limitat; **limited company** = societate *f* cu răspundere limitată (SRL)

limiting *adjective* restrictiv; **limiting clause** = clauză restrictivă (a unui contract)

line *noun* linie *f;* **airline** = companie *f* de transport aerian; **assembly line** = linie de asamblare; **product line** = gamă *f* de produse; **production line** = linie *or* secție *f* de producție; **shipping line** = linie maritimă

liner *noun* transatlantic *n*

link *verb* a corela; a indexa; **to link salaries to the cost of living** = a indexa salariile în raport cu costul de trai

liquidate *verb* **(a)** a achita; **to liquidate a debt** = a achita o datorie **(b) to liquidate stock** = a lichida stocul existent **(c)** a da faliment

liquidation *noun* **(a)** *(of a debt)* achitare *f* **(b)** *(of a company)* lichidare *f*

list 1 *noun* listă *f or* catalog *n;* **list price** = preț de catalog; **price list** = listă de prețuri 2 *verb* a enumera *or* a înșira

literature *noun* documentație *f*

Lithuania *noun* Lituania *f* NOTE: capital: **Vilnius;** currency: **Lithuanian litas** = litas lituanian

Lithuanian *noun & adjective*
lituanian(ă)

litigation *noun* litigiu *n or* conflict *n*

livestock *noun* şeptel *n*

Lloyd's of London *noun* Compania *f*
de Asigurări Lloyd

load 1 *noun* încărcătură *f;* **commercial
load** = capacitate *f* utilă de încărcare (a
unui camion, etc.); **maximum load** =
capacitate maximă de încărcare 2 *verb*
a încărca; **to load a ship, lorry** = a
încărca un vapor, camion

loan 1 *noun* împrumut *f;* **bank loan** =
împrumut bancar; **home loan** =
împrumut pentru cumpărarea unei
locuinţe; **personal loan** = împrumut
personal; **short-term loan** = împrumut
pe scurtă durată 2 *verb* a da cu
împrumut

local *adjective* local; **local authority** =
administraţia locală; **local call** =
convorbire *f* telefonică loco *or* urbană

lock up *verb* a investi capital în
proprietăţi care nu pot fi vândute
imediat

locus sigilli *Latin phrase* locul
sigiliului (L.S.), spaţiu rezervat pentru
ştampilă

log 1 *verb* a înregistra; **to log phone
calls** = a nota într-un registru
convorbirile telefonice 2 *noun* jurnal *n*
de bord

long-term *adjective* pe termen lung;
long-term investment = investiţii *fpl* pe
termen lung; **long-term loan** =
împrumut *n* pe termen lung

loose *adjective* vărsat *or* neambalat; **to
sell loose sugar** = a vinde zahăr vărsat;
loose change = mărunţiş *n*

lorry *noun* camion *n*

lose *verb* a pierde; **the bank lost over
£1m in bad debts** = banca a pierdut
peste un milion de lire din
împrumuturi neachitate; **to lose
customers** = a pierde clienţi; **he lost his
job when the sales dropped dramatically**
= şi-a pierdut slujba când vânzările au
scăzut drastic

loss *noun* pierdere *f or* deficit *n;* **at a
loss** = în pierdere; **profit and loss
account** = cont *n* de profit şi pierderi

loss-leader *noun* articol *n* vândut în
pierdere cu scopul de a atrage clientela

lump *verb* **(a)** a aduna la grămadă,
fără discriminare **(b)** a acumula

lump sum *noun* sumă de bani plătită
în întregime

Luxembourg *noun* Luxenburg *m*
NOTE: currency: **Luxembourg franc** =
franc luxenburghez

Luxembourger *noun & adjective*
luxenburghez(ă)

luxury *noun* lux *n;* **luxury items** =
articole *npl* de lux

Mm

machine *noun* maşină *f;* **adding machine** = maşină de adunat; **copying machine** = maşină de copiat *or* copiator `Xerox'; **dictating machine** = dictafon *n*

machine-tool *noun* maşină-unealtă *f*

macro-economics *noun* macroeconomie *f*

Madagascan *noun & adjective* malgaş(ă)

Madagascar *noun* Madagascar *m* NOTE: capital: **Antananarivo**; currency: **Malagasy franc** = franc malgaş

magazine *noun* revistă *f;* **computer magazine** = revistă de informatică; **fashion magazine** = revistă de modă

magistrate *noun* magistrat *m;* judecător *m* de pace; **magistrates' court** = judecătorie de pace

magnate *noun* magnat *m;* **media magnate** = magnat al presei

mail 1 *noun* **(a)** poştă *f;* **mail box** = cutie *f* poştală; **mail order** = comandă *f* prin poştă; **to put a letter in the mail** = a pune o scrisoare la poştă **(b)** corespondenţă *f* (scrisori, pachete, etc.); **mail room** = registratură *f* 2 *verb* a expedia prin poştă

mailing *noun* **(a)** expediţie *f* **(b)** expediere *f;* **direct mailing** = expedierea de material publicitar clienţilor potenţiali; **mailing list** = listă *f* cuprinzând numele şi adresele clienţilor, cărora li se trimit regulat broşuri publicitare şi cataloage de produse

mail-order *adjective* **mail-order selling** = vânzare prin poştă *or* din cataloag

main *adjective* principal; **the accounts department is situated in the main building** = contabilitatea se află în clădirea principală

mainframe *noun* minicalculator *n;* **the company decided to replace the mainframes with PCs** = compania a hotărât înlocuirea minicalculatoarelor cu PC-uri (personal computer)

mainly *adverb* **(a)** în special; **the company is interested mainly in selling its products abroad** = compania este interesată în special în desfacerea produselor sale peste hotare **(b)** în majoritate

maintain *verb* **(a)** a menţine; **to maintain good relations with somebody** = a menţine relaţii cordiale cu cineva **(b)** a întreţine; **to maintain a machine** = a menţine o maşină

maintenance *noun* întreţinere *f;* reparaţii *fpl;* **maintenance costs** = cheltuieli *fpl* de întreţinere

major *adjective* important; **major shareholder** = acţionar important

majority *noun* majoritate *f*

make 1 *noun* marcă *f;* model *n;* **what make is your car?** = ce marcă este maşina Dvs? 2 *verb* **(a)** a produce *or* a fabrica; **in this factory they only make**

furniture for export = în această fabrică se produce mobilă destinată exclusiv exportului; **made in England** = fabricat în Anglia **(b) to make a deal** = a semna un contract; a încheia o tranzacţie **(c)** a câştiga; **she made £3,000 by selling her shares** = a câştigat £3.000 din vânzarea acţiunilor sale; **the shop makes a lot of money from the sale of souvenirs to tourists** = magazinul câştigă bani frumoşi din vânzarea de suveniruri turiştilor

make up *verb* a compensa; **to make up a loss** = a compensa o pierdere

make up for *verb* a compensa

maker *noun* producător *m or* fabricant *m;* **car maker** = fabricant de automobile; **decision maker** = persoană *f* cu putere executivă

making *noun* producere *f or* fabricaţie *f*

maladminister *verb* a administra necorespunzător

Malaysia *noun* Malaezia *f* NOTE: capital: **Kuala Lumpur;** currency: **Malaysian ringgit** = ringgit malaezian

Malaysian *noun & adjective* malaezian(ă)

malicious damage *noun* daune *fpl* cauzate intenţionat (pentru încasarea primei de asigurare)

Malta *noun* Malta *f* NOTE: capital: **Valetta;** currency: **Maltese lira** = liră malteză

Maltese *noun & adjective* maltez(ă)

man 1 *noun* persoană *f; muncitor m* 2 *verb* a asigura mână de lucru

manage *verb* **(a)** a conduce; **he manages our branch in London** = el conduce filiala noastră din Londra **(b) to manage to** = a reuşi *or* a se descurca; **they managed to increase productivity by installing new equipment** = au reuşit să mărească productivitatea muncii prin instalarea de echipament nou

managed money *noun* monedă *f* dirijată

management *noun* **(a)** management *n or* conducere *f;* consiliu *n* de administraţie; **management buyout (MBO)** = preluarea *f* majorităţii acţiunilor într-o companie de către echipa de conducere; **management team** = echipă *f* de conducere **(b)** *(action)* gestiune *f*

manager *noun* director *m;* **accounts manager** = director al direcţiei contabilitate; **personnel manager** = şef *m* de birou personal

manageress *noun* directoare *f*

managerial *adjective* managerial *or* administrativ; de conducere; **to be appointed to a managerial position** = a fi numit într-o funcţie de conducere

managing director *noun* director *m* general

mandate *noun* **(a)** mandat *n* **(b) bank mandate** = dispoziţie *f* de plată

mandatory *adjective* **(a)** obligatoriu; forţat; **mandatory retirement** = pensionare obligatorie **(b)** împuternicit

manifest *noun* **(a)** listă *f* cuprinzând încărcătura unui vas comercial **(b) passenger manifest** = listă de pasageri

manipulate *verb* **(a)** a manipula; **to manipulate the market** = a manipula piaţa; **to manipulate share prices** = a influenţa prin mijloace artificiale nivelul preţurilor acţiunilor **(b)** a mânui **(c)** a falsifica; **to manipulate accounts** = a falsifica intrări contabile

manpower *noun* forţă *f* de muncă

manual 1 *adjective* manual; **manual exchange** = centrală telefonică operată manual de telefoniste; **manual labour** = lucru manual; **manual worker** = muncitor *m* necalificat 2 *noun* manual *n or* carte *f* tehnică; **operating manual** = instrucţiuni *fpl* de folosire

manufacture 1 *verb* a fabrica *or* a produce; **the company manufactures computer display systems** = firma produce monitoare pentru calculatoare 2 *noun* fabricaţie *f*

manufacturer *noun* fabricant *m;* **manufacturer's recommended price (MRP)** = preţ *n* minim de vânzare recomandat de fabricant

manufacturing *noun* fabricaţie *f;* **manufacturing overheads** = cheltuieli *fpl* generale de fabricaţie

margin **(a)** margine *f* **(b)** limită *f or* marjă *f;* **profit margin** = marjă de beneficiu

marginal *adjective* **(a)** marginal; **marginal costs** = cheltuieli marginale **(b)** minim; **marginal land** = suprafaţă agricolă cu randament scăzut (a cărei cultivare acoperă doar cheltuielile de producţie); **marginal return on investment** = profit minim realizat dintr-o investiţie

marine 1 *adjective* maritim; **marine accident** = accident maritim; **marine insurance** = asigurare maritimă; **marine underwriter** = agent *m* de asigurări maritime 2 *noun* marină *f;* **merchant marine** = marină comercială

mark down *verb* a reduce preţul

mark-down *noun* **(a)** reducere *f* de preţ **(b)** procentaj *n* de scont

mark up *verb* a majora preţul

mark-up *noun* **(a)** majorare *f* a preţului **(b)** marjă *f* de profit

market 1 *noun* **(a)** piaţă *f or* târg *n;* **vegetables are cheaper in the market than in the food stores** = legumele sunt mai ieftine la piaţă decât în supermagazinele alimentare **(b) the Common Market** = Piaţa Comună **(c)** piaţă; **domestic market** *or* **home market** = piaţă internă; **foreign market** = piaţă externă **(d)** vânzări *fpl or* tranzacţii *fpl* comerciale; comerţ *n;* **free market** = comerţ liberalizat *or* piaţă liberă; **free**

market economy = economie *f* de piaţă; **market rate** = preţul *n* pieţei; **market share** = cotă *f* din piaţă; **market value** = valoare *f* comercială **(e) black market** = bursa *f* neagră; **to pay black market prices** = a plăti preţuri de speculă **(f) grey market** = piaţă paralelă **(g) capital market** = piaţă financiară; **stock market** = bursă de valori **(h) up market** = piaţă selectă 2 *verb* a vinde; a comercializa; **this Japanese make of car is being marketed only in America** = acest model de automobil japonez se vinde numai în America

marketing *noun* marketing *n;* **marketing agreement** = acord *n* comercial; **marketing plans** = politică *f* de marketing *or* planuri *npl* de comercializare

mass-produce *verb* a produce în serie

mass production *noun* producţie *f* de serie

material *noun* material *n;* **building materials** = materiale de construcţie; **materials buyer** = achizitor *m;* **raw materials** = materii *fpl* prime

maternity benefit *noun* (în Marea Britanie) alocaţie *f* acordată mamei la naşterea fiecărui copil

mature economy *noun* economie *f* dezvoltată pe de plin

measure 1 *verb* a măsura; **to measure the contents of a petrol tank** = a măsura conţinutul unui rezervor de benzină 2 *noun* măsură *f;* **made to measure** = croit pe măsură

medical 1 *noun* examen *n* medical 2 *adjective* medical; **medical certificate** = certificat medical; **to retire for medical reasons** = a se pensiona pe motive de sănătate

meet *verb* **(a)** a (se) întâlni; **the manager met the building contractors** = directorul s-a întâlnit cu reprezentanţii trustului de construcţii **(b)** a satisface;

to meet someone's demands = a satisface cerinţele cuiva

meeting *noun* **(a)** şedinţă *f;* **management meeting** = şedinţă de consiliu; **annual general meeting (AGM)** = adunare *f* generală anuală **(b)** întrunire *f or* miting *n*

megabyte (MB *or* **Mb)** *noun* megabait *n or* megabit (unitate de măsură a capacităţii de stocare a informaţiei egală cu 1024 kilobiţi)

megastore *noun* supermagazin *n*

member *noun* membru *m;* **honorary member** = membru onorific; **union member** = membru al unui sindicat

membership *noun* afiliere *f or* calitatea *f* de membru

memo *or* **memorandum** *noun* **(a)** memorandum *n* **(b)** *(informal written message)* notă *f*

mercantile *adjective* comercial *or* mercantil; **mercantile law** = lege *f* comercială; **mercantile marine** = marină *f* comercială

merchandise **1** *noun* marfă *f;* bunuri *npl* de consum **2** *verb* a comercializa; **to merchandise a product** = a comercializa un produs

merchant *noun & adjective* **(a)** comerciant *m* **(b)** **merchant bank** = bancă *f* de comerţ **(c)** **merchant fleet** = flotă comercială

merge *verb* a fuziona; **the two rival companies merged last year** = cele două companii rivale au fuzionat anul trecut

merger *noun* fuziune *f*

metre *noun* metru *m*

metric system *noun* sistem *m* metric

Mexican *noun & adjective* mexican(ă)

Mexico *noun* Mexic *m* NOTE: capital: **Mexico City** = Ciudad de Mexico; currency: **Mexican peso** = peso mexican

micro *or* **microcomputer** *noun* microcalculator *n*

micro-economics *noun* microeconomie *f*

Middle East *noun* Orientul Mijlociu *n*

middleman *noun* intermediar *m*

mile *noun* milă *f* (unitate de măsură pentru distanţe egală cu 1,6 km)

mileage *noun* **(a)** distanţă *f* **(b)** kilometraj *n;* **mileage allowance** = cheltuieli *fpl* de deplasare în interes de serviciu

mill *noun* fabrică *f* (de textile); **cotton mill** = ţesătorie de bumbac; **paper mill** = fabrică de hârtie

millimetre (mm) *noun* milimetru *m* (mm)

million *noun* milion *n*

millionaire *noun* milionar *m*

minicomputer *noun* minicalculator *n*

minimum wage *noun* salariu *n* minim

mining *noun* industria *f* extractivă; **mining concession** = concesiune *f* minieră

minister *noun* ministru *m;* **Minister of Foreign Affairs** = Ministru de Externe (NOTE: in Britain: Foreign Secretary, in USA: Secretary of State)

mint *noun* monetărie *f*

minutes *plural noun* proces *n* verbal; minută *f;* **the chairman asked for the last meeting's minutes** = preşedintele a cerut procesul verbal al şedinţei precedente

miscalculate *verb* a calcula greşit

miscalculation *noun* greşeală *f* de calcul

miscarriage *noun* eşec *n or* eroare *f;* **miscarriage of justice** = eroare judiciară

misconduct *noun* **(a)** comportament *n* necorespunzător **(b)** neglijenţă *f* (în serviciu)

misfeasance *noun* interpretare *f* greşită a legii

misinform *verb* a dezinforma

mismanage *verb* a administra *or* a conduce necorespunzător

misrepresent *verb* a deforma (realitatea, fapte, etc.)

misrepresentation *noun* **(a)** deformare *f* **(b)** dezinformare *f;* **fraudulent misrepresentation** = dezinformare frauduloasă

mistake *noun* greşeală *f or* eroare *f;* scăpare *f;* **to make a mistake** = a comite o eroare; a greşi

misuse *noun* abuz *n;* folosire *f* deficientă

mixed economy *noun* economie *f* mixtă

mobile *adjective* mobil; **mobile workforce** = forţă *f* de muncă mobilă

mobility *noun* mobilitate *f;* **mobility of labour** = mobilitatea forţei de muncă

mock auction *noun* licitaţie *f* simulată

mock-up *noun* machetă *f or* model *n* la scară redusă

monetary *adjective* monetar; **International Monetary Fund (IMF)** = Fondul *n* Monetar Internaţional (FMI); **the international monetary system** = sistemul *f* monetar internaţional; **monetary economy** = economie *f* monetară; **monetary policy** = politică *f* monetară; **monetary unit** = unitate *f* monetară

monetize *verb* **(a)** a monetiza **(b)** a stabili valoarea nominală a monedei

money *noun* **(a)** bani *mpl;* **counterfeit money** = bani falşi; **to earn money** = a câştiga bani (muncind); **he is worth a lot of money** = este foarte bogat; **money market** = piaţă monetară; **paper money** = bancnote *fpl;* **plastic money** = cărţi *fpl* de credit (confecţionate din plastic); **pocket-money** = bani de buzunar; **to put money down** = a plăti un avans în bani peşin; **to put money into the bank** = a depune bani la bancă; **ready money** = bani peşin disponibili **(b)** **danger money** = spor *n* de periclitate **(c)** **hush-money** = mită *f* **(d)** **money-spinner** = articol care se vinde foarte bine

moneylender *noun* persoană *f* sau organizaţie *f* care acordă împrumuturi

money order *noun* mandat *n* poştal; **international money order** = mandat poştal internaţional; **telegraphic money order** = mandat poştal telegrafic

monopoly *noun* monopol *n;* **absolute monopoly** = monopol absolut; **discriminating monopoly** = monopol discriminatoriu; **fiscal monopoly** = monopol fiscal; **legal monopoly** = monopol legal; **public or state monopoly** = monopol public

monopsony *noun* monopolul *n* cumpărătorului

month *noun* lună *f;* **calendar month** = lună *f* calendaristică

Moroccan *noun* & *adjective* marocan(ă)

Morocco *noun* Maroc *m* NOTE: capital: **Rabat;** currency: **Moroccan dirham** = dirham marocan

mortgage **1** *noun* ipotecă *f;* împrumut *n* pentru cumpărarea de locuinţe; **to take out a mortgage** = a contracta un împrumut pentru cumpărarea unei locuinţe **2** *verb* a ipoteca; **to pay off her debts she had to mortgage her house** = a trebuit să-şi ipotecheze casa pentru a-şi achita datoriile

most-favoured-nation clause *noun* clauza *f* naţiunii celei mai favorizate

motel *noun* motel *n or* hotel *n* (pentru automobilişti)

motion *noun* moţiune *f* *or* propunere *f;* **abandoned motion** = moţiune abandonată (care nu a fost supusă la vot); **to table a motion** = a prezenta o propunere

motorway *noun* autostradă *f* (în Marea Britanie)

moveable *adjective* mobil; **moveables** = bunuri mobile

Mozambiquan *noun & adjective* mozambican(ă)

Mozambique *noun* Mozambic *m*
NOTE: capital: **Maputo;** currency:

Mozambique metical = metical mozambican

MRP (Manufacturer's Recommended Price) preţ minim de vânzare recomandat de producător

multilateral *adjective* multilateral; **multilateral trade** = comerţ multilateral

multinational *adjective* multinaţional

mutual *adjective* mutual *or* reciproc; **mutual agreement** = acord mutual; **mutual company** = companie mutuală

Nn

nation *noun* naţiune *f or* ţară *f*

national *adjective* naţional; **national advertising** = publicitate la scară naţională; **national debt** = datorie naţională; **national currency** = monedă naţională; **national economy** = economie naţională; **national income** = venit naţional

nationalize *verb* a naţionaliza; **the government nationalized the mining industry** = guvernul a naţionalizat industria extractivă

nationalization *noun* naţionalizare *f*

nationwide *adjective* la scară naţională; **nationwide strike** = grevă *f* la scară naţională (generală)

natural *adjective* **(a)** natural; **natural gas** = gaze naturale; **natural resources** = resurse naturale **(b)** obişnuit *or* firesc

navy *noun* flotă *f* marină *f*; **merchant navy** = marină comercială

Near East *noun* Orientul Apropiat *n*

negotiable *adjective* negociabil; **negotiable instrument** = document negociabil (bancnote, titluri la purtător, etc.)

negotiate *verb* **(a)** a negocia; **the trade union negotiated the new pay package with the management** = sindicatul a negociat noile salarii cu conducerea **(b)** a încheia un contract financiar; **to negotiate a bank loan** = a aranja obţinerea unui împrumut la bancă

negotiation *noun* negociere *f*; **wage negotiations** = negocierea salariilor

neighbourhood *noun* cartier *n*; vecinătate *f*

Nepal *noun* Nepal *m* NOTE: capital: **Kathmandu**; currency: **Nepalese rupee** = rupia nepaleză

Nepalese *noun & adjective* nepalez(ă)

net **1** *adjective* net; **net income** = venit net; **net price** = preţ net; **net profit** = profit net; **net salary** = salariu net; **net weight** = masă netă; **net worth** = valoare netă; **net yield** = randament net **2** *verb* a câştiga *or* a obţine (net); **the company netted a profit of £500,000** = firma a obţinut profituri nete de £500.000

Netherlands *noun* Olanda *f* NOTE: capital: **Amsterdam**; currency: **Dutch guilder** = gulden olandez

network **1** *noun* reţea *f*; **computer network** = reţea de calculatoare; **distribution network** = reţea de distribuţie **2** *verb* a transmite *or* a emite; **to network a television programme** = a transmite un program de televiziune tuturor receptoarelor din reţea

new *adjective* nou; **brand new** = nou-nouţ

news *noun* **(a)** informaţii *fpl* **(b)** ştiri *fpl*; buletin *n* de ştiri; **news release** = comunicat *n*

newsagent *noun* vânzător *m* de ziare şi reviste

newsletter *noun* buletin *n* informativ intern

newspaper *noun* ziar *n*

New Zealand *noun* Noua Zeelandă *f* NOTE: capital: **Wellington**; currency: **New Zealand dollar** = dolar neozeelandez

New Zealander *noun* neozeelandez(ă)

Nicaragua *noun* Nicaragua *f* NOTE: capital: **Managua**; currency: **Nicaraguan córdoba** = córdoba nicaraguană

Nicaraguan *noun & adjective* nicaraguan(ă)

niche *noun* nişă *f* (loc special ocupat de o firmă pe piaţă)

nickel *noun* monedă *f* de 5 cenţi în SUA

nil *noun* nimic *n or* zero *n;* **the funds for the project were cut to nil** = fondurile destinate proiectului au fost suprimate total

nominal *adjective* **(a)** simbolic; **nominal charge** = sumă simbolică percepută **(b)** nominal; **nominal capital** = capital nominal

nominate *verb* **(a)** a numi (în funcţie); **he was nominated head of the research team** = a fost numit şeful echipei de cercetări **(b)** a (-şi) depune candidatura

non-convertible *adjective* neconvertibil (despre monedă)

non-recurring expense *noun* cheltuieli *fpl* extraordinare

non-taxable income *noun* venit *n* neimpozabil

Norway *noun* Norvegia *f* NOTE: capital: **Oslo**; currency: **Norwegian krone** = coroană norvegiană

Norwegian *noun & adjective* norvegian(ă)

notarial *adjective* notarial; **notarial act** = act notarial

notary public *noun* notar *m*

note **1** *noun* notă *f or* aviz *n;* **advice note** = aviz de expediere; **cover note** = poliţă *f* provizorie de asigurări; **credit note** = notă de credit *or* de stornare; **debit note** = notă de debitare **2** *verb* a nota

notice *noun* **(a)** aviz *n or* avizare *f* **(b)** preaviz *n;* **she left her job without giving the required one month's notice** = şi-a părăsit slujba fără a prezenta cuvenitul preaviz de o lună de zile **(c)** avertisment *n;* **to serve notice on someone** = a da un avertisment (oficial) cuiva

notice-board *noun* avizier *n*

notify *verb* a notifica; a aviza; a anunţa (oficial); **the managing director notified the union that further job cuts were to follow shortly** = directorul general a avizat sindicatul că măsuri de reducere a personalului aveau să fie puse în practică în curând

nought *noun* cifra *f* zero

null *adjective* nul; **to declare null and void** = a declara nul şi neavenit

number **1** *noun* **(a)** *(quantity)* număr *n or* cantitate *f* **(b)** **opposite number** = omolog *m;* **the British Prime Minister met his French opposite number** = Primul Ministru britanic s-a întâlnit cu omologul său francez **2** *verb* a numerota

Oo

oath *noun* jurământ *n;* **to give evidence under oath** = a depune mărturie sub jurământ

object 1 *verb* a se opune; **the manager objected to the clause in the contract** = directorul s-a opus clauzei din contract **2** *noun* **(a)** obiect *n* **(b)** scop *n;* **the object of the company** = scopul pentru care compania a fost înfiinţată

obligation *noun* **(a)** datorie *f or* obligaţie *f;* **moral obligation** = datorie morală; **the building company did not fulfil its contractual obligations** = trustul de construcţii nu şi-a îndeplinit obligaţiile contractuale **(b)** datorii *fpl;* **to meet one's obligations** = a-şi plăti datoriile

obligatory *adjective* obligatoriu; **they were told that their attendance at the meeting was obligatory** = ei au fost anunţaţi că prezenţa la şedinţă era obligatorie

oblige *verb* **(a)** a obliga; **the sharp fall in sales obliged the factory to reduce production** = scăderea bruscă a volumului vânzărilor a obligat fabrica să reducă producţia **(b)** a îndatora; **I am much obliged to you for your help** = vă sunt îndatorat pentru ajutorul acordat

obsolescence *noun* uzură *f* (fizică sau morală); **built-in obsolescence** = uzură planificată

obsolescent *adjective* desuet *or* demodat; depăşit din punct de vedere tehnic

obsolete *adjective* depăşit; **these days 286 computers are considered obsolete** = la ora actuală calculatoarele 286 sunt considerate depăşite

occupation *noun* **(a)** ocupare *f;* **occupation of a building** = ocuparea unei clădiri **(b)** *(profession)* ocupaţie *f or* profesie *f*

occupational *adjective* profesional; de muncă; **occupational accident** = accident *n* de muncă; **occupational hazards** = riscuri profesionale

odd *adjective* **(a)** neobişnuit; **odd sizes** = măsuri neobişnuite (de îmbrăcăminte, pantofi, etc.) **(b)** incomplet, care nu e întreg; **ten pounds-odd** = 10 lire şi câţiva pence **(c)** fără soţ *or* impar; **odd numbers** = numere impare (3, 5, 7, etc)

off 1 *adverb & preposition* **(a) the shirts were 10% off the normal price** = cămăşile erau reduse cu 10 % **(b) time off** = concediu *or* timp liber **(c) he is off sick** = absentează pe motive de sănătate **(d) the deal is off** = tranzacţia a fost anulată

offence *noun* infracţiune *f;* **tax offence** = infracţiune fiscală

offer 1 *noun* ofertă *f;* **they made him an offer he could not refuse** = i s-a făcut o ofertă pe care n-a putut să o refuze **2** *verb* a oferi *or* a propune; **because he**

was an established customer he was offered a special deal = din cauză că era un client vechi i s-a oferit o tranzacţie în condiţii avantajoase; **to offer for sale** = a oferi spre vânzare

office *noun* (a) **branch office** = filială *f* *or* sucursală *f;* agenţie *f;* **head office** = sediu *n* central; **office staff** = personal *n* administrativ (b) **booking office** = casă *f* de bilete (c) departament *n or* minister *n* (în Marea Britanie); **the Foreign Office** = Ministerul *n* de Externe; **the Home Office** = Ministerul de Interne (d) **information office** = ghişeu *n or* birou *n* de informaţii (e) **register office** = oficiul *n* de stare civilă

office-bearer *noun* titular *m* de post

officer *noun* (a) funcţionar *m;* **customs officer** = vameş *f;* **fire safety officer** = responsabil cu prevenirea incendiilor; **personnel officer** = şef *m* de birou personal (b) **ship's officer** = căpitan *m* al unui vas comercial; ofiţer *m* cu răspundere pe vas

official 1 *adjective* oficial; **the official exchange rate** = schimbul de valută oficial; **the official documents were examined by the investigation committee** = documentele oficiale au fost studiate de către comisia de anchetă 2 *noun* demnitar *m;* **British businessmen met high officials during their visit** = oameni de afaceri britanici s-au întreţinut cu înalţi demnitari de stat pe timpul vizitei lor

off-licence *noun* (în Marea Britanie) (a) autorizaţie de comercializare a băuturilor alcoolice pentru acasă (b) *(shop)* magazin *n* de băuturi alcoolice

offload *verb* a descărca

off-peak *adjective* în afara orelor de vârf; **off-peak rate** = tarif *n* redus (pentru consumul de energie electrică, gaz metan, etc.) în afara orelor de vârf

offset 1 *verb* (a) a compensa; **to offset losses against tax** = a deduce pierderi

din impozite (b) a contrabalansa 2 *noun (printing)* tipar *n* înalt *or* ofset *n*

offshore *adjective & adverb* (a) departe de ţărm; **offshore oil platform** = platformă petrolieră marină (b) străin *or* de peste hotare; **he transferred all his money to an offshore bank** = şi-a transferat toţi banii într-o bancă străină; **offshore funds** = fonduri *npl* depuse în bănci străine (deseori din motive fiscale)

oil *noun* (a) petrol *n or* ţiţei *n;* **crude oil** = ţiţei brut; **oil-exporting countries** = ţări exportatoare de petrol; **oil-producing countries** = ţări *fpl* producătoare de petrol; **oil rig** = sondă petrolieră; **oil well** = puţ *n* petrolier (b) *(cooking)* ulei *n* (de gătit); **we import olive oil from Greece** = importăm ulei de măsline din Grecia (c) lubrifiant *n*

old age *noun* bătrâneţe *f;* **old age pension** = pensie *f* de limită de vârstă

old-established *adjective* renumit; (despre o companie, etc.) de bună reputaţie, care se află în afaceri de multă vreme

old-fashioned *adjective* demodat; desuet; **old-fashioned typewriters have been replaced by computers and printers** = maşinile de scris demodate au fost înlocuite cu calculatoare şi imprimante

oligarchy *noun* oligarhie *f*

oligopsony *noun* piaţă *f* cu un număr restrâns de cumpărători

omnibus 1 *adjective* complet; general; **omnibus agreement** = acord general; **omnibus edition** = ediţie completă 2 *noun* autobuz *n*

oncosts *plural noun* cheltuieli *fpl* fixe

online *adverb* conectat direct la un calculator central; gata de folosire (despre echipament periferic)

one-off *adjective* unic; **one-off deal** = tranzacţie unică (avantajoasă)

open-door policy *noun* politică *f* de liberalizare a comerțului

open-ended *adjective* care poate fi modificat; **open-ended agreement** = acord *n* flexibil

opening 1 *noun* (a) deschidere *f;* **opening hours** = orar *n* de funcționare (b) inaugurare *f;* **the local MP was invited to the opening of the new shopping mall** = senatorul local a fost invitat la inaugurarea noului complex comercial (c) **job openings** = posturi vacante 2 *adjective* (a) inaugural (b) inițial; **opening bid** = ofertă inițială; **opening price** = primul curs (la bursă)

operate *verb* (a) a intra în vigoare *or* a se aplica; **the new rules will operate from the beginning of the financial year** = noile reguli vor intra în vigoare la începutul anului financiar (b) a manipula *or* a opera; **it took him three months to learn how to operate the new equipment** = i-au trebuit trei luni să învețe să manipuleze noul echipament

operating *noun* funcționare *f;* exploatare *f;* **operating costs** = cheltuieli de exploatare; **operating profit** = beneficiu de exploatare

operative 1 *noun* muncitor *m* 2 *adjective* activ; operativ; **to become operative** = a intra în exploatare; a intra în vigoare

operator *noun* (a) operator *m;* **computer operator** = operator calculator; **keyboard operator** = operator preluare data (b) telefonist(ă) (c) **tour operator** = agenție *f* de turism

optimum *adjective* optim; ideal; **optimum conditions for sales** = condiții optime pentru vânzare

option *noun* alegere *f or* opțiune *f;* **to take up an option** = a exercita dreptul de alegere

optional *adjective* facultativ; opțional; **the redundancy cover is optional** = asigurarea în caz de șomaj este facultativă

order 1 *noun* (a) ordine *f;* **chronological order** = ordine cronologică; **the stock cards are arranged in alphabetical order** = fișele de magazie sunt aranjate în ordine alfabetică; **numerical order** = ordine numerică (b) **working order** = stare *f* de funcționare (c) comandă *f;* **to fulfil an order** = a onora o comandă; **on order** = comandat; **order-book** = registru *n* de comenzi; **order form** = formular *n* de comandă; **outstanding order** = comandă neonorată (încă); **telephone order** = comandă prin telefon; **we placed an order for office furniture** = am făcut comandă de mobilier de birou (d) **banker's order** = dispoziție *f* de plată (e) **order of the day** = ordine de zi (în ședințe) (f) **order not to pay** = cec *n* blocat 2 *verb* (a) *(give orders, command)* a da ordine *or* a comanda (b) a comanda; **they ordered new electronic scales for the mail room** = au comandat un cântar electronic nou pentru registratură

organization *noun* (a) organizare *f;* **organization chart** = organigramă *f* (b) organizație *f;* **employer's organization** = organizație a patronilor

organized labour *noun* muncitori *mpl* afiliați la un sindicat

organizer *noun* organizator *m*

origin *noun* origine *f or* proveniență *f;* **country of origin** = țară *f* de origine; **software of American origin** = software de proveniență americană

ounce *noun* uncie *f* (măsură de greutate egală cu 28 de grame)

outbid *verb* a întrece la licitație oferind cea mai mare sumă

outflow of capital *noun* scurgere *f* de capital în afara țării

outgoings *plural noun* cheltuieli *fpl*

outlay *noun* cheltuială *f; advertising outlay* = cheltuieli publicitare

outlet *noun* piaţă *f* de desfacere; debuşeu *n*

out of date *adjective* demodat; depăşit

out of order *adjective* deranjat; care nu funcţionează corespunzător

out of pocket *adjective & adverb* în pierdere

out of stock *adjective* epuizat; **the books you wish to order are out of stock** = stocul de cărţi pe care doriţi să le comandaţi s-a epuizat

out of work *adjective & adverb* fără lucru; **he has been out of work for more than six months** = este şomer de mai bine de şase luni

output *noun* (a) producţie *f;* productivitate *f or* randament *n;* **gross output** = producţie brută; **to increase output by 5%** = a mări producţia cu 5%; **net output** = producţie netă; **output bonus** = primă *f* de productivitate; **output per hour** = producţie pe oră (b) informaţii *fpl* prelucrate de calculator gata de folosire

outsell *verb* a vinde mai mult decât competiţia

outstanding *adjective* (a) neplătit *or* neachitat; **outstanding debts** = datorii neplătite (b) neonorat; **outstanding orders** = comenzi neonorate

outturn *noun* producţie *f*

outward cargo *noun* încărcătură *f* destinată exportului

overbid *verb (make a higher bid than)* a întrece la licitaţie

overboard *adverb* peste bord; **to throw the cargo overboard** = a arunca încărcătura peste bord

overbuy *verb* a cumpăra mai mult decât necesar

overcharge 1 *noun* preţ *n* sau tarif excesiv 2 *verb* (a) *(a lorry, a ship)* a supraîncărca (b) *(an account)* a încărca exagerat un cont

overdraft facilities *noun* facilitate *f* de descoperit

overdraw *verb* a-şi depăşi suma din cont; **to be overdrawn** = a avea balanţă negativă în bancă

overdue *adjective* (a) datorat (demult); **he received a letter from the bank regarding the overdue payments** = a primit o scrisoare de la bancă privitoare la plăţile datorate (b) întârziat; **the train is overdue** = trenul este întârziat

overheads *plural noun* cheltuieli *fpl* generale; **manufacturing overheads** = cheltuieli de fabricaţie

overload *verb (a lorry, a ship)* a supraîncărca

overloaded economy *noun* economie *f* supraîncărcată, în care cererea e mai mare decât oferta iar preţurile sunt menţinute la un nivel scăzut de guvern

overmanning *noun* exces *n* de personal

overpay *verb* a plăti în exces

overpayment *noun* plată *f* în exces

overrated *adjective* supraevaluat; exagerat

overseas 1 *adjective* din străinătate; străin; internaţional; **overseas bank** = bancă străină; **overseas call** = convorbire telefonică internaţională; **overseas trade** = comerţ exterior 2 *noun* străinătate *f*

overspend *verb* a cheltui excesiv; **to overspend one's budget** = a cheltui mai mult decât este prevăzut în buget

overstock 1 *verb* a acumula stocuri excesiv 2 *plural noun US* **overstocks** = stocuri în exces (în SUA)

overtime *noun* ore *fpl* suplimentare; **at busy times workers are encouraged to do overtime** = în perioadele de vârf angajaţii sunt încurajaţi să presteze ore suplimentare

overvalue *verb* a supraevalua *or* a supraestima

owe *verb* a datora; **he owes me £50** = îmi datorează 50 de lire

own 1 *adjective* propriu *or* personal; **the manager uses his own car for business trips** = directorul foloseşte maşina personală pentru călătorii în interes de serviciu **2** *verb* a poseda *or* a fi în posesia a ceva; **he owns 10% of the shares of the company** = posedă 10 % din totalul acţiunilor companiei

owner *noun* proprietar *m;* deţinător *m;* **the stolen goods were returned to the owner** = bunurile furate au fost înapoiate proprietarului

ownership *noun* calitatea *f* de proprietar; proprietate *f;* **common ownership** = proprietate comună; **state ownership** = proprietate de stat

Pp

pack 1 *noun* (a) lot *n;* **pack of items** = lot de articole (b) pachet *n;* **pack of cigarettes** = pachet de ţigări 2 *verb* a ambala; a împacheta; **the books were packed and dispatched yesterday** = cărţile au fost împachetate şi expediate ieri

package *noun* (a) ambalaj *n* (b) pachet *n;* colet *n;* **airtight package** = pachet (închis) ermetic; **the package was delivered to her door** = coletul a fost livrat la domiciliul ei (c) **package tour** = excursie *f* organizată

package deal *noun* (a) tranzacţie *f* globală (b) ofertă *f* globală (cuprinzând diverse condiţii)

packaging *noun* (a) *(action)* ambalare *f or* împachetare *f* (b) *(material)* ambalaj *n*

packet *noun* pachet *n;* colet *n;* **packet of biscuits** = pachet de biscuiţi; **postal packet** = colet poştal

packing *noun* (a) *(action)* ambalare *f or* împachetare *f;* **postage and packing (p&p)** = preţul *n* pentru francare şi ambalare (b) *(material)* ambalaj *n*

packing-case *noun* ladă *f* de ambalaj

Pakistan *noun* Pakistan *m* NOTE: capital: **Islamabad**; currency: **Pakistani rupee** = rupia pakistaneză

Pakistani *noun & adjective* pakistanez(ă)

Panama *noun* Panama *f* NOTE: capital: **Panama City** = Ciudad de Panama; currency: **Panamanian balboa** = balboa panameză

Panamanian *noun & adjective* panamez(ă)

panel *noun* (a) panou *n;* **advertising panel** = spaţiu *n* publicitar alocat într-o publicaţie; **display panel** = panou de expoziţie (b) **panel of experts** = grup *n* de specialişti

paper *noun* (a) hârtie *f;* **carbon paper** = indigou; **graph paper** = hârtie milimetrică; **lined paper** = hârtie liniată; **wrapping paper** = hârtie de împachetat (b) **paper bag** = pungă *f* de hârtie (c) **papers** = documente *npl* (d) **on paper** = (i) în teorie; (ii) în scris (e) valori *fpl;* **bankable paper** = valori acceptate de bănci; **negotiable paper** = titluri *npl* negociabile (f) **paper profit** = profit *f* teoretic (g) **paper money** = bancnote *fpl* (h) periodic *n;* publicaţie *f;* **newspaper** = ziar *n;* **evening paper** = ziar cotidian de seară; **trade paper** = periodic profesional

paper-clip *noun* agrafă *f* de birou

par *noun* (a) egalitate *f;* la acelaşi nivel; **on a par with** = cu aceeaşi valoare (b) **par value** = valoare nominală (c) **par of exchange rate** = paritatea ratei de schimb

Paraguay *noun* Paraguay *m* NOTE: capital: **Asunción**; currency: **Paraguayan guarani** = guaran paraguayan

Paraguayan *noun & adjective* paraguayan(ă)

paralyze *verb* a paraliza; **lack of raw materials paralyzed production** = lipsa de materii prime a paralizat producţia

parcel 1 *noun* (a) pachet *n;* colet *n;* **parcels office** = mesagerie *f* (b) **parcel of shares** = pachet de acţiuni 2 *verb* (a) *(action)* a împacheta (b) a împărţi în acţiuni; **to parcel out** = a distribui în părţi egale

pari passu *Latin phrase* în ritm egal; în etape egale; în aceleaşi condiţii

parity *noun* paritate *f;* **parity price** = preţ *n* de paritate

park 1 *noun* (a) parc *n;* **industrial park** = platformă *f* industrială (b) **car park** = parcare *f* 2 *verb* a parca (maşina)

part *noun* (a) parte *f;* fragment *n;* **the factory shipped just a part of the consignment** = fabrica a livrat numai o parte din comandă (b) **in part** = în parte; parţial; **to pay the costs in part** = a contribui la plată parţial (c) **spare part** = piesă de schimb; **to replace a part** = a înlocui o piesă (d) **part exchange** = schimb parţial (completat cu bani); **part payment** = plată parţială; **part order** = comandă parţială (e) **part time** = jumătate *f* de normă; **she works part time in a bank** = lucrează cu o jumătate de normă într-o bancă; **part time worker** = lucrător *m* cu jumătate de normă

partial *adjective* parţial; **partial compensation** = despăgubire parţială

participation *noun* participare *f;* implicare *f;* **workers' participation** = participarea muncitorilor la gestionarea întreprinderii

particular 1 *adjective* special; **this ink jet printer works with a particular type of paper** = această imprimantă cu cerneală funcţionează numai cu un tip special de hârtie 2 *noun* **in particular** = în special

particulars *plural noun* (a) detalii *fpl* (b) semne *fpl* particulare

partner *noun* asociat *n* or partener *m;* **active or working partner** = partener activ or participant; **sleeping partner** = asociat comanditar; **trading partner** = partener comercial

partnership *noun* asociere *f* or parteneriat *n;* societate *f;* **general partnership** = societate comercială; **limited partnership** = societate în comandită, cu răspundere limitată

part-owner *noun* copropietar *m*

party *noun* (a) *(to a contract)* parte *f* (la un contract) (b) grup *n;* **working party** = grup de lucru (c) **political party** = partid *n* politic

pass 1 *noun* permis *n* or legitimaţie *f;* **gate pass** = permis de intrare 2 *verb* (a) a aproba; a adopta; **to pass a document** = a aproba un document; **to pass a law** = a adopta o lege (b) **to pass a dividend** = a omite plata de dividende

pass-book *noun* libret *n* or carnet *n* de economii

passenger *noun* (a) pasager *f;* **passenger ship** = transatlantic *n* or vas *n* de pasageri; **passenger train** = tren *n* de pasageri (b) *(informal)* muncitor *m* ineficient

passport *noun* paşaport *n;* **your passport is out of date** = paşaportul dumneavoastră este expirat

patent 1 *noun* brevet *n;* licenţă *f* or patent *n;* **patent office** = oficiu de patente şi mărci 2 *verb* **to patent an invention** = a breveta o invenţie

pattern *noun* (a) tipar *n;* **pattern book** = colecţie *f* de tipare (de croit) (b) *(sample)* model *n* or mostră *f* (c) structură *f;* **pattern of prices** = structură a preţurilor; **trade pattern** = structură a comerţului

pawn 1 *noun* obiect *n* de amanetat; **to put something in pawn** = a amaneta ceva; **to take something out of pawn** = a recupera un obiect amanetat **2** *verb* a amaneta; **he had to pawn his watch in order to get some cash** = pentru a face rost de bani a trebuit să-și amaneteze ceasul

pawnbroker *noun* proprietar *m* de unui munte de pietate; cămătar *m*

pawnshop *noun* Munte *m* de pietate

pay 1 *noun* (a) salariu *n;* **back pay** = restanță de salariu; **basic pay** = salariu de bază; **holidays with pay** = concediu plătit; **pay day** = ziua *f* de salariu; **pay rise** = majorarea *f* salariului; **we haven't had a pay rise for two years** = salariile noastre nu au fost majorate în ultimi doi ani; **pay slip** = chitanță *f* de salariu; **take-home pay** = salariu net (b) **pay desk** = casă *f,* unde se plătește pentru bunuri cumpărate (c) **pay phone** = telefon *n* public **2** *verb* (a) a plăti; **we paid £75,000 for this house** = am plătit 75,000 de lire pe această casă; **to be paid by the hour** = a fi plătit cu ora; **pay-as-you-earn (P.A.Y.E.)** = sistem fiscal de reținere a impozitului din salariu (în Marea Britanie); **to pay by cheque** = a plăti cu cec; **to pay by credit card** = a plăti cu cartea de credit; **to pay cash** = a plăti în numerar; **to pay in advance** = a plăti în avans; **to pay in instalments** = a plăti în rate (lunare); **to pay on demand** = a plăti pe loc (b) a achita; **to pay a bill** = a achita o notă de plată; **(c) to pay back** = a rambursa; a achita; **to pay back a loan** = a achita un împrumut

payable *adjective* plătibil; **accounts payable** = bani *mpl* datorați de o firmă *or* de plătit; **payable in advance** = plătibil în avans

payback *noun* (a) rambursare *f;* **payback clause** = clauza *f* rambursării (într-un contract de împrumut) (b) *(reward)* recompensă *f* pecuniară

payee *noun* (a) salariat *m* (pe statul de plată) (b) *(person who receives a payment)* beneficiarul plății

payer *noun* plătitor *m;* **slow payer** = restanțier *m*

paying 1 *adjective* rentabil; **paying business** = afacere profitabilă **2** *noun* plată *f*

paying-in book *noun* carnet *n* de depuneri

payload *noun* încărcătură *f* utilă (de marfă sau pasageri)

payment *noun* plată *f;* **cash payment** = plata în numerar; **down payment** = plata pe loc *or* aconto *n* (în numerar); **full payment** = plată integrală; **incentive payments** = bonificație de producție; **payments in kind** = plată în natură (mărfuri sau servicii); **he agreed to pay the debt in 6 monthly payments** = a consimțit să plătească datoria în 6 rate lunare

pay off *verb* a achita; **to pay off a mortgage** = a achita plata ipotecii

payoff *or* **paying off** *noun (of a loan, etc.)* lichidarea unei datorii *or* rambursare

payroll *noun* stat *n* de plată

PC = PERSONAL COMPUTER

peak *noun* vârf *n;* **peak period** = perioadă *f* de vârf; **peak output** = randament *n* maxim

pecuniary *adjective* pecuniar; bănesc; monetar; **pecuniary reward** = recompensă bănească

peg *verb* a fixa; a menține; **to peg prices** = a menține prețurile

penalize *verb* a penaliza *or* a sancționa; **he was penalized for failing to perform his basic duties** = a fost sancționat pentru neîndeplinirea sarcinilor de serviciu

penalty *noun* penalizare *f;* amendă *f;* **penalty interest** = dobândă *f* de întârziere; **penalty rates** = tarif *n* de penalizare

penny *noun* monedă *f* de 1 penny, (plural = pence); **100 pence = 1 liră sterlină; to be left without a penny** = a rămâne fără un ban în buzunar; **penny shares** or *US* **penny stock** = acțiuni care se vând la prețuri sub 10 pence sau $1; **penny-wise** = chibzuit or econom

pension 1 *noun* pensie *f;* **pension contributions** = cotizații *fpl* în fondul de pensii; **pension fund** = fond *n* de pensii; **retirement pension** = pensie de limită de vârstă; **state pension** = pensie de stat 2 *verb* **to pension someone off** = a pensiona pe cineva

pensioner *noun* pensionar *m*

per annum *Latin phrase* pe an; **he gets £10,000 per annum (p.a.)** = câștigă 10.000 de lire pe an

per cent (%) *phrase* la sută; **our commission is 10 %** = comisionul nostru este de 10 % (10 la sută)

percentage *noun* procentaj *n;* **percentage increase** = creștere a procentajului

peripherals *plural noun* echipament *n* periferic (pentru calculatoare)

perishable 1 *adjective* perisabil; **perishable goods** = bunuri perisabile 2 *plural noun* **perishables** = perisabilități *fpl* pierderi *fpl*

perk *noun* bonificație *f;* avantaje *npl* oferite unor salariați

permit 1 *noun* permis *n;* autorizație *f;* **import permit** = autorizație de import; **work permit** = permis de lucru (pentru străini) 2 *verb* a permite

person *noun* (a) persoană *f* fizică sau juridică; **fictitious person** = persoană fictivă (b) **in person** = în persoană

personal *adjective* personal; **personal allowance** = sumă din salariu scutită de taxe (în Marea Britanie); **personal assistant** = secretar personal; **personal computer (PC)** = calculator personal; microcalculator *f;* **personal effects** = efecte personale; **personal estate** = bunuri mobile

personnel *noun* personal *n* or cadre *npl;* **personnel manager** = șef *m* serviciu personal

Peru *noun* Peru *m* NOTE: capital: **Lima;** currency: **Peruvian inti =** inti *m* peruvian

Peruvian *noun* & *adjective* peruvian(ă)

petrodollar *noun* petrodolar *m*

petrol *noun* benzină *f;* **car with low petrol consumption** = o mașină cu consum scăzut de benzină

petroleum *noun* țiței *n;* **crude petroleum** = țiței brut

petty *adjective* neînsemnat or minor; **petty cash** = fond *n* pentru cheltuieli minore; fond de piață; **petty expenses** = cheltuieli *fpl* minore

Philippines *noun* Filipine *fpl* NOTE: capital: **Manila;** currency: **Philippine peso** = peso filipinez

phone 1 *noun* telefon *n;* **to book a table by phone** = a rezerva o masă la restaurant prin telefon; **to order by phone** = a comanda prin telefon; **phone book** = carte *f* de telefon; **phone call** = convorbire *f* telefonică; **phone number** = număr *n* de telefon; **portable phone** = telefon portabil or mobil 2 *verb* a telefona

photocopier *noun* mașină *f* de copiat or copiator *m*

photocopy 1 *noun* copie *f* 2 *verb* a copia

pick 1 *noun* alegere *f;* **the pick of the group** = cel mai bun dintr-un lot; **take your pick please** = alegeți, vă rog 2 *verb* a alege; **the personnel manager picked the most suitable candidate for the vacancy** = șeful serviciului personal a ales pe cel mai potrivit candidat pentru postul vacant

picket *noun* pichet *n* (de grevişti)

picking *noun* alegere *f;* selecţionare *f;* **order picking** = selecţionare de articole pentru o comandă

pick up *verb* a se îmbunătăţi; a se ameliora; a creşte (din nou); **sales have picked up after a bad patch** = vânzările au crescut din nou după o perioadă de stagnare

pickup (truck) *noun* camionetă *f;* furgonetă *f*

piece *noun* bucată *f;* **by the piece** = la bucată; **piece goods** = baloturi *npl* de materiale textile; **piece market** = piaţă de desfacere a textilelor; **piece work** = lucrul în acord; **piece worker** = lucrător în acord

pie chart *noun* grafic *n* circular

pint *noun* pintă *f* (unitate de măsură pentru lichide, egală cu 0,568 litri în Marea Britanie şi 0,473 litri în Statele Unite)

piracy *noun* (a) piraterie *f* (b) **literary piracy** = plagiat *n*

pirate 1 *noun* (a) pirat *m* (b) plagiator *m* 2 *adjective* **a pirate copy of a video** = copie *f* ilegală *or* `pirat' a unei casete video

pit *noun* puţ *n;* mină *f* de cărbune

pitch *noun* tarabă *f* în piaţă sau pe stradă

plaintiff *noun* reclamant *m*

plan 1 *noun* plan *n or* proiect *n;* **contingency plan** = plan (în caz de) de urgenţă; **economic plan** = plan economic; **investment plan** = plan de investiţii; **town plan** = ghidul oraşului 2 *verb* a planifica; a alcătui un plan

plane *noun* avion *n;* **my colleague is arriving in Bucharest on the 3 o'clock plane from Heathrow** = colegul meu va sosi la Bucureşti cu avionul de ora 3 de la Heathrow

planned economy *noun* economie *f* planificată

planning permission *noun* autorizaţie *f* de construcţie

plant *noun* (a) instalaţii *fpl* tehnice; **plant-hire firm** = firmă *f* de închiriere de echipament (b) uzină *f;* **central-heating plant** = centrală termică (pentru încălzirea locuinţelor); **chemical plant** = uzină *f* chimică

platform *noun* (a) peron *n or* linie *f;* **the train for Manchester leaves from platform 10** = trenul de Manchester va pleca de la linia 10 (b) platformă *f;* **oil platform** = platformă petrolieră marină

plea *noun* (a) pledoarie *f* (a acuzatului) (b) declaraţie *f* a pârâtului ca răspuns la acuzaţia adusă

plead *verb* a se declara vinovat sau nevinovat; **the defendant pleaded guilty** = acuzatul şi-a recunoscut vina

plummet *or* **plunge** *verb* a plonja *or* a scădea rapid (despre preţuri, etc.)

plutocracy *noun* plutocraţie *f*

pocket 1 *noun* buzunar *n;* **pocket calculator** = calculator *n* de buzunar; **pocket edition** = ediţie *f* de buzunar; **to be £40 in pocket** = a obţine un profit de 40 de lire; **to be £20 out of pocket** = a pierde £20 (într-o tranzacţie) 2 *verb* (a) *(put into one's pocket)* a băga în buzunar (b) a-şi însuşi; **from the total sum he paid a small commission and pocketed the rest** = din toată suma a plătit un mic comision şi şi-a însuşit restul

point 1 *noun* (a) punct *n;* **break-even point** = punct mort (vânzările acoperă cheltuielile, fără profit realizat) (b) centru *n;* **point of sales** = centru de vânzare *or* desfacere 2 *verb* a arăta; **to point out** = a semnala; **he pointed out that without new equipment productivity would suffer** = a semnalat faptul că productivitatea va scădea fără introducerea de echipament nou

Poland *noun* Polonia *f* NOTE: capital: **Warsaw** = Varşovia; currency: **Polish zloty** = zlot polonez

Pole *noun* polonez(ă)

policy *noun* **(a)** politică *f;* **economic policy** = politică economică; **government policy on imports** = politică guvernamentală referitoare la importuri **(b)** politică *f or* tactică *f;* **our policy is to cut the costs and be as efficient as possible** = politica noastră este să reducem costurile şi să devenim eficienţi **(c)** *(insurance)* poliţă *f;* **an accident policy** = poliţă de asigurări împotriva accidentelor; **comprehensive policy** = poliţă de asigurări împotriva tuturor riscurilor; **insurance policy** = poliţă de asigurări; **to make out a policy** = a emite o poliţă de asigurări; **policy holder** = deţinător al unei poliţe *or* persoană asigurată; **to take out an insurance policy** = a contracta o poliţă de asigurări

Polish *adjective* polonez(ă)

political *adjective* politic; **political economy** = economie politică; **political levy** = cotizaţie plătită de un membru de partid; **political party** = partid politic

poll 1 *noun* **(a)** alegeri *fpl* **(b) opinion poll** = sondaj *n* de opinie 2 *verb* **(a)** a sonda opinia publică **(b)** a vota **(c)** *(receive so many votes)* a obţine voturi; **he polled 500 votes** = a obţinut 500 de voturi

pool 1 *noun* **(a) typing pool** = birou *n* de dactilografie (în cadrul unei întreprinderi) **(b) a pool of unemployed labour** = resurse *fpl* umane nefolosite **(c) the pools** = pronosport *n* 2 *verb* a uni

poor *adjective* **(a)** sărac **(b)** inferior *or* modest; scăzut; **poor quality** = calitate inferioară; **poor results** = rezultate modeste; **poor service** = serviciu de proastă calitate

port *noun* **(a)** port *n;* oraş *n* cu port; **autonomous port** = port autonom; **to call at a port** = a face escală la un port;

free port = port liber; **port authority** = autorităţi portuare; **port installations** = instalaţii portuare; **port of call** = port de escală; **the port of Constanza** = portul Constanţa; **port of entry** = port de intrare **(b)** *(computers)* conexiune *f* periferică a unui calculator

Portugal *noun* Portugalia *f* NOTE: capital: **Lisbon** = Lisabona; currency: **Portuguese escudo** = escudo portughez

Portuguese *noun & adjective* portughez(ă) *or* lusitan(ă)

post 1 *noun* **(a)** *(system)* poştă *f;* **to send something by post** = a trimite ceva prin poştă; **to send payment by post** = a trimite plata prin poştă; **parcel post** = mesagerie *f or* coletărie *f* **(b)** *(letters)* corespondenţă *f* **(c)** *(job)* post *n or* poziţie *f;* **to apply for a post as shop assistant** = a solicita un post de vânzător 2 *verb* **(a)** a expedia prin poştă; **to post a letter** = a expedia o scrisoare **(b) to post an entry** = a efectua o intrare (contabilă); **to post up** = a aduce la zi

postage *noun* tarif *n* poştal; **postage paid** = tarif poştal achitat (în avans); **postage stamp** = timbru *n* poştal

postal *adjective* poştal; **postal clerk** = oficiant; **postal meter** = maşină *f* de francat; **postal order** = mandat poştal

postcard *noun* carte *f* poştală

postcode *noun* cod *n* poştal

postdate *verb* a postdata; **postdated cheque** = cec postdatat

poste restante *noun* (serviciu) post *n* restant

postmark 1 *noun* ştampila *f* poştei 2 *verb* a ştampila (o trimitere poştală)

post office *noun* oficiu *n* poştal; poştă *f;* **post office box** = căsuţă poştală

postpone *verb* a amâna; **to postpone payment** = a amâna plata; **the meeting was postponed to next week** = şedinţa a fost amânată pe săptămâna viitoare

postponement *noun* amânare *f*

potential 1 *adjective* potenţial *or* posibil; **potential customers** = clienţi potenţiali; **potential market** = piaţă potenţială 2 *noun* potenţial *n or* resurse *fpl;* **earning potential** = potenţial de câştig

pound *noun* (a) *(weight)* livră *f* (egală cu 0,45 Kg); **to sell vegetables by the pound** = a vinde legume la livră (b) *(money)* **pound sterling** = liră sterlină (£); **a pound coin** = o monedă de o liră; **a fifty pound note** = o bancnotă de cincizeci de lire

poverty *noun* sărăcie *f;* **poverty line** = nivel *n* minim de subzistenţă; **poverty-stricken** = extrem de sărac

power 1 *noun* (a) putere *f;* **buying power** = putere de cumpărare; **executive power** = putere executivă (b) energie *f;* **electrical power** = energie electrică; **power point** = priză *f;* **power station** = centrală electrică (c) **power of attorney** = împuternicire *f* 2 *verb* a aproviziona cu energie (electrică)

PR = PUBLIC RELATIONS relaţii *fpl* cu publicul

practice *noun* (a) practică *f or* metode *fpl;* **code of practice** = conduită *f* profesională; **industrial practices** = practici *fpl* industriale; **restrictive practices** = metode *fpl* restrictive; **sharp practice** = metode lipsite de scrupule; **trade practices** = practici comerciale (b) cabinet *n* medical particular; **Dr X opened a practice in Harley Street** = Doctorul X şi-a deschis un cabinet medical particular pe Strada Harley; **dental practice** = cabinet stomatologic particular

precinct *noun* zonă *f;* **shopping precinct** = zonă (pietonală) comercială

preference shares *plural noun* acţiuni *fpl* privilegiate

preferential *adjective* preferenţial; **preferential payments** = plăţi *fpl;*

preferenţiale; **preferential tariff** = tarif preferenţial; **preferential treatment** = tratament preferenţial

preferred *adjective* preferat; privilegiat; **preferred creditor** = creditor privilegiat

prejudice 1 *noun* prejudiciu *n* 2 *verb* a prejudicia

premises *plural noun* local *n;* incintă *f;* sediu *n;* **commercial premises** = sediu comercial; **on the premises** = în incintă

premium *noun* (a) **premium offer** = ofertă *f* specială (b) **insurance premium** = primă *f* de asigurări; **risk premium** = primă de risc

prepaid *adjective* plătit în avans; achitat anticipat; **prepaid carriage** = transport *n* plătit în avans

present 1 *verb* (a) a prezenta (documente, etc.); **to present a bill for acceptance** = a prezenta o factură spre aprobare (b) *(give as a gift)* a dărui 2 *noun* (a) *(time)* prezent *n* (b) *(gift)* cadou *n;* **his colleagues gave him a watch as a present when he retired** = colegii i-au făcut cadou un ceas când a ieşit la pensie

press *noun* presă *f;* **the national press** = presa naţională; **press release** = comunicat *n* (de presă)

pre-tax *adjective* brut *or* gros; **pre-tax profits** = profituri *npl* înainte de deducerea impozitelor; **the bank reported a pre-tax profit of over £500m** = banca a declarat un profit brut de peste 500 de milioane de lire

prevailing *adjective* predominant; neîntrerupt; **prevailing economic depression** = criză economică predominantă; **prevailing prices** = preţuri predominante (ridicate)

preventive *adjective* preventiv; **preventive measures** = măsuri preventive; **to take preventive measures against fire, theft, fraud** = a lua măsuri de prevenire a incendiilor, furtului, fraudei

price 1 *noun* preț *n;* curs *n;* **actual price** = preț real; **administered price** = preț fixat de producător; **agreed price** = preț convenit; **all-in price** = preț inclusiv; **asking price** = curs cerut; **average price** = preț mediu; **bargain price** = preț redus *or* foarte convenabil; **bid price** = curs cerut la licitație; **closing price** = cursul la închidere; **competitive price** = preț competitiv; **cost price** = preț de cost; **to cut prices** = a reduce prețurile; **factory price** = preț de fabrică; **keen price** = preț competitiv; **list price** = preț de catalog; **net price** = preț net; **opening price** = primul curs (la bursă); **price ceiling** = preț maximal; **price-earnings ratio** = raport *n* cost-beneficiu; **the price of crude oil has increased** = prețul țițeiului brut a crescut; **price list** = listă de prețuri *or* catalog; **price war** = războiul *n* prețurilor; **retail price** = preț cu amănuntul; **retail price index** = indice *m* de prețuri cu amănuntul; **selling price** = preț de vânzare 2 *verb* a evalua; a stabili prețul

priceless *adjective* neprețuit *or* foarte valoros

pricing *noun* determinarea *f* prețurilor; referitor *n* la prețuri; **pricing policy** = politică *f* de prețuri; **pricing system** = regimul *n* prețurilor

primary *adjective* prim; **primary commodities** = materii *fpl* prime; **primary industry** = industrie *f* primară (de bază)

prime *adjective* principal; fundamental; **Prime Minister** = Prim Ministru *n;* **prime rate** = dobândă *f* preferențială

principle *noun* principiu *n;* **in principle** = în principiu; **agreement in principle** = acord de principiu

print 1 *noun* (a) tipar *n* (b) tipăritură *f;* **a book in print** = o carte în circulație;

out of print = epuizat (despre publicații) 2 *verb* (a) a tipări (b) *(write in block letters)* a scrie cu litere majuscule

printer *noun* (a) *(printing works)* tipografie *f;* **the manuscript was ready to be sent to the printer** = manuscrisul era gata pentru a fi trimis la tipografie (b) *(machine)* imprimantă *f;* **dot-matrix printer** = imprimantă matricială; **laser printer** = imprimantă laser

printing works *plural noun* tipografie *f;* atelier *n* tipografic

prior *adjective* anterior; **prior agreement** = acord anterior; **prior to** = înainte de

priority *noun* prioritate *f;* **to give priority** = a acorda prioritate; **to have priority** = a avea prioritate

private *adjective* personal; privat; particular; **private bank** = bancă particulară; **private enterprise** = întreprindere particulară; **private investor** = investitor particular; **private property** = proprietate privată; **private sector** = sector (economic) particular; **to see someone in private** = a avea o întrevedere particulară cu cineva; **private transport** = transport particular

privatization *noun* privatizare *f*

privatize *verb* a privatiza

pro *preposition* pentru; **to consider all the pros and cons** = a examina toate argumentele pentru și împotriva

proceed *verb* (a) **to proceed against somebody** = a da pe cineva în judecată (b) *(continue)* a continua

proceedings *plural noun* dezbateri *fpl;* **legal proceedings** = acțiuni *fpl* în justiție

proceeds *plural noun* profit *n* *or* beneficiu *n;* **the proceeds of a sale** = profituri din vânzare

process 1 *noun* proces *n;* procedeu *n;* **industrial processes** = procedee de fabricație 2 *verb* (a) a prelucra materii prime **(b) to process figures** = a efectua calcule

processing *noun* procesare *f;* prelucrare *f;* **data processing** = prelucrarea *f* de date pe calculator

processor *noun* procesor *n*

procuration *noun* procură *f;* mandat *n*

produce 1 *noun* produs *n;* **farm produce** = produse agricole; **produce exchange** = bursă *f* de mărfuri 2 *verb* **(a)** a prezenta; **to produce documents** = a prezenta documente **(b)** a produce *or* a fabrica; **to mass produce** = a produce în serie

producer *noun* producător *m or* fabricant *n;* **car producer** = fabricant de automobile

product *noun* **(a)** produs *n;* **basic product** = produs de bază; **by-product** = produs secundar *or* subprodus; **end product** = produs final; **product range** = gamă *f* de produse **(b) gross national product (GNP)** = produs național brut (PNB)

production *noun* **(a)** prezentare *f* **(b)** producție *f;* **mass production** = producție de serie; **production cost** = cost *n* de producție; **production line** = secție *f or* linie *f* de producție; **production rate** = ritm *n* de producție; **to speed up production** = a mări ritmul de producție

productive *adjective* productiv *or* eficient; activ; **productive capital** = capital activ; **productive consumption** = consum eficient

productivity *noun* productivitate *f*

profession *noun* profesi(un)e *f;* meserie *f;* **doctor by profession** = de profesie medic; **to exercise a profession** = a practica o profesie *or* a profesa; **legal profession** = avocatură *f*

proficiency *noun* expertiză *f*

proficient *noun & adjective* expert *m*

profit 1 *noun* beneficiu *n;* profit *n or* câștig *n;* **after-tax profit** = profit după deducerea impozitelor; **book profit** = beneficiu contabil; **gross profit or pretax profit** = profit brut; **to make a profit** = a obține profituri; **net profit** = profit net; **percentage profit** = profit procentual; **profit and loss account** = contul *n* de profit și piederi; **profit margin** = marjă *f* de beneficiu; **profit-sharing** = participarea la beneficii; **to show a profit** = a întregistra profituri; **windfall profit** = profit neașteptat 2 *verb* **(a)** a profita; a beneficia **(b)** a câștiga

profit-making *adjective* rentabil; profitabil

profitability *noun* rentabilitate *f*

profitable *adjective* profitabil *or* rentabil

profiteer *noun* speculant *m*

profiteering *noun* obținere *f* de profituri excesive

program 1 *noun* *(computer)* program *n;* **accounting program** = program de contabilitate pe calculator; **computer program** = program de calculator (set de instrucțiuni) 2 *verb* a programa; **to program a computer** = a programa un calculator

programme *noun* program *n;* **development programme** = program de dezvoltare

programmable *adjective* programabil

programmer *noun* analist *m;* programator *m*

programming *noun* programare *f;* **programming language** = limbaj *n* de programare

project *noun* proiect *n;* **developing project** = proiect de dezvoltare; **draft project** = schiță *f* de proiect

projected *adjective* **(a)** proiectat **(b)** prevăzut; estimat; **projected sales** = vânzări estimate

promissory note *noun* bilet *n* la ordin (titlu cambial ce conţine o promisiune de plată)

promote *verb* **(a)** a promova; **he was promoted to chief accountant** = a fost promovat contabil şef **(b)** *(publicize)* a face reclamă

promotion *noun* **(a)** promovare *f or* avansare *f* **(b)** *(publicity)* reclamă *f*

promotional *adjective* publicitar *or* de publicitate; **promotional material** = material de publicitate

propensity *noun* înclinaţie *f or* tendinţă *f*; **propensity to save** = înclinaţie spre a economisi

property *noun* **(a)** proprietate *f*; **private property** = proprietate particulară; **public property** = proprietate de stat; **property tax** = impozit *n* funciar **(b)** clădiri *fpl*; imobile *npl*; **we are looking to buy a property for our new branch** = vrem să cumpărăm un imobil pentru noua noastră filială **(c)** **property company** = societate imobiliară

proposal *noun* propunere *f*; **to put forward a proposal** = a înainta o propunere; **to turn down a proposal** = a refuza o propunere

propose *verb* a propune; **to propose an amendment** = a propune un amendament

proprietary *adjective* brevetat; **proprietary drug** = produs farmaceutic brevetat

proprietor *noun* **(a)** *(owner)* proprietar *m* **(b)** deţinător *m* al unui patent

proprietress *noun* proprietăreasă *f*

protect *verb* a proteja

protectionism *noun* protecţionism *n*

protective cover *noun* fond *n* de acoperire *or* protector

protective tariff *noun* tarif *n* protecţionist

proxy *noun* **(a)** *(document)* procură *f*; delegaţie *f* **(b)** delegat *m*

public 1 *adjective* public; obştesc; **public company** = societate anonimă; **public holiday** = sărbătoare legală; **public opinion** = opinie publică; **public ownership** = proprietate obştească; **public property** = proprietate de stat; **public sector** = sector public (al economiei) *or* de stat; **public servant** = funcţionar *m* de stat; **public transport** = transport *n* în comun *or* public; **public works** = lucrări publice 2 *noun* public *n*

public relations (PR) *noun* relaţii *fpl* cu publicul

publicity *noun* publicitate *f or* reclamă *f*; **publicity bureau** = agenţie *f* publicitară; **publicity campaign** = campanie *f* publicitară; **publicity matter** = material *n* publicitar

publicize *verb* **(a)** a face reclamă **(b)** a face cunoscut

publish *verb* **(a)** a publica; **to publish a book** = a publica o carte **(b)** a anunţa; **the latest interest rate changes have not yet been published** = noile valori ale dobânzilor nu au fost anunţate încă

publisher *noun* editor *m or* editură *f*

Puerto Rican *noun & adjective* portorican(ă)

Puerto Rico *noun* Porto Rico *m* NOTE: capital: **San Juan**; currency: **US dollar** = dolar *m* american

purchase 1 *noun* cumpărare *f*; achiziţie *f*; **bulk purchase** = achiziţii en gros *or* cu ridicata; **cash purchase** = achiziţie cu numerar; **purchase agreement** = contract de achiziţie; **purchase order** = comandă *f* de achiziţie 2 *verb* a cumpăra; a achiziţiona

purchaser *noun* achizitor *m*

purchasing power *noun* putere *f* de cumpărare

put *verb* **(a)** a pune; a fixa; **to put into force** = a pune în vigoare *or* a aplica **(b) to put money into a business** = a investi într-o afacere **(c) to put back a meeting** = a amâna o şedinţă **(d) to put in a claim** = a depune o cerere de despăgubiri

put up *verb* **(a) to put up prices** = a majora preţurile **(b) to put up for sale** = a oferi spre vânzare, la licitaţie

Qq

qualification *noun* calificare *f or* aptitudine *f*; **professional qualifications** = aptitudini profesionale

qualify *verb* a se califica; a obține (un titlu); **he has qualified as an engineer** = a obținut diploma de inginer

qualified *adjective* **(a)** calificat; **highly qualified** = cu înaltă calificare **(b) qualified acceptance** = acceptare condiționată

qualifying period *noun* perioadă *f* de probă

qualifying shares *plural noun* acțiuni *fpl* ale administratorilor

quality *noun* calitate *f*; **bad quality** = calitate inferioară; **good quality** = calitate superioară; **quality control** = control *n* tehnic de calitate

quantity *noun* cantitate *f*; **he got a good discount by buying a large quantity of stationery** = a obținut un bun scont cumpărând o cantitate mare de articole de papetărie; **quantity discount** = scont *n* pentru achiziții en gros

quart *noun* quart *n* (măsură de 1,136 litri)

quarter *noun* **(a)** sfert *n*; **a quarter of a litre** = un sfert de litru (250 ml); **I have been waiting for a quarter of an hour** = aștept de un sfert de oră **(b)** *(fourth part)* pătrime **(c)** *(three months)* trimestru; **we pay the rent at the end of each quarter** = plătim chiria la sfârșitul fiecărui trimestru **(d)** *(Canada and USA)* monedă de 25 de cenți (în Canada și Statele Unite)

quarterage *noun* plată *f* trimestrială (regulată)

quarterly **1** *adverb* trimestrial **2** *adjective* trimestrial; **quarterly bill** = factură trimestrială **3** *noun* revistă *f* cu apariție trimestrială

quartile *noun* măsură *f* de diviziune în patru

quay *noun* chei *n*

query **1** *noun* problemă **2** *verb* a pune întrebări; a chestiona

question **1** *noun* **(a)** întrebare *f* **(b)** problemă *f or* chestiune *f*; **to raise a question in a meeting** = a ridica o problemă într-o ședință **2** *verb* **(a)** a interoga; **the police questioned the manager about the industrial accident** = poliția l-a interogat pe director în legătură cu accidentul de muncă **(b)** a pune la îndoială; **to question somebody's competence** = a pune la îndoială competența cuiva

questionable *adjective* îndoielnic; dubios; **questionable practices** = metode dubioase

questionnaire *noun* chestionar *n*; **the customer was kindly asked to fill in the questionnaire** = clientul a fost rugat politicos să completeze chestionarul

queue **1** *noun* coadă *f or* rând *n*; **to join the queue** = a se așeza la coadă **2** *verb* a sta la coadă; a forma o coadă

quick *adjective* rapid *or* iute; **quick assets** = fonduri *npl* de rulment *or* capitaluri *npl* circulante; **quick recovery** = redresare *f* rapidă; **quick return** = profit *n* imediat

quiet *adjective* inactiv; stagnant (despre situația pieței)

quit *verb* a abandona serviciul (de bună voie) *or* a-și da demisia; **she quit her job to continue her studies** = și-a abandonat slujba ca să-și continue studiile

quota *noun* cotă *f*; **export quota** = cota la export; **import quota** = cota la import; **quota restrictions** = restricții *fpl* la cotele la import sau export; **quota system** = sistem *n* de contingentare

quotation *noun* **(a)** *(Stock Exchange)* cotă *f* **(b)** *(estimate)* deviz *n*; estimare *f*

quote *verb* a întocmi un deviz

quoted company *noun* societate *f* comercială cu acțiuni la bursă

Rr

race *noun* cursă *f;* **horse race** = cursă de cai

rack *noun* **(a)** stand *n;* **display rack** = stand expoziţional **(b) rack rent** = chirie *f* exorbitantă

racket *noun* comerţ *n* ilicit; contrabandă *f*

racketeer *noun* escroc *m* *or* speculant *m;* afacerist *m*

racketeering *noun* escrocherie *f;* comerţ *n* ilicit

raffle *noun* tombolă *f;* loterie *f* cu premii în obiecte (organizată de obicei în scopuri caritabile)

raid *noun* atac *n* brusc; **bear raid** = vânzarea *f* masivă de acţiuni pentru a forţa preţurile titlurilor să scadă; **dawn raid** = achiziţionare *f* masivă de acţiuni la deschiderea bursei

rail *noun* cale *f* ferată; **to travel by rail** = a călători cu trenul; **free on rail** = vagon franco

railhead *noun* punct *n* terminus; cap *n* de linie

railway *noun* cale *f* ferată; **railway station** = gară *f*

raise 1 *verb* **(a)** a strânge; **to raise funds for a charity** = a strânge fonduri pentru o societate caritabilă **(b)** a organiza; **to raise a loan** = a aranja obţinerea unui împrumut **(c)** *(informal)* **to raise the wind** = a face rost de bani rapid **(d)** a colecta; **to raise subscriptions** = a colecta cotizaţii (pentru abonamente) **(e) to raise an invoice** = a emite o factură **(f)** a majora; **to raise tax levels** = a majora impozitele 2 *noun US* mărire *f* de salariu; **we haven't had a raise for two years** = salariile noastre nu au fost majorate în ultimii doi ani

rake in *verb* a strânge *or* a aduna (bani) *(informal)* **to rake it in** = a câştiga mulţi bani

rake-off *noun* comision *n;* **the agency got a £10,000 rake-off for its services** = agenţia a câştigat un comision de £10.000 pentru serviciile prestate

ramp *noun* rampă *f;* **loading ramp** = rampă de încărcare

random *adjective* aleatoriu *or* întâmplător; **at random** = la întâmplare; **random check** = control prin sondaj; **random error** = eroare aleatorie

range 1 *noun* gamă *f* *or* sortiment *n;* **product range** = gamă de produse; **we stock a wide range of power tools** = vindem o gamă largă de unelte electrice 2 *verb* a varia *or* a diferi

rank 1 *noun* **(a)** rang *n* *or* grad *n;* **in rank order** = în ordinea importanţei **(b)** categorie *f* 2 *verb* a clasifica (în ordinea importanţei)

rank and file *noun* membrii *mpl* (de rând) ai unui sindicat

rapid *adjective* rapid; **rapid recover** = redresare rapidă

rate 1 *noun* (a) preţ *n* or tarif *n;* **all-in rate** = preţ cu amănuntul; tarif inclusiv; **full rate** = preţ întreg (fără scont); **the going rate** = preţul curent; **the market rate** = preţul pieţei; **reduced rate** = preţ redus (b) procentaj *n;* **flat rate** = procentaj fix (c) rată *f;* curs *n;* **bank base rates** = ratele de bază ale dobânzilor bancare; **discount rate** = rata de scont; **exchange rate** = cursul de schimb valutar; **fixed exchange rate** = curs fix de schimb valutar; **interest rate** = rata dobânzilor (d) coeficient *n;* **depreciation rate** = coeficient de amortizare (e) **birth rate** = natalitate *f* (f) ritm *n;* **rate of sales** = ritm de vânzare 2 *verb* a aprecia or a evalua

ratify *verb* a ratifica or a aproba oficial

ratification *noun* ratificare *f* or aprobare *f;* **the agreement will be presented for ratification** = contractul va fi prezentat spre aprobare

ratio *noun* raport *n* or proporţie *f;* **ratio of success to failure** = raportul dintre succes şi eşec

ration 1 *verb* a raţionaliza or a limita; **to ration investment capital** = a limita fonduri de investiţie 2 *noun* raţie *f*

rationalization *noun* raţionalizare *f*

rationalize *verb* a raţionaliza

rationing *noun* raţionalizare *f;* normare *f;* **rationing of foreign exchange** = controlul alocării devizelor controlul schimbului valutar

rat race *noun* luptă *f* (aprigă) pentru supravieţuire; **to get out of the rat race** = a se retrage din afaceri

raw *adjective* crud; neprelucrat; în stare naturală; **raw data** = informaţii *fpl* neprelucrate; **raw materials** = materii *fpl* prime

reach 1 *noun* accesibilitate *f;* acces *n;* **within reach** = accesibil 2 *verb* (a) a ajunge; **to reach an agreement** = a ajunge la o înţelegere (b) a atinge; **to**

reach a high price = a atinge un preţ ridicat

react *verb* (a) a reacţiona (b) a-şi pierde valoarea or a scădea; **the shares reacted sharply to the news of the devaluation of the pound** = preţurile acţiunilor au scăzut dramatic imediat după devaluarea lirei sterline

ready-made *adjective* de gata (despre îmbrăcăminte şi încălţăminte)

real *adjective* (a) real; original or autentic; **real income** = venit real; **real wages** = salariu real (b) **real estate** = proprietate *f* imobiliară; **real estate agent** = agenţie *f* imobiliară (în SUA)

realize *verb* (a) a realiza or a-şi da seama; **he realized that he could not meet the next instalment** = a realizat că nu va putea plăti următoarea rată (b) a îndeplini; **to realize a plan** = a îndeplini un plan (c) *(sell for cash)* a lichida proprietăţi sau mijloace fixe

realizable *adjective* convertibil în bani lichizi (despre mijloace fixe)

realtor *noun* US agenţie *f* imobiliară (în SUA)

realty *noun* US proprietate *f* imobiliară (în SUA)

reasonable *adjective* (a) rezonabil; **reasonable prices** = preţuri rezonabile or accesibile (b) moderat

reassess *verb* a reevalua

rebate *noun* (a) rabat *n;* reducere *f;* **to offer a rebate of 15 %** = a oferi o reducere de 15 % (b) scutire *f;* reducere *f;* **tax rebate** = reducere a impozitului

receipt 1 *noun* (a) chitanţă *f;* recipisă *f;* **customs receipt** = chitanţă vamală; **sales receipt** = chitanţă de vânzare; **receipt book** = chitanţier *n* (b) primire *f;* **to acknowledge receipt of payment** = a confirma primirea plăţii 2 *verb* a semna de primirea bunurilor

receivable *adjective* **accounts receivable** = bani *mpl* datoraţi unei firme, de primit

receive *verb* a primi; **he received his mail order within three days of payment** = a primit comanda prin poştă trei zile după ce a plătit

receiver *noun* **(a)** destinatar *m or* primitor *m* **(b) official receiver** = executor *m* judecătoresc; **the company is in the hands of the receivers** = compania se află în lichidare

receivership *noun* lichidare *f*

reception *noun* recepţie *f;* **reception clerk** = recepţioner *m;* **reception desk** = recepţie *f*

recession *noun* recesiune *f or* criză *f* economică

recipient *noun* beneficiar *m*

reciprocal *adjective* reciproc *or* bilateral; **reciprocal contract** = contract bilateral; **reciprocal trade agreement** = acord *n* reciproc de reducere a taxelor vamale

reciprocity *noun* reciprocitate *f*

reckon *verb* **(a)** a calcula *or* a estima; **to reckon the costs** = a estima cheltuielile **(b) to reckon on** = a se bizui pe

reclaim *verb* a recupera; a reintroduce în circuitul productiv; **to reclaim land** = a recupera teren arabil

reconstruction *noun* reconstrucţie *f;* restaurare *f;* **economic reconstruction** = reconstrucţie economică

record 1 *noun* **(a)** document *n;* **on the record** = (în mod) oficial; **off the record** = (în mod) neoficial **(b) records** = arhivă; **all the copy invoices are kept in the company's records** = toate cópiile facturilor sunt păstrate în arhiva companiei **(c) criminal record** = cazier *n* judiciar 2 *verb* a înregistra *or* a nota; **your order has been recorded** = comanda Dvs. a fost înregistrată

recorded delivery *noun* trimitere *f* poştală recomandată

recording *noun* înregistrare *f;* notare *f*

recourse *noun* recurs *n;* **to have recourse to the courts** = a face recurs împotriva unei hotărâri judecătoreşti

recover *verb* **(a)** *(get something back)* a recupera; **they recovered their money after taking the supplier to court** = şi-au recuperat banii după ce l-au dat în judecată pe furnizor **(b)** a (se) reface *or* a se redresa; **after a period of deep recession the economy started to recover** = economia a început să se redreseze după o perioadă de recesiune accentuată

recoverable *adjective* recuperabil

recovery *noun* **(a)** *(getting back something which has been lost)* recuperare *f* **(b)** redresare *f or* refacere *f;* **economic recovery** = redresare economică

recruit *verb* a recruta *or* a angaja; **we will recruit 20 staff for the new warehouse** = vom angaja 20 de persoane pentru noul depozit

recuperate *verb* a reveni la valoarea iniţială (despre preţul acţiunilor)

recycle *verb* a recicla (resurse)

red tape *noun* birocraţie *f*

redeem *verb* **(a)** a plăti *or* a lichida; **to redeem a debt** = a lichida o datorie **(b)** *(a mortgage)* a amortiza **(c) to redeem a bond** = a vinde un bon de tezaur

redeemable *adjective* rambursabil; care poate fi amortizat

redemption *noun* rambursare *f or* amortizare *f;* **redemption before due date** = amortizare anticipată; **redemption of a mortgage** = amortizarea unei ipoteci

redevelopment *noun* renovare *f* urbanistică

redistribution of income *noun*
redistribuirea *f* veniturilor

reduce *verb* a reduce *or* a diminua; **to reduce expenditure** = a reduce cheltuielile; **to reduce taxes** = a reduce impozitele

reduction *noun* reducere *f;* diminuare *f;* **price reduction** = reduceri de prețuri; **reduction in demand** = diminuarea cererii; **staff reduction** = restructurarea *f or* reducerea personalului

redundancy *noun* pierderea *f* serviciului *or* concediere *f;* **redundancy payment** = plată *f* oferită unui angajat pentru a renunţa voluntar la post; **voluntary redundancy** = renunţarea *f* de bună voie la slujbă (pentru o sumă de bani)

redundant *adjective* **(a)** *(more than is needed)* excesiv **(b)** concediat; **to make staff redundant** = a concedia personal

re-export 1 *noun* reexportare *f* 2 *verb* a reexporta

reflation *noun* readucerea *f* preţurilor la un nivel acceptabil (intervenţie a guvernului)

refresher course *noun* curs *n* de reciclare; **50 of our staff were sent on a refresher course** = 50 din angajaţii noştri au fost trimişi la un curs de reciclare

refund 1 *noun* ramburs *n;* **full refund** = ramburs total 2 *verb* a rambursa

refundable *adjective* rambursabil; **refundable deposit** = garanţie rambursabilă

refunding *noun* rambursare *f;* **refunding of a loan** = rambursarea unui împrumut

refuse *verb* a refuza; **the businessman refused to be interviewed** = omul de afaceri a refuzat interviul

register *noun* **(a)** registru *n;* **to enter something in a register** = a opera o intrare în registru; **electoral register** or

register of electors = listă electorală; **shareholders' register** = lista *f* acţionarilor **(b) cash register** = maşina *f* de casă **(c) land register** = cadastru *n* 2 *verb* **(a)** a nota în registru **(b) to register a letter** = a trimite o scrisoare recomandată cu valoare declarată

registered *adjective* **(a) registered shares** = acţiuni *fpl* nominale **(b) registered post** = trimitere *f* poştală cu valoare declarată

registrar *noun* **(a)** arhivar *m* **(b)** ofiţerul *m* stării civile

registration *noun* înregistrare *f;* **certificate of registration** = certificat *n* de înregistrare

registration number *noun* **(a)** număr *n* de înregistrare **(b)** *(of a car)* număr *n* de înmatriculare (auto) **(c)** număr de expediţie

registry (office) *noun* oficiul *n* de stare civilă

regular *adjective* **(a)** normal **(b)** regulat *or* constant; **regular flight** = zbor regulat; **regular income** = venit *n* constant

regulate *verb* **(a)** a regla; a ajusta **(b)** a regula *or* a controla; **government-regulated prices** = preţuri *npl* controlate de guvern

regulation *noun* reglementare *f;* dispoziţie *f*

reinsure *verb* a asigura din nou; a încheia o nouă asigurare

related *adjective* **(a)** afiliat; înrudit; **related company** = companie afiliată **(b)** **earnings-related pension** = pensie *f* calculată în funcţie de salariu

relation *noun* **(a)** legătură *f;* **in relation to** = în legătură cu *or* privitor la **(b) relations** = relaţii *fpl;* **industrial relations** = relaţii de muncă; **public relations** = relaţii cu publicul

release *noun* **press release** = comunicat *n* de presă

relief *noun* (a) reducere *f;* **tax relief** = reducere de impozite (b) **relief shift** = tură *f* de schimb

remainder 1 *noun* (a) rest *n* (b) *(cheap books)* **remainders** = stoc *n* (de carte) nevândut 2 *verb* a comercializa stocuri de mărfuri nevândute la preț redus

remit *verb* (a) a remite (b) **to remit by cheque** = a trimite un cec pentru o plată

remittance *noun* (a) transfer *n* bancar (b) giro *n*

remunerate *verb* a remunera *or* a plăti

remuneration *noun* remunerație *f or* salariu *n*

render *verb* a prezenta; **to render an account** = a prezenta un cont *or* o factură

renew *verb* a reînnoi; **to renew an insurance policy** = a reînnoi o poliță de asigurare; **to renew a subscription** = a reînnoi un abonament

rent 1 *noun* (a) chirie *f;* **contractual rent** = chirie contractuală; **rack rent** = chirie exorbitantă; **rent control** = reglementarea chiriei (b) rentă *f;* **land rent** = rentă funciară 2 *verb* (a) a închiria (b) **to rent out** = a da cu chirie

renunciation *noun* renunțare *f;* **letter of renunciation** = scrisoare *f* de renunțare

reorder 1 *noun* comandă *f* suplimentară 2 *verb* a reînnoi o comandă

rep *noun* = REPRESENTATIVE

repay *verb* a rambursa

repayable *adjective* rambursabil; **a loan repayable over 3 years** = un împrumut rambursabil în 3 ani

repayment *noun* rambursare *f;* plată *f;* **repayment period** = perioadă de

rambursare; **terms and conditions of repayment** = modalități de rambursare

represent *verb* a reprezenta; **he represents his firm in London** = își reprezintă firma la Londra

representation *noun* reprezentare *f*

representative 1 *adjective* reprezentativ; specific 2 *noun* (a) reprezentant *m;* **we sent our representative to discuss the sales contract** = l-am trimis pe reprezentantul nostru să discute contractul de vânzare (b) resprezentant comercial

repudiate *verb* a repudia; a rezilia; **to repudiate a contract** = a rezilia un contract

request 1 *noun* cerere *f;* **her request for a loan was granted** = cererea ei de împrumut a fost aprobată; **on request** = la cerere; **to put in a request for** = a face o cerere pentru 2 *verb* a cere *or* a solicita

require *verb* (a) a avea nevoie de; **they require a computer specialist** = au nevoie de un expert în sisteme de calcul (b) *(demand)* a solicita; a necesita

requirement *noun* cerință *f;* necesitate *f*

requisition *noun* (a) rechiziție *f;* **materials requisition** = rechiziție de materiale (b) document *n* oficial de rechiziție

resale *noun* revânzare *f*

rescind *verb* (a) a rezilia *or* a anula; **to rescind a contract** = a rezilia un contract (b) a revoca

research 1 *noun* cercetare *f;* **applied research** = cercetare aplicată; **consumer research** = studiul comportamentului consumatorilor; **research institute** = institut *n* de cercetări; **research worker** = cercetător *m;* **the company decided to allocate £1m to research** = compania a decis alocarea unei sume de 1 milion de lire pentru cercetare **2** *verb* a cerceta; a studia

researcher *noun* cercetător *m*

reservation *noun* rezervare *f;* **to make a reservation on a train** = a rezerva un bilet de tren

reserve 1 *noun* rezervă *f;* **bank reserves** = rezerve bancare; **gold reserves** = rezerve în aur; **operating reserve** = rezerve de exploatare; **reserve funds** = fonduri *npl* de rezervă; *(at an auction)* **reserve price** = preț minim acceptabil (la o licitație); **reserve ratio** = raportul dintre rezerve și moneda în circulație **2** *verb* a rezerva

resign *verb* a-și da demisia

resignation *noun* demisie *f*

resources *plural noun* resurse *fpl;* **financial resources** = resurse financiare; **human resources** = resurse umane; **natural resources** = resurse naturale

responsibility *noun* responsabilitate *f*

restitution *noun* **(a)** *(restoring a thing to its owner)* restituire *f* **(b)** *(reparation for an injury, etc.)* compensație *f*

restraint *noun* restricție *f;* **pay restraint** = plafonarea salariilor; **restraint of trade** = restricții ale schimburilor comerciale; **restraints on imports** = restricții la importuri

restrict *verb* a limita; a restrânge; **to restrict imports** = a limita importurile

restriction *noun* restricție *f;* limită *f*

restrictive *adjective* restrictiv; limitativ; **restrictive trade practices** = practici comerciale restrictive

retail 1 *noun* comerț *n* cu amănuntul; **retail price** = preț cu amănuntul; **retail price index** = indice *m* de prețuri cu amănuntul; **retail trade** = comerț cu amănuntul **2** *verb* a desface *or* a vinde cu amănuntul

retailer *noun* vânzător *m or* negustor *m* cu amănuntul

retire *verb* a ieși la pensie; a se retrage din afaceri

retrain *verb* a recicla

retraining *noun* reciclare *f* profesională

retroactive *adjective* retroactiv

return 1 *noun* **(a)** profit *n;* **return on investment** = profit din investiții **(b)** **official return** = declarație *f* oficială **(c)** **returns** = cărți *fpl* nevândute returnate editurii **(d) return ticket** = bilet dus întors **2** *verb (give back)* a înapoia

revalorization of currency *noun* revalorizarea *f* monedei

revaluation *noun* reevaluare *f;* **revaluation of assets** = reevaluarea mijloacelor fixe și investițiilor

revalue *verb* a reevalua

revenue *noun* **(a)** venit *n;* **average revenue** = venit mediu **(b)** impozit *n or* bani *mpl* încasați în bugetul statului; **Inland Revenue** = Administrația *f* Financiară *or* Fiscul *n* (în Marea Britanie); **revenue office** = fisc *n;* administrație *f* financiară; **revenue officer** = inspector *m* financiar

review 1 *noun* revistă *f* **2** *verb* a revizui; **she was told that they would review her salary after 6 months** = i s-a spus că salariul ei va fi revizuit după 6 luni =

rider *noun* clauză *f* adițională

rig 1 *noun* **oil rig** = sondă *f* petrolieră **2** *verb* a manipula; **to rig the market** = a manipula piața

right to bargain *noun* dreptul *n* de negociere a contractului colectiv

right to strike *noun* dreptul *n* la grevă

Riksbank *noun* Banca *f* Centrală Suedeză

ring 1 *noun* cartel *n* 2 *verb* a telefona; she rang to cancel the order = a telefonat ca să anuleze comada

rip-off *noun* (preţ de) speculă *f*

rise 1 *noun* (a) creştere *f or* majorare *f;* price rise = majorarea preţurilor (b) mărire *f* de salariu 2 *verb* a creşte *or* a spori

risk 1 *noun* risc *n;* financial risk = risc financiar; insurable risk = risc care poate fi asigurat; to run a risk = a risca 2 *verb* a risca

risky *adjective* riscant

robotics *noun* robotică *f*

rocket *verb* a creşte vertiginos (despre preţuri)

rolling stock *noun* material *n* rulant

Romania *noun* România *f* NOTE: capital: **Bucharest** = Bucureşti; currency: **leu** = leu *f*

Romanian 1 *noun* român(că) 2 *adjective* român, românesc, română, românească

Romanian Central Bank *noun* Banca Naţională a României (BNR)

royalties *plural noun* drepturi *npl* de autor

ruin 1 *noun* ruină *f* 2 *verb* a ruina

run 1 *noun* regim *n* de lucru (al unei maşini); test run = probă *f* de lucru 2 *verb* (a) a fi valabil; your insurance policy runs for one year = poliţa Dvs de asigurări este valabilă un an de zile (b) a conduce *or* a organiza (c) a funcţiona; she noticed that the computer was not running properly = a observat că ordinatorul nu funcţiona corespunzător

runaway inflation *noun* inflaţie *f* galopantă

running costs *plural noun* cheltuieli *fpl* de exploatare

Russia *noun* Rusia *f* NOTE: capital: **Moscow** = Moscova; currency: **rouble** = rublă *f*

Russian *noun & adjective* rus(ă); rusesc, rusească

Rwanda *noun* Ruanda *f* (Urundi) NOTE: capital: **Kigali**; currency: **Rwandan franc** = franc ruandez

Rwandan *noun & adjective* ruandez(ă)

Ss

sack 1 *noun* sac *n;* **to sell vegetables by the sack** = a vinde legume în saci **(b) to get the sack** = a fi concediat 2 *verb* a concedia; **she was sacked for bad time-keeping** = a fost concediată din cauză că nu era punctuală

safe 1 *noun* seif *n;* **every night the manager puts the cash and the cheques in the safe** = în fiecare seară directorul pune banii şi cecurile în seif 2 *adjective* sigur *or* în siguranţă; **safe investments** = investiţii sigure

safeguard 1 *noun* pază *f;* protecţie *f* 2 *verb* a păzi; a proteja; **to safeguard the interests of the customers** = a proteja interesele clienţilor

safe-keeping *noun* custodie *f or* păstrare *f*

safety *noun* securitate *f or* siguranţă *f;* **safety margin** = coeficient *n* de siguranţă; **to take safety measures** = a lua măsuri de siguranţă

sag *verb* a scădea (despre preţuri)

salary *noun* salariu *n;* **she was told that they would review her salary after 6 months** = i s-a spus că salariul ei va fi revizuit după 6 luni; **gross salary** = salariu brut; **net salary** = salariu net; **salary deductions** = popriri *fpl* pe salariu; **salary increase** = majorarea salariului

salaried *adjective* angajat *or* salariat; **salaried staff** = angajaţi permanent (care primesc salarii, spre deosebire de cei care primesc indemnizaţii)

sale *noun* **(a)** vânzare *f;* **bill of sale** = act *n* de vânzare; **forced sale** = vânzare impusă (de o hotărâre judecătorească); **jumble sale** = vânzare de mărunţişuri pentru strângerea de fonduri pentru societăţi caritabile; **on sale** = în vânzare *or* pe piaţă; **private sale** = vânzare particulară **(b) for sale** = de vânzare; **to put a house up for sale** = a oferi o casă spre vânzare **(c) sales** = vânzări *fpl;* **domestic sales** = vânzări pe piaţa internă; **overseas sales** = vânzări peste hotare; **sales force** = personal *n* de vânzări; **sales tax** = impozit *n* pe vânzări; **sales volume** = volum *n* de vânzări **(d)** *(selling goods cheaply)* sold *n;* vânzare *f* la preţ redus; **closing-down sale** = lichidare *f* **(e)** *(auction)* licitaţie *f;* **sale room** = sală *f* de licitaţii

saleable *adjective* vandabil; care are căutare pe piaţă

sales clerk *noun (in shop)* vânzător *m*

salesman *noun* **(a)** *(in shop)* vânzător *m* **(b)** reprezentant *m*

salesmanship *noun* arta *f* de a vinde; arta de a convinge cumpărătorii

saleswoman *noun* vânzătoare *f*

El Salvador *noun* Salvador *m* NOTE: capital: **San Salvador;** currency: **Salvadorian colón** = colón salvadorian

Salvadorian *noun & adjective* salvadorian(ă)

salvage 1 *noun* **(a)** salvare *f;* operaţiune *f* de salvare; **salvage money** = primă *f* de salvare (plătită de un armator echipei de salvare); **salvage vessel** = vas *n* de salvare **(b)** *(things saved)* bunuri *npl* salvate **(c)** supravieţuire *f* financiară (după o criză) **2** *verb* **(a)** *(business)* a se redresa **(b) to salvage cargo from a wreck** = a salva încărcătura de pe o epavă

sample 1 *noun* mostră *f;* exemplar *m;* **free sample** = exemplar gratuit **2** *verb* a proba

sampling *noun* sondaj *n;* colectare *f* de mostre

sanction 1 *noun* **(a)** permisiune *f;* aprobare *f;* **she needs the sanction of the council to open a nursery** = are nevoie de aprobarea primăriei pentru a deschide o creşă **(b) economic sanctions** = sancţiuni economice **2** *verb* **(a)** a aproba **(b)** a ratifica; **the expenditure budget was sanctioned by the board** = bugetul de cheltuieli a fost ratificat de consiliul de administraţie

sandwich course *noun* curs *n* în care teoria alternează cu practica (în producţie)

sandwich man *noun* om-reclamă *m*

satellite office *noun* sucursală *f* a unei firme

satisfaction *noun* mulţumire *f;* satisfacţie *f;* **customer satisfaction** = mulţumirea clientului

satisfy *verb* a mulţumi; a satisface; **the manager is very satisfied with the results of the team** = directorul este foarte mulţumit de rezultatele echipei; **to satisfy a demand** = a satisface o cerere; **to satisfy the demand for** = a satisface cererea pentru

saturation *noun* saturaţie *f;* **saturation point** = punct *n* de saturaţie

saturate *verb* a satura; **to saturate the market** = a satura piaţa; **the market for cameras is saturated** = piaţa aparatelor de fotografiat este saturată

Saudi Arabia *noun* Arabia Saudită *f* NOTE: capital: **Riyadh;** currency: **Saudi Arabian riyal** = riyal saudit

Saudi (Arabian) *noun & adjective* (arab) saudit(ă)

save *verb* a economisi (bani); **he is saving to buy a new car** = el economiseşte ca să-şi cumpere o maşină nouă; **to save energy** = a folosi raţional energia (electrică); **in order to save time they bought a faster printer** = pentru a economisi timpul, au cumpărat o imprimantă cu viteză de lucru mai mare

saving 1 *noun* **(a)** economisire *f* **(b) savings** = economii *fpl;* **savings account** = cont *n* de economii; **savings bank** = casă *f* de economii **2** *adjective* econom

scab *noun* spărgător *m* de grevă

scale 1 *noun* **(a)** scară *f or* gamă *f;* **on a large scale** = de mare anvergură; pe scară mare; **scale of prices** = gamă de preţuri **(b) scales** = cântar *n;* balanţă *f* **2** *verb* **to scale down** = a reduce preţurile

scarcity *noun* lipsă *f;* criză *f;* **scarcity of raw materials** = criză de materii prime

schedule 1 *noun* **(a)** orar *n or* program *n;* plan *n;* **to finish a project ahead of schedule** = a termina o lucrare înainte de termen; **schedule of events** = program de activităţi **(b)** listă *f* **2** *verb* **(a)** a anunţa (preţuri) oficial; **scheduled prices** = preţuri oficiale **(b)** a planifica; a prevedea; **scheduled flight** = zbor regulat (potrivit orarului stabilit)

scrap 1 *noun* **(a)** bucăţică *f or* fragment *n* **(b)** resturi *npl;* **scrap metal** = fier *n* vechi; **scrap value** = valoare *f* reziduală **2** *verb* a arunca la gunoi

sea *noun* mare *f;* **by sea** = pe cale maritimă *or* cu vaporul; **sea-captain** = căpitan *m* de vas (comercial)

seafood *noun* peşti *mpl* şi moluşte *fpl* comestibile

seaport *noun* port *n* maritim

seaworthy *adjective* în bună stare de navigabilitate

seal 1 *noun* sigiliu *n;* ştampilă *f;* **company's seal** = sigiliul companiei 2 *verb* (a) a ştampila (b) a sigila (un plic, pachet, etc.); **sealed envelope** = plic sigilat

season *noun* (a) anotimp *n* (b) sezon *n;* **busy season** = sezon de vârf; **low season** = sezon mort; **tourist season** = sezon turistic (c) **season ticket** = abonament *n* (de călătorie)

seasonal *adjective* sezonier; **seasonal unemployment** = şomaj *n* sezonier *or* temporar

secondary *adjective* secundar; **secondary industry** = industrie secundară

second-class 1 *adverb* clasa a doua; **to travel second-class** = a călători cu clasa a doua 2 *adjective* de calitate inferioară

second-hand *adjective & adverb* **second-hand goods** = mărfuri *fpl* de ocazie; **to buy something second-hand** = a cumpăra ceva de ocazie

second-rate *adjective* de calitate inferioară

seconds *plural noun* solduri *npl*

secretary *noun* secretar *m or* secretară *f;* **company secretary** = secretarul companiei

Secretary of State *noun* (a) *(GB)* ministru *m;* **Home Secretary** = Ministru de Interne (b) *(USA)* Ministru *m* de Externe

secretary-general *noun* Secretar *m* General (autoritatea supremă într-o organizaţie internaţională)

sector *noun* sector *n;* **economic sector** = sector economic; **private sector** = sector (economic) particular; **public sector** = sector public

secure 1 *adjective* sigur; **secure investment** = investiţie sigură 2 *verb* a garanta

securities *plural noun* titluri *npl;* valori *fpl;* **gilt-edged securities** = valori de prim ordin (sigure), emise de stat

security *noun* (a) *(safety)* siguranţă *f* (b) *(guarantee)* garanţie *f* (c) **social security** = asigurări *fpl* sociale (ajutor de stat pentru bătrâni, şomeri, bolnavi, etc.); **to live on social security payments** = a trăi din ajutorul social

self-contained *adjective* complet echipat (despre o casă, birou, etc.)

self-employed 1 *adjective* autonom; pe cont propriu 2 *noun* **the self-employed** = persoane *fpl* care lucrează pe cont propriu

self-financed *adjective* autofinanţat

self-financing *noun* autofinanţare *f*

self-made man *noun* persoană *f* care a izbutit în viaţă prin eforturi proprii

self-service store *noun* magazin *n* cu autoservire

self-sufficient economy *noun* economie *f* independentă

self-supporting *adjective* independent (din punct de vedere financiar)

sell 1 *noun* vânzare *f;* **hard sell** = vânzare sub presiune, forţată 2 *verb* a vinde; **they sell at £2 each** = se vinde la preţul de £2 bucata; **to sell at a loss** = a vinde în pierdere; **to sell in bulk** = a vinde cu ridicata *or* în vrac; **to sell off** = a lichida; **to sell out** = a epuiza stocul; **this item does not sell well** = acest articol nu se vinde prea bine

seller *noun* (a) vânzător *m* (b) **good seller** = articol care se vinde bine

selling *noun* vânzare *f;* **direct selling** = vânzare directă; **mail-order selling** = vânzare prin poştă *or* din catalog; **selling cost** = cheltuieli *fpl* de desfacere (vânzare); **selling price** = preţ _n_ de vânzare

semi-skilled _adjective_ semicalificat; **semi-skilled worker** = muncitor _m_ semicalificat

send _verb_ a trimite; a expedia; **he sent the parcel by airmail** = a expediat coletul par avion

sender _noun_ expeditor _m_

Senegal _noun_ Senegal _m_ NOTE: capital: **Dakar;** currency: **CFA franc** = franc CFA

Senegalese _noun_ & _adjective_ senegalez(ă)

senior _adjective_ principal; de primă importanţă; **senior partner** = asociat principal

sequester _verb_ a sechestra _or_ a confisca

sequestration _noun_ sechestrare _f or_ confiscare _f_

servant _noun_ servitor _m;_ supus _m;_ **civil servant** = funcţionar _m_ de stat

serve _verb_ a (de)servi; **to serve a customer** = a servi un client

service 1 _noun_ (a) serviciu _n or_ muncă _f;_ **length of service** = vechime _f_ în muncă (b) **after-sales service** = service post-vânzare _or_ service în garanţie; **service agreement** = contract de întreţinere; **service centre** = centru _n_ de reparaţii; **service engineer** = tehnician _m_ de întreţinere; **service industry** = industria _f_ serviciilor (c) **service station** = staţie _f_ de benzină; atelier de reparaţii auto (d) **to be in service** = a lucra ca servitor 2 _verb_ (a) a repara (b) a presta servicii (c) **to service a debt** = a plăti dobânzile la un împrumut

servicing _noun_ **servicing of debts or debt servicing** = plătirea _f_ de dobânzi pentru o datorie

set 1 _noun_ set _n;_ trusă _f;_ **set of tools** = trusă de scule 2 _adjective_ fix; stabilit; **set menu** = meniu _n_ stabilit; **set prices** = preţuri _npl_ fixe 3 _verb_ (a) a stabili _or_ a fixa (preţuri) (b) **to set against** = a deduce (costuri)

set aside _verb_ (a) a lăsa de-o parte (b) **to set aside money** = a economisi bani

settle _verb_ (a) a stabili (b) a plăti; **to settle an account** = a plăti o datorie (c) **to settle a claim** = a conveni asupra plăţii unei despăgubiri (d) **to settle out of court** = a ajunge la un acord înainte de a porni acţiunea judecătorească (într-o dispută)

settlement _noun_ _(payment)_ achitarea _f_ unei datorii; **cash settlement** = plata _f_ unei facturi în numerar

set up _verb_ a înfiinţa; a fonda

severance pay _noun_ compensaţie _f_ pentru concediere

share 1 _noun_ (a) participare _f or_ cotă _f;_ **market share** = cotă din piaţă; **share of profit** = cotă din profit (b) acţiune _f or_ titlu _n;_ **he holds £2000 worth of shares in a gas company** = deţine acţiuni în valoare de £2000 într-o companie de distribuire a gazului metan`A' share or `B' share** = acţiuni ordinare de tip A sau B; **bonus share** = acţiune gratuită; **cash share** = acţiune de vânzare contra numerar; **ordinary shares** = acţiuni ordinare; **preference share** = acţiune privilegiată cumulativă; **qualifying shares** = acţiuni ale administratorilor; **registered share** = acţiune nominală; **share allotment** = alocare _f_ de acţiuni; **share capital** = capital _n_ în acţiuni; **share certificate** = titlu; **share issue** = emiterea _f_ de acţiuni 2 _verb_ a împărţi; **to share profits** = a împărţi profiturile

shareholder _noun_ acţionar _m;_ **shareholders' meeting** = adunare _f_ a acţionarilor

shareholding _noun_ deţinere _f_ de acţiuni _or_ participare _f_

shift 1 *verb* a transfera plata unui impozit indirect (de obicei de la vânzător la cumpărător) 2 *noun* **(a)** tură *f;* **night shift** = tura de noapte; **shift work** = munca *f* în ture **(b) shift key** = tasta *f* de (litere) majuscule **(c)** *(change)* schimbare *f* (de strategie)

ship 1 *noun* vapor *n;* vas *n* comercial; **cargo ship** = vas comercial 2 *verb* a expedia mărfuri

shipment *noun* **(a)** *(the act of sending something)* expediere *f* **(b)** *(cargo)* încărcătură *f*

shipowner *noun* armator *m*

shipper *noun* expeditor *m*

shipping *noun* **(a)** marină *f;* **shipping agent** = agent *m* maritim de navlosire; **shipping line** = linie *f* maritimă *or* companie *f* maritimă **(b)** expediere *f or* expediție *f;* **shipping clerk** = funcționar *m* răspunzător de expediție **(c) shipping bill** = permis *n* de încărcare

shipyard *noun* șantier *m* naval

shop 1 *noun* **(a)** magazin *n;* **computer shop** = magazin de calculatoare **(b)** atelier *n;* **machine shop** = atelier mecanic; **repair shop** = atelier de reparații 2 *verb* a face cumpărturi; **to shop around** = a compara prețurile din magazine (pentru un articol anume)

shop assistant *noun* vânzător *m or* vânzătoare *f* (în magazin)

shopkeeper *noun* (mic) proprietar *m* de magazin

shoplifter *noun* hoț *m* din magazine

shopper *noun* cumpărător *m*

shopping *noun* cumpărături *fpl;* **shopping basket** = coș *n* de cumpărături

shopping centre *noun* centru *n* comercial

shopping mall *noun* complex *n* comercial

shopping precinct *noun* zonă *f* comercială pietonală

short *adjective* **(a)** scurt; **short delivery** = livrare *f* cu minusuri **(b) to be short of** = a lipsi; a nu avea (suficient); **to be short of money** = a nu avea bani

short-haul flight *noun* zbor *n* de scurtă durată

short-term *adjective* scurtă durată; **short-term loan** = împrumut *n* pe scurtă durată

shortage *noun* lipsă *f;* criză *f;* **shortage of energy** = criză energetică

shorten *verb* a reduce; a scurta; **to shorten credit terms** = a reduce perioada de rambursare a datoriilor

shorthand *noun* stenografie *f;* **shorthand typist** = stenodactilograf(ă)

shortlist 1 *noun* preselecție *f;* listă *f* preferențială 2 *verb (a candidate)* a alege candidați la un post pentru interviul final

short time *noun* normă *f* redusă de lucru; săptămână *f* redusă de lucru

show 1 *noun* **(a)** expoziție *f;* **computer show** = expoziție de echipament de calcul **(b)** *(entertainment)* spectacol *n* 2 *verb* a arăta *or* a indica; **to show losses** = a indica pierderi

showcase *noun* vitrină *f* cu exponate

showroom *noun* **(a)** sală *f* de expoziții **(b)** salon *n* de prezentare

shrinkage *noun* pierderi *fpl* financiare prin neglijență; minus-valoare

shut down *verb* a înceta producția; a închide (temporar) o fabrică

sick leave *noun* concediu *n* medical

sick pay *noun* indemnizație *f* de concediu medical

sickness benefit *noun* ajutor *n* financiar plătit de asistența socială în caz de boală (în Marea Britanie)

sign 1 *noun* firmă *f* de magazin 2 *verb* (a) a semna; **he forgot to sign the cheque** = a uitat să semneze cecul (b) **to sign on** = a semna un contract de muncă

signatory *noun* semnatar *m;* **signatories of an international treaty** = semnatari ai unui tratat internaţional

signature *noun* semnătură *f*

silo *noun* siloz *n*

silver *noun* (a) argint *n* (b) monedă *f* de argint (sau din aliaj de cupro-nichel, de culoarea argintului)

single *adjective* **single ticket or single fare** = bilet *n* de dus

sink *verb* (a) a (se) scufunda; **the ship was sunk in a violent storm** = vasul a fost scufundat de o furtună violentă (b) *(prices)* a scădea brusc

sinking fund *noun* fond *n* de amortizare

sister ships *plural noun* nave *fpl* comerciale construite după acelaşi model

sit-down strike *noun* grevă *f* cu ocuparea întreprinderii

skilled labour (a) mână *f* de lucru calificată (b) muncă *f* calificată

slash *verb* a reduce sever; **to slash output** = a reduce producţia drastic; **to slash prices** = a reduce preţuri substanţial

sleeping-car *noun* vagon *n* de dormit *or* cuşetă *f*

sliding scale *noun* scală *f* mobilă (de valori); **sliding scale of charges** = scală mobilă a tarifelor

slip *noun* recipisă *f;* chitanţă *f;* **he produced the sales slip and asked for a refund** = a arătat chitanţa de vânzare şi a cerut rambursarea banilor; **pay slip** = chitanţă de salariu

slip up *verb* a greşi *or* a comite o eroare

slip-up *noun* eroare *f;* scăpare *f*

Slovakia *noun* Slovacia *f* NOTE: capital: **Bratislava;** currency: **koruna** = coroană *f*

Slovakian *noun & adjective* slovac(ă)

Slovenia *noun* Slovenia *f* NOTE: capital: **Ljubljana;** currency: **tolar**

Slovenian *noun & adjective* sloven(ă)

slump *noun* (a) *(rapid fall)* scădere *f* bruscă (a preţurilor) (b) *(depression)* depresiune *f* economică; criză *f*

small business *noun* întreprindere *f* mică

smallholding *noun* mică fermă *f* agricolă (1-50 de pogoane)

smuggle *verb* a face contrabandă

smuggler *noun* contrabandist *m*

smuggling *noun* contrabandă *f*

snap check *noun* control *n* inopinat

snap up *verb* a cumpăra pe loc (la un preţ avantajos)

social *adjective* social; **social costs** = cheltuieli sociale; **social legislation** = legislaţie socială; **social report** = bilanţ social; **social security** = asigurări sociale; **social welfare** = bunăstare socială; **to live on social security payments** = a trăi din ajutorul social

society *noun* (a) societate *f;* **consumer society** = societate de consum (b) club *n or* organizaţie *f;* societate *f* mondenă

soft *adjective* moale *or* blând; **soft currency** = monedă convertibilă cu greutate; **soft loan** = împrumut *n* în condiţii avantajoase

software *noun* software *or* program *n* (de calculator); componente *npl* logice

sole *adjective* unic *or* exclusiv; **sole agency** = reprezentanţă exclusivă; **sole rights** = drepturi *npl* exclusive; **sole trader** = comerciant *m* individual

solicitor *noun* avocat *m*

solvent *adjective* solvabil

solvency *noun* solvabilitate *f*

Somali *noun & adjective* somalez(ă)

Somalia *noun* Somalia *f* NOTE: capital: **Mogadishu**; currency: **Somali shilling** = şiling somalez

source *noun* sursă *f*; **source of income** = sursă de venit; **income from all sources must be declared to the tax authorities** = veniturile din toate sursele trebuie declarate autorităţilor fiscale

South Africa *noun* Africa de Sud *f* NOTE: capital: **Pretoria**; currency: **South African rand** = rand sudafrican

South African *noun & adjective* sudafrican(ă)

space bar *noun* bara *f* de spaţiu (a claviaturii unei maşini de scris sau calculator)

Spain *noun* Spania *f* NOTE: capital: **Madrid**; currency: **Spanish peseta** = peseta spaniolă

Spanish *noun & adjective* spaniol(ă)

spare part *noun* piesă *f* de schimb

special deposits *plural noun* depuneri *fpl* speciale (de sume mari)

specialist *noun* specialist *m* or expert *m*; **specialist in tax law** = expert în legislatură fiscală

specialization *noun* (a) diviziunea *f* muncii (b) specializare *f*

specie *noun* (a) *(coins)* monezi *fpl*

specimen *noun* (a) **specimen signature** = specimen *n* de semnătură (b) *(example)* mostră *f*

speculate *verb* (a) a juca la bursă; a face speculaţii la bursă (b) *(invest riskily)* a investi riscant

speculation *noun* joc *n* la bursă; operaţiuni *fpl* de bursă

speculative *adjective* speculativ; **speculative builder** = antrepriză *f* de

construcţii care cumpără teren în scopul realizării de profituri

speculator *noun* speculant *m*

spend *verb* (a) a cheltui; **he spent most of his money buying a new house** = şi-a cheltuit aproape toţi banii pe cumpărarea unei case noi (b) a petrece (timpul); **she spent an hour photocopying the invoices** = fotocopierea facturilor i-a luat o oră

spending *noun* cheltuială *f*; **spending money** = bani *mpl* de cheltuială; **spending power** = putere *f* de cumpărare

spiral *noun* spirală *f*; **inflationary spiral** = spirala inflaţiei; **wage-price spiral** = spirala preţurilor şi salariilor

sponsor *noun* sponsor *m*; **the local football team found a sponsor for the new season** = echipa de fotbal locală a găsit un sponsor pentru noul campionat

spot cash *noun* bani *mpl* peşin *or* plata *f* pe loc

spot check *noun* control *n* inopinat

spot delivery *noun* livrare *f* imediată

spot goods *noun* bunuri *npl* gata de livrare

spread **1** *noun* diferenţa *f* dintre preţul de cost şi preţul de vânzare **2** *verb* a (se) extinde

square **1** *adjective* (a) pătrat; **square metre** = metru pătrat (m^2); **square root** = rădăcină pătrată (b) cinstit *or* echitabil; **square deal** = tranzacţie echitabilă **2** *noun* *(open space surrounded by buildings)* piaţă *f* or scuar *n* **3** *verb* **to square up** = a-şi încheia socotelile, a-şi achita datoriile

squeeze **1** *noun* restricţie *f* or limitare *f*; **credit squeeze** = limitarea creditelor oferite de bănci; **pay squeeze** = limitarea majorării salariilor (deseori impusă de guvern) **2** *verb* a strânge; **to squeeze**

profits = a strânge profituri (deseori, indiferent de mijloace)

stability *noun* stabilitate *f;* **price stability** = stabilitatea preţurilor

stabilization *noun* stabilizare *f;* **stabilization fund** = fond *n* de stabilizare

stabilizer *noun* stabilizator *m*

staff 1 *noun* personal *n;* **member of staff** = angajat *m* al unei întreprinderi; **office staff** = personal *n* administrativ 2 *verb* a angaja *or* a încadra personal

staffing *noun* încadrare *f* de personal; **staffing levels** = nivele *npl* ale încadrării de personal

stag *noun* (a) speculant *m* la bursă (b) *US* agent *m* de bursă independent 2 *verb* a cumpăra acţiuni în scopul revânzării

stagflation *noun* (*informal*) stagnare *f* economică combinată cu inflaţie şi rată ridicată a şomajului

stagger *verb* a eşalona; **staggered holidays** = concedii eşalonate

stagnant *adjective* stagnant; **stagnant economy** = economie stagnantă

stake 1 *noun* (a) capital *n;* participare *f* (b) (*amount of money gambled at races*) sumă *f* de bani pariată la curse 2 *verb* (a) (*place a bet*) a paria (b) a risca; **she staked everything on convincing him to continue his studies** = a riscat totul convingându-l să-şi urmeze studiile

stamp 1 *noun* (a) ştampilă *f or* sigiliu *n;* **rubber stamp** = ştampilă de cauciuc (b) **postage stamp** = timbru *n* poştal; **he bought three £2 stamps** = a cumpărat trei timbre de £2 (c) **stamp duty** = timbru fiscal 2 *verb* (a) a ştampila; **the immigration officer stamped his passport** = funcţionarul de la Biroul Imigrări i-a ştampilat paşaportul (b) a aplica timbre pe o trimitere poştală (c) a franca

standalone *adjective* (*computer*) de sine stătător *or* independent

standard *noun* standard *n or* normă *f;* nivel *n;* **production standards** = norme de producţie; **standard of living** = nivel de trai 2 *adjective* normal *or* standard; **standard agreement** = formular *n* de contract (tipărit); **standard charges** = tarif standard; **standard deviation** = abatere *f* admisibilă; **standard time** = ora *f* oficială

standardization *noun* standardizare *f*

standby fund *noun* fond *n* de rezervă

standing order (a) reguli *fpl* procedurale (b) (*instruction to a banker to make regular payments*) ordin *n* de plată fixă la intervale regulate

standstill *noun* (a) paralizare *f or* încetare *f;* **the lack of raw materials brought production to a standstill** = lipsa de materii prime a paralizat producţia (b) impas; **the negotiations have come to a standstill** = negocierile sunt în impas (c) **standstill agreement** = extinderea *f* termenului de plată a unei datorii externe

state 1 *noun* (a) stat *n or* ţară *f;* **state bank** = bancă *f* de stat; **state enterprise** = întreprindere *f* de stat; **state planning** = planificare *f* de stat (b) **state of affairs** = situaţie *f;* poziţie *f* actuală 2 *verb* a declara *or* a afirma

state-controlled *adjective* naţionalizat *or* controlat de stat

state-managed *adjective* în regie

statement *noun* (a) (*of account*) extras *n* de cont; **bank statement** = extras de cont bancar (b) declaraţie *f;* **the businessman's lawyer issued a statement regarding the incident** = avocatul omului de afaceri a emis o declaraţie privitoare la incident

state-of-the-art *adjective* cel mai modern, cel mai pus la punct din punct de vedere tehnologic

stationery *noun* articole *n* de papetărie

statistical *adjective* statistic; **statistical analysis** = analiză statistică

statistics *plural noun* statistică *f*

statistician *noun* statistician *m*

status *noun* situaţie *f*; **financial status** = situaţie financiară

stenographer *noun* stenograf(ă)

sterling *noun* & *adjective* **(a) pound sterling** = liră *f* sterlină; **sterling area** = zonă *f* de influenţă a lirei sterline **(b) sterling silver** = argint *n* cu puritate de 92,5%

steward *noun* steward *m*

stewardess *noun* stewardesă *f*

sticker *noun* etichetă *f*

stiff *adjective* **(a)** acerb *or* dur; **stiff competition** = competiţie acerbă **(b) stiff price** = preţ pipărat

stimulate *verb* a stimula *or* a încuraja; **to stimulate trade with the eastern European countries** = a stimula comerţul cu ţările Europei de Est

stock 1 *noun* **(a)** rezerve *fpl* de materii prime; stoc *n*; **out of stock** = epuizat; **stock book** = registru *n* de magazie; **stock control** = inventar *n*; **stock control card** = fişă *f* de magazie; **to take stock** = a face inventarul; **we have a large selection of footwear in stock** = avem o gamă largă de încălţăminte în stoc **(b) stock** *or* **livestock** = şeptel *n*; **stock breeder** = crescător *m* de animale **(c)** acţiuni *fpl or* titluri *npl*; **common stock** = acţiuni ordinare; **preferred stock** = acţiuni preferenţiale; **stock certificate to bearer** = certificat *n* de acţiuni la purtător **(d) rolling stock** = material *n* rulant 2 *verb* a stoca

stock account *noun* cont *n* de capital

stockbroker *noun* agent *m* de schimb; agent de bursă

stock company *noun* societate *f* pe acţiuni

stock exchange *noun* bursa *f* de valori

stockholder *noun* deţinător *m* de acţiuni

stockist *noun* distribuitor *m*; angrosist *m*

stocklist *noun* listă *f* de inventar

stockpiling *noun* stocare *f*; acumulare *f* de stoc de rezervă

stockroom *noun* magazie *f*; depozit *n*

stocktaking *noun* inventariere *f*

stock up *verb* a acumula (stoc)

stop 1 *noun* **(a)** oprire *f or* încetare *f*; **to come to a stop** = a (se) opri *or* a înceta **(b) bus stop** = staţie *f* de autobuz **(c)** suspendarea *f* livrării; **account on stop** = cont *n* blocat 2 *verb* **(a)** a opri **(b) to stop a cheque** = a bloca o filă de cec (în caz de pierdere sau furt)

stop over *verb* a face o scurtă escală

stopover *noun* scurtă escală *f*

stoppage *noun* **(a)** suspendare *f*; întrerupere *f*; **stoppage of work** = întreruperea lucrului; grevă *f* **(b)** reţineri *fpl* pe salariu

storage *noun* **(a)** *(keeping in warehouse)* depozitare *f* **(b)** *(cost of storage)* taxă *f* de magazinaj **(c)** stocare *f* de informaţii pe calculator *or* memorizare *f*; **this hard disk has a storage capacity of 170 Mb** = acest disc (intern) are o capacitate de memorizare de 170 Mb

store 1 *noun* **(a)** *(place where goods are kept)* magazie *f or* antrepozit *n* **(b)** *(provisions)* rezerve *fpl or* provizii *fpl* **(c)** US magazin *n*; **department store** = magazin universal 2 *verb* **(a)** *(keep goods in a warehouse)* a depozita **(b)** *(make provisions)* a strânge provizii

storekeeper *noun* **(a)** *(owner of a shop)* proprietar *m* de (mic) magazin; comerciant *m* **(b)** *(person in charge of a warehouse)* magazioner *m*

straight-line depreciation *noun* amortizare *f* uniformă

strike 1 *noun* grevă *f;* **general strike** *or* **all-out strike** = grevă generală; **to go on strike** = a face grevă; **nationwide strike** = grevă la scară naţională; **sit-down strike** = grevă cu ocuparea întreprinderii; **strike call** = convocare *f* la grevă; **strike pay** = ajutor *n* de grevă; **token strike** = grevă simbolică; grevă de avertisment 2 *verb* (a) a face grevă (b) **to strike an agreement** = a încheia un acord

strikebound *adjective* paralizat de grevă (despre un sector economic, serviciu, etc.)

strikebreaker *noun* spărgător *m* de grevă

striker *noun* grevist *m*

strongbox *noun* safe *n or* seif *n;* casă *f* de bani

strongroom *noun* safe *n or* seif *n;* tezaur *n* (într-o bancă)

stub *noun* cotor *n;* **cheque stub** = cotorul carnetului de cecuri

sub-editor *noun* redactor *m*

sublease or sublet 1 *noun* subarendare *f or* subînchiriere *f* 2 *verb* a subînchiria *or* a subarenda; **he subleased a room in a big flat** = a subînchiriat o cameră într-un apartament spaţios

submit *verb* a prezenta *or* a înainta (spre aprobare); **to submit a project for approval** = a înainta un proiect spre aprobare

subordinate *noun & adjective* subaltern (m); subordonat (m)

subpoena 1 *noun* citaţie *f* 2 *verb* a cita

subscribe *verb* a (se) abona (la o publicaţie); **she subscribed to her favourite magazine** = s-a abonat la revista ei preferată

subscriber *noun* abonat *m*

subsidiary *adjective* subsidiar *or* secundar; **subsidiary company** = sucursală *f;* companie *f* subsidiară

subsidize *verb* a subvenţiona; **the government subsidizes heavy industry** = guvernul subvenţionează industria grea

subsidy *noun* (a) subvenţie *f;* subvenţionare *f;* **public subsidy** = subvenţionare de către guvern (b) primă *f;* **export subsidy** = primă de export

subsistence *noun* subzistenţă *f*

subtenancy *noun* contract *n* de subînchiriere

subvention *noun* subvenţie *f*

subway *noun* US metrou *n* (în SUA)

Sudan *noun* Sudan *m* NOTE: capital: **Khartoum;** currency: **Sudanese pound** = liră sudaneză

Sudanese *noun & adjective* sudanez(ă)

sue *verb* a da în judecată; **the company was sued for breach of contract** = compania a fost dată în judecată pentru încălcarea contractului

suit *noun* proces *n;* acţiune *f* civilă

suite *noun* apartament *n* (la hotel); **he booked a hotel suite for himself and his family** = a rezervat un apartament la hotel pentru el şi familia sa

sum *noun* (a) sumă *f;* **sum insured** = sumă asigurată *or* valoarea maximă pentru care compania de asigurări va plăti despăgubiri (b) total *n*

summary *noun* sumar *n;* variantă *f* prescurtată a unui document

summons *noun* citaţie *f* (la tribunal); **she rang her lawyer after receiving the summons** = i-a telefonat avocatului ei după ce a primit citaţia; **originating summons** = citaţie preliminară

sundries or sundry items *plural noun* articole *npl* diverse

superannuation *noun (payment made to a retired person)* pensie *f;* **superannuation fund** = fond *n* de pensii

superstore *noun* supermagazin *n*

supplier *noun* furnizor *m;* **the supplier delivered the order in time** = furnizorul a livrat comanda la timp

supply 1 *noun* aprovizionare *f;* ofertă *f;* **composite supply** = ofertă combinată; **law of supply and demand** = legea *f* cererii şi ofertei; **supply price** = preţ *n* de ofertă **2** *verb* a aproviziona

surety *noun* girant *m*

surplus *noun* **(a)** excedent *n or* surplus *n;* **economic surplus** = surplus economic; **surplus value** = plusvaloare *f;* **wheat surplus** = surplus de cereale **(b)** profit *n;* **acquired surplus** = profituri dobândite prin creşterea dobânzilor

Swede *noun* suedez(ă)

Sweden *noun* Suedia *f* NOTE: capital: **Stockholm;** currency: **Swedish krona** = coroană suedeză

Swedish *adjective* suedez(ă)

swing *noun* oscilaţie *f or* fluctuaţie *f;* **periodic swings** = fluctuaţii periodice

Swiss *noun & adjective* elveţian(ă)

Switzerland *noun* Elveţia *f* NOTE: capital: **Bern** = Berna; currency: **Swiss franc** = franc elveţian

switchboard *noun* centrală *f* telefonică

Syria *noun* Siria *f* NOTE: capital: **Damascus** = Damasc; currency: **Syrian pound** = liră siriană

Syrian *noun & adjective* sirian(ă)

system *noun* sistem *n;* **systems analyst** = inginer *m* de sistem (de calcul)

Tt

table 1 *noun* **(a)** masă *f;* **to lay on the table** = a supune discuţiei **(b) table of contents** = tabla *f* de materii **(c)** tabel *n* 2 *verb* a supune atenţiei (într-o şedinţă); **to table a proposal** = a înainta o propunere

tacit *adjective* tacit; **tacit approval** = aprobare tacită

take-home pay *noun* salariu *n* net

take over *verb* **(a)** a prelua; **to take over a company** = a prelua conducerea unei companii; a achiziţiona o companie **(b)** a înlocui; **Mr Popescu took over from Mrs Marin** = Domnul Popescu a înlocuit-o pe Doamna Marin

takeover *noun* preluare *f;* **takeover bid** = ofertă *f* de preluare

taker *noun* cumpărător *m;* persoană *f* care acceptă o ofertă

takings *plural noun* încasări *fpl;* **the shop assistant was caught stealing the takings** = vânzătorul a fost prins furând încasările

tally 1 *noun* pontaj *n;* marcaj *n;* **tally clerk** = pontator *m;* **tally sheet** = borderou *n;* foaie *f* de pontaj 2 *verb* a corespunde *or* a concorda; **the figures do not tally** = cifrele nu corespund

tanker *noun* **(a)** *(ship)* petrolier *n* **(b)** *(railway)* vagon *n* cisternă

Tanzania *noun* Tanzania *f* NOTE: capital: **Dodoma**; currency: **Tanzanian shilling** = şiling tanzanian

Tanzanian *noun & adjective* tanzanian(ă)

target 1 *noun* ţintă *f;* obiectiv *n;* **to set targets** = a fixa obiective; **target figure** = cifră *f* de plan *or* normă *f* 2 *verb* a ţinti *or* a viza; **to target a market** = a viza o anume piaţă de desfacere

tariff *noun* **(a)** taxă *f;* **customs tariff** = taxă vamală; **General Agreement on Tariffs and Trade (GATT)** = Acordul *n* General de Tarife şi Comerţ; **protective tariff** = tarif *n* de protecţie; **retaliatory tariff** = tarif punitiv **(b)** tarif *n* *or* preţ *n* **off-peak tariff** = tarif redus pentru energia electrică

tariff barriers *noun* **(a)** bariere *fpl* vamale **(b)** politică *f* tarifară

task *noun* sarcină *f* de muncă *or* îndatorire *f;* **task force** = grup *n* operativ; **task work** = muncă *f* în acord; **task worker** = lucrător *m* în acord

tax 1 *noun* **(a)** taxă *f;* impozit *n;* **capital gains tax** = impozit progresiv pe avere; **capital transfer tax** = impozit pe transferul de capital; **corporation tax** = impozit pe profiturile societăţilor cu răspundere limitată (în Marea Britanie); **council tax** = impozit perceput de primării (în Marea Britanie); **direct tax** = impozit direct; **federal tax** = impozit federal (general) (în SUA şi în Canada); **income tax** = impozit pe venit (salariu); **indirect tax** = impozit indirect; **progressive tax** = impozit progresiv; **regressive tax** = impozit regresiv; **sales tax** = impozit pe vânzări **(b)** *US* **tax assessor** = inspector *m* fiscal (în SUA); **tax avoidance** = evaziune *f* fiscală; **tax base** = baza *f* de impunere; **tax code** = cod *n* al impozitului pe venit (în Marea Britanie); **tax-exempt** = scutit de impozite; **tax exemption** = scutire *f* de impozite; **tax relief** = degrevare *f* de impozite; **tax year** = an *m* fiscal **2** *verb* a percepe impozite; a impune taxe

taxable *adjective* impozabil; **taxable income** = venit impozabil

taxation *noun* percepere *f* de impozite *or* impunere *f* a unei taxe; **double taxation** = dublă impunere

taxi *noun* taxi *n;* **taxi fare** = costul călătorie cu taxiul

taxpayer *noun* contribuabil *m*

technocracy *noun* tehnocraţie *f*

technology *noun* tehnologie *f;* ştiinţe *fpl* tehnice aplicate

telecommunications *plural noun* telecomunicaţii *fpl*

telegram *noun* telegramă *f;* **to send a telegram** = a trimite o telegramă; **radio telegram** = telegramă transmisă prin radio *or* radiogramă *f*

telegraph 1 *noun* telegraf *n* **2** *verb* a trimite o telegramă *or* a telegrafia

telegraphic *adjective* **(a)** telegrafic; **telegraphic transfer** = mandat telegrafic **(b)** **telegraphic address** = adresă prescurtată

telephone 1 *noun* telefon *n;* **to book a table by telephone** = a rezerva o masă la restaurant prin telefon; **to order by telephone** = a comanda prin telefon; **portable telephone** = telefon portabil *or* mobil; **telephone call** = convorbire *f* telefonică; **telephone directory** = carte *f* de telefon; **telephone exchange** = centrală *f* telefonică; **telephone number** = număr *n* de telefon; **telephone order** = comandă *f* telefonică **2** *verb* a telefona

telephonist *noun* telefonistă *f*

teleprinter *noun* teleimprimatoare *f*

telesales *plural noun* vânzări *fpl* prin telefon

telex *noun* **(a)** telex *n* **(b)** *(message transmitted through telex)* mesaj *n* prin telex

teller *noun* casier *m*

tenancy *noun* **(a)** *(agreement)* contract *n* de închiriere **(b)** *(period)* perioadă *f* de închiriere

tenant *noun* **(a)** chiriaş *m;* **tenant at will** = chiriaş liber să rezilieze contractul de închiriere la cerere **(b)** **tenant farmer** = arendaş *m*

tender *noun* **(a)** ofertă *f* în numerar (de achitarea unui împrumut) **(b)** ofertă *f* de servicii din partea unui furnizor, etc.; **to submit a tender** = a prezenta o ofertă **(c)** *(boat)* şalupă *f* **2** *verb* **(a)** a face o ofertă (avantajoasă) **(b)** **to tender one's resignation** = a demisiona; **he tendered his resignation** = şi-a dat demisia

tenderer *noun* ofertant *m* (persoană *or* organizaţie)

term *noun* **(a)** perioadă *f;* termen *m;* **the minimum term of the lease is 12 months** = perioada minimă de închiriere este de 12 luni; **long-term** = (pe) termen lung; **short-term** = (pe) termen scurt; **term deposit** = depunere *f* pe termen **(b)** **terms** = termeni *mpl or* condiţii *fpl;* **payment terms** *or* **terms of payment** = condiţii de plată; **terms of sale** = condiţii de vânzare; **terms of trade** = condiţii de schimb

terminal 1 *noun* **(a)** terminus *n or* capăt *n* de linie **(b)** **computer terminal** = terminal de calculator **(c)** **air terminal** = terminal aerian (aerogară); **ocean terminal** = terminal maritim **2** *adjective* final *or* de încheiere

terminus *noun* terminus *n*

territorial waters *plural noun* ape *fpl* teritoriale

tertiary industry *noun* industrie *f* a serviciilor

test *noun* examen *n*

testimonial *noun* *(certificate of conduct or qualifications)* caracterizare *f;* recomandare *f or* atestat *n*

Thai *noun & adjective* thailandez(ă)

Thailand *noun* Thailanda *f* NOTE: capital: **Bangkok;** currency: **Thai baht** = baht thailandez

third party *noun* terţa parte *f*

Third World *noun* Lumea *f* a Treia

three-part *adjective* *(document)* în trei exemplare

throughput *noun* **(a)** *(industry)* capacitate *f* de producţie **(b)** *(computing)* cantitatea *f* de informaţie pe care un calculator o poate prelucra în unitate de timp

ticket *noun* tichet *n;* bilet *n*

time *noun* timp *m;* **time lag** = decalaj *n;* **time rate** = tarif *n* pe oră; **time scale** = programă *f;* **time sheet** = foaie *f* de pontaj

time-keeping *noun* punctualitate *f*

timetable *noun* **(a)** program *n* **(b)** orar *n;* **according to the timetable our train leaves from platform 2** = potrivit orarului trenul nostru va pleca de la linia 2

tip 1 *noun* bacşiş *n;* **he gave the taxi driver a generous tip** = i-a dat şoferului de taxi un bacşiş generos 2 *verb* a da bacşiş

Togo *noun* Togo *m* NOTE: capital: **Lomé;** currency: **CFA franc** = franc CFA

Togolese *noun & adjective* togolez(ă)

token *noun* simbol *n;* **token strike** = grevă *f* simbolică *or* grevă de avertisment

toll *noun* taxă *f* percepută pentru folosirea autostrăzilor şi tunelelor de către automobilişti

toll call *noun* convorbire *f* telefonică interurbană (în SUA)

toll free *adverb* gratuit; **to call toll free** = a telefona gratuit (servicii speciale cu prefix 800 în SUA)

ton *noun* **long ton or British ton** = tona *f* britanică (= 1016.05 kg); **short ton** = tonă nordamericană (= 907 kg)

tonne *noun* tonă *f* (1000 kg)

tonnage *noun* tonaj *n;* **gross tonnage** = tonaj brut

total 1 *adjective* total; întreg; **total amount** = cantitatea totală *or* suma totală; **total cost** = cost total; **total loss** = pierderi totale (când bunurile asigurate sunt distruse complet) 2 *verb* a totaliza 3 *noun* total *n;* sumă *f;* **grand total** = total general

tourism *noun* turism *n*

tourist *noun* turist *m;* **tourist bureau** = birou *n* de informaţii turistice; **tourist class** = clasă turistică *or* clasa a doua (în călătoriile cu avionul sau vaporul)

tour operator *noun* agenţie *f* de turism

tow *verb* a remorca (un vas, etc.)

towage *noun* remorcare *f*

trade 1 *noun* **(a)** comerţ *n;* **domestic trade or home trade** = comerţ interior; **favourable balance of trade** = balanţă *f* de comerţ pozitivă; **foreign trade** = comerţ exterior; **multilateral trade** = comerţ multilateral; **trade agreement** = acord *n* comercial; **trade discount** = rabat *n* comercial; **trade gap** = deficit *n* comercial; **trade mark** = marcă *f* înregistrată; **trade price** = preţ *n* de mic gros **(b)** **trade association** = sindicat *n* patronal 2 *verb* a face comerţ; a face afaceri

trader *noun* comerciant *m;* om *m* de afaceri; **sole trader** = comerciant individual

trade union *noun* sindicat *n* profesional

trading *noun* comerţ *n;* **trading account** = cont *n* de exploatare *or* de exerciţiu; **trading company** = societate *f* comercială; **trading partner** = partener *m* comercial

traffic 1 *noun* trafic *n or* circulaţie *f;* transport *n;* **we arrived late because of the heavy lorry traffic on the motorway** = am ajuns târziu din cauza traficului intens de camioane de tonaj pe autostradă; **traffic warden** = agent *n* de circulaţie 2 *verb* a trafica

trailer *noun* (a) remorcă *f* (b) *US* rulotă *f* (c) *(film)* scurt metraj *n* publicitar al filmului de vizionat

train 1 *noun* tren *n;* **freight train or goods train** = tren de marfă *or* mărfar; **passenger train** = tren de pasageri 2 *verb* a educa *or* a instrui

trainee *noun* ucenic *m;* practicant *m;* **graduate trainee** = stagiar *m*

training *noun* ucenicie *f or* pregătire *f* profesională

transaction *noun* tranzacţie *f;* operaţiune *f* comercială

transfer 1 *noun* (a) transfer *n;* **bank transfer** = transfer bancar; **electronic transfer** = transfer electronic (de fonduri); **transfer payments** = plăţi *fpl* prin transfer (b) transbordare *f;* **transfer service** = serviciu *n* de transbordare (c) **mail transfer** = mandat *n* poştal 2 *verb* (a) a transfera; a muta; **he asked to be transferred to a different department** = a rugat să fie transferat în altă secţie (b) *(change from one type of travel to another)* a transborda

transferable *adjective* transferabil

transit *noun* tranzit *n;* **goods damaged in transit** = bunuri *npl* deteriorate în tranzit; **transit visa** = viză *f* de tranzit

translate *verb* a traduce

translator *noun* traducător *m*

transport 1 *noun* transport *n;* **air transport** = transport aerian; **means of transport** = mijloc *n* de transport; **private transport** = transport particular; **transport costs** = cheltuieli *fpl* de transport 2 *verb* a transporta

travel 1 *noun* călătorie *f;* **travel agency** = agenţie *f* de voiaj 2 *verb* a călători

traveller *noun* (a) călător *m;* **traveller's cheque** = cec *n* de călătorie la purtător (b) **commercial traveller** = comis *m* voiajor

Treasury *noun* Minister *n* de Finanţe; **treasury bonds** = bonuri *npl* de tezaur

treaty *noun* (a) acord *n;* **private treaty** = acord particular (b) tratat *n or* acord *n* (internaţional); **commercial treaty** = acord comercial internaţional

trial period *noun* perioadă *f* de probă

truck *noun* camion n

trust 1 *noun* (a) încredere *f* (b) *(commercial)* trust *n;* **trust company** = companie *f* fiduciară 2 *verb* a avea încredere

trustee *noun* curator *m;* adminstrator *m* fiduciar

Tunisia *noun* Tunisia *f* NOTE: capital: **Tunis;** currency: **Tunisian dinar** = dinar tunisian

Tunisian *noun & adjective* tunisian(ă)

Turk *noun* turc(ă)

Turkey *noun* Turcia *f* NOTE: capital: **Ankara;** currency: **Turkish lira** = liră turcească

Turkish *adjective* turc(ă); turcesc, turcească

turnover *noun* **(a)** cifră *f* de afaceri; **turnover tax** = impozit pe cifra de afaceri **(b)** rotaţie *f;* **turnover of staff** = rotaţia cadrelor

two-part *adjective* (în) duplicat; în două exemplare

tycoon *noun* magnat *m*

type *verb* a dactilografia

typing *noun* dactilografiere *f;* **typing error** = greşeală *f* de dactilografiere

typist *noun* dactilograf(ă)

Uu

Uganda *noun* Uganda *f* NOTE: capital: **Kampala**; currency: **Ugandan shilling** = şiling ugandez

Ugandan *noun & adjective* ugandez(ă)

Ukraine *noun* Ucrainia *f* NOTE: capital: **Kiev**; currency: **karbovanets**

Ukrainian *noun & adjective* ucrainian(ă)

ullage *noun* (a) ulaj *n* (b) volumul *n* de lichid al unei cisterne sau butoi (rămas după scurgeri şi evaporări) pe care se percepe taxa vamală

ultimate consumer *noun* consumator *m* final

umbrella *noun* (a) umbrelă *f* (b) protecţie *f or* patronaj *n;* **umbrella organization** = organizaţie *f* importantă sub patronajul căreia se alflă altele mai mici

umpire *noun* arbitru *m*

unable *adjective* incapabil; **he is unable to deal with his finances on his own** = este incapabil să-şi administreze finanţele singur

unauthorized *adjective* neautorizat; **unauthorized expenditure** = cheltuieli neautorizate

unavailable *adjective* care lipseşte de pe piaţă, care nu poate fi găsit

unavoidable costs *plural noun* cheltuieli *fpl* inevitabile *or* cheltuieli fixe

unbalanced *adjective* dezechilibrat

unconvertible *adjective* neconvertibil (despre monedă)

unclaimed *adjective* nereclamat *or* nerevendicat; **unclaimed prize** = premiu nerevendicat

undated *adjective* nedatat *or* fără dată; **the bank returned his undated and unsigned cheque** = banca i-a returnat cecul nedatat şi nesemnat

underdeveloped *adjective* subdezvoltat; **underdeveloped countries** = ţări *fpl* subdezvoltate

underemployment *noun* (a) forţă *f* de lucru nefolisită deplin (din cauza lipsei acute de lucru) (b) şomaj *n* parţial

underground *noun* metrou *n* (în Marea Britanie)

underproduction *noun* subproducţie *f*

undersell *verb* (a) a vinde mai ieftin decât competiţia (b) a vinde sub valoarea reală

underspend *verb* a cheltui mai puţin decât prevede bugetul

undertake *verb* (a) a întreprinde; a încerca (b) *(promise)* a promite

undertaker *noun* (a) antreprenor *m* (b) antreprenor *m* de pompe funebre

undertaking *noun* (a) promisiune *f* solemnă (b) declaraţie *f* (în scris); depoziţie *f* (c) *(business)* întreprindere *f*

undervalued currency *noun* monedă *f* depreciată

underwrite *verb* **(a)** a-şi scoate o poliţă de asigurare **(b)** a gira (emiterea de acţiuni) **(c)** a garanta (o plată)

underwriter *noun* **(a)** expert *m* în asigurări care evaluază riscuri şi stabileşte primele de sigurări **(b)** girant *m;* garant *m*

unearned income *noun* venit *n* provenit din dobânzi

uneconomic *adjective* neeconomic

unemployed *adjective* fără lucru *or* şomer; nefolosit; **the unemployed** = şomerii *mpl*

unemployment *noun* şomaj *n;* **disguised unemployment** = şomaj ascuns (situaţia în care se află o parte a populaţiei care, deşi fără lucru, nu poate pretinde ajutor de şomaj, deci nu figurează în cifrele oficiale); **seasonal unemployment** = şomaj sezonier; **unemployment benefit** = ajutor *n* de şomaj

unfair *adjective* nedrept; neloial; **unfair competition** = concurenţă *f* neloială; **unfair dismissal** = concediere *f* pe nedrept

unfulfilled order *noun* comandă *f* neonorată

unilateral *adjective* unilateral; **unilateral contract** = contract *n* unilateral

uninsured *adjective* neasigurat

union *noun* **(a)** unire *f;* fuzionare *f* **(b)** sindicat *n;* *US* **labor union** = sindicat profesional (în SUA); **trade union** = sindicat profesional (în Marea Britanie)

unionism *noun* sindicalism *n*

unionist *noun* sindicalist *m*

unit *noun* **(a)** unitate *f;* **unit cost** = cost *n* per bucată *or* cost unitar; **unit price** = preţ *n* unitar **(b)** element *n* **(c)** unitate *f;* secţie *f;* **business unit** = unitate

comercială; **factory unit** = fabrică *f;* **production unit** = secţie *f* de producţie **(d) monetary unit** = unitate monetară

unit trust *noun* societate *f* de investiţii

United Kingdom (UK) *noun* Regatul Unit (RU) NOTE: capital: **London** = Londra; currency: **pound sterling (£)** = liră sterlină (£)

United Nations (UN) Organizaţia Naţiunilor Unite (ONU)

United States of America (USA) *noun* Statele Unite ale Americii (SUA) NOTE: capital: **Washington;** currency: **American dollar ($)** = dolar american ($)

unitized handling *noun* transport *n* de mărfuri în containere

unlawful *adjective* ilegal; ilicit

unlisted securities *noun* valori *fpl* necotate; **unlisted securities market** = piaţă *f* de valori necotate

unofficial *adjective* neoficial; **unofficial rate of exchange** = rata *f* de schimb (valutar) neoficială

unpaid *adjective* **(a)** neplătit; **unpaid bills** = note *fpl* de plată *or* facturi *fpl* neplătite **(b)** fără plată; **unpaid holiday** = concediu fără plată; şomaj temporar

unprofitable *adjective* neprofitabil; nerentabil

unsecured *adjective* fără garanţie; negarantat; **unsecured loan** = împrumut *n* fără garanţie

unseaworthy *adjective* care nu e dotat corespunzător pentru navigaţie (despre un vas)

unskilled work force *noun* mână *f* de lucru necalificată

unsold items *noun* articole *npl* care nu se vând, fiind de obicei returnate furnizorului

update **1** *noun* actualizare *f;* modernizare *f* **2** *verb* a actualiza; a moderniza; **we update our data base**

every other month = actualizăm banca de date la două luni

up front *adverb* în avans; **money up front** *or* **up front payment** = plată *f* în avans; aconto *n*

upgrade 1 *noun* îmbunătăţire *f;* **on the upgrade** = care progresează; în curs de perfecţionare 2 *verb* **(a)** a aduce îmbunătăţiri *or* a perfecţiona (un sistem de calcul, etc.); **he upgraded his computer by adding more RAM chips =** a îmbunătăţit performanţa calculatorului său adăugând module de RAM (Random Access Memory) **(b)** a promova (în funcţie)

up to date *adjective* actual *or* la zi

Uruguay *noun* Uruguay *m* NOTE: capital: **Montevideo;** currency: **Uruguayan peso** = peso uruguayan

Uruguayan *noun & adjective* uruguayan(ă)

usage *noun* utilizare *f;* folosire *f*

use 1 *noun* folos *n or* folosinţă *f* 2 *verb* a (se) folosi; a utiliza; **we use a laser printer for printing brochures** = pentru tipărirea broşurilor utilizăm o imprimantă laser

useful *adjective* util *or* folositor

useless *adjective* inutil

user *noun* **(a)** utilizator *m;* **user's manual** = carte *f* tehnică (de exploatare) **(b)** uzufructuar *m;* **user costs** = cheltuieli *fpl* uzufructuare

user-friendly *adjective* uşor de folosit

usufruct *noun* uzufruct

usury *noun* **(a)** camătă *f;* dobândă *f* **(b)** cămătărie *f*

usurer *noun* cămătar *m*

utilize *verb* a utiliza

utilization *noun* utilizare *f*

Vv

vacancy *noun* **(a)** post *n* vacant; **she found out about the vacancy in the local newspaper** = a aflat de postul vacant în ziarul local **(b) vacancies** = camere *fpl* neocupate (într-un hotel) **(c) vacancy rate** = procentaj *n* de proprietăți neînchiriate

vacant *adjective* vacant; neocupat

vacation *noun* **(a)** perioadă *f* când tribunalele sunt închise (în Marea Britanie) **(b)** *US* vacanță *f*; concediu *n*

valid *adjective* **(a)** valid *or* valabil; **valid ticket** = bilet *n* valabil **(b)** legal *or* valabil; **valid passport** = pașaport *n* valabil

validate *verb* a valida; a confirma

valorization *noun* valorizare *f*; sprijinire *f* artificială a prețurilor și a monedei

valuable *adjective* valoros; prețios; **valuable information** = informații prețioase

valuables *plural noun* valori *fpl*; lucruri *npl* de valoare; **most of his valuables were destroyed in the fire** = aproape toate lucrurile sale de valoare au fost distruse de incendiu

valuation *noun* evaluare *f*; **she asked for a valuation of her jewellery collection** = a cerut evaluarea colecției sale de bijuterii

value 1 *noun* valoare *f*; preț *n*; **discounted value** = valoare de scont; **face value** = valoare nominală; **intrinsic value** = valoare nominală; **market value** = valoare comercială; **scrap value** = valoare reziduală; **(cash) surrender value** = valoare de răscumpărare a unei polițe de asigurări; **value added tax (VAT)** = taxa *f* asupra valorii adăugate (TVA) **2** *verb* a evalua; **the property was valued at £150,000** = proprietatea a fost evaluată la £150.000

valuer *noun* evaluator *m*

variable *adjective* variabil; **variable budget** = buget *n* variabil; **variable costs** = costuri *npl* variabile; **variable factor** = factor *n* variabil

variety *noun* varietate *f* *or* diversitate *f*; **variety of items and prices** = diversitate de articole și prețuri; **variety store** = magazin *n* popular care practică prețuri reduse (în SUA)

VAT = VALUE ADDED TAX

vault *noun* **(a)** *(safe)* casă *f* de bani **(b)** *(place of storage in a bank)* tezaur *n*

velocity of circulation *noun* viteză *f* de circulație

vendee *noun* cumpărător *m* (al unei proprietăți)

vendor *noun* **(a)** vânzător *m* (al unei proprietăți) **(b) street vendor** = vânzător ambulant

Venezuela *noun* Venezuela *f* NOTE: capital: **Caracas;** currency: **Venezuelan bolivar** = bolivar venezuelan

Venezuelan *noun & adjective*
venezuelan(ă)

venture 1 *noun* afacere *f;* tranzacţie *f*
comercială; întreprindere *f* (care
implică o doză de risc); **joint venture =**
întreprindere în participaţie; **venture
capital =** capital *n* de speculaţie 2 *verb*
a risca în afaceri; a specula

verbal *adjective* verbal *or* oral; **verbal
agreement =** înţelegere *f* verbală; **verbal
order =** comandă *f* verbală

verify *verb* a verifica

verification of assets *noun*
efectuarea *f* reviziei mijloacelor fixe (de
către un revizor)

vertical *adjective* vertical; **vertical
integration of industry =** integrarea
verticală a industriei

vested interests *plural noun* interese
npl personale

veto *noun* veto *n;* respingere *f;* **right of
veto =** drept *n* de veto

viability *noun* viabilitate *f*

viable *adjective* viabil

videotape *noun* video-casetă *f or*
casetă *f* video

Vietnam *noun* Vietnam *m* NOTE:
capital: **Hanoi;** currency: **Vietnamese
dong =** dong vietnamez

Vietnamese *noun & adjective*
vietnamez(ă)

visa *noun* viză *f;* **entry visa =** viză de
intrare; **tourist visa =** viză turistică; **visa
application form =** formular *n* de viză

void 1 *adjective* nul *or* fără valoare 2
verb a anula (un contract, decret, etc.)

voluntary redundancy *noun* şomaj
n voluntar *or* renunţarea *f* de bună voie
la slujbă pentru o sumă de bani

vote 1 *noun* vot *n;* **vote of confidence =**
vot de încredere 2 *verb* a vota

voter *noun* votant *m;* alegător *m*

vouch for *verb* a garanta

voucher *noun* bon *n;* chitanţă *f;* **cash
voucher =** bon de casă; **refund voucher**
= bon de rambursare

Ww

wage *noun* salariu *n;* **average wage** = salariu mediu; **basic wage** = salariu de bază; **to earn a good wage** = a câştiga bine; **gross wage** = salariu brut; **guaranteed wage** = salariu (minim) garantat; **incentive wage** = sistem *n* de salarizare care stimulează productivitatea; salarizare *f* în acord; **minimum wage** = salariu minim; **net wage** = salariu net; **wage brackets** = scala *f* salariilor; **wage ceiling** = plafon *n* de salarii; **wage freeze** = îngheţarea *f* salariilor; **wage levels** = nivele *npl* de salarizare; **wage negotiations** = negocierea *f* salariilor

wage-earner *noun* salariat *m* *or* angajat *m*

wagon *noun* vagon *n*

wagonage *noun* **(a)** vagonaj *n* **(b)** transport *n* (pe cale ferată)

waive *verb* a renunţa la o despăgubire

waiver *noun* clauză *f* de renunţare

Wall Street *noun* centrul *n* financiar american; numele popular al bursei new-yorkeze (stradă în New York unde se situează Bursa)

want *noun* **(a)** carenţă *f;* necesitate *f* **(b)** **want ads** = mica publicitate *or* rubrica `cumpărări'

war *noun* război *n;* **price war** = războiul preţurilor

warehouse 1 *noun* **(a)** depozit *n;* **bonded warehouse** = depozit vamal;

warehouse manager = şef *m* de depozit **(b)** antrepozit *n* 2 *verb* a depozita

warehouseman *noun* magazioner *m*

warehousing *noun* depozitare *f*

warrant 1 *noun* **(a)** autorizaţie *f;* document *n* oficial; procură *f* **(b)** mandat *n* **(c)** **share warrant** = certificat *n* de acţionar (la purtător) 2 *verb* **(a)** a garanta **(b)** a justifica

warrantee *noun* persoană *f* care primeşte o garanţie

warranty *noun* (certificat de) garanţie *f;* **12 months warranty** = garanţie de 12 luni; **express warranty** = condiţii *fpl* de garanţie; **implied warranty** = garanţie implicită

wastage *noun* pierderi *fpl;* **natural wastage** = pierderea de personal prin pesionări şi demisii

waste 1 *noun* **(a)** daune *fpl* cauzate de chiriaşi **(b)** risipă *f;* pierdere *f;* **waste of money** = risipă de resurse financiare; **waste of time** = pierdere de timp **(c)** reziduuri *npl* industriale; **nuclear waste** = reziduuri nucleare (radioactive) 2 *verb* a risipi

water power *noun* energie *f* hidraulică

waterproof *adjective* impermeabil

waybill *noun* scrisoare *f* de trăsură; fraht *n*

wealth *noun* (a) prosperitate *f* (b) avere *f;* bogăţie *f;* **wealth tax** = impozit *n* pe avere

wear and tear *noun* uzură *f* (fizică) a mijloacelor fixe cauzată de folosinţă îndelungată şi scurgerea timpului

week *noun* săptămână *f*

weigh *verb* a cântări; **this parcel weighs 3.5 kilos** = acest colet cântăreşte 3,5 kilograme

weighbridge *noun* pod *n* basculă

weight *noun* greutate *f or* masă *f;* **gross weight** = greutate brută; **net weight** = greutate netă

welfare *noun* (a) bunăstare *f;* **social welfare** = bunăstare socială; **welfare state** = stat al bunăstării sociale (b) asistenţă *f* socială; ajutor social oferit de stat

Western European Time *noun* Ora *f* Europei Occidentale

wharf *noun* chei *n* (de mărfuri)

white-collar worker *noun* funcţionar *m*

White Paper *noun* document *n* oficial emis de guvernul britanic

wholesale 1 *noun* vânzare *f* cu ridicata; **wholesale price** = preţ *n* cu ridicata; **wholesale trade** = comerţ *n* en gros *or* cu ridicata 2 *adverb* **to sell wholesale** = a vinde cu ridicata

wholesaler *noun* angrosist *m*

will *noun* testament *n*

windfall profit *noun* profit *n* neaşteptat

wind up *verb* a lichida (o întreprindere, afacere)

winding up *noun* lichidare *f*

winding up sale *noun* vânzare *f* forţată de o hotărâre judecătorească

withdraw *verb* a retrage bani de la bancă

withdrawal *noun* retragere *f;* operaţiune *f* de restituire

work 1 *noun* (a) muncă *f or* lucru *n;* **casual work** = lucru ocazional; **work force** = forţa de muncă; **work in progress** = lucru în curs; **work permit** = permis de lucru (pentru străini) (b) serviciu *n;* **he goes to work by train** = merge la serviciu cu trenul 2 *verb* a munci

worker *noun* muncitor *m;* **blue-collar worker** = muncitor manual; **clerical worker** = funcţionar *m;* **worker participation** = participarea *f* muncitorilor la beneficii şi luarea deciziilor

working week *noun* săptămână *f* de lucru

workload *noun* cantitatea *f* de lucru; normă *f*

works *plural noun* (a) fabrică *f;* întreprindere *f* (b) **public works** = lucrări *fpl* publice

workshop *noun* atelier *n;* secţie *f*

wreck *noun* epavă *f*

wreckage *noun* bunuri *npl* recuperate de pe o epavă

writ *noun* citaţie *f;* ordonanţă *f*

write down *verb* (a) a nota (într-un carnet, etc) (b) a reduce valoarea mijloacelor fixe

writedown *noun* depreciere *f* (a mijloacelor fixe)

write off *verb* (a) a anula (plata unei datorii) (b) a casa mijloace fixe

Xx Yy Zz

Xerox (machine) *noun* maşină *f* de copiat *or* copiator `Xerox'

yard *noun* (a) curte *f* or incintă *f* (b) unitate *f* de măsură egală cu 0.91m (c) depozit *n* (d) şantier; **shipyard** = şantier *n* naval

year *noun* an *m;* **calendar year** = an calendaristic; **financial year** = an fiscal *or* financiar

yearbook *noun* anuar *n*

yearly *adjective & adverb* anual

yield *noun* (a) randament *n* *or* rentabilitate *f;* grad *n* de valorificare (a resurselor naturale) (b) profit *n;* **net yield** = profit net (c) dividend *n*

Zaire *noun* Zair *m* NOTE: capital: **Kinshasa;** currency: **zaïre** = zair *m*

Zairean *noun & adjective* zairez(ă)

Zambia *noun* Zambia *f* NOTE: capital: **Lusaka;** currency: **Zambian kwacha** = kwacha zambian

Zambian *noun & adjective* zambian(ă)

zero *noun* (cifra) zero *n*

zero-rated *adjective* neimpozabil

zip code *noun* US cod *n* poştal (în SUA)